SharePoint Online Modern Experience Practical Guide

2nd Edition

Migrate to the modern experience and get the most out of SharePoint including Power Platform

Bijay Kumar Sahoo

www.bpbonline.com

First published: 2019

Second published: 2024

Published by BPB Online
WeWork
119 Marylebone Road
London NW1 5PU

UK | UAE | INDIA | SINGAPORE

ISBN 978-93-5551-577-3

www.bpbonline.com

Dedicated to

My late sister

Nini

About the Author

Bijay Kumar Sahoo is a ten-time Microsoft MVP (Most Valuable Professional) with over seventeen years of technical experience in Microsoft technologies, with a spotlight on SharePoint. His vast experience spans both SharePoint on-premises and SharePoint Online. Throughout his journey, he's been an integral part of esteemed corporations such as HP, TCS, and KPIT, holding pivotal roles as a SharePoint architect. Currently, he helms TSinfo Technologies Pvt Ltd, a premier SharePoint development company that provides innovative solutions to clients across the United States and Europe.

But his impact doesn't stop there. Bijay is the mastermind behind two renowned SharePoint websites, SPGuides.com and EnjoySharePoint.com. These platforms are not just businesses but serve as lifelines to the SharePoint community. For his continued contributions and unparalleled expertise, Microsoft has consecutively recognized him as an MVP for the past decade. Beyond his business endeavors, Bijay has a passion for education. He shares his wealth of SharePoint knowledge with a global audience through his YouTube channel, "EnjoySharePoint", making the complexities of the platform accessible to all.

Acknowledgement

I want to express my deepest gratitude to my co-worker Preeti Sahu who helped me in this journey, and gave us her valuable feedback and suggestions on the book.

I also want to give my love to my daughter Tamanna who encouraged me on this journey without knowing the importance of this book

I am also grateful to BPB Publications for their guidance and expertise in bringing this book to fruition. It was a long journey of revising this book, with valuable participation and collaboration of reviewers, technical experts, and editors.

I would also like to acknowledge the valuable contributions of my readers from my SharePoint web sites SPGuides.com and EnjoySharePoint.com, who have taught me so much and provided valuable feedback on my work.

Finally, I would like to thank all the readers who have taken an interest in my book, and for their support in making it a reality. Your encouragement has been invaluable

Preface

Building enterprise applications is a complex task that requires a comprehensive understanding of the latest technologies and programming languages. C# and .NET are powerful tools that have become increasingly popular in the field of enterprise development.

This book is designed to provide a comprehensive guide to building enterprise applications with C# and .NET. It covers a wide range of topics, including the basics of C# programming, advanced concepts such as object-oriented programming, and the use of the .NET platform for building robust and scalable applications.

Throughout the book, you will learn about the key features of C# and .NET and how to use them to build enterprise applications that are efficient, reliable, and easy to maintain. You will also learn about the best practices and design patterns for building enterprise applications and will be provided with numerous practical examples to help you understand the concepts.

This book is intended for developers who are new to C# and .NET and want to learn how to build enterprise applications. It is also helpful for experienced developers who want to expand their knowledge of these technologies and improve their skills in building robust and reliable applications. I hope you will find this book informative and helpful.

Chapter 1: Introduction to SharePoint Online- explains everything needed for the reader to know the overview of Microsoft 365 and SharePoint including all its plans and subscriptions. Furthermore, the chapter also gives an idea about Microsoft 365 Admin Center and all the interface Components. Moreover, the reader will get to know what SharePoint Online is, why we use it and what SharePoint Online Admin Center is, including its key settings. This chapter also walks through the overview of Classic SharePoint and its benefits.

Chapter 2: SharePoint Modern Team Site – presents the detailed overview of Moden Team site in SharePoint exploring their key features, creation, customization, and management. From understanding site settings and navigation to exploring site templates and permissions, readers will equip with the knowledge they need to harness the power of SharePoint. Throughout, this chapter covers a range of topics, from site usage analytics to integrating with Microsoft Teams and even handling the complexities of subsites.

Chapter 3: SharePoint Communication Sites - covers the details overview of Communication site in SharePoint exploring why it is important to create Communication site, exploring their key features, creation, customization, and management. The readers will learn about site settings, how to make your site easy to navigate, using different templates, setting permissions, and connecting with Microsoft Teams. This chapter will also explain managing subsites, which are deeper components of the Communication site, and monitoring how it is used. Furthermore, this chapter shows how you can share the Communication site with your team members.

Chapter 4: SharePoint Online Modern List - is a guide to SharePoint Online lists. The reader will explore what they are, their advantages, and how to create and manage them effectively. This chapter will also equip the readers with creating list columns, managing items, setting permissions, filtering data, and customizing the list's appearance. This chapter will go through the templates, views, and even add, edit and delete options. By the end, the reader will be well-versed in making the most of SharePoint Online lists.

Chapter 5: SharePoint Online Modern Library - is a guide to SharePoint Online modern libraries. It covers the advantages of using them, how to create and manage document libraries, working with columns, settings, and files, as well as version history, templates, permissions, audience targeting, custom views, exporting to Excel, and backup/restore procedures. Whether you are new to SharePoint or looking to deepen your knowledge, this chapter provides practical insights to make the most of SharePoint Online modern libraries.

Chapter 6: SharePoint Modern Pages - explores the basic concepts of modern SharePoint pages in a simple way. Readers will start learning the difference between site pages and web part pages. Further, they will learn the benefits of using SharePoint site pages and this chapter guides you through creating and customizing them. Readers will also learn how to save your pages as templates, redirect them, and manage page navigation. This chapter also covers features like hiding certain properties, tracking comments, likes, and views, and using audience targeting to make your pages more relevant to specific groups of people. Additionally, this chapter explains breadcrumbs and introduces you to features like "Save for Later," "Send by Email," and how to delete a SharePoint site page. This chapter is an easy-to-follow guide to making the most of modern SharePoint Online pages.

Chapter 7: Modern Web Parts in SharePoint Online - explains with detail and numerous practical examples various SharePoint Online Web Parts, and how to insert a web part in SharePoint Online Modern Page. This chapter also allows the reader to learn how to delete the SharePoint Web Part, how to move and make duplicate a SharePoint web part in the modern page. Here the reader will get to know some of the important Web parts in SharePoint Online like Text, Image gallery, Quick links, News, People, and many more.

Chapter 8: Power Apps - explains what is Power Apps, their advantages, along with all the drawbacks, permissions, connectors etc. This chapter covers practical examples of Power Apps integrating with SharePoint, various Power Apps controls including saving and publishing the application. Also, the reader will get to know what Delegation in Power Apps is and how to share the Power Apps with other users including various scenarios.

Chapter 9: Power Automate - explores the world of automation in an easy-to-understand way. This chapter starts introducing "Power Automate" and its advantages in simplified way. It will also guide you through the "Connectors" and "Types of Actions" that make this tool so versatile. The reader will learn about triggers and actions, and what a "Flow" is, along with the different types available. Also, this chapter will teach readers how to create a flow using SharePoint, create manual triggers, use APIs to create SharePoint lists, discover how to share your flows, turn them on/off, and delete them as needed.

Chapter 10: Power BI - covers "What is Power BI" and introduces "Power BI Desktop" and its key features. Readers will learn about "Power BI Reports," the data sources it connects to, including SharePoint. This chapter explains the powerful "Power Query" for data transformations and provides an overview of "Visualization in Power BI. Readers will discover how to "Create Power BI Reports" using SharePoint data. The chapter also touches on "Power BI Service," teaching readers how to "Publish and Share Reports" and embed them with SharePoint Online. Further, this chapter guides readers through "Creating Power BI Dashboards" and explain how "Power BI SharePoint Data Refresh" keeps your data up-to-date automatically

Chapter 11: SharePoint Framework - covers the introduction to SPFx, helps readers to set up their development environment, and guides them in creating their first client-side web part. They will learn about web part properties and the property pane. Readers also explore SharePoint Framework Extensions, including application customizers, field customizers, command sets, and form customizers. Whether the readers are new to SPFx or looking to expand their skills, this chapter will make readers proficient in building customized solutions for SharePoint.

Code Bundle and Coloured Images

Please follow the link to download the
Code Bundle and the *Coloured Images* of the book:

https://rebrand.ly/b6w1znl

The code bundle for the book is also hosted on GitHub at:
https://github.com/bpbpublications/SharePoint-Online-Modern-Experience-Practical-Guide-2nd-Edition.
In case there's an update to the code, it will be updated on the existing GitHub repository.

We have code bundles from our rich catalogue of books and videos available at **https://github. com/bpbpublications**. Check them out!

Errata

We take immense pride in our work at BPB Publications and follow best practices to ensure the accuracy of our content to provide with an indulging reading experience to our subscribers. Our readers are our mirrors, and we use their inputs to reflect and improve upon human errors, if any, that may have occurred during the publishing processes involved. To let us maintain the quality and help us reach out to any readers who might be having difficulties due to any unforeseen errors, please write to us at :

errata@bpbonline.com

Your support, suggestions and feedbacks are highly appreciated by the BPB Publications' Family.

Did you know that BPB offers eBook versions of every book published, with PDF and ePub files available? You can upgrade to the eBook version at www.bpbonline.com and as a print book customer, you are entitled to a discount on the eBook copy. Get in touch with us at :

business@bpbonline.com for more details.

At **www.bpbonline.com**, you can also read a collection of free technical articles, sign up for a range of free newsletters, and receive exclusive discounts and offers on BPB books and eBooks.

Piracy

If you come across any illegal copies of our works in any form on the internet, we would be grateful if you would provide us with the location address or website name. Please contact us at **business@bpbonline.com** with a link to the material.

If you are interested in becoming an author

If there is a topic that you have expertise in, and you are interested in either writing or contributing to a book, please visit **www.bpbonline.com**. We have worked with thousands of developers and tech professionals, just like you, to help them share their insights with the global tech community. You can make a general application, apply for a specific hot topic that we are recruiting an author for, or submit your own idea.

Reviews

Please leave a review. Once you have read and used this book, why not leave a review on the site that you purchased it from? Potential readers can then see and use your unbiased opinion to make purchase decisions. We at BPB can understand what you think about our products, and our authors can see your feedback on their book. Thank you!

For more information about BPB, please visit **www.bpbonline.com**.

Join our book's Discord space

Join the book's Discord Workspace for Latest updates, Offers, Tech happenings around the world, New Release and Sessions with the Authors:

https://discord.bpbonline.com

Table of Contents

CHAPTER 1
Introduction to SharePoint Online

Introduction

This chapter will go through every aspect of SharePoint in depth, from the fundamentals to the more complex features, such as what Microsoft 365 is and its subscriptions, the advantages of utilizing Microsoft 365, and how to sign up for a Microsoft 365 trial.

Also, we will overlook everything related to the Microsoft 365 Admin Center, including its functions, how to access it, information on Microsoft 365 Users, etc.

The readers will also learn more about SharePoint Online, Modern SharePoint Online, why a company would utilize SharePoint Online, what the SharePoint Online Admin Center is and how it can be used.

At last, we will learn the differences between modern SharePoint and traditional SharePoint, as well as the benefits of modern SharePoint online, how to go from a classic experience in SharePoint to a modern experience, and much more.

Structure

This chapter describes everything related to Microsoft 365 and SharePoint Online, including the reasons why people use it, the types of subscriptions it offers, and its costs.

Additionally, we will go over everything there is to know about SharePoint Online, including its advantages, incentives, and an overview of the SharePoint Online Admin Center.

The entire list of topics we will be covering in this chapter are:

- Overview of Microsoft 365
- Microsoft 365 subscriptions
- Microsoft 365 trial
- Overview of Microsoft 365 admin center
- Adding users in Microsoft 365
- What is SharePoint Online?
- Benefits of using SharePoint Online for an organization
- Overview of SharePoint Online admin center
- Overview of classic SharePoint
- Overview of Modern SharePoint Online
- Advantages of Modern SharePoint Online
- Enabling the Modern experience at Tenant Level

Objectives

If you are unfamiliar with Microsoft 365 SharePoint Online, this chapter will help you gain a thorough understanding of SharePoint Online, how to sign up for a free trial of Microsoft 365, how to utilize the Microsoft 365 Admin Center, and its benefits.

Likewise, the reader will be able to comprehend topics like how to add users in Microsoft 365, the differences between a modern and classic version of SharePoint, how to enable the modern experience at the tenant level, and more.

Overview of Microsoft 365

The cloud-based platform for collaboration known as Microsoft 365, which offers Office apps and other services, is available for anyone to subscribe to. Additionally, you may use the internet to access emails, contacts, calendars, and other office programs like OneNote, Excel, Word, PowerPoint, and Outlook.

Office 365 was renamed Microsoft 365 on April 21, 2020, to highlight the service's current inclusion of goods and services outside the core Microsoft Office software family (including cloud-based productivity tools and artificial intelligence features).

Exclusive intelligent features like ideas in Excel, researcher in Word, real-time communication, Teams as the center of teamwork, and cutting-edge security features are all part of Microsoft 365 Apps for Enterprise.

You can have the most recent Microsoft Office programs by subscribing to Microsoft 365. You may install Microsoft 365 on all your devices with Microsoft 365 family, allowing you to log in to five devices simultaneously and use Office from any location or device.

Benefits of using Microsoft 365

Some of the top advantages listed below illustrate why we chose Microsoft 365:

- Microsoft Teams, Outlook, Word, Excel, and other top-tier office applications are all included with Microsoft 365.

- It is possible to install Microsoft 365 on PCs, Macs, tablets, and phones.

- It provides 1 TB of OneDrive cloud storage.

- You can install Office with a user-based license on up to five PCs or Macs, five tablets, and five mobile devices.

- With such ease of use and flexibility, it is fairer to permit your staff to work remotely without compromising productivity or important data. Employing Microsoft Office 365 similarly makes it simpler for staff to collaborate while not being present in the same location.

- You can always get the most recent office applications from Microsoft with the help of the subscription service of Microsoft 365.

Microsoft 365 subscriptions

There are three varying plans available with Microsoft 365. They are,

- For home

- For business

- For enterprise

For home

There are two different kinds of home plans offered by Microsoft 365, namely

- Paid yearly

- Paid monthly

Paid yearly

The following table gives details about the yearly plan of home Microsoft 365:

Microsoft 365 Family $99.99/year	Microsoft 365 Personal $69.99/year
For one to six people.	For one person.
Use up to five devices simultaneously.	Use up to five devices simultaneously.
Works on PC, Mac, iPhone, iPad, and Android phones and tablets.4	Works on PC, Mac, iPhone, iPad, and Android phones and tablets.4
Up to 6 TB of cloud storage (1 TB per person).	1 TB of cloud storage.
Additional features in the Family Safety mobile app.	

Table 1.1: Microsoft 365 Paid yearly Subscriptions

Paid monthly

The following table gives details about the monthly plan of home Microsoft 365:

Microsoft 365 Family $9.99/month	Microsoft 365 Personal $6.99/month
For one to six people.	For one person.
Use up to five devices simultaneously.	Use up to five devices simultaneously.
Works on PC, Mac, iPhone, iPad, and Android phones and tablets.4	Works on PC, Mac, iPhone, iPad, and Android phones and tablets.4
Up to 6 TB of cloud storage (1 TB per person).	1 TB of cloud storage.
Additional features in the Family Safety mobile app.	

Table 1.2: Microsoft 365 Paid monthly Subscriptions

To know more details about this Microsoft 365 home plans, you can refer to this MSDN below:

https://www.microsoft.com/en-us/microsoft-365/buy/compare-all-microsoft-365-products

For business

In Microsoft 365, there are four different kinds of business plans accessible such as,

Microsoft 365 Business Basic $6.00 user/month	Microsoft 365 Business Standard $12.50 user/month	Microsoft 365 Business Premium $22.00 user/month	Microsoft 365 Apps for business $8.25 user/month
Web and mobile versions of Microsoft 365 apps only	Desktop versions of Microsoft 365 apps with premium features	Advanced security	Desktop versions of Microsoft 365 apps with premium features
Chat, call, meet up to 300 attendees	Easily host webinars	Access and data control	1 TB of cloud storage per user
1 TB of cloud storage per user	Attendee registration and reporting tools	Cyberthreat protection	Standard security
Business-class email	Manage customer appointments		Anytime phone and web support
Standard security			
Anytime phone and web support			

Table 1.3: Microsoft 365 Subscriptions For business

To know more details about this Microsoft 365 Business Plans, you can refer to this MSDN below:

https://www.microsoft.com/en-us/microsoft-365/business/compare-all-microsoft-365-business-products

For enterprise

The three types of Microsoft 365 Enterprise plans are as follows:

- Microsoft 365 E3

- Microsoft 365 E5

- Microsoft 365 F3

The following table describes these in detail:

	Microsoft 365 E3 $36.00 user/month	Microsoft 365 E5 $57.00 user/month	Microsoft 365 F3 $8.00 user/month
Microsoft 365 Apps	Yes	Yes	Yes
Email and calendar	Yes	Yes	Yes

	Microsoft 365 E3 $36.00 user/month	Microsoft 365 E5 $57.00 user/month	Microsoft 365 F3 $8.00 user/month
Meetings and voice	Yes	Yes	Yes
Device and app management	Yes (Including Windows Autopatch)	Yes (Including Windows Autopatch)	Yes (Excluding Windows Autopatch)
Social and intranet	Yes	Yes	Yes
Files and content	Yes	Yes	Yes
Work management	Yes	Yes	Yes
Advanced analytics	Yes (Excluding Power BI Pro)	Yes (Including Power BI Pro)	No
Identity and access management	Yes (Excluding Azure Active Directory Premium plan 2)	Yes (Including Azure Active Directory Premium plan 2)	Yes (Excluding Azure Active Directory Premium plan 2)
Threat protection	Yes (Excluding Microsoft 365 Defender, Microsoft Defender for Endpoint P2, Microsoft Defender for Office 365, Microsoft Defender for Identity)	Yes (Excluding Microsoft Defender for Endpoint P1)	Yes (Excluding Microsoft 365 Defender, Microsoft Defender for Endpoint P1, Microsoft Defender for Endpoint P2, Microsoft Defender for Office 365, Microsoft Defender for Identity)
Information protection	Yes (Excluding Azure Information Protection P2, Microsoft Defender for Cloud Apps)	Yes	Yes (Excluding Azure Information Protection P2, Microsoft Defender for Cloud Apps)
Security management	Yes	Yes	Yes

	Microsoft 365 E3 $36.00 user/month	Microsoft 365 E5 $57.00 user/month	Microsoft 365 F3 $8.00 user/month
Compliance management	Yes (Excluding Rules-based automatic retention policies, Advanced eDiscovery, advanced audit, Insider Risk Management, Built-in third-party connections)	Yes	Yes (Excluding Basic org-wide or location-wide retention policies, Rules-based automatic retention policies, Advanced eDiscovery, Advanced audit, Insider Risk Management, Built-in third-party connections)

Table 1.4: Microsoft 365 Subscriptions For enterprise

To know more details about this Microsoft 365 Enterprise plans, you can refer to this MSDN below:

https://www.microsoft.com/en-us/microsoft-365/compare-microsoft-365-enterprise-plans

Microsoft 365 trial

Since no Microsoft 365 Enterprise plan can now offer a free SharePoint trial due to Microsoft's upgrade, we can go with a Microsoft 365 Business subscription instead.

The first method to obtain the SharePoint Online trial is by using one of Microsoft 365's business plans, specifically Microsoft 365 Business Premium.

Microsoft 365 business premium's advantages

Over the other business plans, this Microsoft 365 Business Premium package provides a few extra benefits such as:

- Each user has access to 1 TB of OneDrive cloud storage, allowing you to manage your files from anywhere.

- Establishing a secure connection to your data and assisting iOS, Android, Windows, and macOS devices running safely.

- Always use the latest versions of Word, Excel, PowerPoint, and other software.

- Exchange, Outlook, and Microsoft Teams can all be used to communicate with clients and employees.

- Use encryption to limit access to sensitive information and avoid the accidental sharing of data.

Trial for SharePoint with Microsoft 365 business premium plan

To try out the SharePoint Online with Microsoft 365 Business Premium Plan, we can refer to the instructions below:

Step 1:

 a. Open Microsoft 365 Plans by using this URL: **https://www.microsoft.com/en-in/ microsoft-365/business/compare-all-microsoft-365-business-products**

 b. Microsoft 365 plans come in two different types. For example, **For home** and **For business**. Select **For business**.

 c. There are four types of plans listed under **For business** Plan:

  o Microsoft 365 Business basic

  o Microsoft 365 Apps for business

  o Microsoft 365 Business standard

  o Microsoft 365 Business premium

Select **Try free for one month2** under the **Microsoft 365 Business Premium** free for a month. It provides more services than other Microsoft 365 plans (including SharePoint) as shown in the following screenshot:

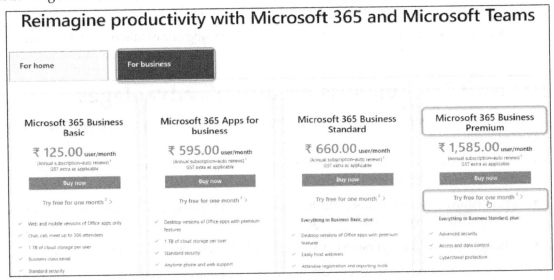

Figure 1.1: Microsoft 365 Business Premium Licensing, Pricing, Trial details

Step 2:

a. You will then be taken to the setup page where you must enter your **Email** address from work or school.

b. After you provide your email, they will determine whether you need a new account to use the Microsoft 365 Business Premium Trial. Choose **Next**.

Additionally, as seen in the following screenshot, you may view all the plan advantages and product highlights on the right side of the page:

Figure 1.2: Enter your email address in Microsoft 365 Business Premium Trial Setup

Step 3:

• It will then go to the account setup page, where you can create a new account and set up your account. Then select **Set up account** as shown in the following screenshot:

Figure 1.3: Set up account for Microsoft 365 Business Premium Trial

Step 4:

a. In this step, Microsoft will try to learn more about your company, its size, and your nation.

b. Give details about your **First name**, **Middle name**, **Surname**, **Business phone number**, **Company name**, **Company size**, and **Country or Region**.

c. Finally, select the Microsoft agreement in accordance with your needs before clicking **Next**.

Note: Make sure to provide a working business phone number that is both visible and accessible.

Figure 1.4 represents the setup page where you need to provide the user details like First name, Middle name, Surname, etc.

Figure 1.4: Tell about yourself in setup page

Step 5:

a. Self-verification is another important step that must be completed before proceeding. This is why it is crucial to provide a reliable mobile number.

b. Check out one of the two options listed below: **Text me** or **Call me**, Choose any of these possibilities and hit the **Send verification code** button as shown in the following screenshot:

Figure 1.5: Send verification code

c. A code would be sent to the specified mobile number since we selected the text confirmation method. After entering the verification code, click **Verify** as shown in the following screenshot:

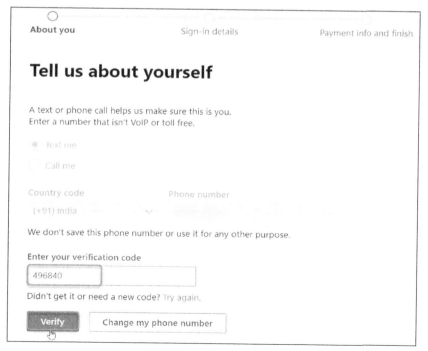

Figure 1.6: Enter verification code and Click verify

Step 6:

    a. For your business, this step is crucial. Enter the name of your company here. By default, the username and domain name are displayed together: `PreetiSahu@ TSinfoTechnologies787.onmicrosoft.com`

    b. This domain name is merely an example. You can change a custom domain whenever you want.

    c. After entering your desired password, confirm it. Select **Next** as shown in the following screenshot:

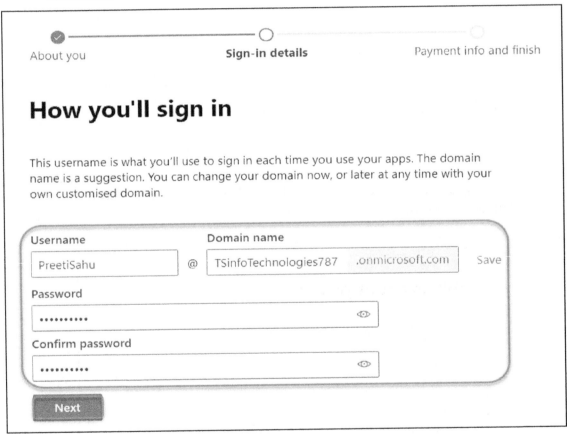

Figure 1.7: Sign-in details

    d. Now the account will be established. You will be instructed not to refresh the page until you create an account as shown in the following screenshot:

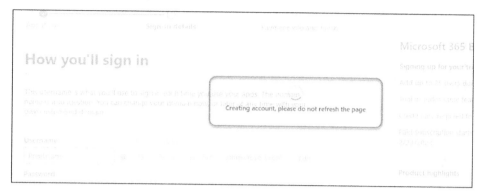

Figure 1.8: Creating a Microsoft 365 trial account

Step 7:

a. You must add a payment method in the final step to qualify for the one-month free trial of SharePoint.

b. Choose the amount and press the **Add payment method** button on the **Quantity and payment** page as shown in the following screenshot:

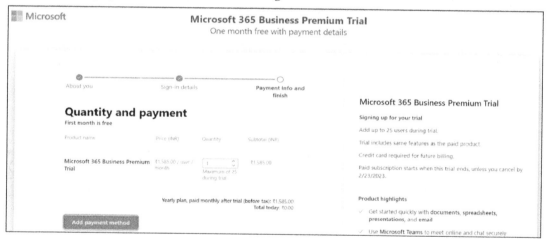

Figure 1.9: Add Quantity and tap payment method

c. Enter all the card information, including the **Card number**, **Security code**, **Expiration month**, **Expiration year**, etc., on the following payment method page. Lastly, select **Save** as shown in the following screenshot:

Add payment method

First month is free

Add a payment method
Your first month is free. You need to add a payment method because the free trial will be automatically converted to a paid subscription after the trial period.

We accept the following cards:

VISA ●●

Card number *

| | VISA |

Security code * ⓘ

Expiration month *   Expiration year *

| ▽ | | ▽ |

First name *   Last name *   Name on card *

| Preeti | | Sahu | | |

Address line 1 *   Address line 2 (Optional)

| F-105, SJR Residency | | Bellandur |

Address line 3 (Optional)

| |

City *

| Bangalore |

State *

| Karnataka   ▽ |

Postal Code *

| 560103 |

Country/Region *

| India   ▽ |

By clicking the button below to continue, you consent to tokenize and save this card. You'll be redirected to your bank's website for verification.

Learn more about tokenization

| Save | | Cancel |

Figure 1.10: Enter payment details

Step 8:

a. You will then be directed to the **Review and Confirm** page, where you will be asked for your **Tax ID** (either it should be a **GST ID** or **PAN ID**). Here, we need the **PAN ID**.

b. Enter your PAN ID both in the Tax ID field and beneath the PAN Registration number. Click **Save** in the **Registration and Tax ID** sections as shown in the following screenshot:

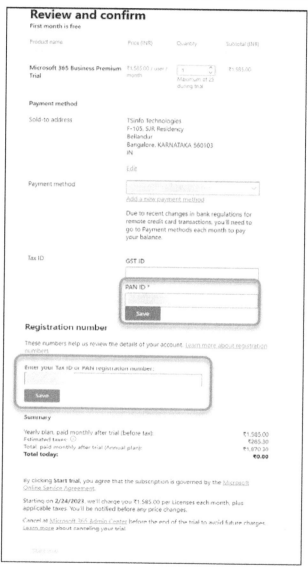

Figure 1.11: Review and confirmation pane

Once you save this information, you can see that the **Start Trial** button will become active, select **Start trial** as shown in the following screenshot:

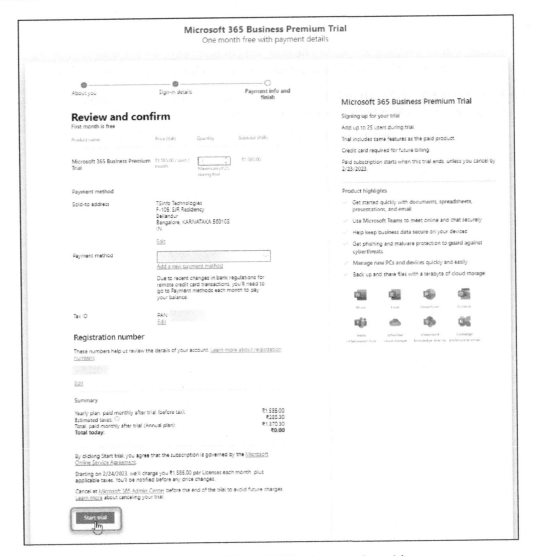

Figure 1.12: Start Microsoft 365 business premium trial

Step 9:

a. When you choose the **Microsoft 365 Business Premium Trial**, the following screen will appear to thank you. It also offers some advice on how you could make use of it to your benefit.

b. Click **Start using Microsoft 365 Business Premium Trial** button as shown in the following screenshot:

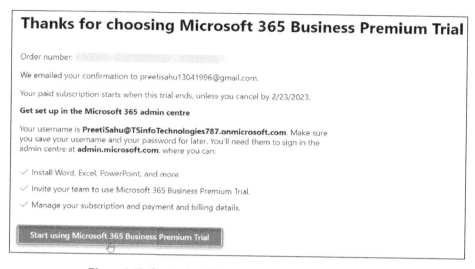

Figure 1.13: Start using Microsoft 365 Business Premium Trial

Step 10:

a. Enter your correct login information (**Username** and **Password**) on the following Microsoft Sign-in screen, and then click on **Sign in**.

b. Click **Yes** if you wish to stay logged in as shown in the following screenshot:

Figure 1.14: Sign-in to Microsoft 365 business premium trial

c. When everything is finished, you may view the Microsoft 365 admin center as displayed below. Here, you can perform any tasks for your company, such as:

  i.   If you want to add a new user, click the **+ Add user** button.

  ii. If you wish to alter the password for your account, use the **Reset password** option.

  iii. You can set up a custom domain for email.

  iv. Among many others, the most recent Microsoft 365 apps can be installed or shared as shown in the following screenshot:

Figure 1.15: Display Microsoft 365 admin center

Step 11:

a. To access your Microsoft 365 tenant at any time, click on any of the URLs mentioned below. Use any of the following URLs to sign into Microsoft 365:

    i. **https://admin.microsoft.com/** or

    ii. **https://portal.office.com/** or

    iii. **https://office.com/**

b. You will be asked to enter the Microsoft credential (your tenant admin credentials) when you click one of the URLs below. If you have already signed in, it will not ask you for your credentials.

c. Choose **SharePoint** from the **App Launcher** as shown below to access your SharePoint Online:

d. The following figure represents Microsoft 365 App Launcher.

Figure 1.16: Microsoft 365 App Launcher

e. You can also get to your SharePoint Online Admin Center page by entering the following URL:

https://<Your tenant's name>-admin.sharepoint.com/

Example: **https://tsinfotechnologies787-admin.sharepoint.com/**

f. To visit your company's SharePoint homepage, enter the following URL:

https://<Your tenant's name>.sharepoint.com/

Example: **https://tsinfotechnologies787.sharepoint.com/**

Check out the following screenshot to see how the SharePoint Home page looks like:

Figure 1.17: SharePoint Home Page

The instructions mentioned describe how to obtain a free trial of SharePoint through the Microsoft 365 Business Premium Plan. Next, we will see how to join a Microsoft 365 Developer Program account.

Join Microsoft 365 Developer program for free

Microsoft has introduced a developer program designed specifically for programmers who can produce Microsoft 365 applications that function across desktop, web, and mobile platforms.

We can create Microsoft Teams apps, Office Add-ins for Word, Excel, PowerPoint, Outlook, or SharePoint Add-ins, using Microsoft Graph, the SharePoint Framework, Power Apps, Microsoft Power BI, Power Automate, etc.

You can access a Dev Tenant with 25 Microsoft 365 E5 membership packs for a 90-day trial through the Microsoft 365 Developer Program. There is a 90-day trial period for the Microsoft developer program, but if you regularly use it for testing, it will automatically renew for a longer amount of time.

Microsoft 365 Developer program advantages

The following are the advantages of this program:

- The fact that the Microsoft 365 Developer Program includes 25 Microsoft 365 E5 user licenses is the most significant aspect.

- It contains all the Microsoft 365 Apps (comprising Exchange Online, SharePoint Online, Microsoft Teams, OneDrive, Word, Excel, and more).

- It offers security and business mobility (EMS).

- Power BI Advanced analytics are available with this Microsoft 365 Developer plan.

- It also features Azure Active Directory (With Azure AD Premium P2 Licenses).

We will now go through the process of joining the Microsoft 365 developer program by following these steps:

Step 1:

a. First, make sure you have a Microsoft Accounts or Azure Active Directory-enabled email account, such as *Outlook.com*, *Hotmail.com*, etc., before applying for the Microsoft 365 Developer Program.

b. Click the following link to access the Microsoft 365 Developer Program webpage: **https://developer.microsoft.com/en-us/microsoft-365/dev-program**

c. Sign in using your Hotmail, Outlook, or Microsoft account details in the top right corner of the page as shown in the following screenshot:

Figure 1.18: Microsoft 365 Dev Center

d. Enter your email address, then select **Next**.

e. After entering your password, click **Sign in** as shown in the following screenshot:

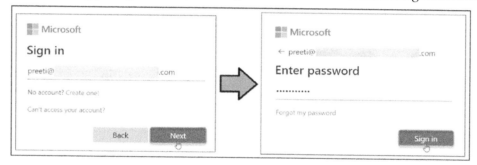

Figure 1.19: Sign in with Microsoft 365 Dev center

f. Click **Join now** to sign up for the **Microsoft 365 Developer Program today** after successfully signing in. Refer to the following figure:

Figure 1.20: Join Microsoft 365 Developer Program

Step 2:

a. You will then see a **Join the Microsoft 365 Developer Program today!** screen that asks for information such as your Country or region, Company, Preferred language, etc.

b. Next, select and agree to the **terms and conditions of the Microsoft 365 Developer Program.**

c. You can tick the **I would like information, tips, and offers about the Microsoft 365 Developer Program** box if you would like to hear from Microsoft about new features and other updates. s seen in the following screenshot, click **Next**.

d. The following figure specifies entering the company information. Further, accept terms and conditions:

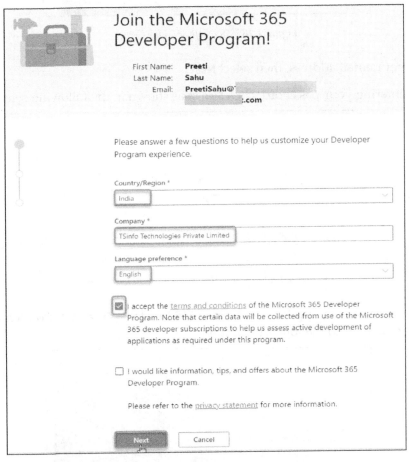

Figure 1.21: Provide Company Details and accept the terms & conditions

Step 3:

a. After that, a primary focus page will appear where you must enter your preferences so that Microsoft may personalize your experience.

b. As a developer, choose at least one **primary focus as a developer** before clicking **Next** as shown in the following screenshot:

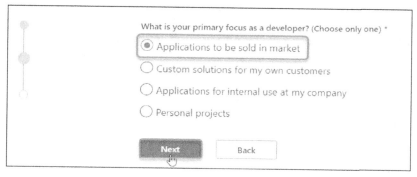

Figure 1.22: *Choose your primary focus as a developer*

Step 4:

a. Select the **Microsoft 365 development** areas in which you are interested in the following page. To get you going, they will demonstrate your available resources, tools, and training.

b. Click **Save** after deciding which areas to select as shown in the following screenshot:

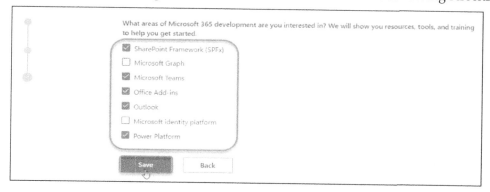

Figure 1.23: *Select Microsoft 365 development areas*

Step 5:

a. Setting up your Microsoft 365 E5 sandbox is the next step. As you can see, there are two different kinds of sandboxes:

   i. **Instant sandbox:** It includes everything you need to build Microsoft 365 applications and solutions. In this sandbox, there are 16 fictitious users, a Microsoft Teams sample data pack with preconfigured App studio and custom apps, and data for Microsoft Graph, SharePoint, and Office Add-ins development.

    ii. **Configurable sandbox:** It builds a personalized sandbox. This subscription needs sample data manually added, and provisioning could take up to two days. The domain name can also be modified.

b. According to your needs, select your **Microsoft 365 E5 developer sandbox**. In the following screenshot, we have chosen **Instant sandbox** in this case. Additionally, the following items can be seen on the right side of the page:

    i. **Domain name**

    ii. **Renewable E5 subscription**

    iii. **Administrator**

    iv. **25 user licenses**

    v. **90/90 days left**

    vi. **Sample data packs**

c. Select **Next** as shown in the following screenshot:

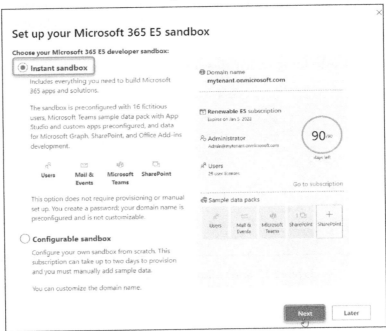

Figure 1.24: Set up Microsoft 365 E5 sandbox

Step 6:

a. You will see the following screen on the next page after selecting the **Instant Sandbox**. Here, you must configure your **Microsoft 365 E5 Instant Sandbox** by providing details about the admins, such as the **Country or region**, **Admin username**, **Admin password**, etc.

b. Additionally, you can verify that you use a different password for each of the 16 fictional users. Select **Continue** as shown in the following screenshot:

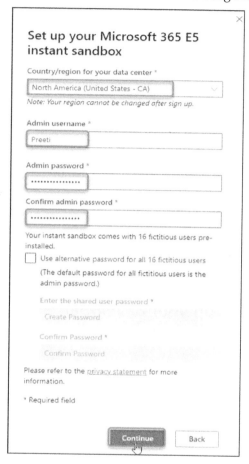

Figure 1.25: Set up Microsoft 365 E5 instant sandbox

Step 7:

a. After that, you can authenticate your identification by entering it on the **Add phone number for security** page, which will soon appear.

b. The country code will automatically be **India (+91)**. You can choose your country from the drop-down option if you wish to alter it.

c. If you use the phone number, they will text you a code that you may use to verify your phone number.

d. You will eventually receive an OTP from them. After entering the code, select **Set up** as shown in the following screenshot to configure the developer subscription as shown in the following screenshot:

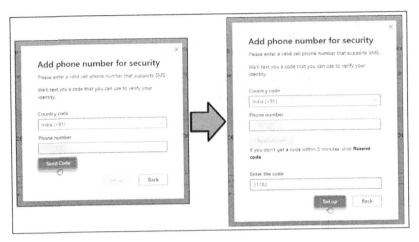

Figure 1.26: Add phone number for security

e. As you can see in the following screenshot, once the page has been set up, the setup process is **In Progress**. It should not take longer than a minute.

Figure 1.27: Developer program is in progress mode

Step 8:

a. Your 90-day trial of your Microsoft 365 developer subscription is now completed.

b. To sign into the developer account, click the **Go to subscription** link as shown in the following screenshot:

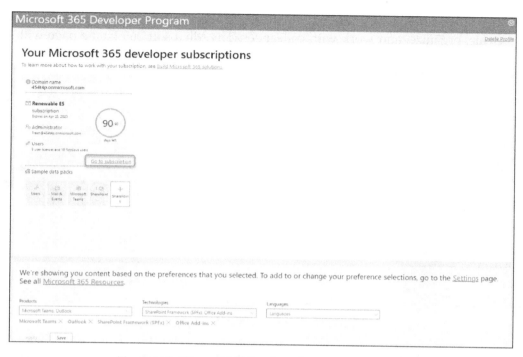

Figure 1.28: Microsoft 365 Developer Program is ready to use

Step 9:

a. You will then be directed to the Microsoft Sign-in box page, where you will be asked to **Enter password**. Select **Sign in** after entering the admin password.

b. To protect your account, the following Microsoft window can show up as in the picture below. If it does, click on **Skip for now (14 days until this is required)**. Then, choose **Next** as shown in the following screenshot:

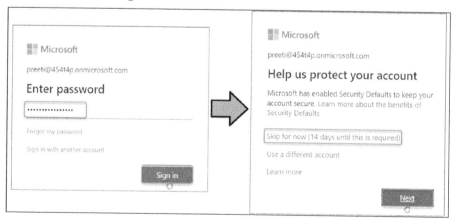

Figure 1.29: Sign in Microsoft 365 Developer Program

c. The Microsoft 365 Welcome page will then appear, giving you a single location to create, organize, and work with colleagues. The Microsoft 365 Home page will then appear after you click the next icon (>) as shown in the following screenshot:

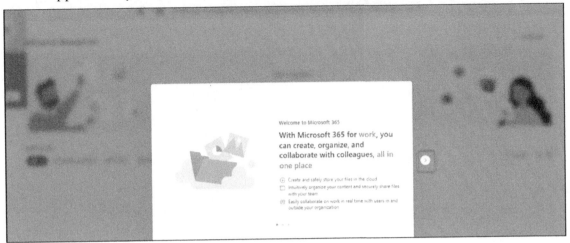

Figure 1.30: Microsoft 365 Welcome page

d. If you want to change any Settings about **Products**, **Technologies**, **Code languages**, or Platforms, you may also click on **Settings** on the Microsoft 365 Developer Program Dashboard page as shown in the following screenshot:

Figure 1.31: Change your preference selections

e. You will be taken immediately to the page with your account preferences, where you can make changes and **Save** them as shown in the following screenshot:

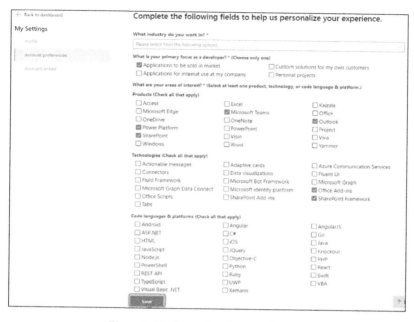

Figure 1.32: Account preferences Settings

Step 10:

a. Choose SharePoint from the App Launcher as shown below to access your SharePoint Online. (Additionally, you can see additional Microsoft applications including OneDrive, Word, PowerPoint, Outlook, etc.). Refer to the following screenshot:

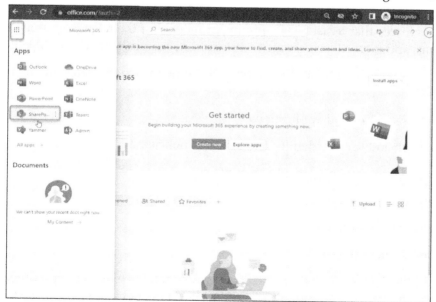

Figure 1.33: Microsoft 365 App Launcher

b. After that, you can see a **Welcome to SharePoint Start Page** like the one below. Click **NEXT** if you want to see news from websites as shown in the following screenshot:

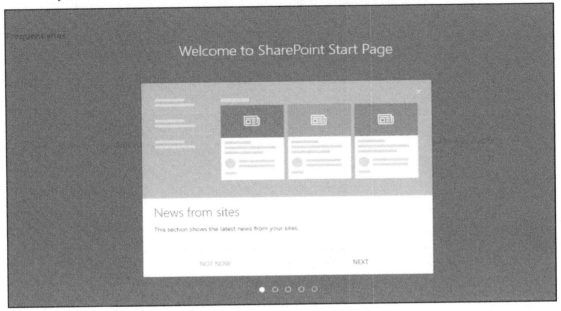

Figure 1.34: *Welcome to SharePoint Start Page*

Overview of Microsoft 365 admin center

Microsoft offers the Microsoft Admin Center, which is made up of a collection of different tools and resources that assist M365 admins in managing their tenants, users, IAM, teams, subscriptions, and more, to coordinate and streamline the many aspects of M365.

Users can check many administrative settings and functions in the Admin Center through the cloud:

- Control services and applications
- Establish and review identity management policies
- Analyze access management and security
- View the data and reports
- Manage teams and users
- Make service requests

Additionally, the Admin Center offers customization options to increase productivity, such as the ability to pin the most important data and tasks on the home screen for quick access.

Access Microsoft 365 admin center

The Microsoft 365 admin center is simple to use and obtain. The following steps can be used to open it:

There are two ways to access Microsoft 365 Admin Center:

1. Open Microsoft 365 Admin Center from Admin Web link:

    a. Using the Admin URL below, we can open the Microsoft 365 Admin Center immediately. **http://admin.microsoft.com**

    b. The Microsoft 365 Admin Center page will launch without requesting any Microsoft credentials if you are already signed in. If not, you must first login before the Microsoft 365 Admin Center page can be accessed.

2. Open Microsoft 365 Admin Center from App Launcher:

    a. Use **https://www.office.com/** to log in.

    b. **Sign in**.

    c. Choose the **App Launcher** tab.

    d. Select **Admin**.

Note: If the Admin symbol is not there, Office 365 administrative permissions are not available in your organization. A person who creates a Microsoft account and purchases an Office 365 business subscription automatically acquires administrator rights and the Office 365 admin account.

The following screenshot represents the Microsoft 365 Admin Center page:

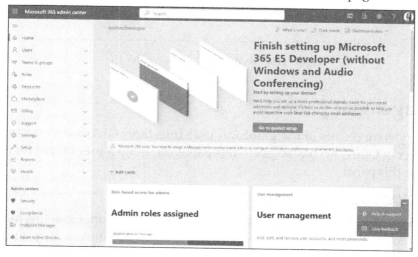

Figure 1.35: Microsoft 365 Admin center

Interface components of Microsoft 365 admin center

Now we will see all the interface components of Microsoft 365 Admin Center. After logging in, you will see three major panels and options in the middle of the Microsoft 365 admin center window (formerly known as Office 365 admin center).

The three panels are:

- Top management panel
- Left navigation panel that contains subsections like Users, Groups, Roles, Resources, etc.
- Admin centers panel

Let us take a closer look at each panel on the Microsoft 365 admin center UI as shown in the following screenshot:

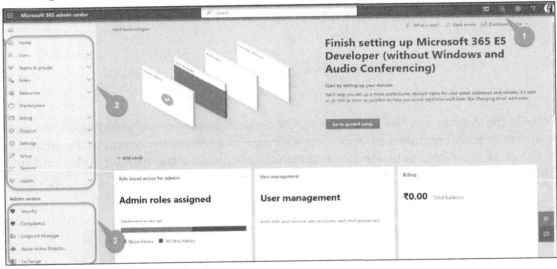

Figure 1.36: Microsoft 365 Admin center UI

Top management panel

The six primary components of the **graphical user interface (GUI)** are in the top horizontal panel. Each user of Office 365 has access to this panel. To set up a user profile for an Office 365 account, utilize this panel.

- **Office 365 Menu (App Launcher)**

  To access the Office 365 menu, click the nine-dot menu icon. From this menu, you can switch to any Office 365 online application that is compatible with your membership plan. Only users with administrator privileges have access to the admin icon.

- **Cloud Shell**

  The Microsoft 365 Admin Center now directly links to the Azure Cloud shell. If you choose that, a PowerShell-style window like the one above will be displayed at the bottom of the page. All your favorite scripts may be launched right here in a web browser as shown in the following screenshot:

Figure 1.37: Microsoft 365 Admin center Cloud Shell

- **Microsoft 365 Admin app**

  With the admin mobile app, you may work efficiently from any location. You may use the app to manage devices, manage users, add users, reset passwords, issue support requests, and more while you are on the go.

- **Settings**

  You may configure your notification settings, contact preferences, and display themes in this menu. You can also change your password.

- **Help**

  In case you require assistance from Microsoft, utilize this menu.

- **My account**

  In the top right corner, click the circle to access your account options. You may check personal information, subscriptions, security and privacy settings, app permissions, apps and devices, and tools and add-ins in your account settings.

Left navigation pane

The Microsoft Office 365 admin center's left navigation pane is the most important since it allows you to access settings for your Office 365 domain and user accounts, manage groups, establish permissions, and more. This navigation pane has parts and subsections that resemble a menu. Let us go over each section one by one.

- **Home**

    To return to the Office 365 admin center's home page (landing page), click the link **https://admin.microsoft.com/#/homepage**. The following components can be seen in the page's center:

    o **+ Add cards**

        For rapid access to commonly used pages, such as Service Health, Setup, message center, Azure AD, Microsoft 365 active users report, and so forth, add cards to your home page. You can move, reorder, and delete the cards to simplify the view.

        You can refer to the image below:

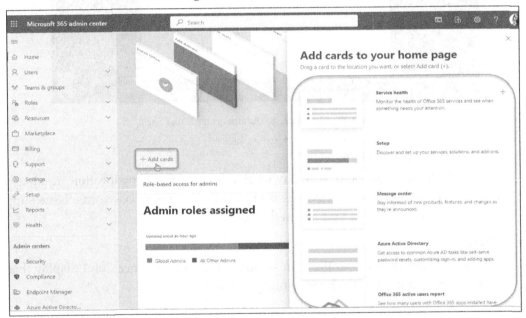

Figure 1.38: Microsoft 365 Admin center Add cards

    o **What's new?:**

        When an important new feature is released, windows users get a message about it in the apps where that feature appears. You can manage which messages your users will see.

    o **Dark mode:**

        Choose your preferred theme. A light mode and a dark mode are selectable. It will be in Light mode by default. Click on **Dark mode** if you want the Microsoft 365 Admin Center theme to be in dark mode.

o **Dashboard view**:

To change the Microsoft 365 Admin center home page view to Simplified or Dashboard, click on it.

- **Users**

Managing user accounts is the most frequent responsibility of administrators. There are four subsections in this section where you can manage employee or student Office 365 user accounts.

o **Active users**:

All users are listed in-depth (in a table), along with their licensing status. A user can be added, user templates may be made, many users can be added, and multi-factor authentication can be enabled or disabled.

You can assign or remove user licenses, reset passwords, manage Office 365 users (add, modify, delete, export users), and utilize filters to pick the required users (which is useful if you have many Office 365 users for your domain).

Active users can be sorted by columns. To sort users by username, for instance, click Username. Below represents the columns:

Display name | Username | Licenses | Choose columns

To choose the columns that will be shown in *Figure 1.39*, click **Choose columns**.

Figure 1.39: Microsoft 365 users

o **Contacts** and **Guest users**:

To create mail contacts for users from outside the company, utilize these options.

o **Deleted users**:

If necessary, you can restore the specified users from a list of deleted users.

- **Teams and groups**

Manage Microsoft teams and Office 365 groups, security groups, distribution lists, and shared mailboxes for your company using these choices. Instead of managing each user individually while managing Office 365 users, it can be helpful to group users into groups and manage those groups.

Collaboration is supported by Microsoft Teams through chat, calls, and online meetings. The teams you add are groups of individuals, items, and resources. Groups are useful since they are collections of people if all you need is a group email address.

New distribution groups and mail-enabled security groups can take up to an hour to appear here.

The following figure represents all about the Microsoft 365 Teams and groups:

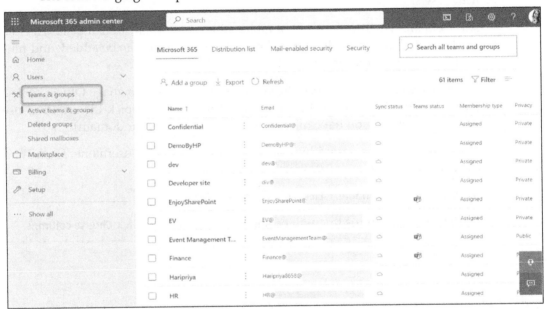

Figure 1.40: Microsoft 365 Teams and groups

- **Roles**

  The global Office 365 admin at your company can provide additional users with different admin roles by using the Microsoft 365 admin center (administrators). This strategy may be helpful if your firm has a huge number of users and you wish to give some control to other administrators who should be concentrating on managing Exchange, licenses, or SharePoint, for example.

  There are two types of Microsoft 365 Admin Center Roles, that is, **Role assignments** and **Administrative units**.

  The Roles page contains a complete list of Office 365 admin roles. To choose which role to provide users, read the description for that role as shown in the following screenshot:

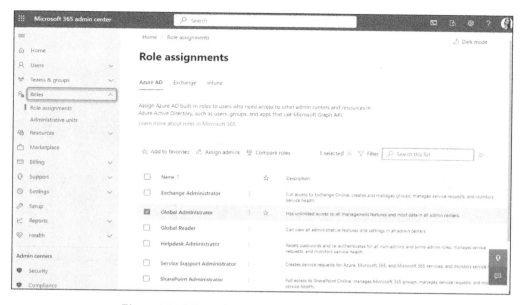

Figure 1.41: *Microsoft 365 Admin center Role assignments*

- **Resources**

  You may create and manage resources, such as sites and conference rooms, using the resources choices. You can view the status of the SharePoint sites and site collections you have developed for user collaboration and external sharing as shown in the following screenshot:

Figure 1.42: *Microsoft 365 Admin center Resources*

- **Marketplace**

  This is the place where we can find out what you may purchase for your company in terms of goods and services. This section has two tabs, **Recommended** and **All products** as shown in the following screenshot:

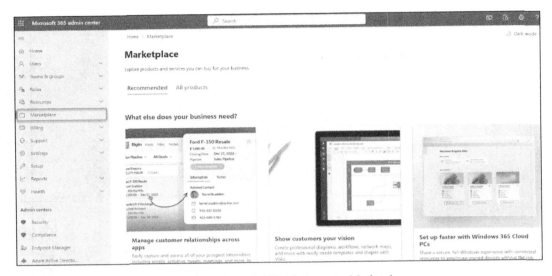

Figure 1.43: Microsoft 365 Admin center Marketplace

- **Billing**

  You can check bills and payments, view your membership status, buy more Microsoft cloud services, set up payment options, and more under this tab. You may also check how many licenses are left in your Office 365 subscription plan as well as see and assign licenses. Check out the following screenshot:

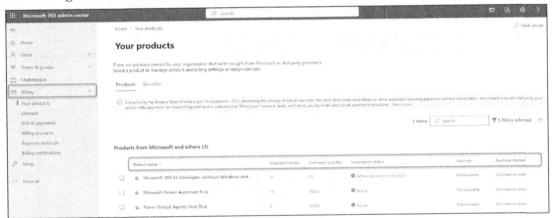

Figure 1.44: Billing in Microsoft 365 Admin center

- **Support**

  In this section, you can monitor current service requests, their status and submit a new support request to Microsoft if necessary. Office 365 admin support is offered by Microsoft. In the following screenshot, you can see all the Data access requests in Microsoft 365 admin center:

Figure 1.45: Microsoft 365 Admin center Support

- **Settings**

    Authentication settings, email settings, calendar settings, external sharing settings, password policy settings, Azure Active Directory integration settings, and other settings for Office 365 applications may all be managed from this section. Changes can be made to calendar settings, release preferences, and password expiration dates.

    To assign or manage software licenses, manage domains, or migrate data, view the product details for your subscription. You can add a domain, buy a new domain, and check the status of an existing domain.

    You can refer to the below screenshot to view all the settings in **Microsoft 365 Admin center**:

Figure 1.46: Microsoft 365 Admin center Settings

- **Setup**

    To assign or manage software licenses, manage domains, or migrate data, view the product details for your subscription. You can add a domain, buy a new domain, and check the status of an existing domain. You may transfer email accounts and email data from a variety of services, including Gmail, Hotmail, and Yahoo, as well as import data from exported PST files, thanks to data migration options as like the following figure:

Figure 1.47: Setup in Microsoft 365 Admin center

- **Reports**

  Get a thorough analysis of how employees at your firm used Office 365 applications over a chosen time period. You may keep track of which programs people prefer and compare dynamics for the chosen time frame (7, 30, 90, or 180 days).

  Reports can help you determine which employees at your organization do not use Office 365 services and may not require the license that has been granted to them. You will also be able to identify the employees who use this service frequently and are on the verge of exceeding quotas (for OneDrive, for example). Refer to the following screenshot:

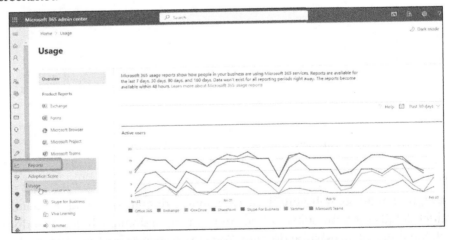

Figure 1.48: Microsoft 365 Admin center Usage Reports

- **Health**

  Check the status of your Office 365 services by opening this section in the Office 365 admin portal. The alert icon is displayed next to the service name if any faults or disruptions occurred. The Status column will show the number of incidents. You can stay updated on recent and upcoming events with the aid of the message center.

  Normally we can see information about your Microsoft 365 apps and services and view suggested steps to keep your business secure and up to date in this section as shown in the following screenshot:

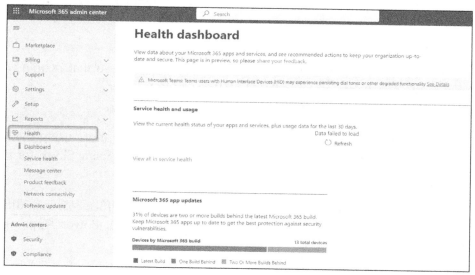

Figure 1.49: Microsoft 365 Admin center Health dashboard

Admin centers panel

To enable the Office 365 company administrator to access all settings from the single interface of the Microsoft 365 admin center, the **Admin centers** section, found at the bottom of the navigation pane, collects all significant configuration options for Office 365 products.

- **Security/Compliance**

  To access the Office 365 security and compliance administration center, select one of these choices.

- **Endpoint Manager**

  The company's exclusive endpoint management tool is called Microsoft's Endpoint Management Admin Center. By logging, tracking, recording, and monitoring all IoT devices linked to a company's network, it aids IT personnel in ensuring security. Using Microsoft Intune, Microsoft Endpoint Management also offers support for the cloud.

- **Azure Active Directory**

  This enables you to define access restrictions for external applications that communicate with Office 365 via Microsoft APIs, manage users, groups, and policies, and configure Azure AD for Office 365 and synchronization with Windows Server Active Directory.

- **Exchange**

  Manage the user accounts and mailboxes for Office 365 by visiting the Exchange Online admin center. Set up group mailboxes, anti-spam filters, mail flow rules, and other features in this section. To safeguard data users' mailboxes, do not forget to do Microsoft Office 365 backup.

- **SharePoint**

  To set up the Microsoft cloud environment for Office 365 so that people within the company can collaborate, open the SharePoint admin center.

- **Teams**

  You can manage teams, set policies, examine reports, and more using the Microsoft Teams admin center. Meetings may be scheduled for teams using Skype for Business.

- **All admin centers**

  It opens a page listing every admin center available for Office 365, including admin centers for OneDrive, Yammer Enterprise, Dynamics 365, Power Apps, Skype for Business, and other services.

  Refer to the screenshot below to view all the interfaces in Microsoft 365 Admin center:

Figure 1.50: Microsoft 365 Admin centers Bottom Panel

Different views in Microsoft 365 Admin center

There are two views in the Microsoft 365 Admin Center:

- **Simplified view:** Simplified view helps in managing the most frequent tasks in smaller organizations.

- **Dashboard view:** The dashboard view has more complex settings and tasks. A button at the top of the admin center allows you to change between them.

Microsoft 365 Admin Center in simplified view

To change the Microsoft 365 Admin Center view to Simplified view, expand the Dashboard view on the top right corner of the home page and then select **Simplified view**.

When a user opens the Microsoft 365 Admin Center, by default, the view will be **Dashboard view**.

On Microsoft 365 Admin Center Simplified view home page, you can see the following functionalities:

- **+ Add user**: You can add a user or member by using the **+ Add user** button.

- **Reset password**: If you want to change the Microsoft 365 password, then you can use the **Reset password** button.

- **Users**: Once you will click on this tab, you can view all the individual user details like **Name, Username for sign-in, Licenses**, etc. Moreover, you can also edit and delete any specific user from the user list.

- **Teams**: Manage teams in Microsoft Teams for communication, meetings, and collaboration, including members, owners, visitors, and email. The organization-wide team will always be expanded by adding new users. If you want to create a new team, then click on the **+ Add a team** button. Here also, you can manage owners, edit the team's name and description, Edit the email address, and delete any specific team.

- **Subscriptions**: By using this, we can view invoices, modify the payment method, and monitor license usage for subscriptions.

- **Learn**: This is the Microsoft 365 admin center's help documentation. If you want to learn more about the Microsoft 365 admin center, you can refer to it. Refer to the following screenshot:

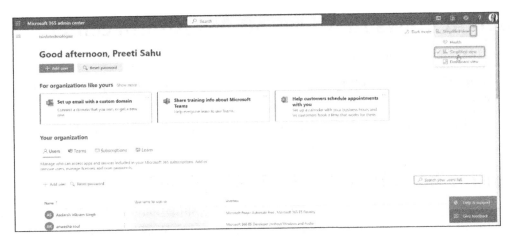

Figure 1.51: Microsoft 365 Admin center Simplified view

Microsoft 365 Admin Center in Dashboard View

As mentioned above, by default, the Microsoft 365 Admin Center Home page will be in **Dashboard view**. If not, you can expand the Dashboard view on the top right corner of the home page and then select **Dashboard view**.

On Microsoft 365 Admin Center Dashboard view home page, you can see the following functionalities:

- **Go to guided setup**

  We can use it to set up the Microsoft 365 domain name for your website and email addresses. To save yourself from subsequently change in email addresses, it is better to complete this as soon as possible.

- **+ Add cards**

  Choose **+ Add cards** or drag a card to the required location in the Microsoft 365 Admin Center Dashboard view. You can add cards like **Service health**, **Setup**, **Message center**, **Azure Active Directory**, etc.

- **Role-based access for admins**

  This card can be seen in the Dashboard view. It is the most recent introduction to the Microsoft 365 Admin center's home page. We may assign roles and provide all the role information by utilizing this card.

- **User management**

  This is another card that will help you add, edit, remove user accounts, and reset passwords directly from the Dashboard page as shown in the following screenshot:

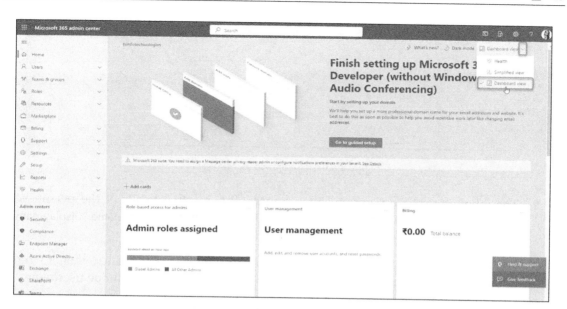

Figure 1.52: *Microsoft 365 Admin center Dashboard view*

Adding users in Microsoft 365 Admin Center

Now, we will see how to add users in Microsoft 365 Admin Center.

In the Microsoft 365 Admin Center, adding users can be done in one of four different approaches:

- Adding users in the Microsoft 365 Admin Dashboard view

- Adding multiple users at a time in the Microsoft 365 Admin Dashboard view

- Adding a single user in the Microsoft 365 Admin Simplified view

- Adding multiple users at a time in the Microsoft 365 Admin Dashboard view (Using CSV File)

Let us explore it one by one.

Adding users in the Microsoft 365 Admin Dashboard view

To add a single user in the Microsoft 365 Admin Dashboard view, refer to the instructions below:

1. On the Microsoft 365 Admin Center, Expand **Users** (From the left navigation) | **Active users** | Click on the **Add a user** button (From the **Active users** page) as shown in the following screenshot:

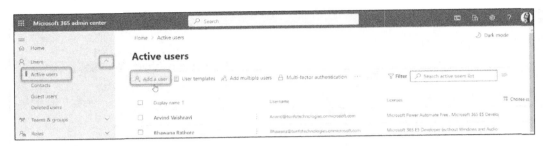

Figure 1.53: Microsoft 365 Active users

2. The following set up page will then appear. Provide the details of the person you are introducing as a user. Some basic details like **First name**, **Last name**, **Display name**, **Username**, **Password**, etc. will have to be mentioned.

3. The **Username** will verify the user. If a specific username already existed, then it would not take the name you suggested. You need to provide any other unique username.

4. Select the suitable option for **Password**. You can either create this automatically, or it will require the user to change their password. This can be done by first signing in, or sending password in email upon completion.

5. Click on **Next** as shown in the screenshot below:

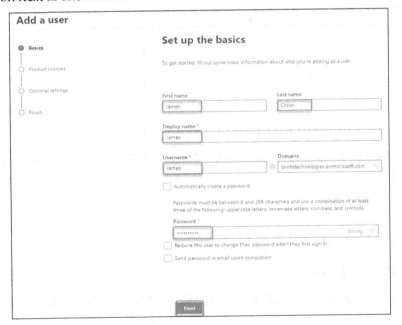

Figure 1.54: Add a user Set up

6. Next, a Product licenses page will appear where you need to select the user location and **assign user a product license**. Click on **Next** as shown in the following screenshot:

Figure 1.55: Assign product licenses to a user

7. On the **Optional settings** window, you can view two types of options:

   a. **Roles (User: no administration access)**

   b. **Profile info**

This can be seen illustrated in the following screenshot:

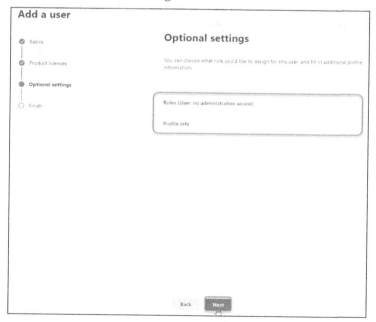

Figure 1.56: Optional settings to add a user

a. **Roles (User: no administration access):**

Users with admin responsibilities are permitted to view data and carry out actions in admin centers. By assigning the least-permissive role, you can give users only the access they require as shown in the following screenshot:

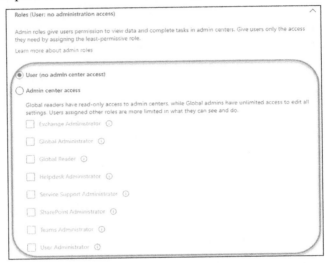

Figure 1.57: Provide Roles to the user

b. **Profile info:**

Once you expand this option, it will ask you to fill in all the user profile information like **Job title**, **Department**, **Office**, **Office phone**, etc.

Once everything is done, click on **Next** as shown in the following screenshot:

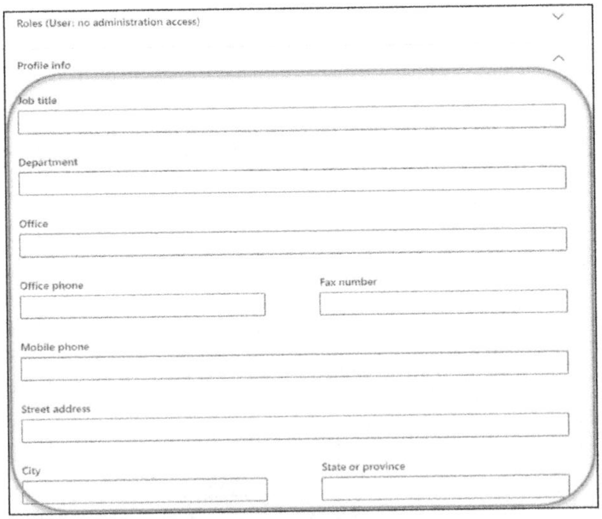

Figure 1.58: Provide Profile info of the user

8. Finally, the **Review and finish** window will display data for you to review all the user information. Once the review is completed, click on the **Finish adding** to create the new user as shown in the following screenshot:

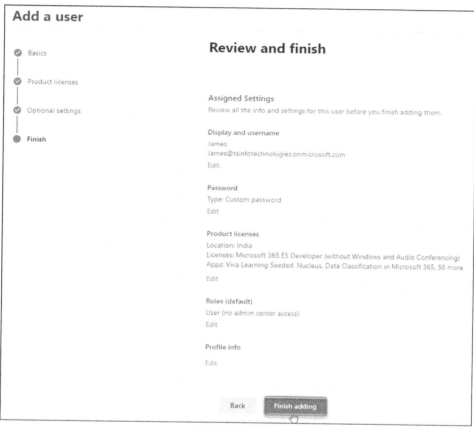

Figure 1.59: Review and finish the user set up

After a while, the specific new user will be created, and will be displayed under the **Active users (Users)** section in the Microsoft 365 Admin center.

Adding a single user in the Microsoft 365 Admin Simplified view

To add a single user in the Microsoft 365 Admin Simplified view, please follow these steps:

1. Sign into the Microsoft 365 admin center using your admin credentials.

2. Convert the admin center view to **Simplified view.**

3. Now, the Dashboard will appear as an option to an add user. Click on the **+ Add user** as shown in the following screenshot (*Figure 1.60*):

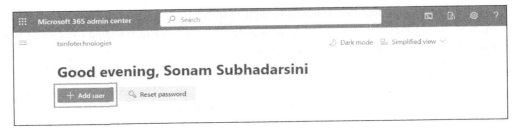

Figure 1.60: Add Single user in Microsoft 365 Admin with Simplified view

4. Add a single user from the SharePoint admin center simplified view

5. Once you click on **Add user,** a page appears where you need to set up the basic information of a user, product licenses, optional settings. The steps are the same as the above topic. (Add Users in the Microsoft 365 Admin Dashboard view).

Add multiple users at a time in the Microsoft 365 Admin Dashboard view (Using CSV File)

To add multiple users to Microsoft 365 Admin center Dashboard view by using the CSV file, you can follow these steps:

1. Sign into the Microsoft 365 Admin center using your administrator account.

2. From the left-hand menu, select **Users** and then click on **Active users**.

3. You can find the option **+ Add multiple users** as shown in the following screenshot:

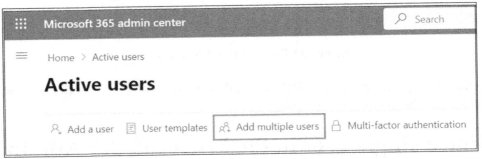

Figure 1.61: Add Multiple users in Microsoft 365 Admin with Dashboard view

4. It will take you to a screen where you can manually add as many as 249 users at once. Choose the options that asks you to upload a CSV with user information if you want to add many users via CSV file.

5. Once you select **Add multiple users** option, it will display two more links. When you click on each link, the respective CSV file will be downloaded to your local system, and you can open that file in any editors to add details. Such option-links are:

a. **Download blank CSV file with the required headers** where you can find required headers such as username, first name, last name, display name, job title, and so on. (Total 16 headers are there).

b. **Download a CSV file that includes example user info** where the file will come with example of a user information as shown in the following screenshot (*Figure 1.62*):

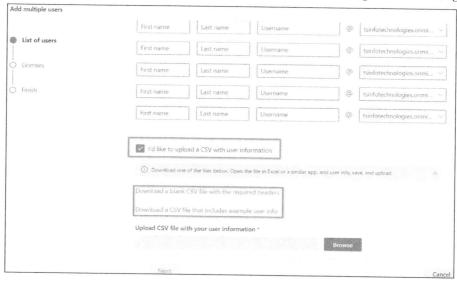

Figure 1.62: Display Download option for prebuilt CSV file template

6. Let us open the CSV file that downloaded from the second link on an editor (ex: Excel). On that excel sheet, insert some user details as per the headers and save the file as like below (*Figure 1.63*):

Figure 1.63: Insert user information in CSV file

7. Now, return to the **Microsoft admin center** page, and upload the CSV file where you inserted the users' information. Click on **Browse | upload the CSV file | Next** as shown in the following screenshot (*Figure 1.64*):

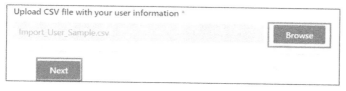

Figure 1.64: Upload CSV file with user information

8. In the next step, it will ask you to set the location and product licenses for the 3 users you are adding. Again, click on **Next** as shown in the following screenshot:

Figure 1.65: Assign Product licenses to the user

9. Finally, it will redirect you to the **Finish** page. Here, click on the **Add users** button as shown in the following screenshot:

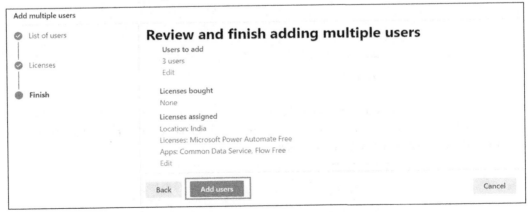

Figure 1.66: Upload CSV file with user information

10. Now, it will send the users' details via your email. Click **Close** as shown in the following screenshot:

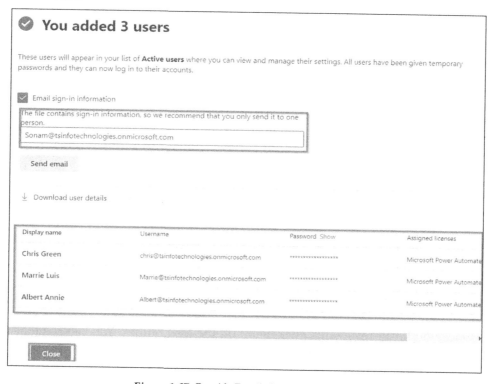

Figure 1.67: Provide Email sign-in information

Adding multiple users at a time in the Microsoft 365 Admin Dashboard view

There is another way through the Dashboard view in the Microsoft 365 Admin Center, where you can add many users at once manually. Using the Microsoft 365 Admin dashboard view, you can add up to 249 people at once. For this, follow these steps:

1. Sign in to the Microsoft 365 Admin Center using your administrator account.

2. By default, the admin center will open with the simplified view. To add multiple users, convert the admin center from simplified view to dashboard view.

3. Navigate to **Users | Active users | Add Multiple users.**

4. It will redirect you to a page containing some fields based on user's information such as first name, last name, username, etc.

5. It also allows you to add and remove the row from the information page as shown in the following screenshot:

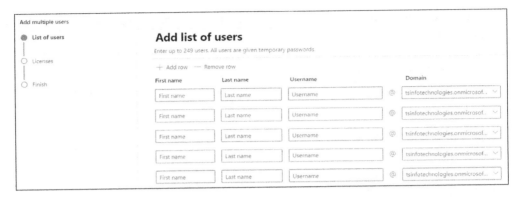

Figure 1.68: Add list of users

6. Once you give the users' details a **Next** button will lighten under this page. Click on that button.

7. Next, it will redirect you to the **Licenses** page where you need to assign the users with their relevant licenses. Click again on the **Next** button.

8. This will take you to the **Finish** page where you can review the added users' details, licensing including **edit** options.

9. Once you finish reviewing, click again on the **Next** button. You can see that multiple users are added to the Microsoft 365 Admin center.

What is SharePoint Online?

SharePoint is a web-based collaboration system that enables corporate teams to collaborate using workflow applications, **list** databases, other web elements, and security features.

Software as a service in the cloud is called SharePoint Online. Information can be shared, stored, and used jointly by users. The program is hosted by Microsoft on its own servers. Companies use a subscription approach to purchase the software.

Microsoft SharePoint is a website creation tool used by businesses. It serves as a safe location where you may store, arrange, share, and access data from any device. A web browser, such as Microsoft Edge, Internet Explorer, Chrome, or Firefox, is all that is required.

A team collaboration platform called SharePoint enables several users to work on the same document. OneDrive is a platform for online file storage and provides shared folder for files.

Benefits of using SharePoint Online for an organization

We will now explore the advantages of utilizing SharePoint Online for a business.

Real-time collaboration

Collaboration is one of the most important advantages of SharePoint. We are all aware of how important real-time collaboration and document sharing are for enhancing workflow, decision-making, and other processes.

Additionally, the procedure becomes a complete disaster when numerous people are working on the same document. As an example, everyone is changing the document and emailing its various versions. Someone can lock the document for editing when you want to modify it.

Several versions of a document are not a problem when working on a single document in the SharePoint environment because all modifications made by the team members are automatically synchronized.

In addition, if you want to see who has made what changes to the document, you can view its entire version history.

Data management

Any professional who wants to increase productivity faces a significant challenge in data management. Users can overcome this difficulty using SharePoint without having to engage in difficult programming.

Using SharePoint, managers of content or data can simply manage several projects at once. SharePoint makes it simple to publish or update website contents like events, blogs, presentation stacks, news, and so on.

You can use professional templates that are available and ready to use. You have complete control over its versions in addition to the content. When you or your team works on a file in SharePoint, it creates and stores numerous versions of that file.

When necessary, you may retrieve any prior versions or use SharePoint to correct any file system issues. To backup, restore, or fix files, you do not require any other tools.

Enhanced security

Cybercriminals are now more sophisticated and creative. To steal data, they can easily defeat even the most sophisticated security safeguards.

Advanced security measures for information sharing are stressed by the government, healthcare, medical, legal, and other industries. While working with these businesses, you must comply with tight security compliance and regulatory requirements.

When utilizing SharePoint, security is not a concern. You can work with other team members and share documents inside and outside your company.

Your communications and documents are all secure. To protect your data, SharePoint has strong data encryption and cloud backup.

Better productivity

One of the most alluring benefits of using SharePoint is increased productivity. You may quickly automate and streamline company procedures with SharePoint. It will be simple and quick for workers to collaborate in real-time. They would also be able to easily converse, track and manage documents, and send data.

Also, collaborating on group projects would be simple. Such advantages will undoubtedly increase organizational performance and effectiveness.

Integration with existing apps

The other business apps in your system can be seamlessly integrated with Microsoft SharePoint. Your Microsoft Office applications (Excel, Word, and PowerPoint), MS Exchange Server, MS Unified Communications, ERP, CRM, and many more back-office systems and earlier versions will all function flawlessly with the product.

Microsoft Edge and Internet Explorer are not the only web browsers that are compatible with SharePoint Online; all current web browsers are compatible with SharePoint.

Document sharing

You should share your documents with other team members for evaluation or feedback, much like when working collaboratively. To organize documents for editing, remark on them, and then return them to the senders might become very difficult for one person.

It only requires saving a file to a SharePoint document collection and granting stakeholders' access. Individuals have access to view, edit, and comment on the document. All revisions and comments are contained in one document.

Saving money

It is possible that you already pay for SharePoint through your Microsoft 365 subscription. Use SharePoint as your go-to productivity tool to save money on unneeded apps and tools for work or personal use.

Overview of SharePoint Online Admin center

Administrators can monitor and manage a SharePoint environment using the SharePoint Online Admin Center. It is organized into various sections and enables administrators to configure and manage SharePoint from a single location, including control of security, monitoring, general settings, system settings, and apps.

The administrator of SharePoint in your company may be a system administrator. If not, the administrator of your system may be aware of the SharePoint administrator and be able to assist you in locating them. You should ask your SharePoint administrator to fix any problems you are having, such as when you do not have enough permissions.

Access SharePoint Online Admin center

To access SharePoint Online Admin Center, refer to the instructions below:

1. To access the Office 365 admin center, open your web browser and navigate to **https://admin.microsoft.com**.

2. Click **Show all (...)** in the left navigation and tap on **SharePoint** to launch a SharePoint Online Admin Center from the list of all **Admin centers** as shown in the following screenshot:

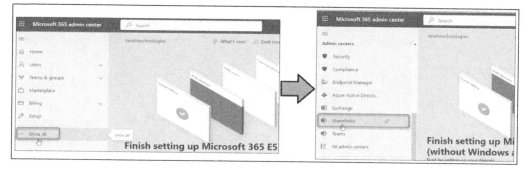

Figure 1.69: Access SharePoint Online Admin Center

3. Use a direct link instead to get to an Office 365 SharePoint admin center, like this:
   https://yourcompany-admin.sharepoint.com as shown in the following screenshot, Where **yourcompany** is your company (tenant) name

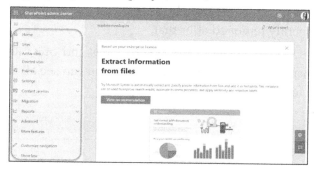

Figure 1.70: SharePoint Online Admin Center Home page

Sites

There are two types of sites in SharePoint Online Admin Center:

- **Active:**

  To manage all your sites, use this page. The list of active sites includes team sites and communication sites, along with details like the site name, URL, storage usage, and primary admin are available here.

  A graph showing the total amount of storage used by all sites is in the upper right corner. The active sites list can be exported to a CSV file using the Export button.

  Sites that are active allow visitors to read pages, download, upload files, and edit and alter existing files as shown in the following screenshot:

Figure 1.71: SharePoint Admin Center Active sites

- **Deleted sites**

  The list of deleted SharePoint sites can be seen on this page of the SharePoint admin center. A deleted site can be restored by a SharePoint administrator within 93 days. The site gets permanently removed after that.

  You can choose a site from the list of deleted sites and press **Restore** to bring it back or press **Permanently delete** to remove it forever. You can see all the SharePoint deleted sites as like the following screenshot:

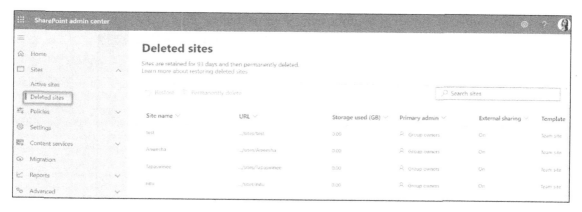

Figure 1.72: *SharePoint Admin Center Deleted sites*

Policies

Sharing policies and Access control settings are present in this section.

- **Sharing:**

  These sharing options are used to regulate sharing in SharePoint and OneDrive at the organizational level. From the least permissive to the most permissive settings, all are available here. There are four levels accessible, and you can share content with:

  o **Anyone**

  o **New and existing guests**

  o **Existing guests**

  o **Only people in your organization**

  More external sharing settings:

  o **Limit external sharing by domain** (select domains from which users can/cannot access shared files)

  o **Allow only users in specific security groups to share externally**

  o **Guests must sign in using the same account to which sharing invitations are sent**

  o **Allow guests to share items they don't own**

  o **Guest access to a site or OneDrive will expire automatically after this many days __**

  o **People who use a verification code must reauthenticate after this many days __**

These options are also shown in the following screenshot:

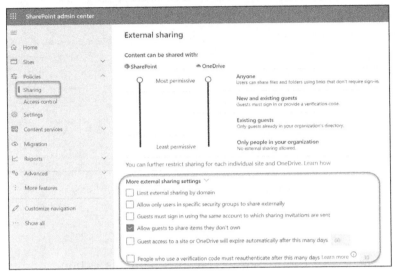

Figure 1.73: SharePoint admin center External sharing

- **File and folder links**:

  In this section, we need to choose the link type when users share files and folders in SharePoint and OneDrive, Choose the Permission, expiration, and other settings as shown in the following screenshot:

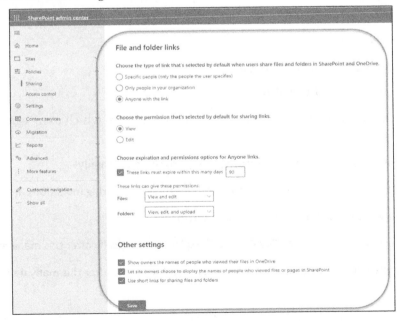

Figure 1.74: SharePoint Online Admin center File and folder links

- **Access control**:

There are four types of Access control in the SharePoint Online Admin Center:

  o **Unmanaged devices**: If specified operating system and web browser combinations are being utilized, or if they don't correspond to the set configuration, you can enable, limit, or block access for those devices.

  o **Idle session sign-out**: Using this option, the SharePoint administrator can specify the amount of inactivity before a user receives a warning and is signed out.

  o **Network location**: You can set SharePoint access to only be granted from trusted IP addresses using this option. You must add your own IP address to the list of permitted IP addresses when configuring this option or you risk blocking yourself.

  o **Apps that don't use modern authentication**: This option permits or prevents access from third-party programs or outdated Microsoft Office applications (Office 2010 and prior versions) that cannot implement device-based limitations.

Refer to the screenshot below:

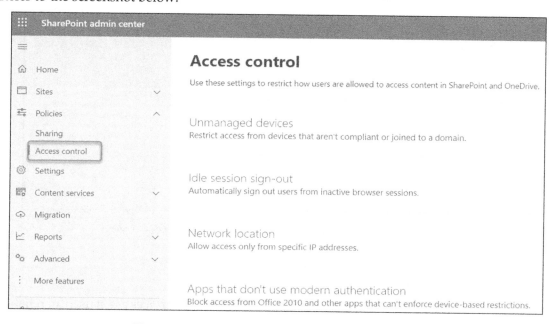

Figure 1.75: SharePoint Online Admin center Access control

Settings

The following settings are available in SharePoint Online admin center:

- **Default admin center**: If this setting is enabled, the SharePoint admin center opens by default with the old version of the admin interface loaded.

- **Pages:** Configure whether people can publish modern pages and leave comments on them.

- **SharePoint notifications:** If users enable notifications for mobile apps, they can utilize this setting to get alerts about news, file activity, and SharePoint content.

- **Site creation:** Activate this setting to allow users to create sites from the SharePoint and OneDrive home pages. A default time zone and a directory where users can establish sites can be chosen.

- **Site storage limits:** These limitations have two configuration options: automatic and manual. You can provide sites with as much storage space as they require if you choose the automated option. If you choose the manual option, you must manually establish the limitations for each site.

All these settings are illustrated in the following screenshot:

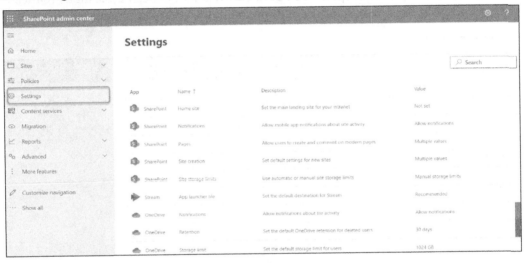

Figure 1.76: SharePoint Online Admin center Settings

Content services

Using metadata in the SharePoint Online Admin Center, content services assist users in reliably entering and sorting data.

- **Term store:**

  A Term store gives SharePoint users extra options for storing and organizing data, including metadata. A term store is a global web directory of terms you use frequently in your company. A SharePoint site's local taxonomy can be edited, terms can be created and edited, and a person or group can be chosen for the term set like the following figure:

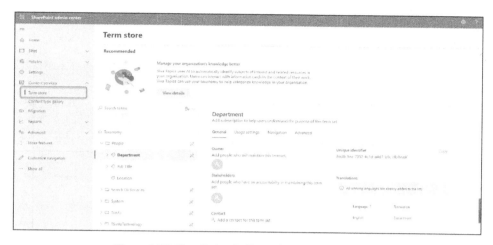

Figure 1.77: SharePoint Online Admin center Term store

- **Content type gallery**:

  Develop various content types, give each one a category, and link the corresponding template to the category. Configurations can be adjusted to force users to utilize a default document template.

  For example, when a user uses a template to create an Excel document and the template is linked to a Timesheet content type, the user consistently creates the same content type using the right and standardized template. Refer the following figure:

Figure 1.78: Content type gallery in SharePoint Online Admin center

Migration

The migration manager and SharePoint migration tool options for moving on-premises file shares to Office 365 are shown in this section (Microsoft 365). To add content to SharePoint Online and Office 365, you can copy it from a standalone SharePoint Server as shown in the following screenshot:

Figure 1.79: SharePoint Online Admin center Migration

Reports

This section constitutes of the following:

- **Content services**:

  The content services navigation area has just been added by Microsoft to the SharePoint Online admin center dashboard's left side. Microsoft's Project Cortex, SharePoint, and Content Services are the main products.

  On the dashboard of the SharePoint admin center, we may build a term store and a content type as shown in the following screenshot:

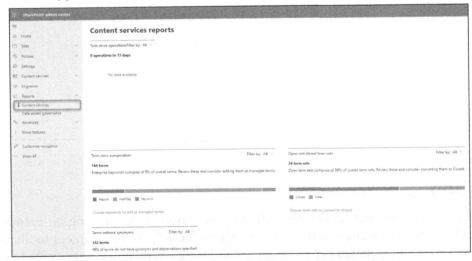

Figure 1.80: SharePoint Online Content services reports

- **Data access governance**:

  Organizations need solutions to help them manage their data as security and compliance regulations become more stringent across industries and the volume of company data increases tremendously.

  Information from data access governance reports can be used to manage user access to SharePoint data. The reports assist you in finding websites with potentially sensitive or overshared content.

  These reports can be used to evaluate and implement the right security and compliance procedures as shown in the following screenshot:

Figure 1.81: SharePoint Online Admin Center Data access governance

Advanced

This section constitutes of the following options:

- **API access**:

  To utilize the app's advanced functionality, you must have access to extra resources outside of SharePoint. To guarantee that the app's functionality is not constrained, access must be granted by a Global Administrator.

  Certain permissions are given directly through app components, while others are given through the SharePoint Admin page.

  You can grant two permissions here:

  o Having access to Azure AD enables you to employ rules in modern forms that are particular to users in particular AD groups by allowing modern forms to query AD group membership.

  o The Calendar web component needs access to Exchange Calendars in order to read Exchange Calendars. If you do not want to show users' Exchange calendars on the web part, you don't need to grant this permission. Refer to the screenshot below:

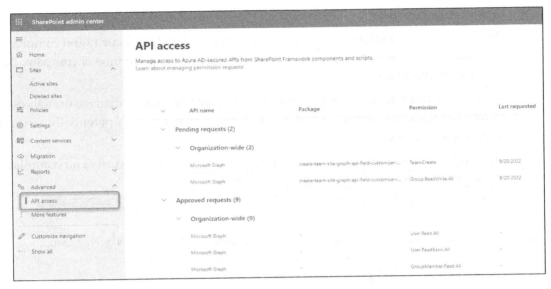

Figure 1.82: SharePoint Online Admin Center API access

- **More features:**

  You can locate recognizable and dated SharePoint features that were present in the previous admin center on this page. To access feature settings, choose the required feature and click on **Open** as shown in the following screenshot:

Figure 1.83: More features in SharePoint Online Admin Center

Overview of classic SharePoint

The *Classic* experience merges SharePoint lists and libraries through a user interface that is highly customizable. The *Modern* interface is mobile-ready, (currently) restricts the amount of visual customization possible, improves producers' experiences through greater intuitiveness, and improves users' experiences through greater collaboration.

To make UI customization simple, the classic UI incorporates SharePoint lists and libraries. You can add your own CSS, jQuery, and other features using the script editor online tool in the traditional experience. The traditional experience, however, is not as updated or optimized for mobile as the contemporary one.

Links, calendars, and announcements sections can be found on the classic SharePoint home page. On the other hand, the most recent SharePoint home page includes a document library, quick connections, and recent site activity.

Wiki pages and blog pages, as well as other Classic web elements, are included with Classic SharePoint sites. These web elements and pages, like everything else in the classic UI, do not offer a seamless user experience and call for customization for numerous modifications. Whereas the modern experience is quicker, simpler to use, and mobile-friendly.

Although the user may simply configure and manage material, there is no current online tool for applying styling.

Time period for a classic SharePoint online experience

As long as the customers continue using classic mode, it will be supported. It is not going away for the **foreseeable future**, according to a new post at Office Development Center.

Until the contemporary library experience allows the same level of customization as the classic one and partners have had enough time to adapt their solutions to the new experience, we will continue to support both mitigations.

Overview of Modern SharePoint Online

Microsoft SharePoint's new user interface is intended to be engaging, flexible, and more productive. Anyone may now easily develop appealing, dynamic sites and pages that are mobile-ready via recent technology.

Every site is a site collection and can be connected to a hub, which is a flat collection of sites that share navigation, branding, and other components, in the current SharePoint experience. This kind of structure is much more adaptable to the shifting requirements of your firm.

Navigation

The most efficient SharePoint sites (as well as websites in general) make it easy for users to locate the information they require, enabling them to make decisions, get knowledge of current events, get access to tools they require, or collaborate with coworkers to find solutions.

Both the classic and modern SharePoint structures can benefit from following the same core guidelines and best practices for site and page navigation. But, depending on the structure of your websites and intranet, you have many possibilities for creating navigation.

Branding

Custom master pages or other CSS configurations are typically necessary for site branding. New default site themes and site designs (or templates) for modern SharePoint are responsive and look beautiful on any device. You can alter your site's logo and colors to represent your business by using site themes better.

Also, you can match your company's branding to the mobile SharePoint app for your users. Site designs give your website distinct layouts and other capabilities. With the use of unique themes or site layouts, additional branding can be accomplished without the fear of a SharePoint update ruining something.

Publishing

If your company has deployed publishing sites or publishing-enabled sites, you are aware of how crucial it is to develop engaging and effective pages to communicate with a broad audience.

Modern communication sites make it simple to build stunning, dynamic, and effective sites and pages that are mobile-ready. Yet, there are several distinctions from traditional publishing and some things to consider before switching to the current experience.

Search

If you want users to find what they are looking for quickly and easily, search is a crucial component of any website. SharePoint offers both a classic and a modern search interface. The modern interface in SharePoint is Microsoft Search.

The Microsoft Search box is now located in the header bar at the top of SharePoint, which is the most noticeable change. The fact that Microsoft Search is personalized and contextual is another distinction.

Even when you search for the same words, the results you receive are different from what other people view. Also, depending on where you are when you search, you will see various results.

Sharing and permissions

SharePoint still offers security groups managed by Azure Active Directory in addition to SharePoint groups. Microsoft 365 Groups, a third grouping choice for SharePoint, are also offered by Microsoft 365.

Security groups and Microsoft 365 groups are comparable, yet Microsoft 365 groups offer many more advantages. A group email account, as well as extra resources including a shared calendar, notebook, planner, and SharePoint Team site, are made available to Microsoft 365 groups.

Performance

SharePoint's new user interface is intended to be engaging, adaptable, and most importantly, more efficient.

The speed at which pages are rendered in the client browser, also known as perceived end-user latency, is the key performance parameter for SharePoint as well as the performance of specific SharePoint components like search, lists, and document libraries.

Multilingual

For your intranet sites' content to be offered in different languages, modern communication sites make use of a multilingual experience. The user's preferred language can be displayed for user interface components like site navigation, site title, and site description.

On communication sites, you can also offer websites and news articles that you translate and display in the user's preferred language. The creation of a similar page on the same site but in a language-specific folder in the Site Pages library is one of the most significant differences between the modern experience and the variants feature, which produces separate subsites for each language.

Advantages of Modern SharePoint Online

The advantages of the Microsoft 365 platform are felt by businesses, now more than ever. The Microsoft 365 toolkit is a cloud-based solution that is always developing and getting better to satisfy the demands of contemporary businesses. Some of the key advantages of utilizing Modern SharePoint are mentioned here.

- **Better performance**: Performance is better, especially for content editors or site managers, due to the SharePoint framework, which executes all web elements on the client side rather than the server. With numerous page reloads in the past, things could be a little clumsy, but SharePoint is now quicker and more flexible.

- **Faster**: As compared to the classic experience, the Modern SharePoint site in Microsoft 365 offers a faster document library and lists.

- **Integration with Microsoft 365 Groups**: We may also use M365 groups' membership services, which make it simple to manage permissions for the hub and related team sites. Microsoft Teams, OneNote, Planner, MS Stream, Power Apps, and other services that are fully integrated with the SharePoint contemporary experience may all be accessed with the help of M365 groups.

- **Responsive**: The responsiveness of modern SharePoint sites is built-in, which is a significant improvement over the classic site. The modern experience offers a layout that works on any screen size, including laptops, desktop computers, tablets, and smartphones. No requirement for side-scrolling is necessary. All browsers have a nicer appearance that is also simpler to use.

- **Modern SharePoint Architecture**: Sites and subsites in SharePoint Classic can only be organized hierarchically. In comparison, modern architecture can be adaptable by using flat architecture to create a hierarchy-like structure through hub and association. Cross-site navigation is possible with Hubs, which also immediately applies a design or theme to the related site. Sites can easily be relocated between hubs.

- **Security and Sharing**: Every modern SharePoint site places a lot of emphasis on security. Permissions in classic SharePoint sites are controlled by several permission groups (that is, Owners, Members, Visitors, and so on). It is simpler to configure and regulate access on a modern SharePoint site. Remember that anyone with access to a modern SharePoint site has access to all the site's content.

As an alternative, you can provide a single file or folder along with a shareable link that allows access to anyone, only people in your organization, or only specific people.

Users can share content with others outside the company, such as partners, vendors, clients, or customers, using SharePoint Online's external sharing features. At the organizational and site levels, external sharing can be controlled.

Enabling the modern experience at tenant level

You can enable the SharePoint Modern experience at the Office 365 Tenant level if you are currently utilizing the SharePoint Classic experience and would like to switch to it.

It is preferable to disable SharePoint's modern experience at the tenant level, at least for production sites, if your company is not ready to use it.

At the Office 365 Tenant level, we can enable or disable the SharePoint Online Modern experience. The best course of action is to disable the new SharePoint Online experience if you do not want to utilize it. To enable or disable the new experience in SharePoint Online, follow these steps:

1. Open **Microsoft 365 admin center** using valid Microsoft credentials. You can open the admin center by clicking the provided link or go to the **App launcher** and click on **Admin,** as shown in the following screenshot:

Figure 1.84: Click Admin from Microsoft 365 App Launcher

2. On Microsoft 365 admin center page, click **SharePoint** under the **Admin centers** section as shown in the following screenshot:

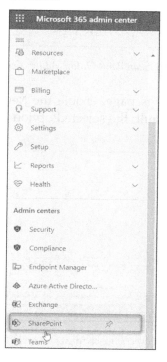

Figure 1.85: Open SharePoint Admin center

3. On the SharePoint admin center page, go to **Settings** (from the left navigation) and Click on the **classic settings page** link as shown in the following screenshot:

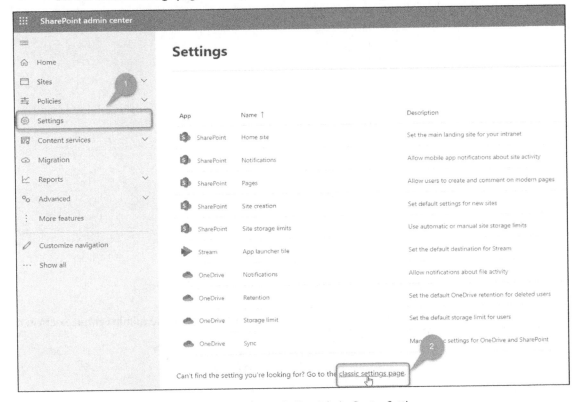

Figure 1.86: SharePoint Online Admin Center Settings

4. On the tenant level Settings page, enable the **New experience** option of **OneDrive for Business experience**. By default, the selected option will be **New experience** as shown in the following screenshot:

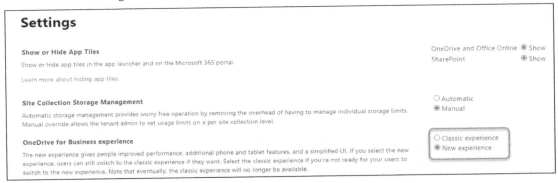

Figure 1.87: Enable New experience settings for OneDrive for Business experience

SharePoint Online list and document library switch to New Experience

We can also enable or disable the modern experience at the SharePoint List level or Document library level to use the new experience in SharePoint Online. To do this, follow these steps:

1. If you want to switch SharePoint Online List to a new experience, then go to the **Settings** icon and click on the **List settings** under the **SharePoint** section.

2. If you want to switch SharePoint Online Document Library to a new experience, then go to the **Settings** icon, click on the **Library settings** under **SharePoint** section and tap on **More library settings** as shown in the following screenshot:

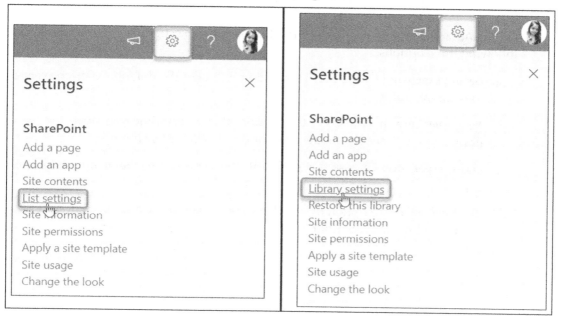

Figure 1.88: SharePoint Online Document List/Library settings

3. On the **List settings** or **Library settings** page, click on the **Advanced settings** option under the **General Settings** section, as shown in the following screenshot:

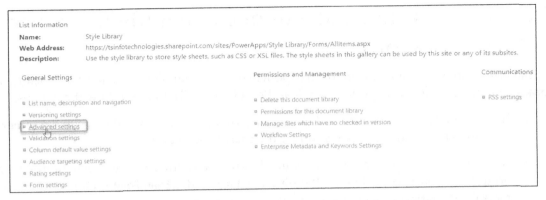

Figure 1.89: SharePoint Online Document List/Library Advanced settings

4. On the **Advanced settings** page, go to the **List experience** section. Here, you can see the following three options:

   a. **Default experience for the site**: This option will take the default experience set by the administrator.

   b. **New experience**: If you select this option, then every time you open the list or library, you will see the modern UI for the specific list or library.

   c. **Classic experience:** Choose this option if you want to use the SharePoint Classic experience.

5. Select the **New experience** option to switch to a new experience and then click on **OK** as shown in the following screenshot:

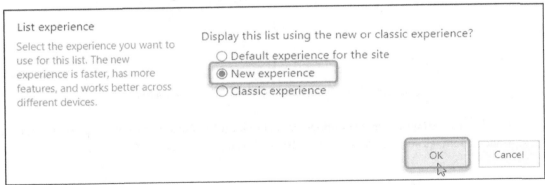

Figure 1.90: Enable New experience under the List experience

Conclusion

In this chapter, we have covered all about Microsoft 365 and SharePoint Online such as what are the various Microsoft 365 subscriptions, and how-to sign-up Microsoft 365 trials.

Also, we learned about Microsoft 365 Admin Center, how to add users in Microsoft 365, everything about SharePoint Online, the benefits of using SharePoint Online, overview of SharePoint Online Admin Center and Modern SharePoint Online, advantages of using Modern SharePoint Online, and how to enable Modern SharePoint experience at tenant level.

In the next chapter, we will discuss what the SharePoint Modern Team site is, why we should create a SharePoint Team site, key features, an Overview of site content, and so on.

Points to remember

You can rapidly read and comprehend some of the chapter's most crucial learning points like:

- Microsoft 365 includes Office applications as well as other services, such as online email, contact, and calendar access, as well as additional software including OneNote, Excel, Word, and PowerPoint.

- Microsoft 365 Subscriptions has three different plans:

    o   For home

    o   For business

    o   For enterprise

- For trial of SharePoint and all the Microsoft 365 apps, there are 4 different plans:

    o   Microsoft 365 Business basic

    o   Microsoft 365 Apps for business

    o   Microsoft 365 Business standard

    o   Microsoft 365 Business premium

- Microsoft 365 Admin Center: A variety of tools and resources are available in the Microsoft 365 Admin Center to help administrators manage their tenant, users, IAM, teams, etc. There are two methods for gaining access to the Microsoft 365 admin center. Such as:

    o   From Admin Web link

    o   From Microsoft 365 App Launcher

- Microsoft 365 Admin Center Interface Components: There are three various types of interface components as:

    o   Top Management panel

    o   Left Navigation panel

    o   Admin centers panel

- Introduction to SharePoint Online:

  o SharePoint is a web-based system for team collaboration that gives businesses the ability to work together utilizing workflow applications, "list" databases, other web components, and security measures.

  o SharePoint Online is a cloud-based software as a service.

  o Companies buy the software via a subscription model.

- Some settings in SharePoint Online Admin Center are, Sites, Policies, Settings, Content services, Migration, Reports, and Advanced

- Overview of Classic SharePoint:

  o SharePoint lists and libraries are combined as part of the Classic experience using a highly customizable user interface.

  o The Modern interface is mobile-ready, limits the degree of visual modification that is currently available, enhances the experiences of producers through increased intuitiveness, and enhances the experiences of users through enhanced cooperation.

  o The classic UI leverages SharePoint lists and libraries to make UI customization simple.

  o In the conventional experience, you can use the script editor online tool to add your own CSS, jQuery, and other features. However, compared to the modern experience, the conventional one is not as modern or mobile-friendly.

- The new user interface for Microsoft SharePoint, that is, Modern SharePoint Online is meant to be more entertaining, adaptable, and useful. Thanks to contemporary technologies, anyone may now quickly create beautiful, dynamic sites and pages that are mobile-ready.

Chapter 2

SharePoint Modern Team Site

Introduction

This chapter will provide you with full information about SharePoint Online team sites, why we should create a team site in SharePoint Online, features of SharePoint team site, and how to create a team site in SharePoint Online.

In this chapter, we will cover how we can customize the SharePoint Modern team site, all about site contents, SharePoint site settings, site navigation, different site templates, changing team site URL, site permission, and many more.

We will see how we can convert the SharePoint team site to a communication site and work on a subsite in the SharePoint team site.

Structure

This chapter is a formidable approach to SharePoint Online team sites. It will describe why it is important to create a team site in SharePoint Online, emphasize the features of a SharePoint team site, and teach you how to create a team site in SharePoint Online. The concept of customizing the SharePoint Modern team site, working on-site contents, and site navigation. We will see how we can work with subsites in SharePoint Online.

The contents of this chapter are listed below:

- Overview of team site in SharePoint

- Creating a SharePoint team site

- Key features of SharePoint Modern team site

- Creating a Modern team site in SharePoint

- Customizing a Modern SharePoint team site

- Overview of site contents

- Introduction to SharePoint site settings

- Navigating SharePoint Online team site and Quick Launch

- SharePoint site template

- Overview of recycle bin

- Changing SharePoint team site URL

- SharePoint site permissions

- Access request settings

- Share SharePoint team site

- SharePoint site usage analytics

- Converting SharePoint Modern team site to communication site

- Connecting Modern SharePoint team site to Teams

- Working with subsites in SharePoint Online

- Deleting a modern team site in SharePoint Online

Objectives

If you are new to SharePoint Online, they will get a detailed view of why they need to create a SharePoint team site and how it is helpful. Also, the user gets to know how to customize the team site so it meets the business needs. Different site settings are available on the SharePoint Team site, what are the different navigations and how we can access them, how to apply site templates, and so on.

Furthermore, the reader gets to know the other aspects of the team site, like how to provide different levels of permissions to the user, change the team site URL, and share the SharePoint team site with another user. Aside from that, the reader also gets to know how they can connect the team site to Microsoft Teams, and how to work on subsites in the SharePoint Online team site.

Overview of team site in SharePoint

This section will discuss the overview of the team site in SharePoint:

- A Team site in SharePoint Online that can help you and your team to connect virtually.

- This SharePoint site also helps your team to connect with various data, information, and applications that you use every day.

- Other than this, a SharePoint team site also includes managing a list of information, storing and working on files, and much more. It also helps team members by keeping them informed using reminders, events, to-do lists, etc.

- When we build a modern team site in SharePoint Online, it immediately creates the Office 365 group, group email address, and the ability to determine if this site includes sensitive information (privacy).

- As we know, the Modern team site is coming with Microsoft 365 groups and allows them to improve collaboration. This group, on the other hand, brings together communications and Outlook calendars, files from SharePoint, tasks from the planner, and many other things into a single space.

Overall, the Modern team site in SharePoint Online is an effective collaboration tool that enables teams to virtually connect, access crucial data and apps, manage information, and keep up to date with events and reminders while maintaining the security of sensitive data.

Creating a SharePoint team site

Here are the reasons why we need to create a team site in SharePoint:

- With a team site we can quickly and easily collaborate with team members on the same project.

- We can host all our documents and contents on the same site so that the team will not go through a massive email chain and document loss.

- A team site in SharePoint Online is extremely simple to create and customize.

- Once it is up and running, you will discover that having a formal space to work together and communicate may greatly improve the overall quality of your projects.

Key features of SharePoint Modern team site

As there are lots of features available on the team site, we will discuss some of them here:

- **Build a team site in a second**: We can build a team site with Microsoft Office 365 group in a second.

- **Easily customize the team site**: You may quickly and effectively change your SharePoint site's appearance to fit your corporate identity. You may select a basic SharePoint theme and modify it as necessary, select a business theme with authorized branding for your organization, or utilize one of the classic experience designs.

- **External sharing feature**: You may use the external sharing features of SharePoint Online to share material with individuals outside your organization if your company works on projects that need document sharing or direct collaboration with suppliers, clients, or customers.

- **Connect your team site to a hub site in SharePoint**: Your sites and content must change as your company's objectives and team structures do. The creation of a full and uniform representation of your project, department, or area is made possible by grouping websites into a hub site that improves content discovery and interaction. Hub sites in SharePoint serve as a crucial intranet-building piece.

- **SharePoint with MS Teams**: Once SharePoint and Microsoft Teams are linked, the world of collaboration will be your ocean and be bursting with opportunities. Workplace connectivity and content collaboration are made possible with SharePoint. The center of teamwork is Microsoft Teams.

Creating a Modern team site in SharePoint

SharePoint Online Modern team sites enable users to interact, exchange documents and messages, and work together. They offer an entirely new experience for users with their straightforward design, responsive UI designed for mobile devices, and quicker page loading.

When you build a site in the SharePoint Online admin center, it automatically generates a modern team and an associated Office 365 group.

To build a modern Team site in SharePoint, follow the below steps:

1. Click on **https://admin.microsoft.com/#/homepage** to access the **Microsoft 365 admin center**, where we can access the SharePoint admin center.

2. Log in to the **Microsoft 365 admin center**, if you are not logged in.

3. Then in the left navigation, under the **Admin centers**, click on **SharePoint**, as you can see in *Figure: 2.1*. Else, you can directly access the SharePoint admin center by writing the URL:

   https://tenantName-admin.sharepoint.com/'

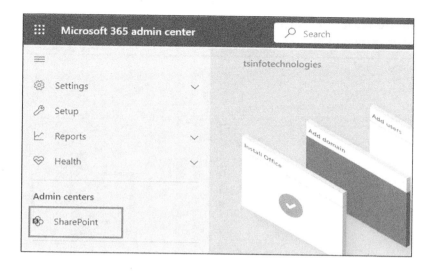

Figure 2.1: Access SharePoint admin center

4. Now in the **SharePoint Admin center**, in the left navigation, you can see the **Sites** category (where we can create, manage, and delete our sites based on our requirements). Under **Sites**, click on **Active sites**.

5. Then, it will redirect to the **Active sites** page. If your organization created sites then you can see different sites on this page. At the top of this page, you can see the 3 options that is, **Create**, **Export**, and **Track view**, from this click on **Create**, as you can see in *Figure 2.2*, to create the team site:

Figure 2.2: Active sites in SharePoint admin center

6. You can see a window, where we get options to create a **Team site**, **Communication site**, and **Other options** (It includes different types of sites like publishing portal, enterprise wiki, etc. Also, you can create a team site that is not associated with Microsoft 365 group).

7. Select the **Team site** (which is associated with Microsoft 365 group) in **Create a Site** window, as shown in *Figure 2.3)*:

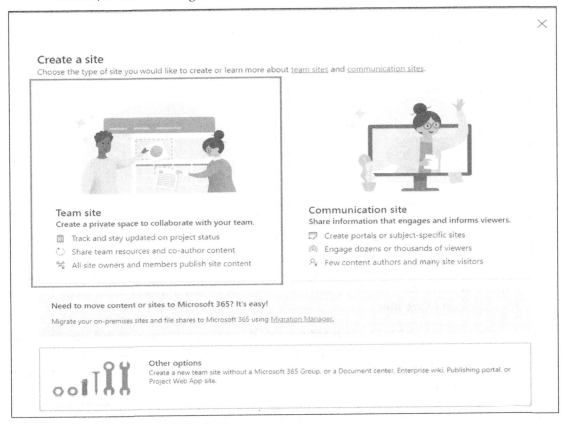

Figure 2.3: *Create SharePoint modern team site*

8. Provide a **Site name**, it will automatically take the **Group email address** and **site address**, illustrated in *Figure 2.4*. Then provide the **Group owner** and **Select the language**.

9. Click on **Advanced settings** and set the **Privacy settings- private - only site members can access this site**, and public (anyone can access this site in the organization).

10. Then provide the **Time zone**, **Site description**, and Storage limit. Click on **Next**.

11. Finally, provide the site members, by providing the name or email address of the **Member** illustrated in *Figure 2.4*.

12. Click on **Finish**.

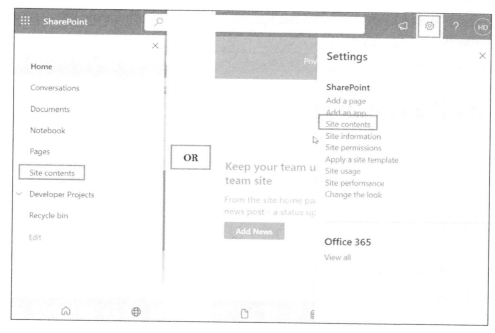

Figure 2.4: Create and add members to the SharePoint Team site

As we have successfully created the Modern Team site, this site will be available in the **Active sites**. In this case, our site **TsInfo Developer** populated in **Active sites** page. By clicking on the **Site name**, you can see the full information about a site based on the category, i.e., **General**, **Activity**, **Permission**, and **Policies**, illustrated in *Figure 2.5*:

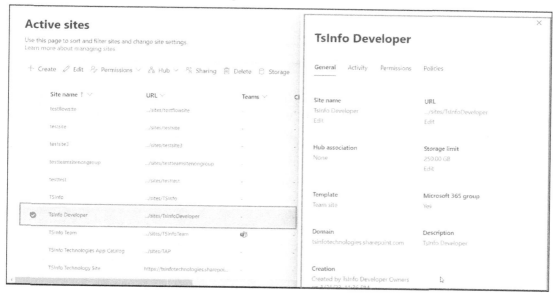

Figure 2.5: SharePoint Modern team site successfully created

Now to access the team site we have created, click on the **URL**, under the **URL** section in the **General** tab, illustrated in *Figure 2.6*:

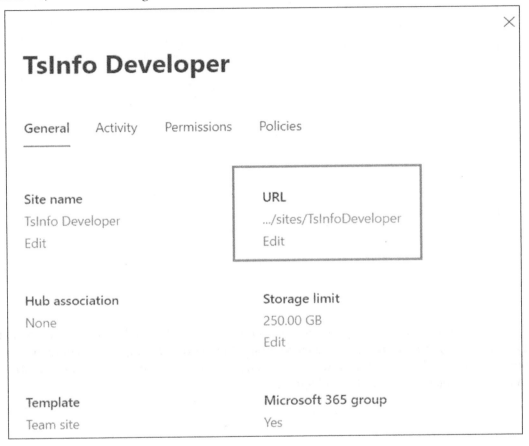

Figure 2.6: *Access the Team site by URL*

Once you click on the URL, you can see the team site is running in the browser, illustrated in *Figure 2.7*, now we can customize, and work with the team site, like adding web parts, creating a list library, and many more based on your requirements:

Figure 2.7: *Team site Look and Feel*

Customizing Modern SharePoint team site

You may quickly and effortlessly change the appearance of your SharePoint Team site to fit your professional style and brand.

We will use the **Change the look** functionality (available in the **Settings** of the team site), to customize the look of the SharePoint team site. Here is the customization we are going to cover for the SharePoint Modern team site.

1. Use the **Theme** to change the color of the SharePoint team site.

2. Customize SharePoint team site **Header**.

3. Customize SharePoint team site **Navigation**.

Note: To do the above customization, the user should have design permission or the user assigned as site owner of the site

Using the theme to change the color of the SharePoint Team site

You can choose one of the classic experience designs or one of the basic SharePoint themes and personalize it as needed. You can even use a business theme with authorized branding for your organization.

To change the color of the SharePoint team site by using **Theme**, follow the below steps:

1. In the SharePoint team site, click on the gear icon ⚙, and select the **Change the look** option.

2. Then select the **Theme** option from the list to customize the theme of the SharePoint site.

Figure 2.8 illustrates the above two steps to change the look of the SharePoint team site:

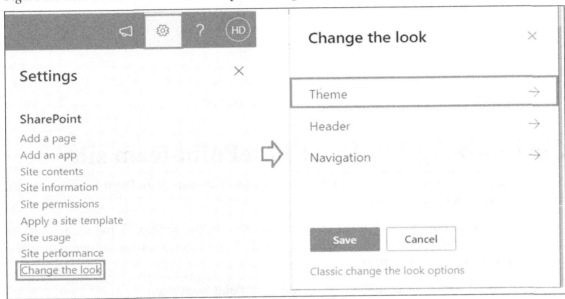

Figure 2.8: *Change the look of the SharePoint team site*

3. To change the color of the SharePoint Team site, select the **Company themes** or **SharePoint themes** illustrated in *Figure 2.9*. And if you want to customize the theme, then you can click on the **Customize** option.

4. Once you choose the theme, click on **Save** as shown in the following screenshot:

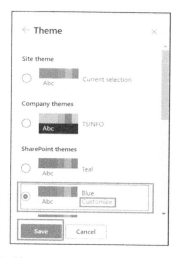

Figure 2.9: Change the theme of the SharePoint team site

Now you can see the theme reflected in the SharePoint team site based on the selected theme.

Customizing SharePoint team site header

Now we will see how we can customize the SharePoint team site header. So, follow the below steps:

1. In the SharePoint team site, click on the gear icon ⚙, and select the **Change the look** option.

2. Then, select the **Header** option from the list to customize the header of the SharePoint site as shown in the following screenshot:

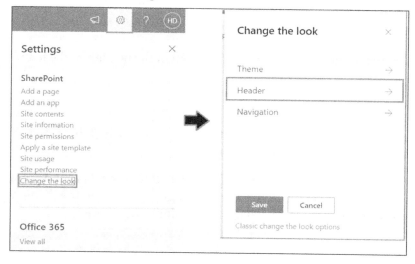

Figure 2.10: Change the header look of the SharePoint team site

Now you can see in *Figure 2.11* the different options to customize the **Layout, Background**, and **Display** of the SharePoint Team site header:

Figure 2.11: *Customize the header of the SharePoint team site*

Let us see the different options to customize the layout of the header on the team site, and how it looks.

Layout 1: Minimal

Reduced height of the header with all content in a single line which included a tiny site logo, site title, site navigation, and site actions and labels.

In *Figure 2.12*, we chose the header as Minimal and changed the background color of the theme to orange. As we change the theme of the site to orange, so based on the theme you choose, it will show you the color option for the background color of the header:

Figure 2.12: *Change the header look to minimal of the SharePoint team site*

Layout 2: Compact

A relatively high layout with the full-size site logo and text on a single line.

In *Figure 2.13*, we choose the header as compact and change the background color of the theme to orange:

Figure 2.13: *Change the header look to the compact of the SharePoint team site*

Layout 3: Standard

A style with the site logo in full size and the information divided into two lines.

In *Figure 2.14* We choose the header as **Standard** and changed the background color of the theme to Orange:

Figure 2.14: *Change the header look to the standard of the SharePoint team site*

Layout 4: Extended

Our most extensive layout, with the text divided into two sections separated by a site logo, title, and an optional background image.

In *Figure 2.15*, We choose the header as extended and change the background color of the theme to Orange:

Figure 2.15: *Change the header look to extended the SharePoint Team site*

Now in the **Display** section, you can customize the **Header** by following:

- **Site Title visibility:** By toggling on/off we can show or hide the title in the header.
- **Site Logo thumbnail:** You can change the logo thumbnail from the site header.
- **Site Logo:** You can **Change** or **Remove** the logo from the site header.

In *Figure 2.16*, you can see the above option illustrated:

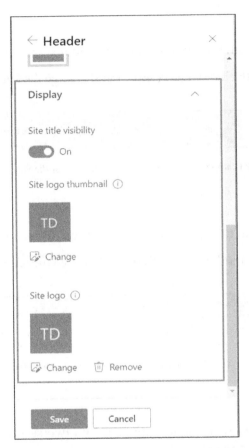

Figure 2.16: Customize the header of the team site in SharePoint

Customizing SharePoint team site navigation

Now we will see how we can customize the style of **Navigation** in SharePoint. So, follow the below steps:

1. In the SharePoint Team site, click on the gear icon ⚙, and select the **Change the look** option.

2. Then select the **Navigation** option from the list to customize the navigation of the SharePoint site. This is illustrated in *Figure 2.17*:

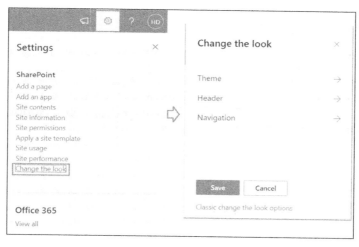

Figure 2.17: Customize the navigation in the SharePoint team site

In the **Navigation** window, you can toggle on/off the visibility of the **Navigation** on the SharePoint team site.

The navigation is divided into two types:

- **Vertical orientation:** This navigation will appear on the left side of the site. It will by default appear when the team site gets created in SharePoint.

- **Horizontal orientation:** This navigation will appear on the top part of the site. It is further divided into two i.e., **Mega menu** and **Cascading**.

In *Figure 2.18* illustrates the types of navigation orientation in SharePoint Team site:

Figure 2.18: Types of navigation orientation in SharePoint team site

Applying mega menu style

Before we start to apply the mega menu, we need to know about the mega menu.

The Mega menu is a style of horizontal orientation navigation. This allows users for quick access to site navigation in SharePoint Online. This raises the value of a site by involving your viewers in discovering more content than they have ever discovered before. Mega menus are suitable for navigation with three levels of hierarchy.

Steps to enable the mega menu:

1. Go to the **Navigation** window.

2. Under **Menu Style**, select **Mega menu**.

3. Click on **Save**.

It is illustrated in *Figure 2.19*:

Figure 2.19: Apply mega menu style in SharePoint Online

4. Then click on the **Edit** option in the navigation. You can see the editing panel open on the left side of the screen. Hover over the mouse for each option to display the **+** icon.

5. Click on the add icon to add a label or link based on your requirements. In *Figure 2.20*, we used the label option and named as **Developer Projects**. Then, add sub-labels to the primary label, by clicking on the add options.

Figure 2.20: Enable mega menu style in SharePoint Online

6. Let us say we created a label **Power BI project** and want to add it as a sub-link for **Developer Projects**. So, hover over the mouse on **Power BI Projects**, click on the more option (...), then select **Make sub link**.

You can see it will reflect as a sub-link in the editor pane, which is illustrated in *Figure 2.21*:

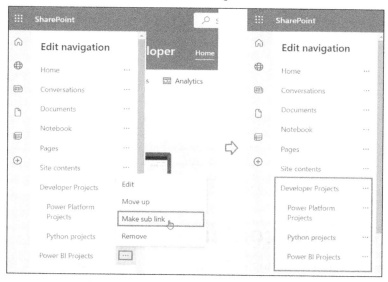

Figure 2.21: Add labels to the navigation pane

7. Once you are done with navigation editing, click on save, and when you hover over the **Developer Projects,** you can see the submenu will display, as illustrated in *Figure 2.22:*

Figure 2.22: Mega menu in SharePoint Online site

Applying cascading style

When the parent dropdown list is selected, a child dropdown list containing items connected to the parent is filled, it is known as cascading.

To change the mega menu style to cascading style follow the given steps:

1. Choose the **Navigation menu style** as **Cascading,** as shown in *Figure 2.23.*

2. Click on **Save**.

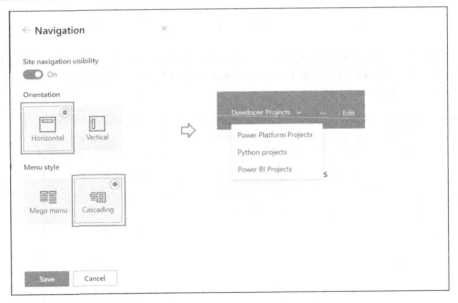

Figure 2.23: Apply cascading menu style to the navigation

Overview of site contents

When working with and maintaining a SharePoint site, there are two major areas to be aware of, site contents and site settings. So, now we will discuss SharePoint site content and later, we will discuss site settings in SharePoint.

The site contents feature in SharePoint allows users to view and manage all the lists, libraries, applications, pages, and subsites in the SharePoint Online site. We can access the **Site contents** from the quick launch and **Settings** menu. This is illustrated in *Figure 2.24*:

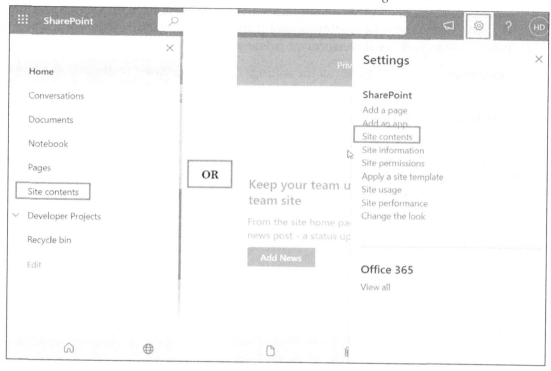

Figure 2.24: Access site content in SharePoint site

Once you access the SharePoint site content, you can create lists, libraries, pages, applications, and subsites. Also, you can see some inbuilt document libraries for **Documents**, **Form templates**, **Site assets**, and **Site library** and page libraries for **Site pages**. Let us discuss the UI of the **Site content** page:

- **+New:** By clicking on the plus icon, you will get a dropdown list to create new **Lists**, **Pages**, document libraries, apps, and **Subsite**.

- **Contents:** By selecting **Contents** tabs to view and interact with all the content on your SharePoint team site, including **Lists**, **Documents**, **Site Assets**, **Pages**, and more.

- **Subsite**: They allow you to see the subsites and the number of views for each, as well as interact with them by selecting the subsite you wish to deal with. To access the **Site contents** page for that subsite, click the ellipses (...).

- **Site usage**: By clicking on the **Site usage** in the SharePoint **Site content** page, the user can view information about the number of viewers who have visited the site, how many times viewers visited the site, and you can see which files received the most views.

- **Site workflows**: Here users can access SharePoint site workflow, which is a pre-programmed mini-application that may automate a variety of business operations. They give criteria, circumstances, and actions for automated behavior as well as activities on SharePoint lists and libraries that create some form of result. A workflow is a process that runs along a flow diagram and evaluates various conditions. Based on how it is designed, it will perform a predefined action based on the stimuli.

- **Site settings**: Here you can see all the settings of your site based on the permission you have.

- **Recycle bin**: Here you can see the list of items that are deleted by the user.

Figure 2.25 illustrates the above 7 features of the SharePoint **Site contents** page:

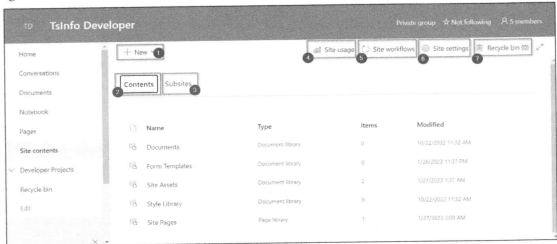

Figure 2.25: SharePoint site content page UI

Introduction to SharePoint site settings

Once a user created the team site, you can access the site settings page which allows you to manage various aspects of your SharePoint site, such as site permissions, site collection features, site design, site content and structure, and site administration. To access the site setting you must have owner or designer permission.

Some common options you can find in site settings include:

- **Site permissions**: Manage site users, groups, and permissions levels

- **Site collection features**: Activate or deactivate features for the entire site collection.

- **Site design**: Change the site's look and feel, master page, and theme.

- **Site content and structure**: Manage lists, libraries, pages, and other site content

- **Site administration**: Manage site policies, site collection administrators, and storage quotas.

To access the site settings page, go to the gear icon ⚙ in the top right corner of your SharePoint site and select **Site Settings**, illustrated in *Figure 2.26*:

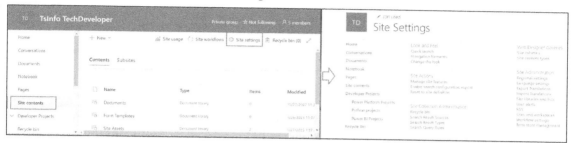

Figure 2.26: *Access site setting in SharePoint Online*

Navigating SharePoint Online team site and Quick Launch

Site navigation in SharePoint Online refers to the groups of controls and connections in your site collections, sites, and pages that assist visitors understand where they are and how to go to other relevant destinations.

Then Site navigation has two elements:

- **Quick Launch:** Quick Launch Navigation Menu in a SharePoint site is a menu that enables users to access material unique to the site they are on using bookmarks (URLs). It shows at the top of the page on communication sites and the left-hand side on all other SharePoint sites (Team Sites with or without an Office 365 Group).

- **Tree View:** The tree view is located on the left side of the SharePoint site page. If both Quick Launch and tree view are active, tree view in the SharePoint site will show underneath Quick Launch. Tree view presents site material in a hierarchical format, such as lists, libraries, and sites in the current site.

Tree view navigation in SharePoint Online is disabled by default, to enable it, follow the given steps:

1. Click the gear icon in the upper-right corner.

2. Go to **Site settings** to activate the tree view.

3. Click tree view in the look and feel section.

4. Tick the **enable tree view** box.

Let us perform some of the functionality of the Quick Launch navigation menu:

- On a team site add a link to the navigation menu.

- Target navigational links to specific audiences.

- Change the order of the menu link.

- Create sublinks on the menu.

- Move the sub link up to the parent link on the menu.

- Remove a link from the menu.

SharePoint Online provides a flexible and configurable navigation menu for team sites that allows users to add, target, reorder, and organize links, as well as build sub-links and move them around, allowing teams to browse the site with ease and efficiency.

To perform the above functionality, you must have permission to edit the navigation.

Adding a link to the navigation menu on a team site

To add a link to the navigation menu, follow the below steps:

1. In the Quick launch of the SharePoint team site, click on the **Edit** button

2. Then where you want to add the link, hover the mouse over there and you can see the plus **+** symbol.

3. Then choose the link from the option and provide the link (here we will provide the site link) and then provide a display name. Check the box of the **Open a new tab**. Click on **OK**.

4. You can see the display name of the link in the Quick Launch. Then click on **Save**.

5. By clicking on the name, we can go to the link we have given. In *Figure 2.27* when we click on the name, it will navigate to the internal site of my organization:

Figure 2.27: On a team site add a link to the navigation menu

Targeting navigational link to specific audiences

Before we add the feature of audience targeting to the team site, we must know what audience is targeting in SharePoint.

The audience targeting function allows you to customize your information to certain SharePoint security groups. This ensures that your users only view information that is relevant to them.

Only site owners can toggle audience targeting on and off. When enabled, any site editor can direct menu links to specific audiences.

Let us follow the steps below to apply this functionality to the Modern team site:

1. Edit the Quick Launch, then at the end, you can toggle on the **Enable site navigation audience targeting**.

2. Then click on the (**...**), **Edit**, beside the link we have added in SharePoint Online.

3. Then provide the group name in the **Audience to target**. Click on **OK**.

4. You can see in *Figure 2.28*, the group icon next to the link to the site. Click on **Save**:

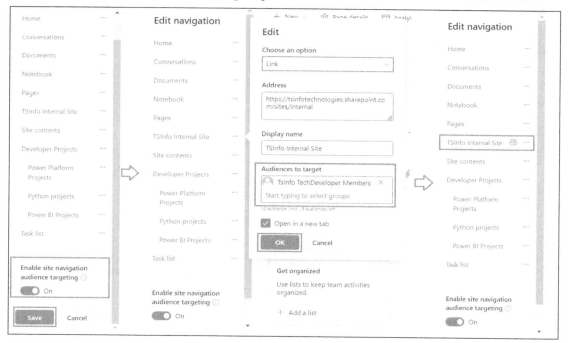

Figure 2.28: Target navigational link to specific audiences

Changing the order of the menu link

To change the order of the menu link, follow the steps below:

1. Select the edit option in the navigation menu.

2. Then in the menu, either drag or drop the link to where you want to place it.

3. Or you click on the (...), then click on **Move up** or **Move down** based on where you want to place the link. Let us say we will move the **Task list** link up by clicking on **Move up**, as you can see in *Figure 2.29*:

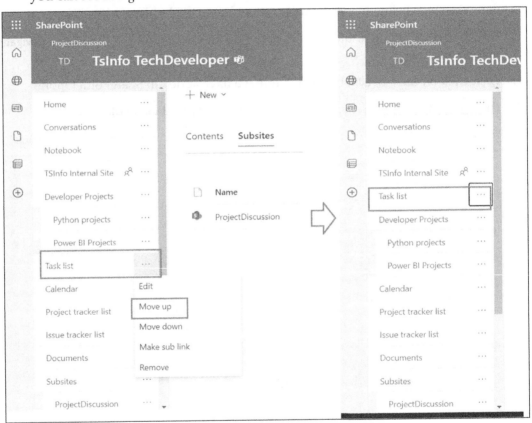

Figure 2.29: Change the order of the menu link

Creating sub-links on the menu

This inserts an indented link beneath another link. A vertical menu in SharePoint can include up to two layers of sub-links. Create the link where you want it to appear, then make it a sub-link of the one above it.

Let us follow the below steps to add sub-links to the navigation menu in SharePoint Online:

1. In the SharePoint team site, Quick launch navigation menu to make the link a sub link, click on the **Edit** button.

2. Then we will make the link/label as sub link, so here, we will use the Power Platform label and make it a sub-link. For this, click on the more icon (...) and then click on **Make Sub link**. Click on **Save**.

Now you can see in *Figure 2.30*, that the **Power Platform** label is set as a sub-link in Quick Launch:

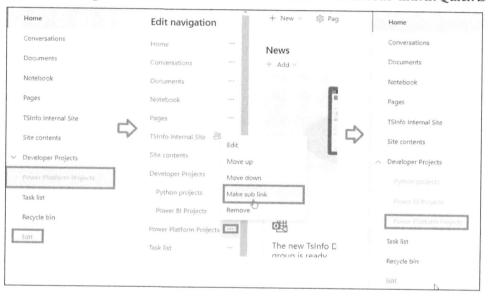

Figure 2.30: Create a sub-link on the menu

Promoting sub-link as the parent link on the menu

To promote the sub-link as the parent link on the Quick Launch menu, follow the below steps:

1. Click on the **Edit** icon in the Quick Launch of SharePoint team site, then to promote the sub-link, click on the More icon (...).

2. Select **Promote sub link**. Then click on save.

3. After that, you can see in *Figure 2.31*, the sub-link is promoted to the parent link in the Quick Launch of SharePoint team site:

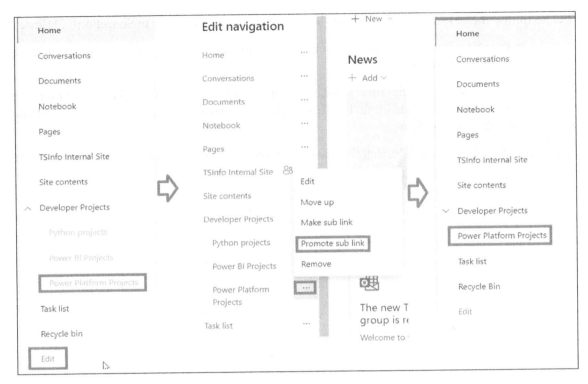

Figure 2.31: Promote sub link as the parent link on the menu

Remove a link from the Quick Launch menu

To remove the link from the Quick Launch menu, follow the below steps:

1. Click on the **Edit** icon in the Quick Launch menu in SharePoint.

2. Now, in the **Edit** navigation, click on the more icon (…), next to the sub-link (**Power Platform Projects**) you want to remove.

3. Click on **Remove** from the list. Click on **Save**.

Now you can see in *Figure 2.32* that the sub-link is removed:

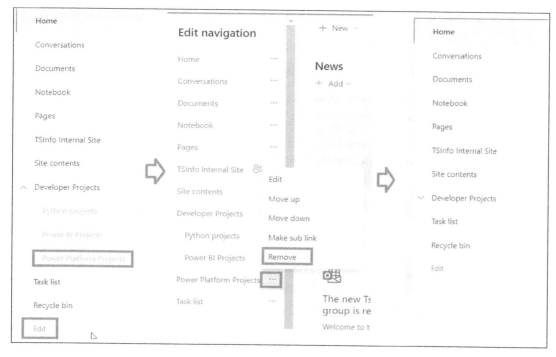

Figure 2.32: *Remove a link from the Quick Launch menu*

SharePoint site template

SharePoint site templates are pre-built configurations that may be used to build new SharePoint sites with a specified structure and set of functionalities. Site templates can save time and effort by offering a pre-configured site with a certain look, feel, and functionality that corresponds to the demands of a given business process or set of users.

SharePoint site designs include a wide range of site kinds, including team sites, communication sites, publishing sites, and custom sites. Each template includes pre-configured lists, libraries, pages, web components, and other site-specific components.

A team site template, for example, may feature a document library, a calendar, and a task list, whereas a communication site template may include news and events web components.

SharePoint also allows users to build custom site templates by saving a site as a template once it has been fully customized to their specifications. This can be a great technique to assure uniformity across numerous locations while also saving time on site setup and maintenance.

Applying built-in site template in SharePoint site

Let us see how we can apply built-in site templates to the team site in SharePoint. Follow the below steps:

1. Click on the site setting gear icon and click on the **Apply a site template** icon from the list.

2. Then Search a template window will open, you can see there will be two tabs:

   a. **From Microsoft**: This shows all the built-in templates in SharePoint.

   b. **From your organization**: This shows all the custom templates, which you have built in your organization.

3. Then select the template based on your requirement, and you can preview the template. Once you are done click on the **Use template** button, as illustrated in *Figure 2.33*:

Figure 2.33: *Access site template in SharePoint Online team site*

4. Then it will show you the screen for **Applying templates**, after that, you can see like in *Figure 2.34*, the templates are applied on the team site:

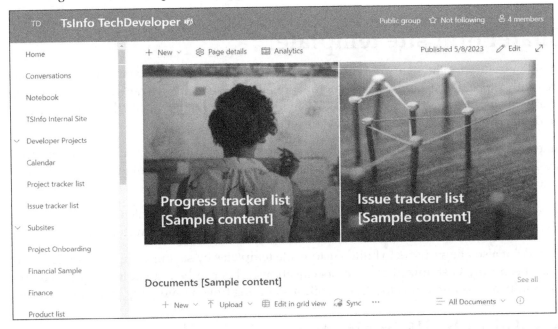

Figure 2.34: *Team site look and Feel after applying template*

Overview of recycle bin

The recycle bin on a SharePoint Online team site functions similarly to the recycle bin in an on-premises SharePoint environment. When a user deletes an object (a document, list, or library), it is relocated to the recycle bin and can be recovered if necessary.

When working with the recycle bin on a SharePoint Online team site, keep the following factors in mind:

- The recycle bin in SharePoint Online has two stages. The first is the recycle bin, and the second is the site collection recycle bin. When an item is removed, it is relocated to the recycle bin, where the person who deleted it can recover it. After 93 days, items in the recycle bin are automatically destroyed. The object is then relocated to the site collection recycle bin, where a site collection administrator can recover it. After 7 days, items in the site collection recycle bin are automatically destroyed.

- SharePoint Online team sites feature two independent recycle bins. The first is unique to each user and can be reached by clicking on the recycle bin link in the Quick Launch menu. The second recycle bin is the site collection recycle bin, which is only available to site collection administrators.

- When an item is deleted, it is initially moved to the first stage of the recycle bin. The item is then transferred to the site collection recycle bin if the user empties their recycle bin.

- Users can restore an item from the recycle bin by selecting the item and clicking the restore button in the toolbar. Users can delete an item permanently by selecting it and clicking the delete button.

- Administrators of site collections can access the site collection recycle bin by navigating to the recycle bin link in the Quick Launch menu and then clicking on the second stage recycle bin link.

Overall, the recycle bin in SharePoint Online team sites acts as a safety net for lost content, allowing users to recover unintentionally deleted things and site collection administrators to recover items removed from user's recycle bins.

Changing SharePoint team site URL

You can change the SharePoint team site URL/address to a Global Administrator or SharePoint Administrator. You can change the URL of the below types of SharePoint sites:

- SharePoint Modern team site without Microsoft 365 group

- SharePoint team site with Microsoft 365 group

- Classic team site
- Communication site

Changing the SharePoint site address is not permitted in the following circumstances:

- The publishing feature is currently enabled, or it was previously enabled for the site.
- If the SharePoint site contains more than 15 million documents.

Now we will see how we can change the SharePoint site address/ URL in the **Admin center**. Follow the below steps:

1. Open **SharePoint Admin center**, go to the **Active sites** available in the **Site** section, then select the site you want to change the URL of.

2. Then click on the **Edit** icon, and it will open the site details pane.

3. Now under the URL, click on the **Edit** option in the **General** tab.

Figure 2.35 illustrates the above 3 points to change the site address:

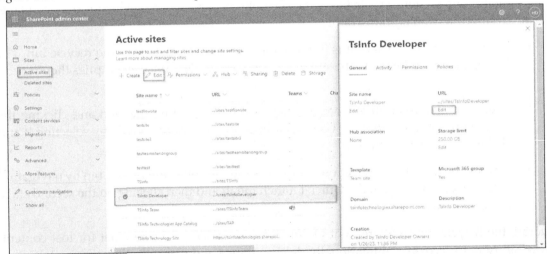

Figure 2.35: Edit the site URL in the SharePoint Admin center

4. Now the **Edit URL** window will open, rename the site URL and click on **Save**. Here, we have changed the **TsinfoDeveloper** to **TSInfoTechDeveloper**.

5. Next, the **Change site name?** window will come, click on **Yes**.

6. You can edit the **Site name** based on your **Site address**. Click on **Save**.

This is illustrated in *Figure 2.36*:

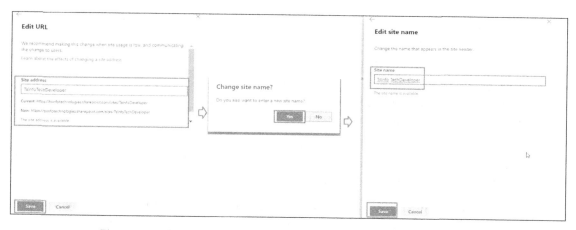

Figure 2.36: Change the site URL and site name in the SharePoint Admin center

7. Now the **site name** and site **URL** got changed, you can see them in the **Active sites** like shown in *Figure 2.37* as well as by opening the site in the browser:

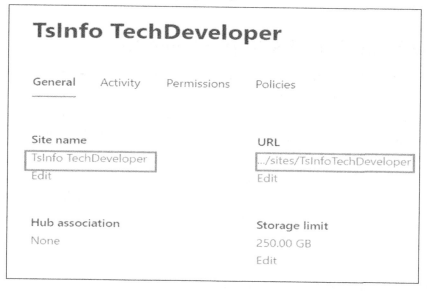

Figure 2.37: Change the site URL and site name of the SharePoint Team site

SharePoint site permissions

A team site in SharePoint is a site collection that allows teams to collaborate on projects, exchange documents, and manage tasks. A team site is built by default with various permissions that grant the site owner and members different levels of access to the site's contents. Here are some common SharePoint team site permissions:

- **Site owner**: Site owners have complete control over the site, including the ability to adjust access, change the site structure, and add new lists and libraries. They may also change the settings of the site and add new members.

- **Site member**: Site members can add, modify, and remove items in the site's lists and libraries since they have contributed access. They may also explore the site, engage in discussions, and create new content.

- **Site visitor**: A site visitor has read-only access to the site, which means they may browse the material but cannot add, edit, or remove things. They may take part in debates, as well as examine lists and libraries.

- **External sharing**: Site owners can enable external sharing, which allows users outside of the company to view the site's contents. The owner can decide how much access external users have to the site.

In addition to these basic rights, SharePoint enables more granular permissions to be defined on lists and libraries inside the team site. This enables the site owner to restrict access to certain content on the site.

Provide SharePoint site permission

Permissions for SharePoint sites can be granted at various levels of the site hierarchy. These are the levels at which you may grant SharePoint site permissions:

- **Site collection level**: At the highest level, SharePoint site collection administrators can manage permissions for the entire site collection, including all subsites, lists, and libraries within the collection.

- **Site level**: Site owners can manage permissions for individual sites within a site collection. They can add and delete users or groups, as well as designate the amount of access each user or group should have.

- **List or library level**: Site owners can also control rights for lists or libraries inside a site. This gives them control over who has access to the contents in that list or library.

- **Folder or item level**: In addition to list and library level permissions, SharePoint allows permissions to be configured on specific folders or objects inside a list or library. This is useful for managing sensitive or secret information.

Access request settings

In a SharePoint Online team site **Access request settings** can be configured by the site owner to allow users to request access to the specific content they do not have permission to view.

Here is how to configure **Access request settings** in a SharePoint Online team site:

1. Navigate to the team site where you want to configure **Access request settings**.

2. Click on the gear icon in the top right corner of the page and select **Site Permission -> Advanced**.

3. In the ribbon at the top, click on **Access Request Settings**.

4. In the **Access Request Settings** dialog box, select **Allow access requests** to enable access requests for the site, as shown in *Figure 2.38*:

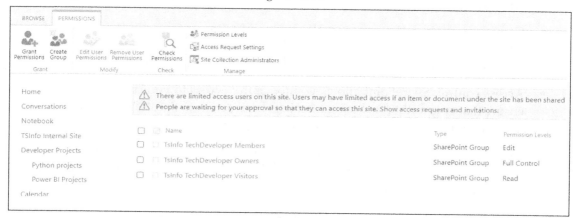

Figure 2.38: *Access Request Setting in SharePoint Permission*

5. Enter the email address of the person or group who should receive access requests in the **Email address** field.

6. Optionally, you can also set the **Group** field to a specific SharePoint group that should receive access requests.

7. Click **OK** to save your changes.

The above points are illustrated in *Figure 2.39*:

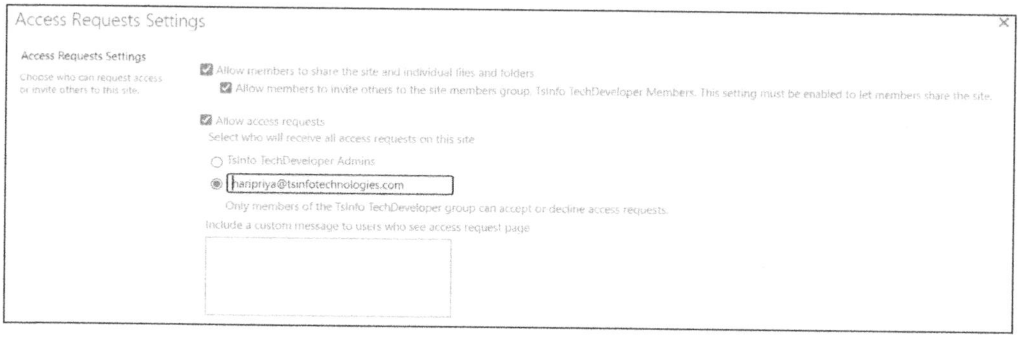

Figure 2.39: *Add email to allow access requests*

Share SharePoint team site

Sharing a team site in SharePoint enables you to collaborate with others by providing them with access to the site and its content. There are several reasons why you might want to share a team site in SharePoint, including:

- **Collaboration:** Sharing a team site in SharePoint Online allows you to work collaboratively with others on a project or task. By providing team members with access to the site, they can contribute their ideas, edit documents, and share feedback with others.

- **Communication:** A team site can also be used to share information and communicate with team members. By sharing the site with others, you can ensure that everyone is up to date on the latest project updates, timelines, and tasks.

- **Access control**: SharePoint allows you to control access to your team site, so you can ensure that only authorized team members have access to the site's content. This helps to ensure the security and privacy of your project information.

- **Increased productivity**: By sharing a team site in SharePoint, you can increase productivity by streamlining workflows, reducing duplication of effort, and promoting collaboration among team members.

Overall, sharing a team site in SharePoint is an effective way to improve communication, increase productivity, and collaborate effectively with others on a project or task.

To share a SharePoint modern team site with others, the SharePoint site owner will give access to the site by adding them as site owners, members, and visitors:

1. Navigate to the **SharePoint** Modern team site you want to share.

2. Click on the gear icon in the upper-right corner of the page to open the **Settings** menu.

3. Select **Site permissions** from the menu.

4. In the **Site permissions** pane that appears, click on the **Add members** button.

5. Then you will see the two options:

    a. **Add members to group:** By adding members to the SharePoint site group, you can give access to all the group resources.

    b. **Share site only:** To give access to the site only. By clicking on the **Share site only** option. Then write the email address of a group or user available in your organization.

6. Once you add an email address to the site, you can permit to edit, read, and full control by clicking on the dropdown.

7. Then write a welcome message to that person in the **Send email** box.

8. Then click on **Add**, as shown in *Figure 2.40*. Sharing a SharePoint Modern team site with colleagues is critical for communication and teamwork. Following these simple procedures, team members can be added to the site and granted access to its resources, allowing them to participate and collaborate more effectively.

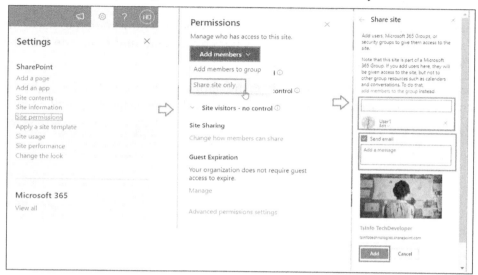

Figure 2.40: Share SharePoint team site

Once you share the site, the users you invited will receive an email with a link to access the SharePoint modern team site. They will need to sign in with their Microsoft account or work or school account to access the site.

SharePoint site usage analytics

Site usage analytics in SharePoint Online team sites provide insights into how the site is being used by site members, including how many people are visiting the site, what pages are being viewed, what files are being accessed, and how users are interacting with the site content.

These usage analytics can be used to track site performance and engagement, and to identify popular content or areas of the site that may need improvement or further development.

Some of the specific information that can be gathered through site usage analytics includes:

- **Number of page views**: This shows how many times each page on the site has been viewed by users.

- **Unique viewers**: This shows how many individual users have viewed the site or specific pages within a given time frame.

- **Popular content**: This shows which files and pages on the site are being accessed the most frequently.

- **Referrers**: This shows which websites or search engines are referring users to the site.

- **User activity**: This shows how users are interacting with the site content, including which files they are editing, which pages they are commenting on, and which files they are sharing with others.

SharePoint Online team site owners and members can use this information to make informed decisions about how to optimize the site for better engagement and to ensure that the site is meeting the needs of its users.

To visualize the SharePoint site usage, click on the settings icon, present on the right-top of the page. Then click on **Site usage**. You can see in *Figure 2.41* the site usage page will open:

Figure 2.41: Site usage in SharePoint teams site

Now from the above Site usage page, you can see some numbers and graphs based on these constraints:

- Views overall and unique visitors to the site.

- A graph showing the growth of views over time.

- A list of the most popular pages and the number of views per page.

- A list of the top referring websites along with the number of views they generated.

You may improve your site's performance by using this information to obtain insight into the user behavior on it. In the Site usage page's top right-hand corner, there is a download button that you can use to download the data to Excel for more analysis.

Converting SharePoint Modern team site to communication site

Since there is no solution to convert SharePoint Modern Team site to Communication site, there are some ways you can try to change the Modern Team site to Modern Communication site. These are:

- There is no left navigation in Quick launch, so you can remove the left navigation from Team site.

- You can create a template of a communication site and use that template in communication site.

- By changing the name and the URL of the team site to create a communication site (with the same name) and migrate data. You can do it by following this link '**https://learn.microsoft.com/en-us/answers/questions/727371/how-to-change-a-team-site-into-a-communication-sit**'.

Connecting Modern SharePoint team site to Teams

We can connect the Modern SharePoint Team site connects to Microsoft Teams. This integration allows you to access your SharePoint team site files, lists, and pages right from Teams, allowing you to collaborate on content and interact with your team all in one place.

To connect the SharePoint Modern team site group to Microsoft Teams, follow the below steps:

1. Login to your Microsoft Teams, and then click on **Teams** from the left navigation.

2. Click on the **Join or create a team** button, then click on **Create team**, as shown in *Figure 2.42*:

Figure 2.42: Create team in Microsoft Teams

3. Select **From a group or team** to create a team from an existing Microsoft 365 group and choose the SharePoint team site you want to connect to Teams.

4. Then select **From a group or team** in the **Create a Team** window, as shown in *Figure 2.43*:

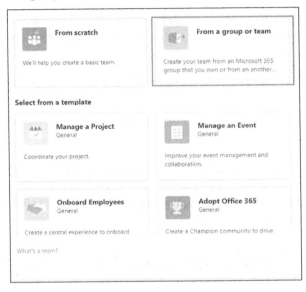

Figure 2.43: Create your team from a group

5. Then select Microsoft 365 group in Create a new team from something you already own window.

6. Then it will open the **Microsoft 365 group** you want to use. Select your modern team site group that is, TsInfo TechDeveloper. Click on **Create**.

7. In the **Teams** tab, you can see in *Figure 2.44*, the team created with the name **TsInfo TechDeveloper**:

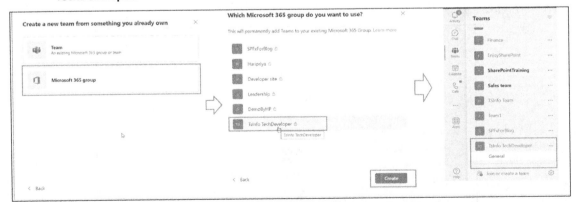

Figure 2.44: Team gets created in Microsoft teams

Once the team site Microsoft 365 group is added, follow the below steps to connect the SharePoint team site to Microsoft Teams:

1. In Microsoft Teams, click on **Teams** on the Left navigation, then expand the **TSinfo Tech Developer** teams.

2. Click on **General**, the general channel window will open on Teams, then click on the **+** icon, shown in *Figure 2.45*:

Figure 2.45: *General channel window in Microsoft Teams*

3. Select **SharePoint**, then there will be two options, in *Figure 2.46*:

   a. **Tsinfo tech developer** site

   b. **SharePoint Site**

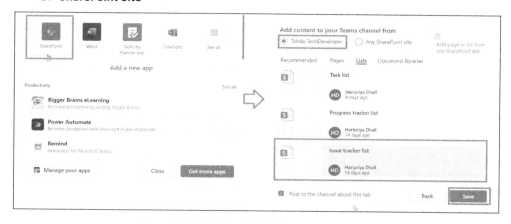

Figure 2.46: *Add SharePoint list to channel Teams*

4. Then choose the resources you selected as tabs, here in *Figure 2.46* you can see we have selected **List**, then select **Issue Tracker list**. Click on **Save**.

5. You can see in *Figure 2.47*, the issue tracker list from the Team site in Microsoft Teams:

Figure 2.47: Issue tracker list is added to Microsoft teams

From here, you can exchange files, collaborate on content, and interact with your team all in one place. And any modifications you make to your SharePoint material in Teams will be reflected in SharePoint, and vice versa.

Working with subsites in SharePoint Online

A subsite is a site that is built within another site, usually known as the parent site, in SharePoint Online. A subsite is a smaller, more focused site within a larger SharePoint site.

Subsites in SharePoint Online enable users to establish a site hierarchy in which the top-level site is the parent site and subsites are nested within it. This can be useful for organizing content and facilitating collaboration within a specific team or department.

When building a subsite in SharePoint Online, users may choose to inherit access from the parent site or create unique permissions for the subsite. This implies that users may regulate who has access to each subsite and what they can do within it.

Subsites can also have their unique features and settings, such as navigation, site templates, and site columns. This allows users to customize each subsite to meet the needs of its users.

Working with subsites in SharePoint Online team site

Working with subsites in a SharePoint Online team site may help you to organize content, manage permissions, and facilitate collaboration. To work with subsites in a SharePoint Online team site, follow these steps:

1. **Create a subsite**: To create a subsite in the SharePoint Online team site, navigate to the site content page, by clicking on the new button, selecting the subsite, and providing the information of the subsite such as title, description, URL site name, etc.

2. **Customize subsite settings**: Once your subsite has been created, you may modify its settings to match the needs of your team. For example, you can add new lists or libraries, modify navigation, and adjust site columns. You can also configure the subsite's permissions to control who can access the subsite and what actions they can perform.

3. **Create content within the subsite**: You may now begin producing content for your subsite. You may create new documents, lists to manage tasks or issues, and calendars to arrange team events. By keeping content within a subsite, you can ensure that it remains structured and easily accessible.

4. **Collaborate within the subsite**: To collaborate within your subsite, you can use features like document co-authoring, team discussions, and shared calendars. You can also use alerts to stay informed about updates within the subsite.

5. **Manage subsites**: As your team's needs evolve, you may need to create new subsites or modify existing ones in SharePoint Online. You can use the SharePoint Online Admin center to manage subsites across your entire organization. This can include creating new subsites, adjusting permissions, and managing features and settings.

By following the above steps, you can efficiently work with the subsites in the SharePoint Online team site.

Creating a subsite in SharePoint Online team site

To create a subsite in SharePoint Online Team site, follow the below steps:

1. Navigate to your SharePoint Online team site and click on the settings icon (gear icon) in the top right corner of the page.

2. Click on **Site contents** to view the contents of the current site.

3. Click on **New** in the top left corner of the page and select **Subsite** from the dropdown menu. This is illustrated in *Figure 2.48*:

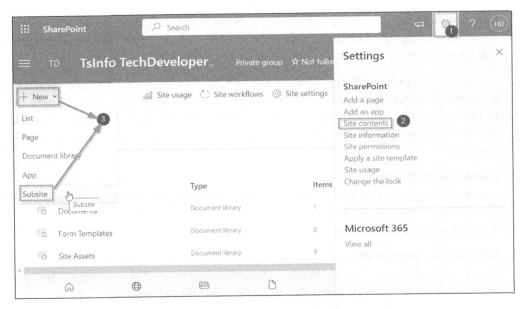

Figure 2.48: Selecting subsite in SharePoint site content page

4. To create a Subsite, provide the title, description, and URL name, and select the language.

5. Then you can use a template under the **Template** section, or else you can use the default Team site.

6. Then under the **User Permission**, we have two options:

    a. **Use same permission as parent site**: You can grant access to your new site to the same user that has access to the parent site.

    b. **Use unique permission**: We can give unique permission to the user in subsite.

7. Display this site on the Quick Launch of the parent site, select yes, if you want to display the site on the quick launch, else no.

8. Display this site on the top link bar of the parent site, select yes, if you want to display it on the top link bar, else no.

9. Use the top link bar from the parent site, and select yes if you want to inherit the top link bar navigation from the parent site.

10. Then click on **Create**.

Figure 2.49 illustrates the above points to create a subsite in SharePoint:

Figure 2.49: Creating subsite in SharePoint team site

Overall, subsites are a useful feature of SharePoint Online that can be used to create a hierarchical structure of sites within a larger SharePoint environment. By using subsites effectively, users can better organize their content, manage permissions, and enable collaboration within their teams.

Deleting a modern team site in SharePoint Online

As we know SharePoint Online is a cloud-based platform that allows businesses to create, share, and collaborate on content, documents, and information. SharePoint Online sites are used to store and manage this material, and users with the necessary permissions can build them.

You may need to delete a SharePoint Online site for several reasons, such as removing unwanted or old sites, reorganizing your organization's information, or freeing up storage space. Nevertheless, before removing a SharePoint Online site, make sure you have backed up any crucial data or material, as the deletion procedure wipes all content from the site forever.

To remove a SharePoint Online site, you must have the necessary permissions. Contact your SharePoint administrator to seek access if you do not have the relevant permissions. After you have the rights, you may visit the site and delete it by following the instructions outlined in the prior answer.

To delete a SharePoint Modern team site in SharePoint Online, follow the below steps:

1. Navigate to the SharePoint site you want to delete.

2. Click on the settings icon (gear icon) in the top right corner of the page.

3. Then click on the **Site Information** option and click on **Delete site** at the bottom of the window.

4. **Delete Microsoft 365 group** window will open, select the check box **yes delete this group and all its associated resources**. Then click on the **Delete** icon.

Figure 2.50 illustrates how we can delete a modern team site in SharePoint:

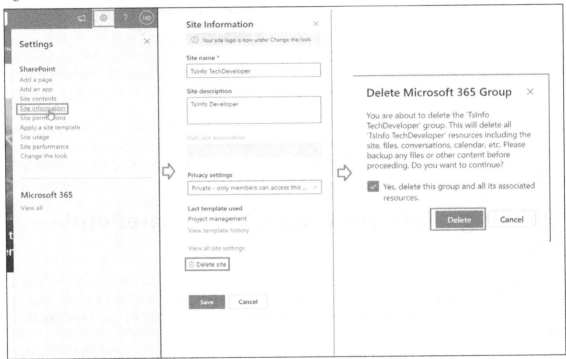

Figure 2.50: *Deleting a Modern team site in SharePoint*

Once you click on delete, you can see the site is removed from the Active site in SharePoint administrator. To restore the sites, you can go to deleted sites under sites, and select the site you want to restore, then click on restore. After that, you can access your site as it is.

Conclusion

Finally, this chapter presents a thorough overview of the capabilities and functionalities of SharePoint team sites, with a particular emphasis on the modern team site in SharePoint Online. From creating and customizing team sites to managing site settings, navigation, and permissions, this chapter covers a wide range of topics that are essential for effective collaboration and teamwork.

Furthermore, the chapter discusses advanced topics such as SharePoint site usage analytics, connecting modern team sites to Microsoft Teams, and converting modern team sites to communication sites. With this knowledge, users can effectively utilize SharePoint to streamline their workflows and enhance their productivity.

In the next chapter, we will see what a modern communication site is, what are the features and functionality so that the user has an idea in which case we will create team site and modern team site.

## Chapter 3

SharePoint Communication Sites

Introduction

In *Chapter 2, SharePoint Modern Team Sites*, we learned all about modern team sites, like what is SharePoint online modern team site, how we can create a modern team site, as well as key features of SharePoint modern team site, customizing modern team site in SharePoint online, and overview of site contents.

After that, we discussed site settings, how a user can change the team site RL, and different types of permissions. Also, we saw how to create a subsite and delete a modern team site.

In this chapter, we will see what SharePoint online communication site is and discuss some of the key features of the SharePoint communication site. Also, moving forward in this chapter, we will see create, customize, and delete the modern communication site.

Lastly, we will see the navigation option in the communication site, how we can access site content and settings, and how to add a footer to the communication site. Also, we will see the site-level permissions for communication sites in SharePoint Online.

Structure

In this chapter, we will cover the following topics:

- Overview of communication site in SharePoint

- Key features of SharePoint modern communication site

- Create a modern communication site in SharePoint

- Customize modern SharePoint communication site

- Overview of navigation in communication site

- Overview of site contents and site setting

- SharePoint communication site permissions

- SharePoint communication site

- Modern SharePoint communication sites

- Delete a modern communication site in SharePoint Online

Objectives

This chapter is a formidable approach to SharePoint online communication sites. It will describe why it is important to create a communication site in SharePoint online, emphasize features of SharePoint communication site, and teach you how to create a communication site in SharePoint online.

By the end of this chapter, you will get an understanding of the concept of customizing SharePoint modern communication site, working on-site contents, and site navigation. Also, we will see how to work with subsites in SharePoint Online.

Overview of communication site in SharePoint online

SharePoint online communication sites are a type of SharePoint site intended for internal or external communication. These sites are perfect for businesses that must communicate with big groups of individuals, such as employees, customers, partners, or stakeholders.

Communication sites in SharePoint online are mobile-friendly and have a clean, modern design that is simple to use and browse. They offer a range of pre-built web parts that may be changed to meet your needs, such as News, Events, Documents, Quick Links, and more.

One of the key benefits of SharePoint online communication sites is that you can simply build and publish content without any coding or technical knowledge. You can rapidly build pages, update content, and publish them to your site, ensuring your users always have the most up-to-date information.

SharePoint online communication sites include significant collaboration tools such as document co-authoring, file sharing, and workflow management. This makes it simple for teams to collaborate and stay organized, even if they are spread across the globe.

Key features of SharePoint modern communication site

SharePoint modern communication sites offer several key features to help organizations improve communication and collaboration among team members, stakeholders, and customers. Here are some of the key features of SharePoint modern communication sites:

- **Responsive design**: Modern communication sites are designed to perform effortlessly across several platforms, including PCs, tablets, and smartphones.

- **The hero web part**: Every communication site you create in SharePoint online includes the hero web part by default.

- **Easy-to-use interface**: SharePoint modern communication sites offer a user-friendly interface allowing users to quickly discover and access the information they need.

- **Customizable layout**: Communication sites in SharePoint online use a flexible layout system that allows you to easily add, remove, and rearrange web parts to create the perfect page layout for your needs.

- **Pre-built web parts**: Modern communication sites have a range of pre-built web parts that may be changed to match the specific needs of your organization, such as News, Events, Documents, Quick Links, and more.

- **Integrated with Office 365 apps**: Communication sites in SharePoint online integrate seamlessly with other Office 365 apps, such as Teams, Outlook, and Yammer, making it easy for your team to communicate and collaborate in one central location.

- **Customization and branding**: SharePoint online communication sites can be easily branded and customized to match your organization's look and feel. You can add your logo, colors, and fonts to make the site a natural extension of your organization's brand.

- **Easy content creation**: SharePoint modern communication sites make creating and publishing content easy without coding or technical expertise. You can quickly create pages, add content, and publish them to your site, ensuring your users can access the latest information.

So, SharePoint online communication sites are valuable for any company seeking to increase communication and collaboration inside their organizations or with external stakeholders. These sites can help you stay connected and productive no matter where you are, thanks to their responsive design, configurable web components, and interaction with other Office 365 products.

SharePoint modern team site vs. communication site

SharePoint modern team sites and communication sites are the two types of SharePoint sites that serve unique features.

Here are a few key differences between the two:

Features	Modern Team site	Modern Communication site
Purpose	Modern team sites are designed for collaboration within a team or department.	Modern communication sites are designed for sharing information with a larger audience, such as employees, customers, partners, or stakeholders.
Security	Modern team site in SharePoint online uses Microsoft 365 group for security purposes.	Modern communication sites in SharePoint online uses the SharePoint group for security purpose.
Navigations	In a modern team site, navigation is accessed on the left side of the site.	Whereas the communication site is accessed at the top of the site.
Access	Typically, modern team sites are only accessible to members of the team or department.	Communication sites are designed to be accessible to a larger audience.
Branding	Typically, team sites can also be customized, but they are typically more focused on team collaboration than branding.	Communication sites may be easily branded and personalized to match the appearance and feel of your organization, making it appear to be a natural extension of your brand.
Features	Modern team sites in SharePoint online offer features that are designed to support team collaboration, such as document libraries, lists, calendars, and team news.	Communication sites in SharePoint online offer features designed to facilitate communication, such as News, Events, Documents, Quick Links, and more.

Table 3.1: SharePoint Team site vs Communication site

Ultimately, your organization's needs will determine the decision between the modern team and communication sites. Modern team sites may be a better choice for collaboration, while communication sites may be for sharing information with a larger audience.

Create a modern SharePoint communication site

These sites are perfect for businesses that must communicate with big groups of individuals, such as employees, customers, partners, or stakeholders.

To create a modern SharePoint communication site, refer to the following steps:

1. Click on **https://admin.microsoft.com/** to access the **Microsoft 365 admin center**, where we can access the SharePoint admin center.

2. If you are not logged in, log in to the **Microsoft 365 admin center**.

3. Then in the left navigation, under the **Admin centers** | Click on **SharePoint**, as shown in *Figure 3.1*. Else, you can directly access the SharePoint admin center by writing the URL **https://tenantName-admin.sharepoint.com/'**:

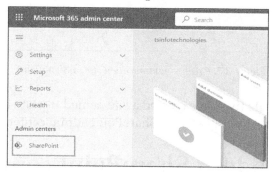

Figure 3.1: *Access SharePoint Admin center*

4. Now in the **SharePoint admin center**, in the left navigation, you can see the **Sites** category (where we can create, manage, and delete our sites based on our requirements). Under **Sites** | click on **Active sites.**

5. Then it will redirect to the **Active sites** page, and if your organization created sites, you can see different sites on this page. You can see the three options on this page: Create, **Export**, and **Track View**. From this, click on **Create** to create the team site. Refer to the following figure:

Figure 3.2: *Active sites in SharePoint Admin center*

6. You can see a window where we get options to create a **Team site**, **Communication site**, and, **Other options** (It includes different types of sites like publishing portal, enterprise wiki, etc. Also, you can create a **Team site** not associated with Microsoft 365 group).

7. Choose the **Communication site**, then provide the required information to create a communication site, like **Site name**, **Site owner**, and **Select a language**. Click on **Finish**. Refer to the following figure:

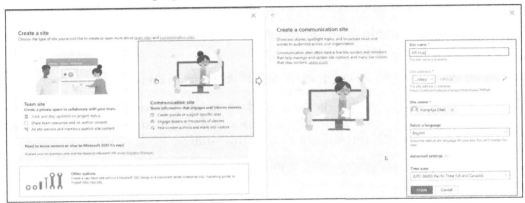

Figure 3.3: Create communication site in SharePoint

Once the communication site (we have created a site named **HR Hub**) is created, you can access the communication site in active sites in the SharePoint admin center.

Customize modern SharePoint communication site

Customizing a modern SharePoint communication site involves several steps that can help you improve your site's overall look and feel and enhance its functionality.

The customization options are:

- Use the theme to change the color of the SharePoint communication site.

- Customize SharePoint communication site header.

- Customize SharePoint communication site navigation.

Microsoft provides the Change the **Look** options to customize the modern communication site in SharePoint online, located under the settings on the right top of the **Communication site**.

Use the theme to change the color of the SharePoint Communication site:

Several pre-built themes are available in SharePoint, or you can use the theme generator to make your own. Go to **Site Settings** | Change the look to modify your site's theme. Let us see how we can do it:

1. Open the **Communication site**, click on **Settings** | click on **Change the look** link |click on **Theme**.

2. You can choose the theme from the list; it will change the look and feel of your communication site. Also, by clicking on **Customize link**, you can choose your color based on your requirements. Refer to the following figure:

Figure 3.4: Customize theme of communication sites

Customize SharePoint communication site header:

You can customize the header to include a navigation menu, search box, and other elements. To customize the header, click **Site Settings** | **Change the look** | **Header**. Let us see how we can customize the header of the communication site:

1. Open the **Communication site**, click on **Settings** | click on **Change the look link** |click on **Header**.

2. You can choose the layout in the Header window as **Minimal**, **Compact**, **Standard**, or **Extended**, which we have done for the team site in SharePoint online.

3. Also, you can change the background theme of the header of the communication site.

4. You can toggle on or off the Site title.

5. You can change or remove the site logo thumbnail. Also, the same goes for the site logo.

6. Once you are done, click on the **Save**, and the changes will reflect on the header of the communication site. Refer to the following figure:

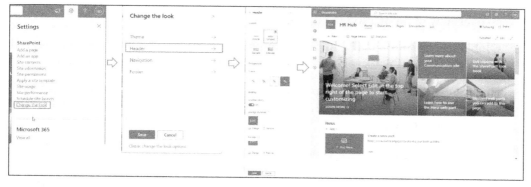

Figure 3.5: Customize header of communication sites

To customize SharePoint communication site navigation:

Customizing site navigation in SharePoint communication site involves several steps that can help you improve your site's overall look and feel and enhance its functionality:

- Open the **Communication site,** click on **Settings** | click on **Change the look link** | click on **Navigation**.

- You can toggle on or off the site navigation visibility.

- Then you can choose the **Menu style** as **Mega menu** and Cascading menu. Click on **Save**. Refer to the following figure:

Figure 3.6: Customize SharePoint communication site navigation

Overview of navigation in communication site

SharePoint online is a powerful platform for creating communication sites that allow users to share news, stories, and other content with their colleagues and external partners. Navigation is an essential element of communication sites, as it allows users to access the different pages and content within the site easily.

In a SharePoint communication site, navigation is a collection of menus and links users can browse the site's content. Navigation is essential to enhance user experience on the website and make it simpler for visitors to obtain the information they require.

Here is an overview of navigation in communication sites in SharePoint online:

- **Global navigation:** This is the main navigation menu at the top of the website. It links to the home page, news, events, and other crucial pages are often included.

- **Hub navigation:** If your communication site is a hub site, you can activate hub navigation to show links to other hub sites. Above the global navigation menu, hub navigation is displayed.

- **Footer navigation:** This is a secondary navigation menu that can be found at the bottom of the website. It typically contains links to pages such as the privacy statement, the legal section, the contact page, and other pages that might not be often visited.

- **Mega menu:** A mega menu is an expanded version of the global navigation that shows a list of pages or sections under the primary navigation menu. Sites with a lot of content frequently employ megamenus.

Let us perform some of the below functionality of the navigation menu:

- Add a link or label to the navigation menu on a communication site.

- Add or edit links and labels in the footer of a communication site.

- Target navigational links to a specific audience.

- Change the order of the menu link.

- Create sub-links on the menu.

- Move sub-links on the menu.

To perform the above functionality, ensure you have the right permission or cannot see the edit link in the navigation menu.

Add a link or label to the navigation menu on a communication site:

To add a link or label to the navigation menu on the Communication site, refer to the following steps:

1. Click on the **Edit** option on the top navigation menu of the communication site.

2. Then click on the **+** icon | **Add** window will open | From **Choose an option**, select **Label**.

3. Provide the **Display name** | click on **OK**. Refer to the following figure:

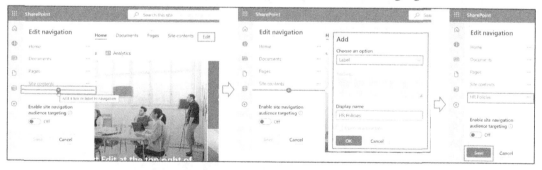

Figure 3.7: *Add a link or label to the navigation menu on a communication site*

Add or edit links and labels in the footer on a communication site:

To add or edit links and labels in the footer on a communication site, refer to the following steps:

1. Click on the **Edit** icon on the footer, then click on the **+** icon in the **Edit** navigation window on the right side.

2. Then select options as **Label**, provide the **Display name,** and click **Ok**.

3. Next, click on **Save**. You can see the label in the footer. Refer to the following *Figure: 3.8*:

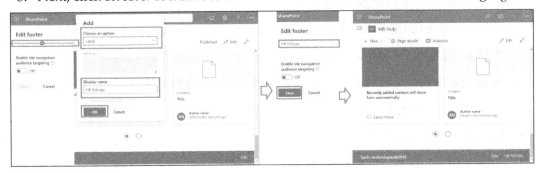

Figure 3.8: *Add or edit links and labels in the footer on a communication site*

Enable site navigation audience targeting

Audience targeting is a powerful feature in SharePoint communication sites that can help organizations to improve the user experience, increase engagement, and drive better business outcomes by delivering targeted and relevant content to specific audiences.

To enable the audience targeting in SharePoint communication site:

1. Click on the **Edit** icon in the Top **navigation**.

2. Then in the **Edit navigation** window | toggle on the **Enable site navigation audience targeting** options. Click on **Save**. Refer to the following *Figure 3.9*:

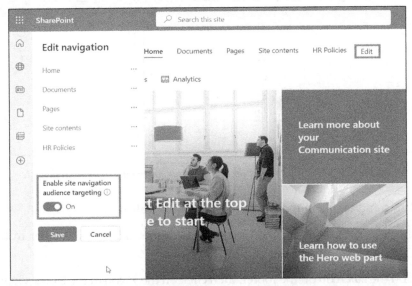

Figure 3.9: *Enable audience targeting on site navigation*

Change the order of menu link

To change the order of the menu link in the top navigation of the communication sites. Refer to the following steps:

1. Click on the **Edit** icon in the navigation menu | which link or label you want to move up or down to change the order, next to that, click on the more icon(...).

2. Then click on the **Move up** option. Click on **Save**. Refer to the following figure:

Figure 3.10: Change the order of menu link

Create sub links on the menu

To create a sub links on the navigation menu of the SharePoint communication site, follow the given steps:

1. Click on the **Edit** icon on the navigation menu.

2. Then click on the more icon next to the link or label you want to make sub-link.

3. Then click on **Make Sub link** option. Click on **Save**.

4. You can see the link created as sub link in the navigation menu. Refer to the following figure:

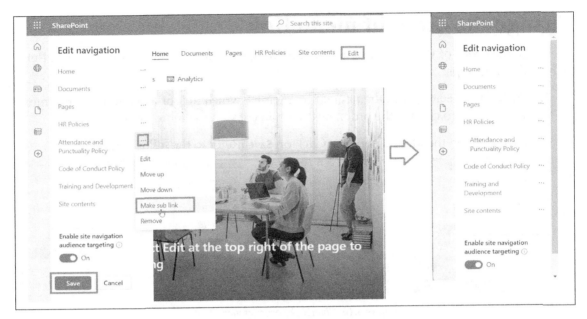

Figure 3.11: Create sub links on the menu

Move a sub links on the menu

To move a sub links on the navigation menu in the SharePoint communication site:

1. Click on the **Edit** icon on the navigation menu.

2. Then click on more icon (...) | click on **Move down**, you can move down the sub link.

3. Click on **Save**. You can see the sub link menu moved down. Refer to the following *Figure 3.12:*

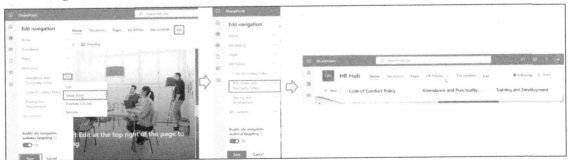

Figure 3.12: Move sub links on the menu

Overview of site content and site settings

SharePoint online communication sites are designed to facilitate information sharing within an organization. Site content in a SharePoint online communication site can be broadly categorized into the following types:

- **Pages**: Pages are the primary content type in a communication site. They present information in a structured manner and can be customized with text, images, videos, and other content. It can be created and managed using the SharePoint page editor.

- **News**: News articles are another important content type in a communication site. They provide a way to share timely information with users and can be customized with images, videos, and links. News articles can be created and managed using the News web part.

- **Documents**: Documents are a fundamental part of any communication site. They can be used to share important information, policies, procedures, and other resources, and it can be uploaded and managed using the SharePoint document library.

- **Lists**: Lists store and manage structured data in a communication site. They can be used for tasks, contacts, events, and other types of information. Lists can be created and managed using the SharePoint list editor.

- **Images and Videos**: Images and videos can be used to enhance the visual appeal of a communication site. They can be uploaded and managed using the SharePoint media library.

- **Web Parts**: Web Parts are pre-built components that can be added to a communication site to provide additional functionality. They can be used for displaying news feeds, documents, calendars, and other types of content. Web Parts can be added and configured using the SharePoint web part gallery.

- **Navigation**: Navigation in a communication site allows users to find and access the content they need easily. It can be customized using the SharePoint navigation settings.

Overall, SharePoint online communication sites provide a flexible and customizable platform for sharing information within an organization. By leveraging the various content types and web parts available, users can create a tailored experience for their audience that meets their needs.

To access the above Site contents in SharePoint Online Communication site, follow the below steps:

1. Click on **Settings** at the top of the SharePoint communication site.

2. Then click on **Site Contents**. Otherwise, you can access the site content from the top navigation. Refer to the following figure:

Figure 3.13: Site contents in SharePoint Communication site

Site settings option in communication site

In SharePoint online, a communication site showcases content to users, such as news, events, and other information. The site settings option in a communication site allows site owners and administrators to configure various settings for the site.

To access the site settings in a communication site, follow the given steps:

1. Go to the Communication site that you want to configure.

2. Click on the **Gear** icon in the top right corner of the page.

3. Select **Site contents** from the option | click on **Site Setting** option, shown in *Figure 3.14*:

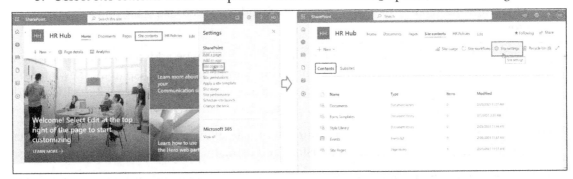

Figure 3.14: SharePoint Communication site-Site Content and Site Setting

4. Here you can see all the options to configure your SharePoint communication site. Refer to the following *Figure 3.15:*

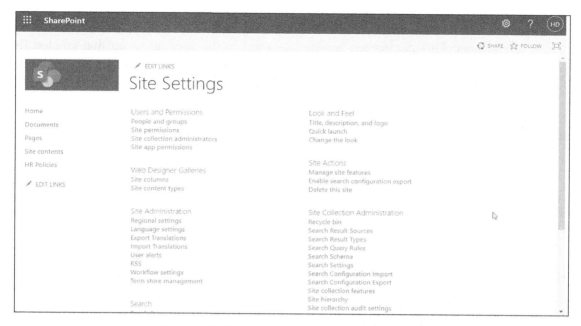

Figure 3.15: *Site settings option in Communication site*

From here, you can configure various settings for the site, including:

- **Site information**: This section lets you update the site's title, description, and logo.

- **Site permissions**: This section allows you to manage the site's permissions, including adding or removing users and groups and setting permission levels.

- **Site features**: This section allows you to activate or deactivate features for the site, such as the SharePoint Server Publishing feature or the Document ID Service.

- **Look and feel**: This section allows you to customize the site's design, including changing the theme, adding a background image, and modifying the navigation.

- **Site administration**: This section allows you to manage various administrative tasks for the site, such as creating a site collection, managing site collections, and configuring search settings. And many more settings you can configure.

SharePoint communication site permissions

SharePoint online communication sites have a unique permission structure that differs from other SharePoint sites. The communication site level permission structure enables collaboration and content sharing while protecting sensitive information.

The permission levels available for communication sites are as follows:

- **Site owner**: This permission level is assigned to the user or group that created the communication site. Site owners have full control over the site, including managing permissions, adding or removing users, creating subsites, and changing site settings.

- **Site member**: This permission level is assigned to users invited to collaborate on the site. Members can view, edit, and contribute to the site's content without managing permissions or changing site settings.

- **Site visitor**: This permission level is assigned to users who only need to view the site's content. Visitors can view all site content without editing or contributing to it.

Additionally, SharePoint online communication sites have unique permissions for specific areas of the site, such as individual pages, documents, and lists. These permissions can be customized to allow or restrict access to specific content as needed.

Here are some of the unique permissions available for specific areas of a communication site:

- **Page-level permissions**: Site owners can set page-level permissions to control who can view or edit individual pages on the site. This can be useful for sharing confidential information with a select group of users or restricting access to specific pages that contain sensitive information.

- **Document-level permissions**: Site owners can set document-level permissions to control who can view, edit, or download specific documents on the site. This can be useful for sharing confidential or sensitive documents with a select group of users.

- **List-level permissions**: Site owners can set list-level permissions to control who can view, edit, or contribute to specific lists on the site. This can be useful for managing access to sensitive or confidential data stored in lists, such as customer or financial information.

- **Folder-level permissions**: Site owners can set folder-level permissions to control who can view, edit, or contribute to specific folders within lists or libraries on the site. This can be useful for managing access to sensitive or confidential data stored in specific folders.

Using these unique permissions, site owners can control access to specific site areas and ensure that confidential information is only accessible to authorized users. To set these permissions, site owners can navigate to the specific area of the site (For example, page, document, list, or folder) and modify the permissions settings as needed.

SharePoint communication site template

SharePoint communication sites are designed to help organizations share news, reports, and other types of content with their employees, customers, or partners. The communication site template is a pre-built site that offers a modern and responsive design, making creating and managing engaging and interactive pages easy.

Here are some key features of the SharePoint communication site template:

- **Customizable design**: The communication site template includes several pre-designed themes, layout options, and color palettes, making it easy to customize the look and feel of your site.

- **News and events**: Communication sites allow you to easily create and publish news articles, events, and announcements. You can also set up a newsfeed to display the latest news and updates on your site's homepage.

- **Page templates**: The communication site includes several pre-built page templates, such as the Hero, Blank, and Topic layouts, to help you quickly create pages that meet your needs.

- **Navigation**: Communication sites offer a streamlined navigation experience that helps users find the content they need quickly and easily.

- **Web parts**: Communication sites come with various web parts that can display text, images, videos, documents, and other types of content. These web parts can be easily customized and configured to meet your needs.

- **Search**: SharePoint communication sites are fully integrated with SharePoint search, making it easy for users to find the content they need across your site.

- **Mobile-friendly**: Communication sites are designed to be responsive and mobile-friendly, ensuring your content looks great and is easily accessible on any device.

Overall, the SharePoint communication site template is a great option for organizations creating a modern and engaging site to share news, information, and other types of content with their employees, customers, or partners.

Modern SharePoint communication site

We can connect a modern SharePoint communication site to Microsoft Teams. By doing so, you can bring together the collaboration capabilities of SharePoint with the communication and teamwork capabilities of Teams.

Here is how you can connect a modern SharePoint communication site to Microsoft Teams:

1. Login to **Microsoft Teams** with Microsoft credentials.

2. Then click on the **Teams** in the left navigation | click on **Join** or **Create a Team**.

3. Then click **Create a Team** from the window | Select what kind of team it will be like **Private**, **Public**, and **OrgWide**. In this case select **Public**. Refer to the following *Figure: 3.16:*

Figure 3.16: Modern SharePoint communication site connect to teams

4. Next, you can provide a **Team name** | Provide description(optional) | Click on **Create**.

5. Add members to **Tsinfo Techno** window will open | here we will add members who can access the Team site. You can skip this part if you do not want to add a team group member. Refer to the following *Figure 3.17*:

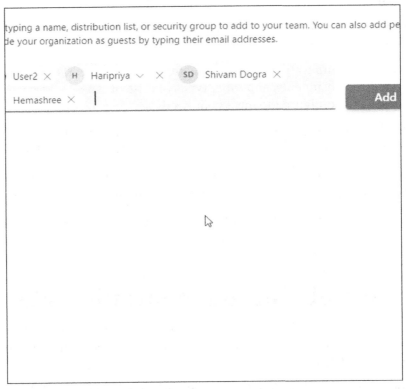

Figure 3.17: Add member to the Team

6. Once the member is added to the Team, the channel **General** is also created by default. Open the channel, click on **+** icon | select **SharePoint**.

7. Select **Add content to your Teams channel from Tsinfo Techno** | select **Pages tab** | select **Page** | click on **Save.** Refer to the following *Figure 3.18:*

Figure 3.18: SharePoint Team site get connected to the Microsoft teams

Connecting a modern SharePoint communication site to Microsoft Teams allows you to share content, documents, and other resources from SharePoint within Teams, and vice versa. This integration can help streamline your workflow and improve your team's productivity.

Add footer to SharePoint communication site

You can add elements to the footer, such as copyright information, links to social media, or contact information. To customize the footer, click **Site Settings** | **Change the look** | **Footer**. Let us see how we can add footer to the SharePoint Communication site:

1. Open the **Communication site**, click on **Settings** | click on **Change the look link** | click on **Footer**.

2. You can toggle on or off enable options based on your requirements.

3. Then you can change the layout of the footer to simple or extended.

4. Now you can see that the footer is added to the SharePoint Communication site. Refer to *Figure 3.19*:

Figure 3.19: Add footer to SharePoint communication site

Delete a modern communication site in SharePoint online

SharePoint online sites that are no longer required, including those made for projects, should be deleted so that only relevant information is accessible. There are many reasons to delete a communication site in SharePoint online.

Here are some of the scenarios where you might want to delete the SharePoint site:

- **The site is no longer needed**: If the site has been created for a specific project or purpose and has been completed, or the site's purpose is no longer relevant, you may want to delete the site to avoid clutter and confusion.

- **The site has been created by error**: If it was created by mistake or with the wrong settings, you might want to delete it and recreate it with the correct settings.

- **The site is causing issues**: If the site is causing issues with performance or functionality, you may want to delete the site and create a new site to avoid these issues.

- **The site is not being used**: If the site has been created but is not used, you may want to delete the site to avoid wasting resources.

Note: To delete the site in SharePoint, you must have permission. If you are SharePoint Administrator or Owner, you can only delete the SharePoint Communication site.

Now let us see how we can delete the SharePoint communication site in **SharePoint** online:

- In The Communication site I Click on the **Gear** icon I Click on **Site information**.

- Then **Site information** window will open I Click on **Delete Site, as** you can see in *Figure 3.20*:

Figure 3.20: Delete modern communication site in SharePoint Online

Now the communication site will get deleted. You can check in the **Active Sites** in the **SharePoint admin center**. If you want to restore the deleted site in case, you can navigate to **Delete sites** under **Sites** in the **SharePoint admin center** I select the site and click on **Restore**. If you do not restore the deleted site in 93 days (about three months), the site will be permanently deleted.

Conclusion

Finally, SharePoint modern communication sites are effective and engaging communication tools within organizations. They include characteristics like responsive design, dynamic web parts, and customized layouts that allow users to construct visually beautiful and user-friendly websites. Users may control permissions and share sites with ease because of simple navigation and rich site contents and settings.

Modern SharePoint communication sites promote information exchange, collaboration, and overall productivity. Finally, the ability to delete sites enables good SharePoint Online maintenance and organization.

In the next chapter, we will delve into the functionality of SharePoint Online lists. We will look at the benefits of modern lists, as well as the method of generating and managing them, as well as various column types and permissions. Additionally, we will cover essential topics such as filtering, list settings, formatting, and views. Furthermore, we will discuss modern list templates and the importance of backing up and restoring SharePoint Online lists. These insights will offer readers a thorough understanding of SharePoint Online lists and enable them to successfully exploit its features.

Join our book's Discord space

Join the book's Discord Workspace for Latest updates, Offers, Tech happenings around the world, New Release and Sessions with the Authors:

https://discord.bpbonline.com

CHAPTER 4
SharePoint Online Modern List

Introduction

This chapter will help you learn more about Modern SharePoint Online lists, including their benefits, creation, adding different types of columns, adding items, and so on. Aside from that, this chapter will help you understand how to add, edit, and delete items from the list, save a list as a template, and filter a list based on specific criteria.

Structure

This chapter contains general information about the Modern SharePoint Online list, such as creation of SharePoint list, adding columns to a SharePoint list, adding items to a list, editing and deleting items from the list, and so on.

The chapter will cover the following topics:

- What is SharePoint Online list?
- Advantages of the SharePoint Online Modern list
- Creating SharePoint Online Modern list
- Creating different types of SharePoint list columns
- Adding items into the SharePoint Online modern list

- Editing and deleting items from SharePoint List
- SharePoint Online Modern list permission
- Filtering a SharePoint Online Modern list
- SharePoint Online list settings
- SharePoint list column formatting
- SharePoint Online modern list view
- Discussing SharePoint Online modern list templates
- Backup and restore of the SharePoint Online modern list

Objectives

After reading this chapter, you will have the overall concept of a SharePoint Online Modern list, its permission labels, and list filtrations based on various criteria. You will also learn about SharePoint online list views, audience targeting, backup and restore, and other topics.

What is SharePoint Online modern list?

Microsoft introduced Modern SharePoint Online with the 2016 version of Microsoft SharePoint where we can create lists, libraries, and many more. Its features are as follows:

- A modern SharePoint list is a collection of data with which you can communicate with members of your team and with those who are granted access. There are several ready-to-use list templates available that can be used to organize list items.

- A SharePoint list, like Microsoft Excel, comprises of rows and columns for storing text and data in the form of a table. List items are the rows in a list; similarly, the columns can be referred to as fields, properties, or metadata.

- Lists can also include assignments that you can use as a spotlight for team collaboration or in a solution. In many cases, lists offer quick, effective solutions that require little or no modification.

- Lists are rich and responsive, with many embedded functions that make them effective for storing, sharing, and collaborating with data.

- SharePoint lists are used to process data and can include attachments such as documents or images.

- Microsoft Flow and Power Apps have been integrated directly into SharePoint Modern lists, allowing users to create a new Power App or add a workflow right from the list layout.

- You can create a list of calendars, tasks, links, contacts, courses, attachments, and so on, as per the business requirements.

- *Figure 4.1* demonstrates an example of a SharePoint Course list. Continue reading to learn how to create a SharePoint Online Modern list:

Course Lists ☆				
Course Title ⌄	Educator ⌄	Course Fee ⌄	Course Duration ⌄	Course Type ⌄
SharePoint	Bijay Kumar Sahoo	₹7,999.00	10	Offline
MariaDB	Aadarsh Vikram Singh	₹3,499.00	8	Online
Python	Arvind Vaishnavi	₹9,999.00	20	Offline
Power Platform	Sonam Subhadarsini	₹14,999.00	35	Offline
SPFx	Preeti Sahu	₹10,499.00	18	Online

Figure 4.1: *Example of Modern SharePoint Online list*

Advantages of the SharePoint Online Modern list

Before creating a SharePoint Online Modern list, we must know about the advantages of SharePoint list. The following is a list of SharePoint's advantages:

- **Access time:** You can simply navigate to the site and open the relevant list with a SharePoint list.

- **Workflow:** You can use Power Apps or Power Automate to create workflows that will run whenever items are added, updated, or deleted from the list.

- **Version management:** When data is stored in a SharePoint list with version control enabled, it is possible to track the version history of every single item. This will show you when the item was modified, who made the changes, and what properties or metadata were modified. It even lets you reload an earlier version, if necessary.

- **Data analytics:** SharePoint Lists have the key advantage of customizable views, which allow you to describe exactly what you want and how it should be presented.

- **User accessibility:** Multiple users can connect and modify items remotely at the same time.

Creating SharePoint Online Modern list

You can build and collaborate lists to keep track of issues, properties, tasks, contacts, storage, and other items. SharePoint allows you to create a list by using a prebuilt template, an Excel file, or from scratch.

Apart from these features, it enables the user to create a custom SharePoint list with custom columns. To construct a list, follow the steps below.

1. Sign in the **Microsoft365** with your Microsoft credentials.

2. Go to **App launcher | SharePoint.** (Or you can find SharePoint from **All apps**)

3. Click on **Open in New tab** to open the app in a new tab.

Figure 4.2 displays where to find the SharePoint app. First, we need to sign in the Microsoft 365 with the respective Microsoft credentials. Once it opens, go to the App launcher and open **SharePoint** in a new tab:

Figure 4.2: *Finding SharePoint Apps from Microsoft 365*

4. Click on the **+New** | **List**, as shown:

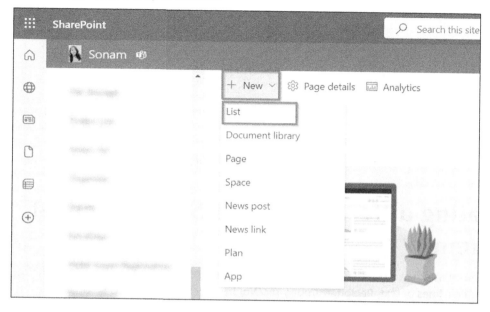

Figure 4.3: Creating new blank list on SharePoint

5. To create a customize list, click on **Blank list**.

6. Specify **Name** and **Description** for the list.

7. Click on **Create** as shown in *Figure 4.4*:

Figure 4.4: Specifying the list name and description

You will now see a new blank list called **Projects Management** with the default column **Title**. It also allows you to add more columns to the list as needed by clicking on **Add Column** as shown in *Figure 4.5*:

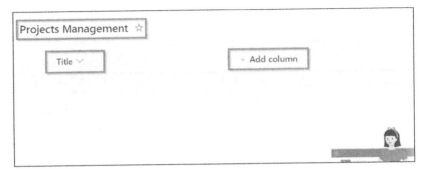

*Figure 4.5: Displaying the **Projects Management** SharePoint list*

Creating different types of SharePoint list columns

SharePoint list allows the user to add different types of columns such as **Text, Choice, Date and time, Multiple lines of text, Person, Number, Yes/No,** Image, Location, and so on as shown in *Figure 4.6*.

We are going to add 6 more columns to the previous SharePoint list **Projects Management**. For example, a **Text** Column (**Project Name**), **Date and time** (**Start Date** and **Due Date**), **Person** (**Project Handler**), and **Choice** (**Project Status**), Currency (**Project Expenditure**).

1. To add a Single line Text column, click on the **Add column** as shown in *Figure 4.6*.

2. Select **Text | Next** as shown in *Figure 4.6*:

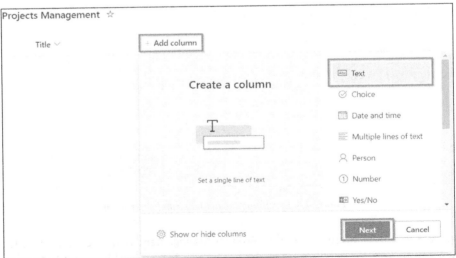

Figure 4.6: Adding a text column to the SharePoint list

3. Give a name to the text column (Example **Project Name**) as shown in *Figure 4.7*.

4. Click on **Save.** The column will display on the SharePoint list as shown in *Figure 4.7*:

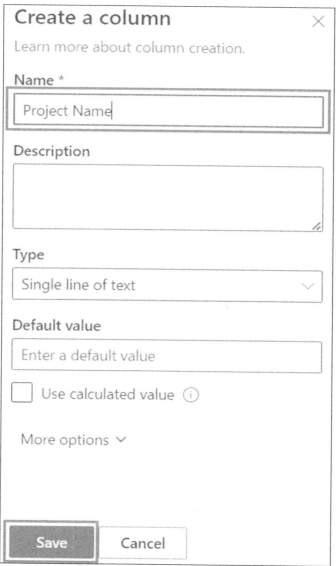

Figure 4.7: Specifying text column name and Save

5. Similarly, to add the Date and time column, click on the **+ Add column | Next**.

6. Give column's **Name | Save as** shown in *Figure 4.8*:

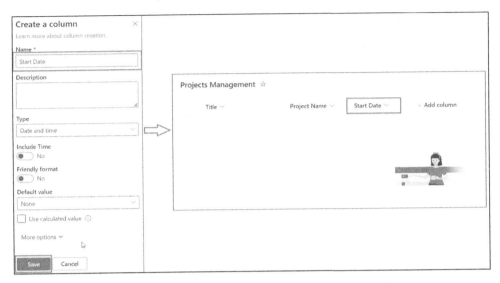

Figure 4.8: Adding date and time column to the SharePoint list

7. Similarly, add another Date and time column for the Due Date. Next, add a Person column for Project Handler. For that, click on the **+ Add column** | **Person** | **Next**.

8. Give a name to the column, that is, **Project Handler** | **Save** as shown in *Figure 4.9*:

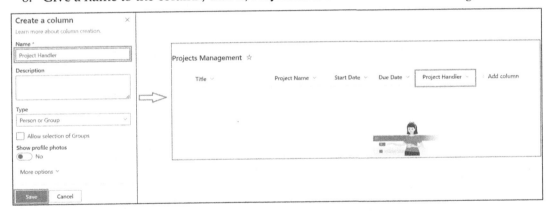

Figure 4.9: Adding a Person column to the SharePoint list

9. Repeat the process to add another field to the above SharePoint list. Click again on + **Add column** | **Choice** | **Next**.

10. Specify the choice column name, that is, **Project Status** and add some choices as per the requirement.

11. Click on **Save** as shown in *Figure 4.10*. Now, the choice column will reflect on the SharePoint list.

Figure 4.10: Adding a choice column to the SharePoint list

Apart from this technique, there is another way to add a column to the SharePoint list via List settings. To add a currency column, that is, **Project Expenditure,** the steps are:

1. On the SharePoint list, click on the **Settings** icon (on the top right bar).

2. Navigate to **List settings**.

3. Go down and select **Create column**.

4. Specify column name **Project Expenditure.**

5. Select the column type, that is, **Currency** as shown in *Figure 4.11*.

6. Specify the currency format as required.

7. Click on **Ok**.

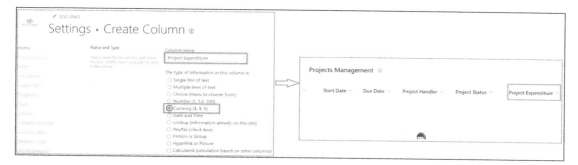

Figure 4.11: Adding a currency column to the list via list settings

Adding items into the SharePoint Online modern list

Once the list is created, it is time to add items into the modern SharePoint list. To add new items to the list, the steps are as follows:

1. On the SharePoint list, click on the **+New** (on the top bar).

2. Fill in all the fields and click on **Save** as shown in *Figure 4.12:*

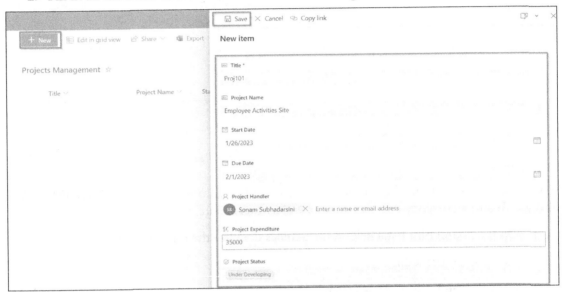

Figure 4.12: Adding an item to the SharePoint list

Note: When you click on the Cancel option, the item will not be saved to the SharePoint list.

Now, the item is saved and reflected to the SharePoint list as shown in *Figure 4.13:*

Figure 4.13: Adding an item to the Modern SharePoint list

Adding several items to the SharePoint list

Rather than adding only one item to the SharePoint list, we can add multiple items at once in the grid view. The steps for the process are as follows:

1. On the SharePoint list, navigate **Edit in grid view**.

2. Enter the item's details one by one.

3. When you click on the **+ Add new item**, a new column will appear with the respective fields.

4. After entering the items, click on the **Exit grid view** as shown in the *Figure 4.14*:

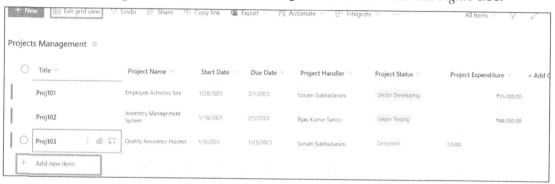

Figure 4.14: Adding several items to the Modern SharePoint list

Now, all the items will be saved and reflected on the Modern SharePoint list.

Adding new list item from URL

We can add a new item from the URL to the SharePoint list. The SharePoint list offers a link or URL while adding a new item. We can copy that link and share it with colleagues to insert the items from the URL. The steps for this process are as follows:

1. Once the SharePoint list is created, click on **+New.**

2. Navigate to **Copy link** as shown in *Figure 4.15*:

Figure 4.15: Adding an item to the list via URL

3. It will display a URL | **Copy** as shown in *Figure 4.16*:

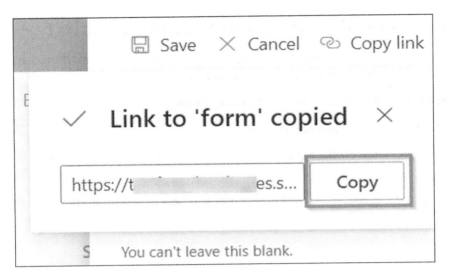

Figure 4.16: Adding a new item to the list via URL

You can share that URL to other users (who have access to the SharePoint list) so they can add new items to the SharePoint list.

Adding calculated columns to the SharePoint Online modern list

Adding calculated columns to a SharePoint Online modern list can provide practical calculated values based on data from other columns or formulas. When you add or edit data in corresponding columns, SharePoint will calculate the value and display the calculated column according to your defined formula.

In the SharePoint list shown above *Figure 4.13*, let us add a calculated column that will calculate the total days depending on the Start Date and Due Date. The following steps are:

1. On the SharePoint list, click on the **Settings** icon.

2. Navigate List settings.

3. Click on **Create columns** | **Calculated**.

4. Specify the column name **Total Days.**

5. Choose the column type i.e., **Calculated.**

6. Insert the formula = **[Due Date] - [Start Date]** on the Formula field as shown in *Figure 4.17*, where Due Date and Start Date are the date and time columns of the SharePoint list:

Name and Type

Type a name for this column, and select the type of information you want to store in the column.

Column name:

Total Days

The type of information in this column is:

○ Single line of text
○ Multiple lines of text
○ Choice (menu to choose from)
○ Number (1, 1.0, 100)
○ Currency ($, ¥, €)
○ Date and Time
○ Lookup (information already on this site)
○ Yes/No (check box)
○ Person or Group
○ Hyperlink or Picture
◉ Calculated (calculation based on other columns)
○ Image
○ Task Outcome
○ External Data
○ Managed Metadata

Additional Column Settings

Specify detailed options for the type of information you selected.

Description:

Formula:

Insert Column:

= [Due Date]- [Start Date]

Compliance Asset Id
Created
Due Date
Modified
Project Expenditure
Project Name
Project Status

Figure 4.17: *Adding a calculated column to the list*

7. Click on **OK**. The calculated column will be added to the SharePoint list. Along with the column will display the total days based on the specified SharePoint columns as shown in *Figure 4.18*:

Projects Management ☆							
Title ⌄	Project Name ⌄	Start Date ⌄	Due Date ⌄	Project Handler ⌄	Project Status ⌄	Project Expenditure ⌄	Total Days ⌄
Proj101	Employee Activities Site	1/26/2023	2/1/2023	Sonam Subhadarsini	Under Developing	₹35,000.00	6
Proj102	Inventory Management System	1/16/2023	2/3/2023	Bijay Kumar Sahoo	Under Testing	₹48,000.00	18
Proj103	Quality Assurance Process	1/3/2023	1/25/2023	Sonam Subhadarsini	Delivered	₹53,000.00	22

Figure 4.18: *Displaying a calculated values in the SharePoint calculated column*

Editing and deleting items from SharePoint List

SharePoint allows you to edit bulk list items at once in a grid view. Sometimes, we might need to delete a SharePoint list from a site (team site or communication site) as well. In this section, you will perform both these functions.

Editing items in the SharePoint list

You can edit bulk items within the grid view of the SharePoint list. The steps to edit are as follows:

1. On the SharePoint list, click on the **Edit in grid view.**

2. It will convert the list into the grid view, so that the user can edit the items as per the requirements.

3. Select the value that you want to edit. For example, let us edit the **Project Name** from the **Employee Activities Site** to **Employee onboarding Apps.** Next, set the **Project Expenditure** from 35,000 to 37,000.

4. Once you edit the items, click on the **Exit grid view** as shown in *Figure 4.19*. It will return to the SharePoint list with the updated value:

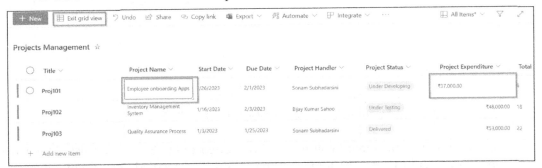

Figure 4.19: Editing items in the SharePoint list grid view

Deleting items in the SharePoint list

We can delete one or more items from the SharePoint list at once. To delete a single item from the SharePoint list, the steps are as follows:

1. Select the specific item(s) | **Delete** (on the top bar of the list) | **Delete** as shown in *Figure 4.20*. It will delete that item(s) from the SharePoint list:

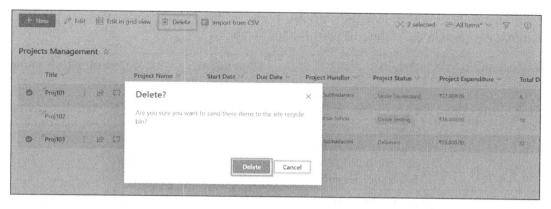

Figure 4.20: Editing items in the SharePoint list grid view

2. If you want to delete a single item from the SharePoint list, select the item | click on the **Ellipses** (vertical three dots) | **Delete** as shown in *Figure 4.21*. This will delete the selected item from the list:

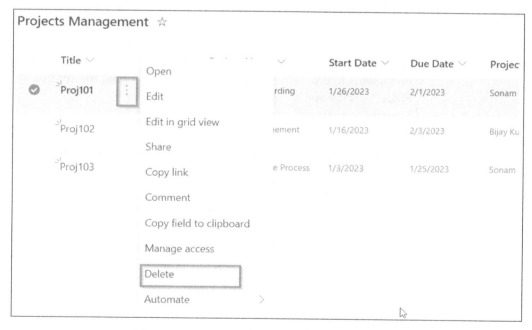

Figure 4.21: Deleting a single item in the SharePoint list

SharePoint Online modern list permission

SharePoint provides various types of permissions that are categorized as list permissions, site permissions, personal permissions, and their like, depending on the objects that can be used. The SharePoint modern list permissions are only applicable to lists and libraries.

The following *Table 4.1* shows the various types of list permissions, their descriptions, dependent permissions, and default permissions levels:

Permissions	Details	Dependent permissions	Default permissions levels
Manage Lists	Lists can be created and deleted, columns can be added or removed from list, and public views can be added or removed.	View items and pages, Open	Edit, design, manage hierarchy, and full control.
Add items	Add items and documents to the SharePoint list and library, respectively.	View items and pages, Open	Add, edit, design, and full control.
Edit items	Edit list items, documents, and Web Part pages in document libraries.	View items and pages, Open	Add, edit, design, and full control.
Delete items	Delete items and documents to the SharePoint list and library, respectively.	View items and pages, Open	Add, edit, design, and full control.
View items	View items and documents to the SharePoint list and library respectively.	View pages and Open	Read, edit, contribute or add, design, full control.
Approve items	Accept or approve a minor version of a list item or document.	Edit items, view items and pages, Open	Design, full control.
Open items	With server-side file handlers, you can see the source of documents.	View items and pages, Open	Read, edit, contribute or add, design, full control.
Create Alerts	You can create alerts.	View items and pages, Open	Read, Contribute, Edit, Design, full Control

Table 4.1: Various permissions in SharePoint Online Modern list

Along with these permissions, you can get more information about the various types of permissions available under the SharePoint server from Microsoft. **(https://learn.microsoft.com/en-us/SharePoint/sites/user-permissions-and-permission-levels?source=docs)**

Customizing SharePoint Online modern list permissions

We can find some default permission levels for the modern SharePoint list. As the owner of a list, you can customize permissions to allow certain people access to data while restricting others.

Note: You cannot break permissions inheritance on a list or library that contains more than 100,000 items. Permissions on the list cannot be inherited again.

These default list permissions levels are:

- **Full control:** The assigned user has full control.

- **Design:** The user can add, view, update, delete, and customize the list.

- **Edit:** It allows the user to add, edit and delete lists. Also, the user can view, add, update, and delete list items and documents.

- **Contribute:** It allows the user to view, add, update, and delete list items and documents from the library.

- **Read:** It enables users to view pages, create lists, and download documents.

- **Restricted view**: The user can view pages, list items, and documents. Documents can be viewed in the browser but not downloaded.

To edit the user permissions on a SharePoint list, the steps are as follows:

1. Open the targeted Modern SharePoint list (Example Projects Management).

2. Navigate to **Settings | List settings.**

3. On the **General Settings**, click on the **Permissions** for the list (under Permissions and Management).

4. Select **Grant permissions** under **Permissions** as shown in *Figure 4.22*.

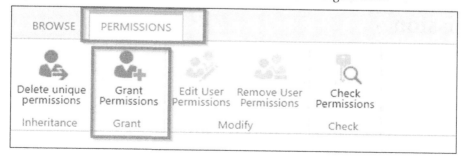

Figure 4.22: Customize SharePoint list permissions

5. Under Permissions, check the box for the permission level that you want for the users or groups.

6. Click on **Edit User Permissions** as shown in *Figure 4.23*:

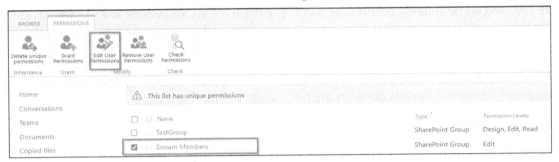

Figure 4.23: Customize SharePoint list user permissions

7. Choose the permissions for the selected user or group as per your requirements.

8. Click **OK** to save the permissions as shown in *Figure 4.24*:

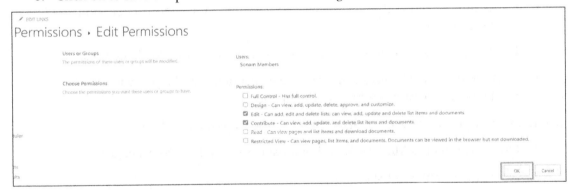

Figure 4.24: Editing User permissions for SharePoint Online list

SharePoint Online modern list item level permission

In SharePoint, the item-level permission specifies which items users can read and edit.

To enable the item-level permission in SharePoint list, the steps are as follows:

1. Open the target in the SharePoint list. (Example, Projects Management)

2. Navigate to the **Settings** gear | **Advanced Settings**.

3. Under the **Advanced Settings**, you can find item-level permissions.

4. By default, Item-level permissions are set as follows:

a. **Read Access** is set to **Read all items** that defines which items users are permitted to read.

b. **Create and edit access** is set to **Create and Edit access** that defines which items users are permitted to read as shown in *Figure 4.25*:

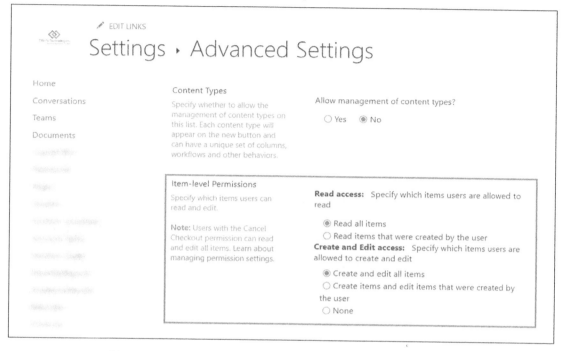

Figure 4.25: Displaying item-level permissions in Modern SharePoint list

5. Here, you can change the item-level permissions to:

   a. **Read items that were created by the user**: It allows users to only see items that they created. They will not be able to see the entries of others. The list views only display items that the user has created.

   b. **Create and edit all items:** It allows users to create items, but they can only edit the items they have created. When a user attempts to edit items created by others, they will receive an error like *Sorry, you don't have access.*

6. Once you customize the item-level permissions as per your need, scroll down the page and click on **OK**. This will save the customized permissions.

Filtering a SharePoint Online Modern list

Filtration limits the number of items displayed in a view to only the information users want to see. A filter selects items that meet certain criteria, such as location, item type, or price range. To filter the modern SharePoint list, the steps are as follows:

1. Open the targeted SharePoint list. (Example Projects Management)

2. Click on the column's heading that you wish to filter by. For example, let us filter the list by project status.

3. Select **Filter by** as shown in *Figure 4.26:*

Figure 4.26: Filtering Modern SharePoint list

4. Choose a column's choice value by which you wish to filter the SharePoint list.

5. Once selected, click on the **Apply (Example Delivered)** as shown in *Figure 4.27:*

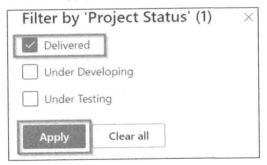

Figure 4.27: Selecting choice value to filter the Modern SharePoint list

6. The filtered data will be visible on the screen with a filter icon beside the column's header, that is, **Project Status** as shown in *Figure 4.28:*

Figure 4.28: Displaying the filter data within the SharePoint list

7. As the view is not saved, it will display an asterisk mark (*) on the **All items** (on the top of the list). If you want to save this filtered view, expand **All items* | Save view as** like in *Figure 4.29*:

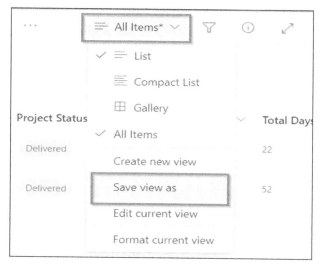

Figure 4.29: Saving filtered view in SharePoint list

8. You can save the filtered view as the current view or save it as a new view. Also, make the filtered view public as well.

Click on **Save**. This will create a new view with filtered data as shown in *Figure 4.30*:

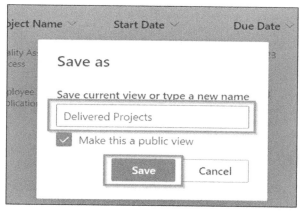

Figure 4.30: Saving filtered view in a new view within SharePoint list

SharePoint Online list settings

A SharePoint list is a versatile way to display and store data. It also allows adjustment of general settings, permissions, and management, which includes list versioning settings, validation settings, audience targeting settings, form settings, enable permissions, workflow settings, metadata and keyword settings, RSS settings, and so on.

To find the SharePoint Online list Settings, the steps are as follows:

1. Open the targeted SharePoint list, go to **Settings** | **List settings** as shown in *Figure 4.31*:

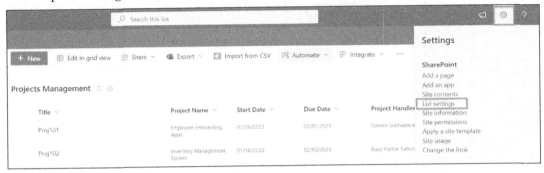

Figure 4.31: SharePoint Online list Settings

2. On the SharePoint list settings, you can edit the list name, description, column ordering, add new columns, permissions, etc. as shown in *Figure 4.32*:

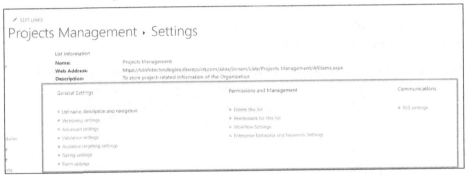

Figure 4.32: Displaying different types of list Settings in SharePoint Online

General settings

In general settings, you can edit and control the navigation, set up the versions, validations, audience targeting, form settings, and many more.

Table 4.2 below shows the various types of settings that come under general settings and their functionalities:

Settings	Functionalities
List name, description, and navigation	Change the list's title, description, and whether it appears in the Quick Launch bar.

Settings	Functionalities
Versioning settings	Set whether submitted items require approval, whether new versions are to be created with each edit, the number of submitted and approved versions, and who can see, edit, and approve draft items.
Advanced settings	Configure the following: • Management of content type • Item-level permissions • Allow attachments • Allow list-comments • Enable folders • Allow items to appear in search result • Reindexing the list • Whether or not non-default views are displayed in search results and so on
Validation settings	Provide a formula for validation and create a message that explains what valid data looks like.
Audience targeting settings	Enable the audience targeting column to filter content based on the context of the user.
Rating settings	Indicate whether this list's items can be rated. That means when you enable ratings, two fields are added to the content types available for this list, and a rating control is added to the list's or library's default view. You can choose between Likes and Star Ratings to rate content.
Form settings	Customize the forms for this list using Microsoft PowerApps where you can change the layout of the form, add images and formatted text, add custom data validation, create new views, and add rules. Microsoft InfoPath is also available for backward compatibility. It is preferable to use PowerApps rather than InfoPath.

Table 4.2: *SharePoint Online General settings*

Permissions and management

In permissions and management settings, you can manage the list's keywords, metadata, workflows, and permissions.

Table 4.3 below shows the various types of settings that come under permissions and management settings and their functionalities:

Settings	Functionalities
Delete this list	It will delete the list completely and redirect to the home page.
Permissions for this list	Set the permission levels for the list for various user groups on the site.
Workflow Settings	Set the types of workflow associations for the list, item, or folder. A workflow can be added, removed, blocked, or restored.
Enterprise Metadata and Keywords Settings	Enable keyword synchronization and add an enterprise keyword column.

Table 4.3: SharePoint Online Permissions and Management

Communications

In the communications settings, you can configure RSS feeds to be sent out when list items change. The RSS settings enable the user to set the following properties:

- Turn on RSS for the list.

- Reduce the length of multiline text fields to 256 characters.

- Set the RSS feed's title, description, and image URL.

- Choose which columns in the list to display in an RSS description.

- Set the maximum number of items to include in the RSS feed as well as the maximum number of days.

SharePoint list column formatting

Column formatting allows you to change how fields in SharePoint lists and libraries appear. The SharePoint list column formatting (as shown in *Figure 4.33*) has no effect on the data in the list item or file. It only changes how data is displayed to users who visit the list. Anyone who can create and manage views in a list can use column formatting to customize how view fields are presented:

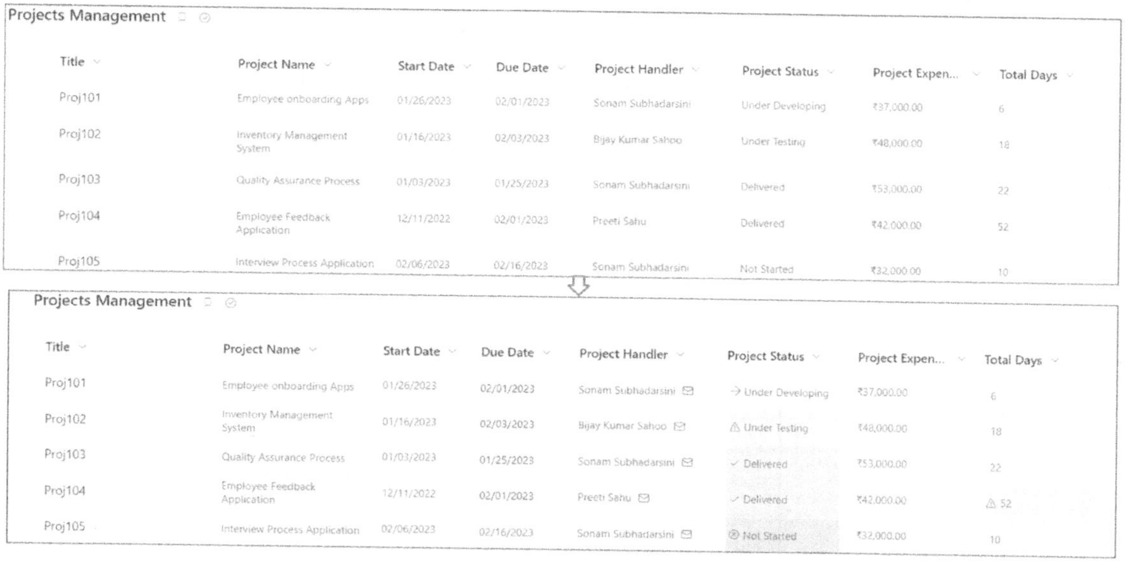

Figure 4.33: *SharePoint list column formatting*

Formatting SharePoint list column using JSON

To accomplish this, create a JSON object that describes the elements that will be displayed when a field is included in a list view, as well as the styles that will be applied to the elements. Microsoft provides some JSON samples in the SharePoint list column formatting, (**https://github.com/pnp/List-Formatting**) from which we can use the JSON directly and format the column as needed.

You can also format the SharePoint list column(**https://learn.microsoft.com/en-us/sharepoint/dev/declarative-customization/column-formatting**) using the direct JSON from the mentioned document provided by Microsoft. Simply copy the JSON and paste it into the column format panel. Remember to change the column names.

Getting started with SharePoint column formatting using JSON

In this section, we will explore how to work with SharePoint Column formatting using JSON.

Data in lists or libraries are unaffected by SharePoint Column formatting. It modifies the way lists and libraries are displayed using different colors, icons, font effects, etc. To do this, we must create a JSON object that contains information on the elements shown in the browser.

Example 1: Formatting choice column in the SharePoint list

To format a choice column within the SharePoint list, the following steps are:

Click on the choice column's header (that is, **Project Status**) | **column settings** | **Format this column** as shown in *Figure 4.34*:

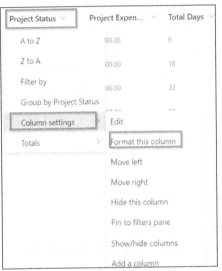

Figure 4.34: SharePoint list choice column formatting

It will redirect to the format panel, go down and select **Advance Mode** | paste the below JSON | **Save** as shown in *Figure 4.35*:

```
{

    "$schema":   "https://developer.microsoft.com/json-schemas/sp/v2/column-
formatting.schema.json",

  "elmType": "div",

  "attributes": {

    "class": "=if(@currentField == 'Delivered', 'sp-field-severity--good', if(@
currentField == 'Under Developing', 'sp-field-severity--low', if(@currentField ==
'Under Testing', 'sp-field-severity--warning', if(@currentField == 'Not Started',
'sp-field-severity--severeWarning',  'sp-field-severity--blocked')))) + '  ms-
fontColor-neutralSecondary'"

  },

  "children": [

    {
```

```
    "elmType": "span",

    "style": {

      "display": "inline-block",

      "padding": "0 4px"

    },

    "attributes": {

    "iconName": "=if(@currentField == 'Delivered', 'CheckMark', if(@currentField
== 'Under Developing', 'Forward', if(@currentField == 'Under Testing', 'Warning',
if(@currentField == 'Not Started', 'ErrorBadge', 'Warning'))))"

    }

  },

  {

    "elmType": "span",

    "txtContent": "@currentField"

  }

 ]

}
```

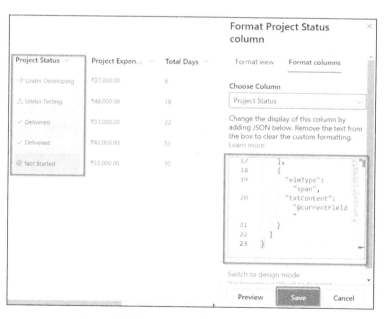

Figure 4.35: Formatting SharePoint text column

Example 2: Formatting date column in the SharePoint list

Similarly, apply the sample JSON below to format the date column within the SharePoint list.

To compare one date/time field value to another, use the Date () method to convert a string to a date. If the value in the **Due Date field** is before **2/05/2023**, the current field is colored blue.

Select the **Due Date | Column settings | Format this column | Advanced mode**. Insert the below JSON and click on **Save** as shown in *Figure 4.36*:

```
{
        "$schema":    "https://developer.microsoft.com/json-schemas/sp/v2/column-
formatting.schema.json",
    "elmType": "div",
    "txtContent": "@currentField",
    "style": {
        "color": {
            "operator": "?",
            "operands": [
                {
                    "operator": "<=",
                    "operands": [
                        "[$DueDate]",
                        {
                            "operator": "Date()",
                            "operands": [
                                "2/05/2023"
                            ]
                        }
                    ]
                },
                "#0000ff",
                ""
```

```
            ]
        }
    }
}
```

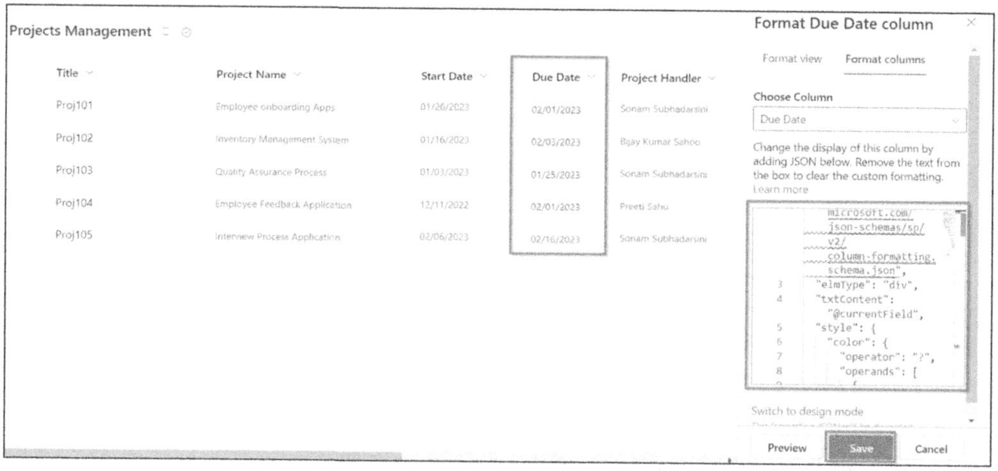

Figure 4.36: Formatting SharePoint date column

The other columns in the SharePoint list can be formatted in the same way. Also, SharePoint allows you to format columns without using JSON.

Formatting SharePoint list column using prebuild formats

SharePoint provides some prebuild formats for formatting the columns based on conditions where we need to manage the rules and conditions.

Let us take the above SharePoint list Projects Management and format different types of columns using the prebuild formats.

Example 1: Formatting the Date column in the SharePoint list

To format the date column within the SharePoint list, select the date column | **Column settings** | **Format this column.**

A format panel will appear where you can edit the date column styles or manage rules using the conditions as shown in *Figure 4.37:*

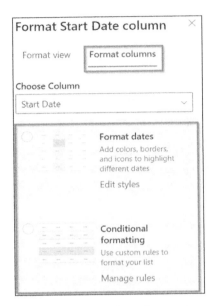

Figure 4.37: Formatting SharePoint date column using prebuild formats

Let us do the conditional formatting on the **Start Date.** Click on the **Manage rules** under the **Conditional formatting**. Manage the rules if the date value of the **Start date** is before **1/1/2023,** then it turns to red color and notifies with a Calendar icon. (You can get this under the **More style** section). Once you click on **Save,** the format will reflect on the date column as shown in *Figure 4.38:*

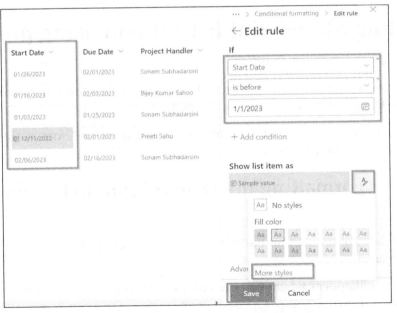

Figure 4.38: Conditional formatting on SharePoint date column

Example 2: Formatting the person column in the SharePoint list

Let us do the conditional formatting in the SharePoint person column. As per the conditional formatting, if the value is equal to a specific value, then the column value will be formatted.

Similarly, navigate to the conditional formatting of the person field and manage the rules as follows:

If **Project Handler** is equal to `Sonam Subhadarsini`, show list item as green color with bold and italics format. The results are shown in *Figure 4.39*:

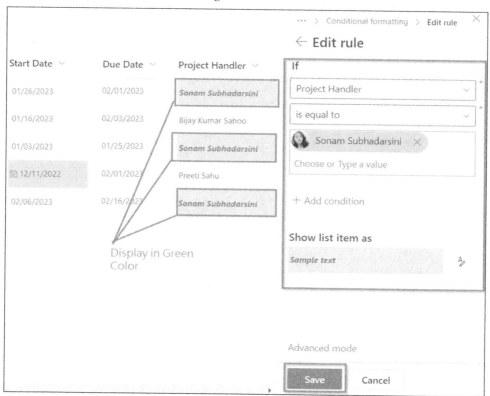

Figure 4.39: *Conditional formatting on SharePoint person column*

You can format the remaining columns in the SharePoint list in a similar manner.

SharePoint Online modern list view

The SharePoint list modern view is used to visualize data from a list or library. At least one view is created by default whenever a list or library is created. The default view for a list is All Items.

Along with organizing and displaying items in a list or document library, you can create custom views. Filtering, sorting, styling, and other features can be added to a custom view.

Aside from that, you can customize your personal views that only you can see and that others cannot. However, you can create public views that can be viewed by other users.

We can create different types of views within the modern SharePoint online list such as **list, calendar, gallery, and board.** Let us create a calendar view within the above SharePoint list by following the given steps:

1. On the command bar of the targeted SharePoint list, expand **All Items | Create new view**.

2. Give a name to the view, select a view (Example **Calendar**) | Choose start date and end date on calendar.

3. Set the visibility as **public or private**.

4. Select the **Title of the items on calendar** (that is, **Project Name**).

5. Click **Create** as shown in *Figure 4.40*:

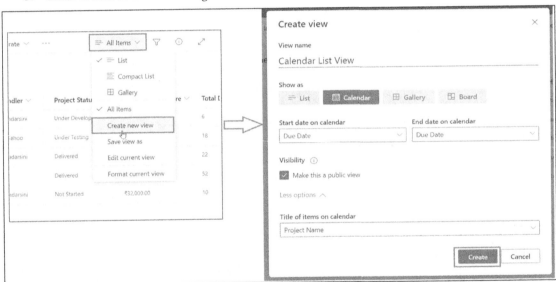

Figure 4.40: Creating a new view on the SharePoint list

Now, the view will reflect on the SharePoint list as below in *Figure 4.41*:

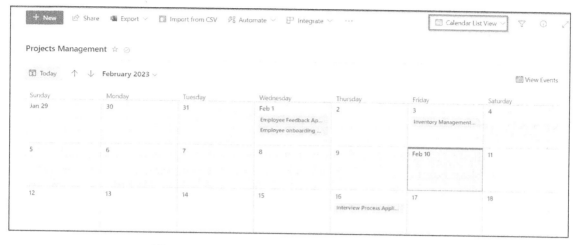

Figure 4.41: Applying created view on the SharePoint list

This view can be saved as the current or default view. As a result, when the list is opened, it will be set to the calendar view by default.

SharePoint Online modern list view edits

Once you set a new view to the SharePoint list, we can edit the current view directly within the list. To edit the current view on the above example of the SharePoint list, the steps are as follows:

1. On the command bar of the targeted SharePoint list, expand the view (that is, **Calendar List View**).

2. Select **Edit current view** as shown in *Figure 4.42:*

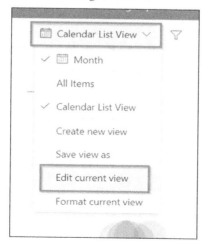

Figure 4.42: Editing SharePoint online list view

3. Make your changes on the **Edit view** page. You can change the order of columns, add sort or filter criteria, set up folders, and more.

4. Once you are done, click on **Save.** The changes will reflect on the SharePoint list.

SharePoint Online modern list view audience targeting

SharePoint audience targeting is a feature that enables you to display certain content to a group of your SharePoint site's users or audiences. You may personalize the user experience by displaying relevant information to certain individuals or groups while hiding it from others who are not part of the target audience by utilizing audience targeting.

Office 365 groups and Azure Active Directory groups can be included in the audience.

There are various types of content where we can use audience targeting in SharePoint list:

- **SharePoint navigation links**: In SharePoint, the navigation links can be found in the quick launch or top link bar. To add, modify, or delete navigation links, you must at least have Contribute permission.

- **Web parts:** Several Web parts promote audience targeting. To add, modify, or delete Web parts, you must at least have Contribute permission.

- **SharePoint list and library items:** To customize the audience targeting, you must have at least the Contribute permission level.

Enabling audience targeting on the SharePoint list

To enable the audience targeting on a specific SharePoint list, the following steps are:

1. Open the targeted SharePoint list, navigate to **Settings**.

2. Then go to the **List Settings**.

3. Under **General settings**, click on the **Audience targeting settings**.

4. It will take you to a screen where you will be asked to enable audience targeting.

5. Click **OK** as shown in *Figure 4.43:*

Figure 4.43: Enabling SharePoint List Audience targeting

Once you are done, an audience field will be added automatically while adding a new item to that SharePoint list as shown in *Figure 4.44*:

Figure 4.44: *Displaying SharePoint List Audience targeting*

SharePoint Online modern list view threshold

In SharePoint, Microsoft set a threshold or limit of not extracting more than 5000 items or files at a time in a single view, so that retrieving items/files from a large SharePoint list or document library does not cause performance issues.

If your list has more than 5000 items, you will get an error message like *the attempted operation is prohibited because it exceeds the list view threshold SharePoint online*. In such a case, you can try the things below to handle the threshold limit while working with the SharePoint list.

- **Use SharePoint list in modern experience instead of classic experience:** Make sure to use the modern SharePoint online list instead of classic SharePoint list to handle the threshold limit of SharePoint list. As a result, items will load as you scroll down the SharePoint list view.

- **Proper planning:** Before working with larger data in a SharePoint list, we need to analyze the data and plan accordingly. This is important so that you can store the data by splitting it into multiple lists and libraries; otherwise, it may display threshold error.

- **Make a filtered list view:** By creating multiple list views, the number of items is limited to 5000. Similarly, applying a filter to SharePoint will return results that are less than 5000.

- **Allow automatic index management:** By enabling `Automatic Index Management` SharePoint the first index is created by Automatic Indexing, and all corresponding indexes are created after sorting any columns.

Discussing SharePoint Online modern list templates

Microsoft provides various types of prebuild list templates that assist you in creating lists by utilizing pre-configured designs that include columns, color formatting, and data structure. You can personalize each list to your needs by changing the formatting to highlight important information, customizing forms to see in brief, and setting reminders to keep you and your team updated of current events.

When you create a list based on a lists template, you have the option of customizing it to meet the needs of your organization.

You can find the different types of list templates, while creating a new list such as **Issue tracker, Employee onboarding, Event itinerary, Asset manager, Work progress tracker, Travel request**, expense tracker, and so on as shown in *Figure 4.45*:

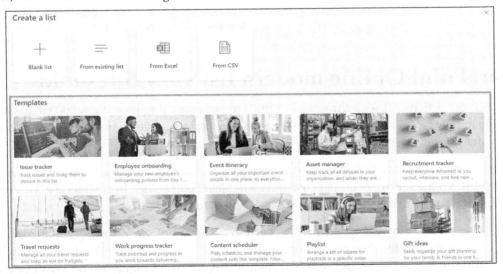

Figure 4.45: Different types of SharePoint list templates

You can select one of the list templates to work on. The following points describe the list of prebuild templates, their uses, and appearance:

- **Issue tracker:** With this template, you can track issues and bring them to closure in this list as shown in *Figure 4.46*:

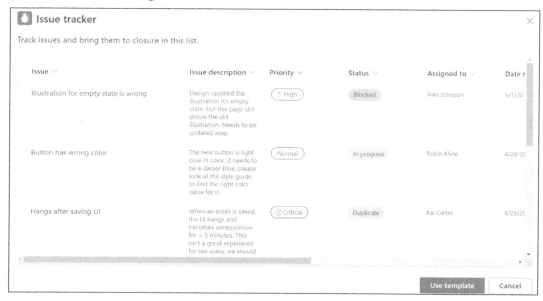

Figure 4.46: Example of SharePoint list templates- Issue Tracker

- **Employee onboarding:** From day one, it will help you manage the employee's onboarding process. With this template, you can share resources and contacts and get your new hire up to speed as soon as possible as shown in *Figure 4.47*:

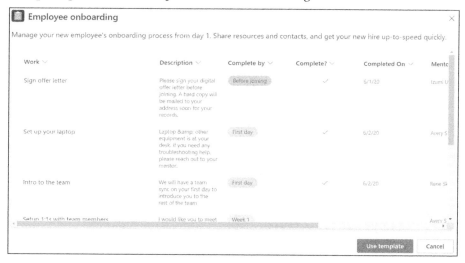

Figure 4.47: Example of SharePoint list employee onboarding

- **Event itinerary:** It will help you to organize details of all important event in one place to ensure a seamless event.

- **Content Scheduler:** This template will help you plan, schedule and manage your content. It is used for filtering items that are due soon or receiving notifications when authors check in their tasks or contents.

- **Expense tracker:** You can keep track of all your expenses in one place with this feature.

- **Work progress tracker:** This will help you keep track of your priorities and progress as you work to deliver products and services.

SharePoint Online modern Calendar list

The SharePoint Online calendar list is a simple and interesting way to organize meetings and events. Calendar lists can be displayed in regular, weekly, and monthly views.

As the calendars have been moved under **Classic Apps**, adding one to a SharePoint Online modern site is slightly complex. The following steps will help you create a calendar list in SharePoint Online:

1. On your modern SharePoint site Home page, click on **New** | **App** as shown in *Figure 4.48*:

Figure 4.48: Building Calendar list from navigating App

2. On the SharePoint page, click on the **Classic Experience** as shown in *Figure 4.49*:

Figure 4.49: Creating SharePoint Online modern Calendar list

Search for **Calendar** | Select the app | Give a name to the app | **Create** as shown in *Figure 4.50*:

Figure 4.50: Giving name to SharePoint Online modern Calendar list

Once the list is created, it will be available on the SharePoint modern site's Site content as shown in *Figure 4.51*:

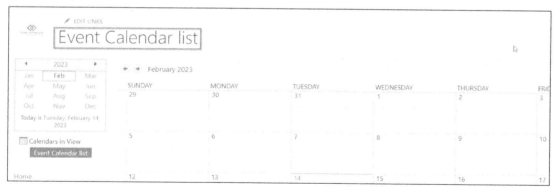

Figure 4.51: Displaying SharePoint Online modern Calendar list

SharePoint Online modern contact list

The most important advantage of the contact list is that it automatically provides the standard metadata associated with a person or contact.

There is no need to create common properties such as First Name, Last Name, Address, Company, Business Phone, Home Phone and so on. These fields are used to find contacts.

To create a modern SharePoint contact list, the steps are as follows:

1. Follow the preceding steps and search for **Contact.**

2. Select the app | give a name to the list. (Example, `TSInfo Employee Contacts`) | **Create** as shown in *Figure 4.52*:

Figure 4.52: Creating SharePoint Online modern contact list

Now, the contact list will appear on the modern SharePoint site as shown in *Figure 4.53*:

Figure 4.53: Displaying SharePoint Online modern contact list

SharePoint Online modern task list

A SharePoint project task list presents a collection of project-related tasks. A task involves working on different items that can be assigned to a single person. A project is typically defined as a set of activities with a beginning, middle, and end.

To create a task list on the modern SharePoint online, the steps are as follows:

1. Similarly, follow the above steps and search for Tasks.

2. Select the app and give a name to the task list (Example **Daily Task Lists**). Press **Create**.

3. The list will appear on the Site Contents of the Modern SharePoint site. By default, the list will appear with classic SharePoint site as shown in *Figure 4.54*:

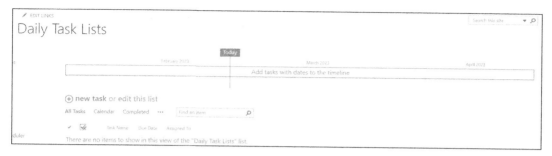

Figure 4.54: Default Classic view of SharePoint Online modern contact list

Change SharePoint Online task list to Modern view

As the task lists in SharePoint Online are created with the Classic experience, it allows to switch its user interface to the new experience user interface or modern experience. The steps are as follows:

1. On the top bar of the task list shown above, click the **List** ribbon.

2. Go to **List settings**.

3. Under **General settings**, click on **Advanced settings.**

4. Select **List experience** as **New experience.** Click **OK** as shown in *Figure 4.55*:

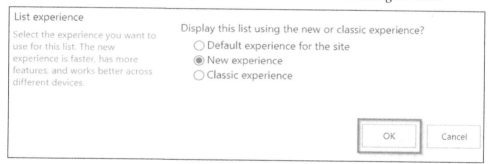

Figure 4.55: Converting Classic view of SharePoint Online modern task list

Now, the list will appear in modern experience within the SharePoint site as shown in *Figure 4.56:*

Figure 4.56: Changing Classic view of SharePoint Online modern task list

Backup and restore the SharePoint Online modern list

SharePoint Online maintains backups of all content for 14 days (about 2 weeks) after it is deleted. If the content cannot be restored using the Recycle Bin or Files Restore, an administrator can contact Microsoft support at any time during the 14-day period to request a restore.

If you mistakenly delete a modern SharePoint list, you can backup that list from the Recycle Bin. The steps for backup are as follows:

1. You can find the Recycle bin option from your SharePoint site or you can find that under the site contents.

2. Select the list that you want to restore.

3. Click **Restore** as shown in *Figure 4.57*:

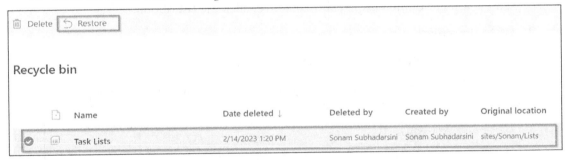

Figure 4.57: Restoring SharePoint Online modern task list

The selected list will be available on your SharePoint site.

Conclusion

In this chapter, we have covered different aspects of SharePoint Online Modern list such as the definition of a modern SharePoint list, creation of modern list, adding items to the list, editing and deleting items from the list, customizing the list, different types of permissions, filtration on SharePoint Online Modern list, understanding the list settings, formatting and creating views, backup and restore the SharePoint Online modern list, etc.

In the next chapter, we will see what modern library is, its advantages, how to create a library, its settings, different types of permissions, and so on.

Points to remember

You can quickly read and learn some of the chapter's most important learning aspects, such as:

- Modern SharePoint Online List helps to use Power Apps or Power Automate to create workflows that will run whenever items are modified from the list.

- Create a Modern SharePoint Online list by using a prebuilt template, an Excel file, or from scratch.

- Add different types of columns to a Modern SharePoint Online list such as:

  o Single line of text

  o Date and time column

  o Number column

  o Choice column

  o Person

- Build calculated column within a SharePoint Online list.

- Edit and delete item(s) from the modern SharePoint Online list.

- Customize the SharePoint Online list permissions based on different scenarios such as:

  o Customizing list level permission in a SharePoint Online

  o Customizing item level permission in a SharePoint Online

- Add filtrations to filtering the SharePoint Online List

- Different types of list settings such as:

  o General settings

  o Permissions and management

  o Communication

- Customize the SharePoint list column using different approaches such as:

  o Format SharePoint list choice column using JSON

  o Format SharePoint list date column using JSON

  o Format SharePoint list column using prebuilt format

- Discussing Modern SharePoint Online modern list view

  o SharePoint Online modern list view edit

- o SharePoint Online modern list view audience targeting

- o SharePoint Online modern list view threshold

- Discussing SharePoint Online list templates

  - o Calendar list

  - o Contact list

  - o Task list

- Backup and restoration of a deleted SharePoint list

Join our book's Discord space

Join the book's Discord Workspace for Latest updates, Offers, Tech happenings around the world, New Release and Sessions with the Authors:

https://discord.bpbonline.com

CHAPTER 5
SharePoint Online Modern Library

Introduction

In this chapter, we will discuss Modern SharePoint Online libraries, including, covering their benefits, how to build them, how to add various types of columns, how to add folders and files, etc. In addition, you will learn how to create custom views, enable audience targeting, work with templates, export libraries to Excel, and many other things in this chapter.

Structure

This chapter will cover general information on the Modern SharePoint Online document library, such as how to define permissions for the library, create a Modern SharePoint Online library, and many other things. An outline of the chapter's contents is provided in the list below:

- Introduction to SharePoint Document library

- Advantages of SharePoint Document library

- Creating a SharePoint document library

- SharePoint document library add columns

- SharePoint library settings

- Working with files in SharePoint library

- SharePoint library version history

- SharePoint library permissions

- Audience targeting

- SharePoint Online document library views

- SharePoint Online document library custom view

- Exporting SharePoint modern library to Excel sheet

- Restore/backup SharePoint modern library

Objectives

After reading this chapter, you will have a general idea of SharePoint Online Modern library, creation of modern library, its permission labels, filtrations of the library based on different criteria. You can also get ideas on SharePoint online library views, audience targeting, how to backup and restore the library, and so on.

Introduction to SharePoint Document library

Microsoft's SharePoint Online collaboration and document management platform includes a web-based file storage system called the document library. Users can store, organize, and access many kinds of documents using it, including Word documents, Excel spreadsheets, PowerPoint presentations, PDFs, photos, and videos, among others.

Users can make and organize documents in the SharePoint Online document library and work with others on shared documents from anywhere. Users can manage and control document access and modification by configuring metadata, access permissions, and versioning.

With SharePoint Online document library, users can also search for specific files and view them in a browser, making it easy to access and share files with other team members. Additionally, SharePoint Online document library can be accessed from any device with an internet connection, making it a versatile and flexible tool for remote work and collaboration.

Figure 5.1 displays an example of SharePoint Online library named **File Storage** that contains different types of files. You can store documents and folders too, as shown:

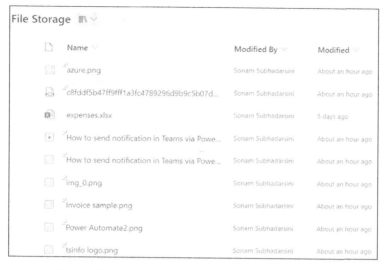

Figure 5.1: *Example of a Modern SharePoint Online library*

Advantages of SharePoint Document library

There are several advantages of using SharePoint Online modern library for document management and collaboration. Some of these advantages include:

- **Modern and intuitive interface:** SharePoint Online modern library provides a streamlined and user-friendly interface that makes it easy for users to upload, manage, and collaborate on documents.

- **Accessibility and mobility**: SharePoint Online modern library can be accessed from any device with an internet connection, making it easy for users to work remotely or on-the-go.

- **Improved collaboration:** SharePoint Online modern library enables users to collaborate in real-time on documents, making it easy to share feedback and updates.

- **Version control:** SharePoint Online modern library provides version control features, allowing users to track changes and revert to previous versions of a document.

- **Customizable metadata:** SharePoint Online modern library enables users to add custom metadata to documents, making it easier to find and organize files.

- **Integration with other Microsoft tools:** SharePoint Online modern library integrates seamlessly with other Microsoft tools such as Teams, OneDrive, and Office applications, allowing for a more cohesive workflow.

- **Enhanced security:** SharePoint Online modern library provides advanced security features such as role-based access controls and encryption to protect sensitive documents.

Creating a SharePoint document library

SharePoint Online document library is used for document management and collaboration, allowing users to store, organize, and share various types of documents, such as Word documents, Excel spreadsheets, PowerPoint presentations, PDFs, images, and videos, among others.

Below is the step-by-step guide that will show you how to create a document library within the SharePoint site:

1. Navigate to the SharePoint site where you want to create a document library.

2. On the Home page of the SharePoint site, click on the **+New** | **Document library**.

3. Enter a name for the document library and, if necessary, add a **Description**.

4. Set whether you want to show the library in site navigation or not.

5. Click on **Create**. A document library will be created and added to your respective SharePoint site, as shown:

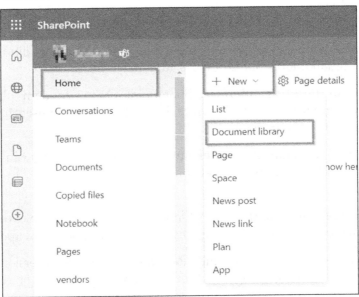

Figure 5.2: Getting started with Modern SharePoint Online library

SharePoint document library add columns

Like a SharePoint list, a SharePoint library lets you add columns. Columns in SharePoint document library are used to store and categorize information about documents, making it easier to find, sort, and filter them.

Using columns in SharePoint document library can help users better manage and organize their documents and make it easier to find the information they need. It is important to choose the right type of columns and use them consistently to ensure that the document library remains well-organized and easy to use.

Here are several approaches for working with columns in a document library in SharePoint:

- **Adding a column:** To add a column, go to the document library and click on **Add column** in the toolbar. Choose the type of column you want to add, such as text, choice, date/time, or lookup, and enter the details for the column, as shown:

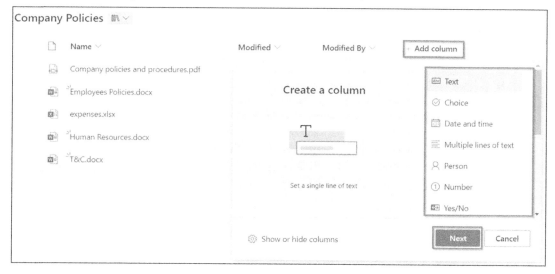

Figure 5.3: Adding column in Modern SharePoint Online library

- **Editing a column**: To edit a column, go to the document library and click on the column name. From there, you can change the column name, data type, description, or other settings:

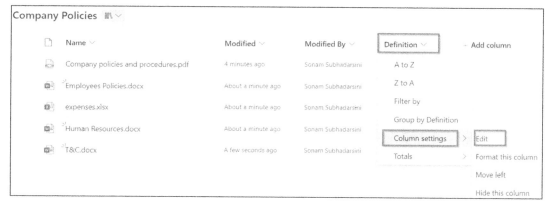

Figure 5.4: Editing column in Modern SharePoint Online library

- **Filtering by column:** To filter documents by column, go to the document library and click on the **Filter by** option. Choose the column you want to filter by and enter the criteria you want to use:

Figure 5.5: Filtering column in Modern SharePoint Online library

- **Sorting by column:** To sort documents by column, click on the column header you want to sort by. Clicking **A to Z** will sort in ascending order, and clicking **Z to A** will sort in descending order, as displayed below:

Figure 5.6: Sorting column in Modern SharePoint Online library

- **Grouping by column:** To group documents by column, go to the document library and click on the **Group by** button. Choose the column you want to group by, and the documents will be grouped accordingly:

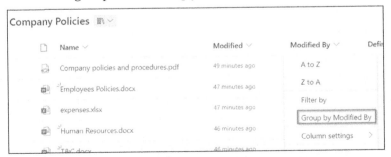

Figure 5.7: Grouping column in Modern SharePoint Online library

SharePoint library settings

SharePoint Online library settings refer to the configuration options available for a document library in SharePoint Online. These settings can be accessed by going to the library settings page.

To find the **SharePoint library settings,** click on the **Gear** icon on the top bar. It will display the Document Library name and Description. There is another option for **More library settings** and once you click on that option, it will redirect to the Settings page that contains different types of settings such as General settings, Permissions and Management settings, and communications. The **More library settings** window will look like this:

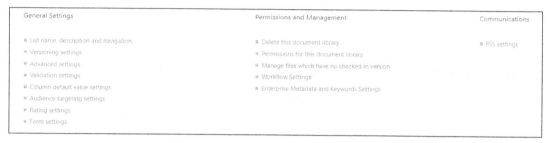

Figure 5.8: Displaying different types of Settings in Modern SharePoint Online library

By configuring these settings, you can tailor the library to meet the specific needs of your organization and make it easier for users to find and manage documents. Let us discuss the different kinds of settings in the next section.

General settings

The general settings in SharePoint Online document library provide basic configuration options for managing the library's properties, versioning settings, and validation settings.

The general settings provide a good starting point for configuring a SharePoint Online document library to meet your organization's needs. *Table 5.1* below gives the specific functions of different settings:

Settings	Functionalities
List name, description, and navigation	This allows you to update the name and description of the document library. Also, set to the navigation to appear in the Quick Launch.
Versioning Settings	This allows you to enable versioning, so you can keep track of changes made to documents in the library. You can also choose how many versions to keep and whether to require check-out before editing.

Settings	Functionalities
Advanced Settings	This allows you to configure other advanced settings such as allowing management of content types, allowing folders, allowing users to edit files in the browser, and others.
Validation Settings	This allows you to set up validation rules to ensure that documents meet specific criteria before they are uploaded or saved in the library.
Audience targeting Settings	It enables the audience targeting column to filter content based on the context of the user.

Table 5.1: *General Settings in SharePoint Document Library*

Permissions and management settings

Permissions and management settings in a SharePoint document library refers to the controls and options that determine who can access, view, edit, and delete the documents in the library and how they can do so. Refer to the following *Table5.2.* for the specific settings:

Settings	Functionalities
Delete this document library	It will delete the document library completely and redirect to the home page
Permissions for this document library	SharePoint allows you to assign specific permissions to individual users or groups of users. You can set permissions to control who can view, edit, or delete documents in the library. You can also create custom permission levels that provide more granular control over actions that users can perform on documents.
Workflow Settings	This setting allows you to configure workflows for the documents in the library, such as approval workflows or custom workflows.
Enterprise Metadata and Keywords Settings	It allows users to input one or more text values in an enterprise keywords field that will be shared with other users and applications to simplify search and filtering as well as consistency and reuse of metadata.

Table 5.2: *Permissions and Management Settings in Document Library*

Communication

The Communications setting in SharePoint document library is a collection of features and settings that enable you to communicate and collaborate with other users within the document library or site.

Under **Communications,** you can find one setting, that is, **RSS settings** that allows you to set up an RSS feed for the document library, enabling users to subscribe to updates and receive notifications when new documents are added or updated. You can look at the figure below for reference:

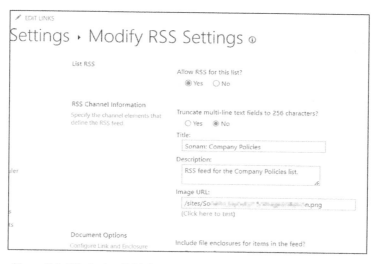

Figure 5.9: Displaying RSS Settings in Modern SharePoint Online library

The Communications setting in SharePoint document library provides a variety of tools and features to help users collaborate, communicate, and stay informed about changes and updates within the document library.

Working with files in SharePoint library

Working with files and folders in SharePoint document library is like working with files and folders on a local computer, with the added benefit of collaborative features such as version control, document approvals, and access controls.

Following these techniques will allow you to easily work with files and folders in the SharePoint document library. These techniques are discussed below:

Uploading files: To upload files to a SharePoint document library, you can either drag and drop the file(s) into the library or click on the **Upload** button and select the file(s) from your local system:

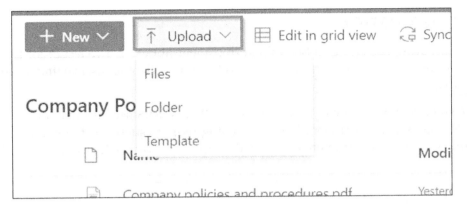

Figure 5.10: Upload files to the Modern SharePoint Online library

Creating folders: To create a new folder in the document library, click on the **New Folder** button and give the folder a name. You can then drag and drop files into the folder or upload new files directly into the folder. Take a look at the following figure for reference:

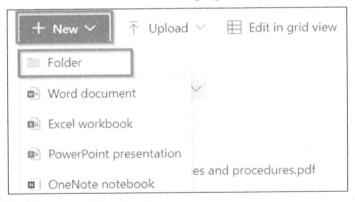

Figure 5.11: Create new folder within the Modern SharePoint Online library

Editing files: To edit a file in SharePoint document library, click on the file name to open it in the associated application (such as Word, Excel, etc.). Once you have made your changes, save the file, and the changes will be automatically updated in the SharePoint document library.

Deleting files and folders: To delete a file or folder in SharePoint document library, select the file or folder, click on the **Delete** button, and confirm the deletion. Or select the files and folders, click on the **Vertical ellipses (...)**, and select **Delete**:

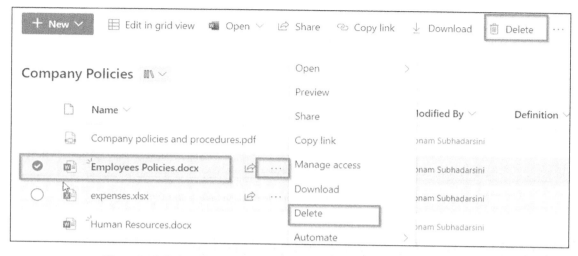

Figure 5.12: Delete files and folders from the Modern SharePoint Online library

Moving files and folders: To move a file or folder in SharePoint document library, select the file or folder, click on the **Move To** button, choose the destination folder, and click **OK**.

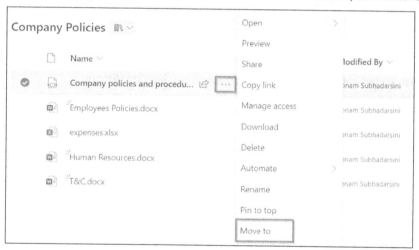

Figure 5.13: Moving files and folders from the Modern SharePoint Online library

Renaming files and folders: To rename a file or folder in SharePoint document library, select the file or folder, click on the **Rename** button, and give it a new name as shown:

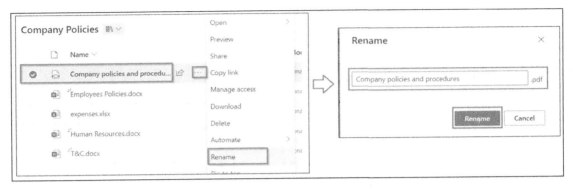

Figure 5.14: Renaming files and folders from the Modern SharePoint Online library

SharePoint library version history

SharePoint library version history is a feature that allows you to track and manage changes made to files and documents in the library over time.

Every time a file is updated, SharePoint creates a new version of the file, which includes information such as the date and time of the update, the user who made the update, and a description of the changes made.

To access the version history of a file in SharePoint document library, select a file | click on the **vertical ellipses** to get more options | Navigate to the **Version History:**

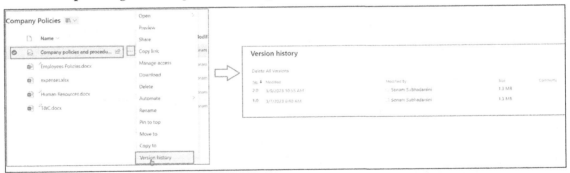

Figure 5.15: Displaying version history of a file in the Modern SharePoint Online library

SharePoint library version history allows you to do the following:

- **View previous versions**: You can view and compare previous versions of a file, including any comments or descriptions made by users.

- **Restore previous versions:** You can restore a previous version of a file, if necessary, which can be useful if you accidentally delete important information or if you need to roll back changes made to a file.

- **Track changes:** SharePoint library version history allows you to track changes made to files over time, which can clarify how a document has evolved and who has made changes to it.

- **Maintain compliance**: Version history can help you maintain compliance with regulatory requirements, such as audit trials and document retention policies.

Overall, SharePoint library version history is a valuable feature that helps you manage and track changes to files and documents in the library, ensuring that you have a complete and accurate history of all changes made to your content.

SharePoint library permissions and Management

SharePoint libraries are used to store and manage documents, files, and other types of content in an organized and secure manner. In SharePoint, you can set permissions for libraries to control who can view, edit, and delete files within them.

SharePoint offers several levels of permissions on the document library, including:

- **Full Control:** Users with this permission level have full control over the library and can perform any action, including changing permissions and deleting files.

- **Design:** Users with this permission level can add, edit, and delete files and folders within the library, but they cannot change permissions or delete the library.

- **Edit:** Users with this permission level can add, edit, and delete files and folders within the library, but they cannot add or delete subfolders.

- **Read:** Users with this permission level can view the files and folders within the library, but they cannot add, edit, or delete anything.

- **Restricted Read:** Users with this permission level can view only certain files and folders within the library.

To find the permissions for a specified SharePoint document library, the following steps are:

1. Open a SharePoint document library.

2. Navigate to the **Library Settings | Permissions for this document library** (under **Permissions and Management**). It will redirect you to a screen, where it will display all the permissions that have been assigned to the respective groups as shown below:

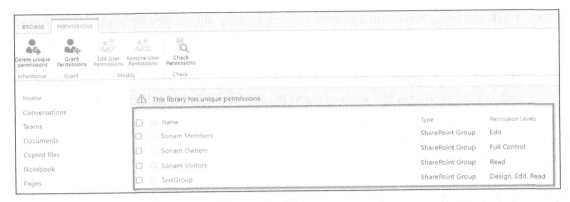

Figure 5.16: Displaying various permissions in the Modern SharePoint Online library

Grant permissions on the SharePoint document library

SharePoint document libraries allow you to grant permissions to control access to the content. This means you can add or remove users or groups and assign them to different permission levels.

Here are the steps to customize the permission on the SharePoint document library:

1. Follow the above steps to reach the **Permissions** window.

2. To add a user or group, click on **Grant Permissions** and enter the user or group name in the **Select Users** or **Select Groups** dialog box.

3. Choose the permission level you want to assign to the user or group, such as **Read**, **Design**, **Full control**, **Restricted View**, **Contribute**, or **Edit.**

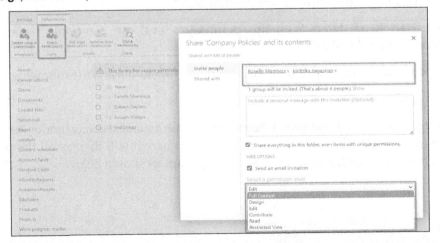

Figure 5.17: Granting permissions in the Modern SharePoint Online library

Create group and assign permissions on the SharePoint document library

Similarly, SharePoint document library allows you to create a new group and assign the permissions. For this, the required steps are:

Follow the above steps to reach the **Permissions** page (Open a SharePoint document library | Library **Settings** | **Permissions for this document library)**

1. Click on **Create Group**.

2. Give a name to the group. (Example: **Custom Permission Group**)

3. Choose **Group Permission for the site**.

4. Click on **Create**.

The following window pops up:

Figure 5.18: *Granting group permissions in the Modern SharePoint Online library*

Edit user permissions on a document library

SharePoint document library allows you to edit the user permissions once the permissions are assigned. To edit user permissions, the following steps are:

1. On the SharePoint document library, navigate to the **Permission** page (Follow the above steps to find the **Permission** page).

2. Select the user or group (Example: **Custom Permission Group**)

3. Once you select the option, the **Edit Users Permissions** will be lightened and click on that option:

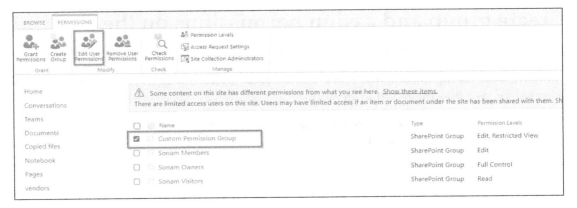

Figure 5.19: Edit user permissions in the Modern SharePoint Online library

4. It will redirect you to another page where you can customize the permissions:

Figure 5.20: Customizing user permissions in the Modern SharePoint Online library

Audience targeting

Audience targeting in SharePoint Modern libraries allows you to show specific content to a specific group of users. This feature enables you to personalize the user experience and make it more relevant to the user.

Here are the steps to set up audience targeting in a SharePoint Modern library:

1. Go to the **SharePoint Modern library** and select the **library settings** from the gear icon.

2. Under the **General settings** section, click on **Audience targeting settings.**

3. Enable the option **Enable audience targeting** and click **OK**, as shown below:

Figure 5.21: Enabling Audience targeting in the Modern SharePoint Online library

Once you enable the **Audience Targeting,** you can now add items to your library and specify which audiences can view them:

1. To do this, select the item, go to **horizontal ellipses (...),** and click on **Details** in the information panel.

2. Under the **Audience targeting** section, select the audience(s) that should be able to view the item:

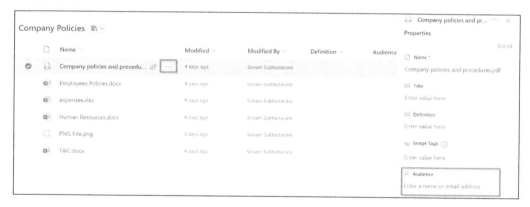

Figure 5.22: Displaying audience targeting in SharePoint Document library

Users who are not part of the targeted audience will not be able to see the item in the library unless they have been granted access through another permission level.

SharePoint Online document library views

SharePoint Online modern document libraries offer a variety of options for customizing and working with views. Here are some steps to help you work with views in a SharePoint Online modern document library:

1. Open your SharePoint Online modern document library.

2. Go to gear icon | **library settings** | **More library settings.**

3. Scroll down the page, under the **View** section, you can find an option that is, **Create View** as shown:

Figure 5.23: Create view in the Modern SharePoint Online library

You can now pick from a variety of view types. Such as:

- **Standard View:** Visualize data on a webpage. There is a selection of display styles available.

- **Datasheet View:** View data in a customizable spreadsheet format that is useful for quick modification and mass editing.

- **Calendar View:** Calendar views of the data can be daily, weekly, or monthly.

- **Gantt View:** To get a graphical representation of how a team's tasks link over time, view list items in a Gantt chart.

The following figure shows these different types:

Figure 5.24: Types of view in the Modern SharePoint Online library

You will get 4 different types of **View Type** such as **Standard View**, **Calendar View**, **Datasheet View**, and **Gantt View**.

You can select any view as per the requirement. Example: Datasheet View.

1. Give a name to the view of the document library.

2. Set the **Audience** that represents the intended audience for this view.

3. Customize the **Columns** that you want to show or hide in this view of this page. To specify the order of the columns, select a number in the **Position from left** box.

4. Also, it allows you to **sort** the columns and **filter** the column based on the requirement. Once the customization is done, click on **OK**:

Figure 5.25: Create a SharePoint library view using the Datasheet view template

The SharePoint document library will appear on a **Datasheet view** as follows:

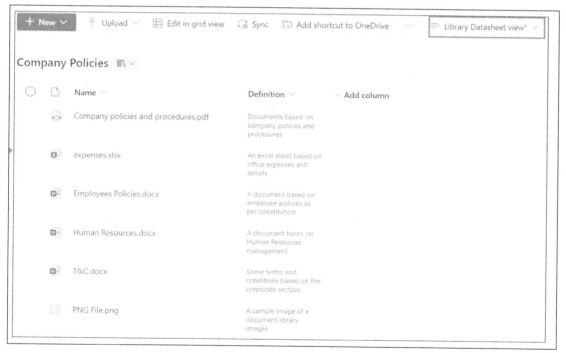

Figure 5.26: Displaying documents in a datasheet view in the SharePoint library

SharePoint Online document library custom view

Here are the steps to create a custom view in SharePoint Online modern document library:

1. Open the SharePoint document library.

2. Click on the **Switch view options** button on the right side of the screen.

3. Select the option **Create new view.**

4. Give a name to the new view and select a view (Example: Gallery).

5. Click on **Create** as shown:

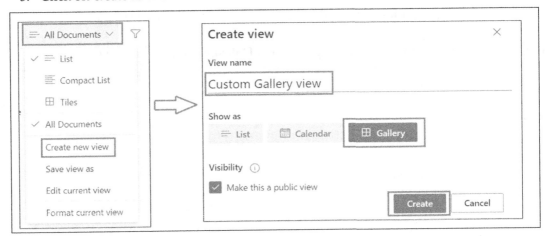

Figure 5.27: Creating a custom view in the Modern SharePoint Online library

6. Now, the SharePoint document library will appear in the gallery view:

Figure 5.28: Displaying documents in gallery view in the SharePoint Online library

Once you have created your custom view, you can share it with other users or set it as the default view for your SharePoint Online modern document library. Custom views are an effective way to organize your documents and make it easier to find the information you need.

Exporting SharePoint modern library to excel sheet

You can export a SharePoint Online modern library to an Excel sheet. When you export a SharePoint Online modern library to an Excel sheet, the library data is copied to the Excel sheet in a tabular format. The exported Excel sheet will include all the columns of the library, as well as any metadata associated with the items in the library.

Exporting a SharePoint Online modern library to an Excel sheet can be useful for a variety of reasons, including:

- **Creating reports:** You can use the exported data to create reports and visualizations that can help you better understand the contents of the library.

- **Data analysis:** You can use Excel's data analysis features to explore the data in the library and gain insights into the information it contains.

- **Offline access:** Exporting the library data to an Excel sheet can provide a way to access the data offline, without requiring an internet connection.

To export a SharePoint Online modern library to an Excel sheet, you can follow these steps:

1. Open the SharePoint Online modern library that you want to export.

2. Click on the **Export to Excel** button located in the toolbar at the top of the library page:

Figure 5.29: Exporting SharePoint Online modern library to excel sheet

3. If prompted, select **Open** to open the Excel sheet in Microsoft Excel or to save the file to your local computer. **Save**

4. Once the Excel sheet opens, you can review and manipulate the library data as needed:

	A	B	C	D	E	F
1	Name	Modified	Modified By	Definition	Item Type	Path
2	Company policies and procedures.pdf	3/14/2023 7:29	Sonam Subhadarsini	Documents based on company policies and procedures	Item	sites/Sonam/Company Policies
3	Employees Policies.docx	3/14/2023 7:31	Sonam Subhadarsini	A document based on employee policies as per constitution	Item	sites/Sonam/Company Policies
4	expenses.xlsx	3/14/2023 7:30	Sonam Subhadarsini	An excel sheet based on office expenses and details	Item	sites/Sonam/Company Policies
5	Human Resources.docx	3/14/2023 7:31	Sonam Subhadarsini	A document bases on Human Resources management	Item	sites/Sonam/Company Policies
6	PNG File.png	3/14/2023 7:32	Sonam Subhadarsini	A sample image of a document library images	Item	sites/Sonam/Company Policies
7	T&C.docx	3/14/2023 7:32	Sonam Subhadarsini	Some terms and conditions based on the corporate section.	Item	sites/Sonam/Company Policies
8						
9						

Figure 5.30: Displaying data in excel sheet exported from SharePoint Online modern library

Note: This method requires Microsoft Excel to be installed on your computer. Additionally, depending on the size of the library and the amount of data being exported, the export process may take several minutes to complete.

However, it is important to keep in mind that the exported Excel sheet will be a static snapshot of the library data at the time of export. Any changes made to the library data after the export will not be reflected in the Excel sheet. Additionally, the Excel sheet may not retain all the functionality of the SharePoint library, such as workflows or customizations.

Restore/backup SharePoint modern library

Restoring a SharePoint document library is an important part of data management and can help to ensure the continuity of business operations and compliance with regulatory requirements. There are several reasons why you may need to restore a SharePoint document library, including:

- **Accidental deletion:** Users may accidentally delete important documents or even the entire library. In such cases, a restore can help recover the lost data.

- **Data corruption:** SharePoint document libraries can get corrupted due to various reasons such as software bugs, power outages, and hardware failure. In such cases, restoring from a backup can help to recover the data.

- **Compliance requirements:** Many organizations have compliance requirements that mandate the retention of data for a certain period. Restoring a document library from a backup can help to ensure that data is retained in accordance with legal and regulatory requirements.

- **Disaster recovery:** In the event of a natural disaster or other catastrophic event, a backup and restore plan can help to quickly recover important data and restore normal operations.

To restore a modern SharePoint document library, the following steps are:

1. Open the SharePoint document library and navigate to the gear icon or **Settings.**

2. Select the option for **Restore this library**, as shown:

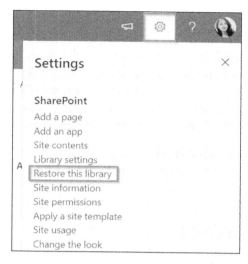

Figure 5.31: Restoring the SharePoint Online modern library

3. Select a date from where you want to take backup. (Example: Yesterday)

4. Select the files that you want to backup and click on **Restore**:

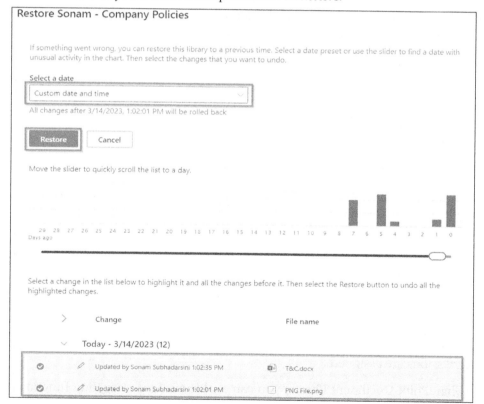

Figure 5.32: Restore or backup the SharePoint Online modern library

Conclusion

In this chapter, we have covered the fundamentals on the SharePoint Online Modern library such as what a modern SharePoint list is, advantages of a document library, how to create a document library, working with columns, library settings, different types of permissions, working with files and folders, library version history, granting permissions, working different types of views using library templates, export library to an excel sheet and so on.

In the next chapter, we will see what modern pages are, their advantages, how to work with SharePoint modern pages such as navigation, quick lunch, title area, comments, like and many more.

Points to remember

You can quickly read and learn some of the chapter's most important learning aspects, such as:

- By using the Modern SharePoint Document Library, users can store, organize, and access many kinds of documents using it, including Word documents, Excel spreadsheets, PowerPoint presentations, PDFs, photos, and videos, among others.

- Create a Document Library within the SharePoint Online, add columns, filter a column, sort a column, and so on.

- Discuss different types of Library settings such as:

  o General Settings

  o Permissions and Management Settings

  o Communication

- Add and delete files to the SharePoint Document Library

- By using the SharePoint library version history, you can manage and track changes to files and documents in the library, ensuring that you have a complete and accurate history of all changes made to your content.

- You can set permissions for SharePoint libraries to control who can view, edit, and delete files within them.

- SharePoint document libraries allow you to grant permissions to add or remove users or groups and assign them to different permission levels.

- SharePoint document library enables you to edit the user permissions once the permissions are assigned.

- In SharePoint Document library, you can enable audience targeting functionality that show specific content to a specific group of users.

- SharePoint Online modern document libraries offer a variety of options for customizing and working with views such as:

  o Standard view

  o Datasheet view

  o Calendar view

  o Gantt view

- You can create custom views in a document library to organize your documents and make it easier to find the information you need.

- You can export a SharePoint Online modern library to an Excel sheet that can be useful for a variety of reasons, including:

  o Creating reports

  o Data analysis

  o Offline access

- Restoring a SharePoint document library is an important part of data management and can help to ensure the continuity of business operations and compliance with regulatory requirements.

Join our book's Discord space

Join the book's Discord Workspace for Latest updates, Offers, Tech happenings around the world, New Release and Sessions with the Authors:

https://discord.bpbonline.com

CHAPTER 6
SharePoint Modern Pages

Introduction

In this chapter, we will be introducing you to SharePoint modern pages, their benefits, and how they differ from web part pages. We will also discuss the reasons for using modern pages. Furthermore, we will examine the modern page creation process, including how to customize the layout, add web parts, use the page design features, and many more.

Structure

This section describes general information about modern SharePoint pages, including how to build modern pages, customize SharePoint pages, talk about layouts, and many other topics. The list below includes the topics we will cover in this chapter:

- Introduction to Modern SharePoint Online Page
- Types of Site pages in SharePoint Online
- Site page vs web part page
- Using SharePoint site pages
- Creating a site page in SharePoint
- Customizing a Modern SharePoint Page

- Header and footer of the SharePoint site Pages
- Layout of SharePoint Modern Page
- Adding background image to SharePoint Page
- Displaying SharePoint Page in Fullwidth
- Adding a table to the SharePoint Site Page
- Adding Bookmark and anchor links to SharePoint Page
- Finding site pages in SharePoint Online
- Redirect a SharePoint modern page
- Audience targeting in a SharePoint Online Modern Page
- Comments, likes, and views in the Site Page
- Disable comments from SharePoint Online Modern Page
- Save for later SharePoint Online Modern Page
- Immersive reader in SharePoint Site Page
- Send your page by email
- Delete a SharePoint site page
- What is SharePoint webparts

Objectives

After reading this chapter, the user will have a general idea of SharePoint Online Modern pages, creation of modern pages, and its customization based on different criteria.

You will also get a tutorial on adding webparts on SharePoint pages, how to give comments, likes, and views, audience targeting, send the modern page via email and so on.

Introduction to Modern SharePoint Online page

SharePoint Online is a web-based collaboration platform that enables organizations to create and manage team sites, document libraries, and lists. One of the key features of SharePoint Online is the ability to create modern pages that offer a visually appealing and intuitive user experience.

Modern SharePoint Online pages are built on a responsive design that automatically adjusts the layout to fit any device, whether it is a desktop computer, tablet, or smartphone. These pages use web parts, which are modular components that can be added, removed, and customized to meet specific needs. Some common web parts include text, images, videos, lists, and document libraries.

In addition to web parts, modern SharePoint Online pages offer a variety of design elements and features that make it easy to create engaging and interactive pages. These include:

- **Section layouts:** Pages can be divided into multiple sections with different column layouts, allowing you to display content in a variety of ways.

- **Themes**: SharePoint Online offers a range of pre-designed themes that can be applied to your pages to give them a consistent and professional look.

- **Customization:** Pages can be customized using CSS and JavaScript to create unique and personalized designs.

- **Publishing:** Pages can be published for specific audiences, such as a team or department, and can be scheduled to go live at a specific time and date.

- **Analytics:** SharePoint Online provides analytics to help you track page views, user engagement, and other metrics.

Modern SharePoint Online pages are easy to create and manage, and they offer a powerful way to communicate with your team, share information, and collaborate on projects. Whether you are building a project dashboard, sharing company news, or creating a knowledge base, modern SharePoint Online pages are a flexible and versatile tool that can help you achieve your goals.

Types of Site pages in SharePoint Online

In SharePoint Online, there are several types of site pages that you can create within a team site:

- **Home Page:** The home page is the default landing page for the team site. It can be customized to include web parts, news articles, announcements, and other content.

- **Wiki Page:** Wiki pages allow users to collaboratively create and edit content. They are often used for knowledge management, documentation, and team collaboration.

- **Web Part Page:** Web part pages allow users to add and customize web parts to display content and functionality. They are often used to create custom dashboards or to display data from other sources.

- **Site Page:** Site pages are a type of modern page that use a modern, responsive design with web parts to add functionality and content. Site pages are customizable and can be used to create dynamic content such as dashboards, team pages, and project pages.

- **News Post:** News posts are a type of site page that is used to share news and updates with team members. They can include images, videos, and formatted text.

- **Document Library Page:** Document library pages allow users to view and manage documents within a document library. They can be customized to include views, filters, and web parts.

- **List Page:** List pages allow users to view and manage items within a list. They can be customized to include views, filters, and web parts.

Note that the types of site pages available may vary depending on the features and settings enabled in your SharePoint Online environment.

Site page vs web part page

SharePoint site pages and web part pages are both types of pages in SharePoint, but they have some differences in their structure and purpose. Here are some of the main differences between SharePoint site pages and web part pages:

- **Structure:** Site pages are structured pages with pre-defined sections, such as header, body, and footer. Web part pages, on the other hand, are more flexible and allow users to add, remove, and arrange web parts to create custom pages.

- **Content:** Site pages are typically used for static content, such as announcements, news, or company information. Web part pages are more dynamic and allow users to add interactive content such as calendars, document libraries, or external data sources.

- **Layout:** Site pages have a fixed layout and are usually created by the site owner or administrator. Web part pages are more customizable and can be created by end-users who have the appropriate permissions.

- **Collaboration:** Site pages are designed for collaboration and can be edited by multiple users. Web part pages can also be edited by multiple users, but they are often used for individual customization and personalization.

- **Compatibility:** Site pages are compatible with most browsers and devices, and they are designed to be responsive to different screen sizes. Web part pages may not always be compatible with all browsers and devices, depending on the web parts used.

To summarize, site pages are best for creating static pages with pre-defined sections, while web part pages are more flexible and allow users to add interactive content and customize the layout.

Using SharePoint site pages

SharePoint site pages provide a way to create and publish web pages within a SharePoint site. Here are some of the main reasons to use SharePoint site pages:

- **Easy to create:** Creating a new page in SharePoint is easy and does not require any technical skills. Users can use the drag-and-drop page builder to add content, images, and web parts to the page.

- **Customizable:** SharePoint site pages are highly customizable, allowing users to add custom branding, colors, and styles to match their organization's brand.

- **Collaboration:** Site pages can be used to collaborate with others, allowing users to work together on the same page in real-time. This can help to improve productivity and ensure that everyone is on the same page.

- **Mobile-friendly:** SharePoint site pages are designed to be mobile-friendly and responsive, ensuring that they can be viewed on any device.

- **Integration:** Site pages can be integrated with other SharePoint features such as lists, libraries, and workflows, allowing users to create powerful and customized solutions for their organization.

- **Security:** SharePoint site pages are secured by the same security mechanisms as the rest of SharePoint, ensuring that users only have access to the pages that they are authorized to view.

Overall, SharePoint site pages provide a flexible and powerful way to create and publish content within a SharePoint site, while also providing collaboration and integration features that can help organizations work more efficiently.

Creating a site page in SharePoint Online

In SharePoint, site pages are web pages that can be used to create and publish content to a site. Site pages are used to create different types of content, such as news articles, announcements, and project updates.

Site pages can be created in both modern and classic SharePoint experiences. In modern experience, users can create a page using one of the pre-built templates, or they can start from scratch with a blank page. The modern experience allows users to add web parts to the page easily, with a simple drag-and-drop interface.

To create a site page in SharePoint Modern Team site, follow the below steps:

1. Navigate to the SharePoint team site where you want to create the page.

2. Then click on **+New** icon | **Page**.

3. Now the Pages window will open, here you can select the template to create a page from saved on this site or built-in, or you can select **Blank page**.

4. Click on the **Create page** button as shown below:

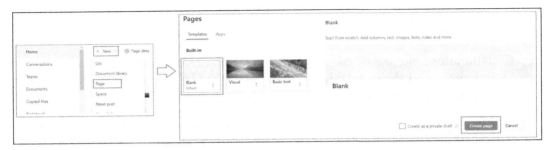

Figure 6.1: Create a blank page on the SharePoint team site

5. It will create a blank page where we need to provide a suitable name for the Site Page. (For example, **Project Onboarding**). This page will reflect all initial phases or onboarding process of projects:

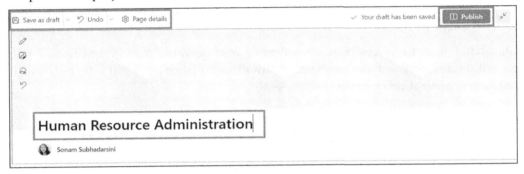

Figure 6.2: Giving a name to the SharePoint site page

6. Here, you can save the page as draft, by clicking on **Save as draft** or clicking on **Publish** to publish the page on the SharePoint team site.

By clicking **page details**, you have options to change the thumbnail, site description, toggle on to use editor to check spelling, grammar, and more. The **page details window** will look like the following figure:

Figure 6.3: Set thumbnail and description to the SharePoint modern site page

Once you have published the SharePoint site page, you can see that the site page is created. Then it will open a navigation page named **help others find your page**. Here you can find the list of options like:

- **Add your page to the navigation**

- **Post as news on this site**

- **Email**

- **Yammer**

- **Save as Page template**

At last, you can get the **Page address**, and note the page address, which we can use to share with other members of our organization. The dialog box will look like the following figure:

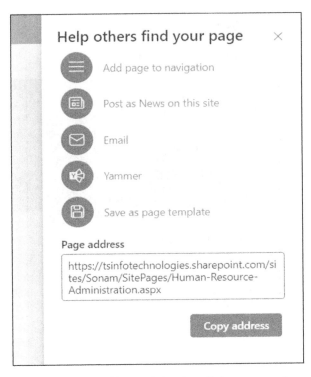

Figure 6.4: Displaying page address to help others find your page after publishing

To access the site page, you can navigate to **Site contents | Site pages**, where you can see all the pages SharePoint site has.

Customizing a Modern SharePoint page

Modern team site pages support rich multimedia material and are quick and simple for the author's convenience. These pages are displayed beautifully on all devices, in browsers, and from the SharePoint mobile app.

Web parts are used to construct SharePoint pages, and you can alter them to meet your requirements. You have the option of adding texts, audio, video, site activities, Yammer feeds, and more. To add content to your page, simply click the plus sign and choose a web element from the toolbox. Here are the steps to customize SharePoint site pages:

1. Navigate to the site page that you want to customize.

2. Click on the **Edit icon** on the top-right corner to edit the page.

3. Once in edit mode, you can add or remove web parts, change the layout of the page, and modify the properties of the web parts. Also, you can set an image to the header of the page as demonstrated in the figure below:

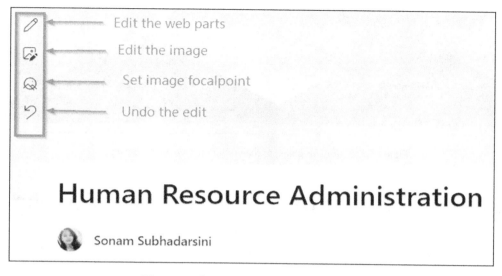

Figure 6.5: Customizing SharePoint site pages

4. On this site page, let us customize the title area by editing the web parts and adding an image to the page title area.

5. To change the webpart layout, click on the **Pencil icon or edit icon.** Select a layout (Ex: **Image and title**). Set the **title's alignment** to **Left or center.** Along with that, it allows us to set other customization options as shown:

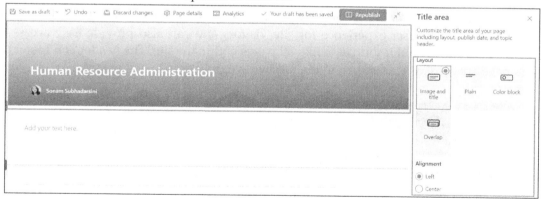

Figure 6.6: Customizing the title area of a SharePoint site page

6. Similarly, let us change the image on the title area. Click on the **image with edit icon** and choose **Image | Insert.** The modification will reflect on the SharePoint site pages:

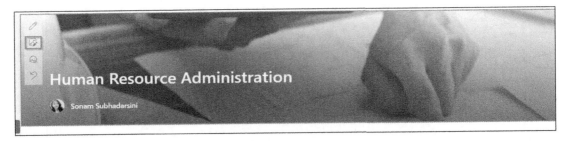

Figure 6.7: Giving an image to the SharePoint site page title area

Header and footer of the SharePoint site page

The header and footer of a SharePoint Online site page are the top and bottom sections of the page that often contain common information or branding elements that remain consistent across all pages within a site.

The header is typically located at the top of the page, and its content and layout can be customized to match the branding and design of the organization or team using the site.

The footer, on the other hand, is located at the bottom of the page and often includes copyright information, links to the site's privacy policy or terms of use, and other general information that is relevant to the site or organization. Like the header, the footer can also be customized to include additional elements or branding elements that are specific to the site or organization.

Customizing the header and footer of a SharePoint Online site page can help to create a more cohesive and branded user experience for site visitors and can also provide easy access to important information and resources across all pages within the site. The header and footer on the site page are displayed as shown in the following figure:

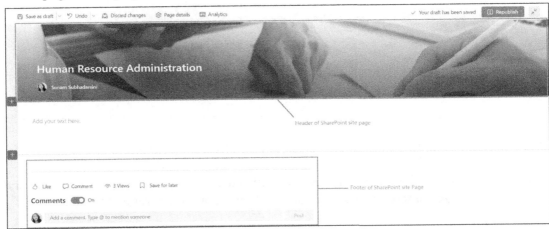

Figure 6.8: Displaying header and footer of the SharePoint site page

By clicking on the **+ icon,** you can add sections, templates and webparts to your SharePoint modern site page. In the upcoming sections we will cover how to add webparts and sections to the page.

Layout of the SharePoint Online Modern Page

A page layout in SharePoint Online is a predetermined design for a page that establishes the layout of the content, the placement of web parts and other page elements, as well as the styles and formatting used on the page. Page layouts are used to give each page on a SharePoint site a unified look and feel, and site administrators can alter them to suit the site's particular requirements.

Currently, there are three-page layouts available in the modern SharePoint Online site pages. They are:

- **Home Page layout:** Without a top banner, the landing page is used.

- **Article Page layout:** Modern websites come with a top banner as part of the standard page layout.

- **Single Part App Page layout:** To maintain one web part.

Adding background image to SharePoint Page

To add a header background image to a SharePoint Online Modern page, follow these steps:

1. Navigate to Modern site page, from **Site Contents** | **Site Pages**, the page where you want to change the header of the background.

2. Click on **Edit**. Then, click on the **Change image** icon on the left corner of the page.

3. Here are some of the sources to upload the background image:

    a. **Recent**

    b. **Stock images**

    c. **Web Search**

    d. **OneDrive**

    e. **Site**

    f. **Upload**

    g. **From a Link**

4. Let us select an image from any source (Example: **Stock images**). Click on **Insert**. The image will be added to the site page as shown:

Figure 6.9: *Adding a background image to the SharePoint site page*

Displaying SharePoint Page in Fullwidth

Displaying a SharePoint Online modern page in full width can provide several benefits, such as:

- **More space for content:** Full width sections allow for more horizontal space on the page, which can be useful for displaying large tables, images, or videos.

- **Enhanced visual appeal:** Full width sections can help make a page look more modern and visually appealing, which can enhance the user experience.

- **Improved readability:** By providing more space for content, full width sections can improve the readability of a page, making it easier for users to consume information.

- **Better compatibility with mobile devices:** Full width sections can help optimize the display of content on mobile devices, where screen real estate is often limited.

Overall, displaying SharePoint Online modern pages in full width can help improve the usability and aesthetics of your site, making it more engaging and easier to use for your audience.

To display the SharePoint Online Modern page in Fullwidth follow the below steps:

1. Open the modern SharePoint site page from the site contents.

2. On the top-right corner, you will find a **Double headed arrow** that indicates to hide headers and navigation. As a result, the site page will appear in full width:

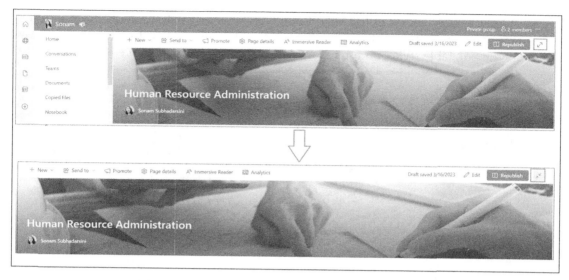

Figure 6.10: *Displaying the SharePoint site pages in fullwidth*

Adding a table to the SharePoint Site page

Tables are a great way to organize information and data in a structured way. By using a table, you can easily present data in rows and columns, which makes it easier for users to read and understand.

To add a table to a SharePoint Online modern page, you can follow these steps:

1. Go to the SharePoint Online modern page where you want to add the table.

2. Click on **Edit.**

3. Select the **Mid-section** of the SharePoint modern page. It will display different types of components to add into the site page.

4. From them click on the **Insert table**. The option for the same is shown in the following figure:

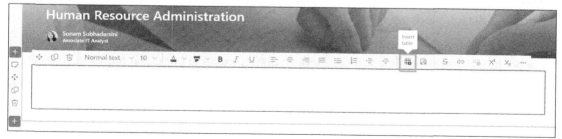

Figure 6.11: *Adding a table to the SharePoint site pages*

5. A table will be added to the SharePoint site page. You will get more editing options, once you press the right click of the table which allows you to add columns, rows, alignment, table styles, and many more. These options can be seen as follows:

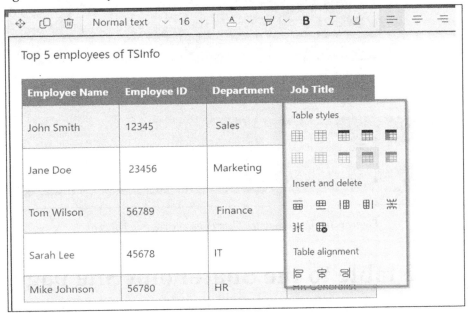

Figure 6.12: Customizing a table in the SharePoint site pages

Adding Bookmark and anchor links to SharePoint page

Page anchor links, also known as anchor tags or bookmarks, allow users to navigate to a specific section or content on a webpage without having to scroll through the entire page.

SharePoint site pages often contain a lot of content, such as text, images, videos, and web parts. The pages can be lengthy, with multiple sections of content. Anchor links can provide a quick and easy way for users to navigate to specific sections of the page, making it easier to find the information they are looking for.

With the text web part, you can add page anchor links to current SharePoint Online pages. To add a bookmark or anchor links to the modern SharePoint site page, the required steps are:

1. On the SharePoint site pages, add contents, and configure the sub-headings using the H1, H2, or H3 heading styles. You can find the heading panel as highlighted:

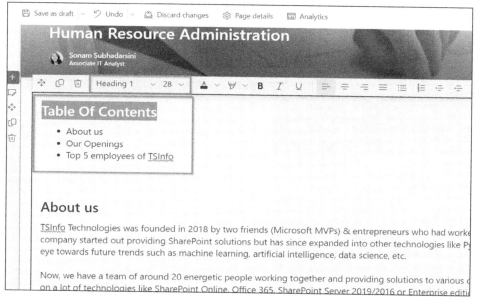

Figure 6.13: Add contents and configure text heading in the SharePoint Page

2. Save the site page and publish.

3. Reopen the page in a new tab and you can find an **Anchor link** beside every heading.

4. Click on **Copy link address** from the published page. The following figure is shown for your reference:

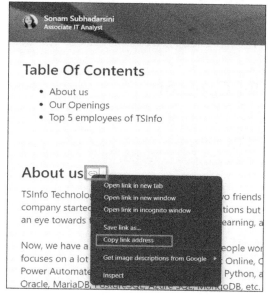

Figure 6.14: Add anchor link to the SharePoint site Page

5. After that, select the text on the site page that you wish to link.

6. Click the **Hyperlink** button in the toolbar while the page is in edit mode.

7. Click on **Save.** Refer to the following figure:

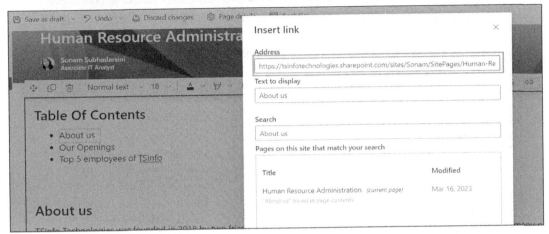

Figure 6.15: Adding anchor link into the SharePoint site Page

8. Again, republish the site page and we can see the link is added to the text as shown below *Figure 6.16*:

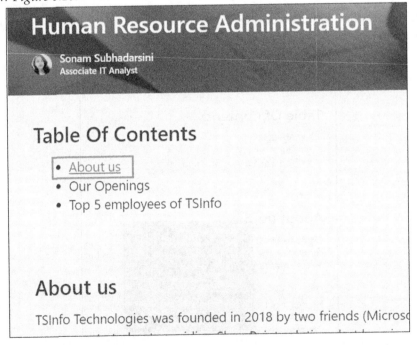

Figure 6.16: Showing anchor link into the SharePoint site Page

Finding site pages in SharePoint Online

Once your site page is published, we might need to find these site pages for further use. To find your site pages in SharePoint Online, you can follow these steps:

1. Go to your SharePoint Online site.

2. Click on **Site Contents** in the left-hand navigation menu.

3. Click on the **Site Pages** option. This will take you to the Site Pages library, which contains all the site pages for your site as shown in the following figure:

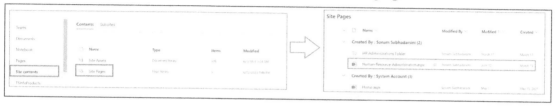

Figure 6.17: Find the site Page from the SharePoint site

Note: The steps to find site pages in SharePoint Online may vary slightly depending on the version and configuration of your SharePoint site. If you are having trouble finding your site pages, you may want to consult the SharePoint Online documentation or ask your site administrator for assistance.

Redirect a SharePoint modern page

Redirecting SharePoint site pages can help ensure a smooth user experience, avoid broken links, and preserve your site's SEO ranking. By redirecting a SharePoint page, user can move from one SharePoint site to another and monitoring the page contents.

SharePoint allows the user to redirect a site page from the modern SharePoint site. To do this, the following steps are:

Approach 1:

1. On your modern SharePoint site, navigate to **Pages** (from the left-navigation bar).

2. It will display all the pages that are contained in your SharePoint site. Select the site page that you want to redirect from the site's home page.

3. Click on the **vertical ellipses (...)** ∣ **Make homepage** as shown below:

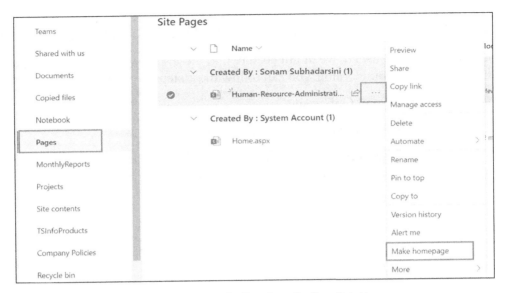

Figure 6.18: Redirecting a site Page from the SharePoint home page

Now, you can find the page on your site home page. Once you click on it, it will redirect you to that site page as shown in the following screenshot:

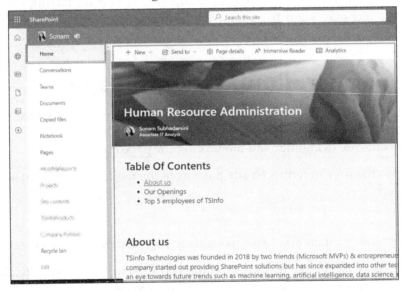

Figure 6.19: Displaying a site Page from the SharePoint home page

Approach 2:

1. Open your SharePoint online site where you want to add site page to redirect.

2. On the left-navigation bar, click on **Edit.**

3. Click on the **+ icon** to add a link to the navigation bar.

4. Insert your site page address in the **Address section** and provide a **Display name.** Refer to the figure below:

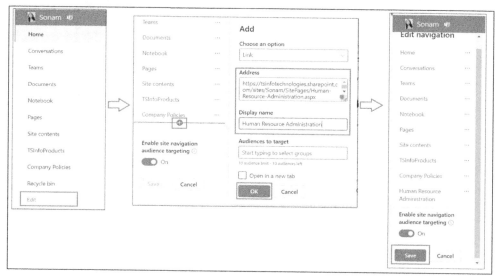

Figure 6.20: Redirecting a site Page from the SharePoint home page via address

The **Page** will be visible on the SharePoint site navigation bar. As a result, the user can redirect to the site page from the SharePoint site navigation bar.

Audience targeting in a SharePoint Site Page

Audience targeting in a modern SharePoint site page is similar to audience targeting in a modern SharePoint online page. It relies on the audiences you have defined in SharePoint. You can define audiences in SharePoint by creating SharePoint groups, security groups, or distribution lists.

Once you have defined your audiences, you can target content to them using the audience targeting web part. This feature is helpful when you want to show or hide specific content to a particular group of people, such as employees or external partners.

To set the audience targeting to a modern SharePoint site page, note the following steps:

1. On your SharePoint site home page, click on **Edit** from the left navigation bar.

2. Click on the context menu of the site page that you have added to the navigation.

3. Click on **Edit** and set the **Audiences to target.**

4. Press **OK** and we can find an audience logo beside the site page on the site navigation bar as shown below:

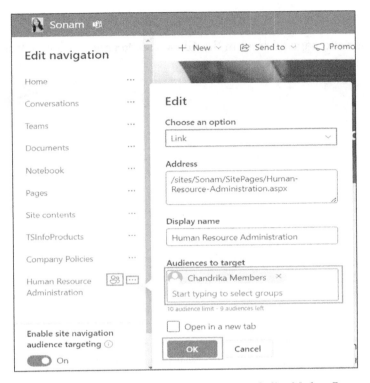

Figure 6.21: Set audience target to the SharePoint Online Modern Page

Comments, likes, and views in the Site Page

Comments, likes, and views are features available in modern SharePoint online pages to promote collaboration, feedback, and engagement within a SharePoint site. These features are explained below:

- **Comments:** Users can leave comments on a SharePoint online modern page, allowing them to share their thoughts and feedback on the content of the page. Comments can be added to individual web parts or the entire page and can be viewed and replied to by other users.

- **Likes:** Users can also express their appreciation for a page or web part by clicking on the **Like** button. The number of likes is displayed alongside the page or web part, providing a quick way to see how popular or well-received it is.

- **Views:** The number of times a page has been viewed is also displayed on the page, allowing users to see how popular or useful it has been to others. This can also help site owners and content creators to track the success and impact of their pages over time. On the footer section of the page, you can find the **comments, likes,** and **views** as shown:

Figure 6.22: Comments, likes, and views in the SharePoint Online Modern Page

Disable comments from SharePoint Site page

SharePoint allows you to disable or hide the comments from the modern SharePoint site page. A site owner or administrator can disable this feature. To disable comments on a SharePoint modern site page, follow these steps:

1. Navigate to the SharePoint admin center.

2. Click on the **Settings** from the left navigation bar | **Pages**.

3. Uncheck the option for **Allow commenting on modern pages**.

4. Click on **Save**. You can find the **comment** section is disabled from the modern SharePoint site pages in the following figure:

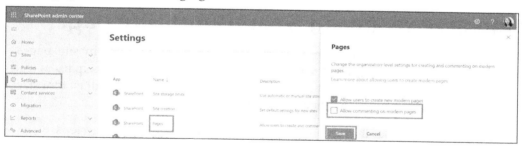

Figure 6.23: Disable comments from the SharePoint Online Modern Page

Save for later online SharePoint site page

Saving SharePoint site pages for later can help you stay organized, save time, and be more productive. It allows you to easily access important information and resources when you need them, without having to search for them again.

You can find the **Save for later** option on the bottom of the page. Once the option is selected, the site page becomes saved for later and the icon appears as filled in. Refer to the following figure:

Figure 6.24: Save for later the SharePoint Online site Page

A list of recently saved items is shown when **Saved for later** is chosen. To view the complete list of saved items, choose **View all saved items** as shown:

Figure 6.25: See all saved items on the SharePoint Online site Page

Immersive reader in SharePoint Site page

SharePoint Online has an **Immersive Reader** feature that can be used in site pages. The immersive reader is a tool that provides a full screen reading experience to help users read and understand content more effectively. It can read out text, highlight words, adjust font sizes and colors, and even translate text into different languages.

To use the Immersive Reader in a SharePoint site page, you can follow these steps:

1. Open the SharePoint site page where you want to use the Immersive reader feature.

2. You can find the **Immersive Reader** option as highlighted below:

Figure 6.26: Immersive Reader on the SharePoint Online site Page

Once you click on the **Play** button, the immersive reader will start reading. On that page, you can find other options to customize the voice speed, voice selection, Text preferences and so on. The customization options are shown in the following figure:

Figure 6.27: Immersive Reader with customization option on the SharePoint site Page

Note: The home page does not have immersive reader features.

Send your SharePoint site page by email

Sending a SharePoint site page by email can be a useful tool for sharing information, collaborating with others, and making content more accessible and convenient.

To send a SharePoint Online site page by email, you can follow these steps:

1. Navigate to the **site page** that you want to send by email.

2. Expand the **Send to** option on the top-bar of the page and select **Email**. The following figure illustrates these steps:

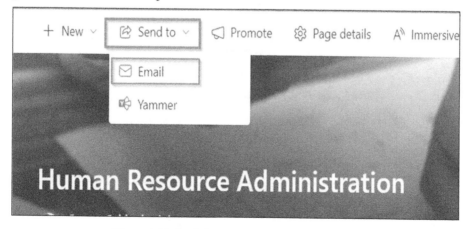

Figure 6.28: Send the SharePoint site Page via email

3. Insert the user's email address or name to email the SharePoint site page. Click on **Send**. The page will be sent to the mentioned user via email.

Note: There is also another option to send the SharePoint site page via Yammer.

Delete a SharePoint site page

The modern SharePoint pages can be quickly removed from a SharePoint site by the site owner or administrator.

To delete pages, you must be the site owner or a SharePoint administrator. If you are the site owner but are unable to delete a page, check to see whether your administrator has disabled this feature.

To delete a site page from your SharePoint site, the following steps are:

1. On the site page itself, under the **Page details**, you can delete your page. Navigate to the site page that you want to delete.

2. Click on the **Page details** on the top bar of the site page.

3. Scroll down the pane and you can find an option to **Delete page.**

4. Give the confirmation to delete the site from the SharePoint site.

The following figure illustrates the steps mentioned:

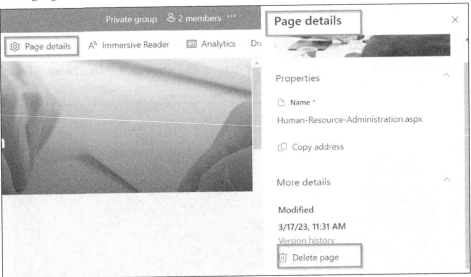

Figure 6.29: Delete the SharePoint site Page from the SharePoint site

What is SharePoint webparts

SharePoint Web Parts are modular components that can be added to SharePoint pages to provide specific functionality to Modern content. They are like building blocks that you can use to create customized pages for your SharePoint site.

Web Parts can display different types of content, such as lists, libraries, images, and videos. They can also provide different types of functionalities, such as search boxes, calendars, and social media feeds.

SharePoint comes with a variety of pre-built Web Parts, but you can also create your own custom Web Parts or download them from third-party vendors.

By adding Web Parts to your SharePoint pages, you can create a more personalized and interactive user experience for your site visitors, making it easier for them to find and access the content they need.

You can get more information on how to add web parts to your SharePoint site pages from *Chapter 7, Modern Webparts in SharePoint Online.*

Conclusion

In this chapter, we have covered the fundamentals of SharePoint Modern pages such as what a modern SharePoint site page is, different types of SharePoint site pages, why to use site pages, how to create a site pages, customizing the site pages, displaying the page in fullwidth, and so on.

In the next chapter, we will see what web parts are, how to add web parts to web pages, working with different types of web parts, and many more features.

Points to remember

You can quickly read and learn some of the chapter's most important learning aspects, such as:

- Modern SharePoint Online pages are built on a responsive design that automatically adjusts the layout to fit any device, whether a desktop computer, tablet, or smartphone.

- SharePoint provides different types of site pages that you can create within a team site:
  o Home Page
  o Wiki Page
  o Web Part Page
  o Site Page
  o News Post
  o Document Library
  o List Page

- Site pages are best for creating static pages with pre-defined sections, while web part pages are more flexible and allow users to add interactive content and customize the layout.

- SharePoint site pages provide a flexible and powerful way to create and publish content within a SharePoint site, while also providing collaboration and integration features that can help organizations work more efficiently.

- Site pages can be created in both modern and classic SharePoint experiences. In modern experience, users can create a page using one of the pre-built templates, or they can start from scratch with a blank page.

- You can customize your SharePoint site page by adding texts, audio, video, site activities, Yammer feeds, and more.

- There are three-page layouts available in the modern SharePoint Online site pages. Such as: Home Page layout, Article Page layout, Single part app page layout.

- Displaying SharePoint Online modern pages in full width can help improve the usability and aesthetics of your site, making it more engaging and easier to use for your audience.

- By using a table, you can easily present data in rows and columns, which makes it easier for users to read and understand.

- By adding anchor tags or bookmarks, users navigate to a specific section or content on a webpage without having to scroll through the entire page.

- SharePoint allows the user to redirect a site page from the modern SharePoint site.

- This feature is helpful when you want to show or hide specific content to a particular group of people, such as employees or external partners.

- Comments, likes, and views are features available in modern SharePoint online pages to promote collaboration, feedback, and engagement within a SharePoint site.

- The immersive reader is a tool that provides a full screen reading experience to help users read and understand content more effectively.

Join our book's Discord space

Join the book's Discord Workspace for Latest updates, Offers, Tech happenings around the world, New Release and Sessions with the Authors:

https://discord.bpbonline.com

CHAPTER 7
Modern Web Parts in SharePoint Online

Introduction

In this chapter, we will introduce SharePoint Web parts, and how to add a web part in SharePoint Online Modern page.

Furthermore, we will also discuss how to remove the web parts from the SharePoint Online page, how to move a specific web part from one section to others, and as well as how we can make a duplicate web part in SharePoint Modern page.

Additionally, by taking different scenarios, we will describe most of the important web parts in SharePoint Online Modern page.

Structure

This section explains the overall information about modern SharePoint Web parts, including how to insert a web part, customize SharePoint web parts, delete a SharePoint Web parts, and examples of several web parts like:

- Introduction to SharePoint Online Web parts
- Add a SharePoint Online Web part
- SharePoint Online Text Web part

- Image gallery Web part in SharePoint Online

- SharePoint Online Quick links Web part

- News Web part in SharePoint Online

- People Web part in SharePoint Online

- SharePoint Online Button Web part

- Call to action Web part in SharePoint Online

- Hero Web part in SharePoint Online

- SharePoint Online Document library Web part

- File and Media viewer Web part in SharePoint Online

- Modern SharePoint Highlighted content Web part

- List Web part in SharePoint Online

- Recent documents Web part in SharePoint Online

- Events Web part in SharePoint Online

- Group calendar Web part in SharePoint Online

- Organization chart Web part in SharePoint Online

- SharePoint Online Microsoft Forms Web part

- Quick chart Web part in SharePoint Online

- Site activity Web part in SharePoint Online

- SharePoint Online World clock Web part

- SharePoint Online Code snippet Web part

- Embed Web part in SharePoint Online

Objectives

After reading this chapter, the reader will have a basic understanding of SharePoint Online Web parts, how to insert one into a modern SharePoint Online page, and how to customize it using various criteria.

Also, the reader will learn how to duplicate, move, and delete a particular web part from a SharePoint Online Modern page. We will also examine numerous web part types in the SharePoint Online page, along with various example types.

Introduction to Web parts in SharePoint Online

To help website pages load quickly, Microsoft has created several modern web parts. SharePoint site pages can be created using many web parts.

Your page can look better with the help of web parts. You can add text, images, lists, libraries, links, etc. to your page as web parts. Also, you can customize web parts as per your needs.

SharePoint Web parts are essentially page components that show content. You put it together like a puzzle to make a SharePoint site page.

SharePoint includes built-in web parts by default. Nevertheless, Microsoft 365 also offers third-party web parts that you can use on your site.

Example:

- To store a file or document, there is a Web part called **Document Library** in SharePoint Site Page.

- Similarly, there is a **Calendar** web part that helps to store an event of an organization.

- Also, to display all the information of every employee of the organization, we can use the **People** web part.

Adding a Web part in SharePoint Online Modern Page

In this section, we will see how to insert a Web part in SharePoint Online Modern Page. Follow the instructions below:

1. First, on the Site page, click on the **+** icon that is present in every section layout. Refer to the following figure:

Figure 7.1: *Add a Web part in SharePoint Online*

2. Once you click on the **+** icon, a web part box will appear on the existing site page, as shown in *Figure 7.2*.

3. In this web part box, you can view different types of web parts like Text, Image, Quick links, News, and so on. Furthermore, Microsoft provides a search box in the web part

box for a user to easily access web parts according to their needs. The following figure illustrates this step:

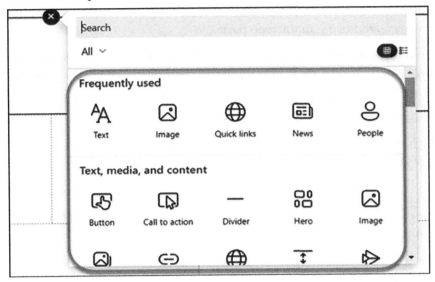

Figure 7.2: Different types of SharePoint Online Web Parts

4. There are two types of views present inside the SharePoint Web part. Such as:

   a. **Grid view**: Once you select this view, then all the web parts will be displayed in a grid system.

   b. **List view**: When you select this view, then all the web parts will be displayed in the list system as shown below:

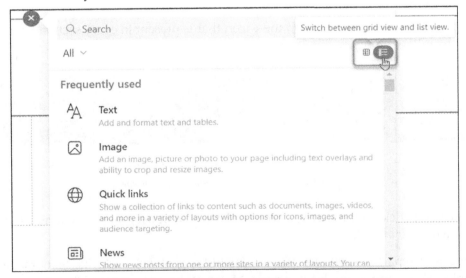

Figure 7.3: SharePoint Online Web part Views

5. Moreover, you can filter the SharePoint web parts as per your need. Once you expand the **All** options (below the search box), you can view all the filters, as shown:

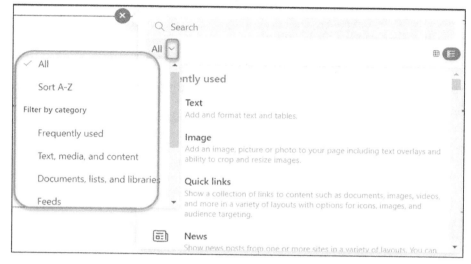

Figure 7.4: SharePoint Online Web Part All Options

6. There are two types of web part filters:

a. **Filter by All**: This All filter helps you to display all the web parts available on the site page. This option has one more filter:

   i. **Sort A-Z:** When you select this filter, then all the web parts will display in ascending or alphabetic order. Refer to the screenshot below:

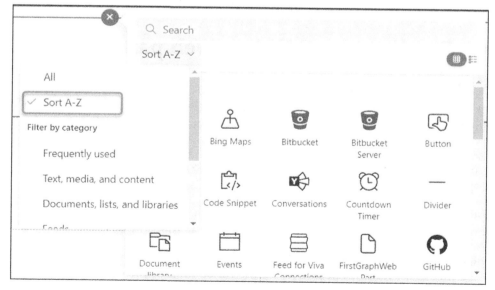

Figure 7.5: SharePoint Online Web part Sort

b. **Filter by category**: If you want to filter the web parts by some categories, then you can select this option. This option has various categories like:

  i. Frequently used

  ii. Text, media, and content

  iii. Documents, lists, libraries and so on

For example, if we select the **Text, media, and content** category, then all these following web parts appear like **Button**, **Call to action**, **Divider**, **Hero**, etc:

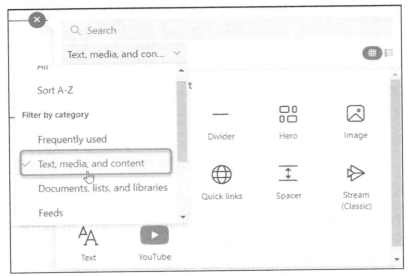

Figure 7.6: SharePoint Web part Filter by category

Move, Duplicate, and Delete Web part in SharePoint Online Modern page

If you select any web part from the SharePoint site page, then you will be able to view the following three options on the top left corner of the specific web part. They are:

- **Move web part**: By using this option, you can move any web part from one section layout to another. You just need to drag the web part and drop wherever you want on the page (within a section).

- **Duplicate web part**: In a similar manner as discussed in the previous option, you can make any specified web part duplicated by using this option.

- **Delete web part**: If you want to remove or delete any specific web part, then click on the trash icon and the specific web part will be removed from the modern site page as shown:

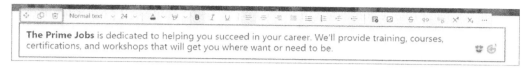

Figure 7.7: Move, Duplicate, and Delete in SharePoint Online Web part

We will now explore some of the important web parts in the following sections.

Text web part in SharePoint Online

You can type text or paragraphs using the Text web part. Follow the given steps:

1. To add the text web part, choose a section on the site page | click on the **+** icon | Select **Text** under the **Frequently used** section as illustrated:

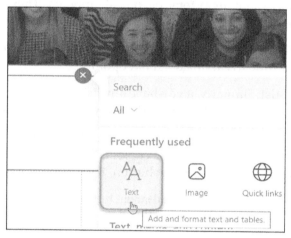

Figure 7.8: SharePoint Online Text Web part

2. Next, a text box will appear on the page where you can enter any text or paragraph as shown below:

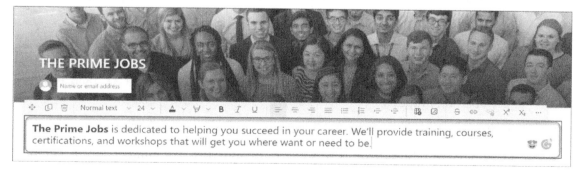

Figure 7.9: Add Text in SharePoint Text Web part

3. You can also provide some design to the text by using some text properties like:

   a. **Normal text**: You can choose the font (like Normal text, Heading 1, Heading 2, etc.) from this dropdown menu.

   b. **Font size**: Specify the size of the font as per your wish.

   c. **Font color**: You can select any color for the specified text or paragraph.

   d. **Highlight color**: You can select any highlight color for the specific font.

   e. **Bold**: By using this property, you can make the text or paragraph bold.

   f. **Italic**: By using this property, you can change the text font to an italic font style.

   g. **Underline**: In case you want to underline some content, then choose this property.

   h. **Alignments**: There are a total of four alignments. They are, Align left, Center, Align right, and Justify. Provide any alignment as per your choice.

   i. **Bulleted list**: If you have any list of contents inside the text web part, then you can use this property to make it bullet points.

   j. **Numbered list**: Similarly, if you have any list of contents inside the text web part, and you want to make it numbered, then you can use this property.

   k. **Increased indent**: The distance is increased between the current paragraph (the selected one or the one where the cursor is placed) and the left page margin. Each time you click the **Increase Indent** button, the left margin increases.

   l. **Decreased indent**: The **Decreased Indent** button moves the paragraph one tab stop to the left. Tab stops are every half inch by default; however, you can change the setting for the same.

   m. **Insert table**: If you want to add a table inside the text web part, then you can use this property.

   n. **Insert image**: If you want to add an image inside the text web part, then you can use this insert image property.

   o. **Strikethrough**: Strikethrough is usually used to indicate incorrect or unnecessary text.

   p. **Hyperlink**: If you want to insert any link to any specific text, then use this hyperlink property.

   q. **Remove link**: To remove the hyperlink, you can use this property.

   r. **Superscript, Subscript**: A superscript or subscript is a number, figure, symbol, or indicator that is smaller than the normal line of type and is set slightly above it (superscript) or below it (subscript).

 s. **More styles**: Once you click on this property, you will be able to view two more properties:

  i. **Clear all formatting**: If you want to clear all the formatting in text web part, then click on this option.

  ii. **More options**: To view more properties in the Text web part, click on this option.

Image gallery web part in Modern SharePoint Online

The image gallery web part is a better option than the image web part if you want to display more than one image on your site.

You can upload as many images as you need from the same sources using this image gallery (including dynamic filtering). To add the image gallery web part:

1. To add the image gallery web part, choose a section on the site page | Click on the + icon | Select **Image gallery** under the **Text, media, and content** section:

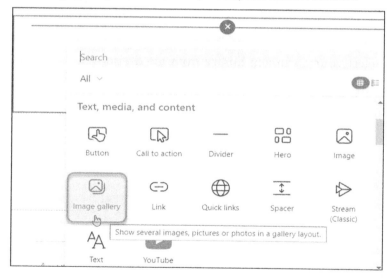

Figure 7.10: SharePoint Online Image gallery Web part

2. Once it is added to the modern page, you can add images by clicking on the **+ Add** button. You can insert the images from various ways like Recent, Stock images, Web search, OneDrive, Site, etc.

3. There are three different layouts available:

 a. **Grid** (Here, you can choose the Aspect ratio)

b. **Brick**

c. **Carousel**

The following image shows these options:

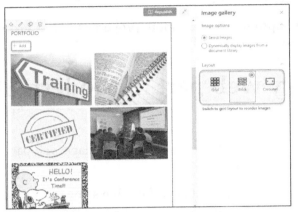

Figure 7.11: Image gallery layout

4. In Image gallery web part, if you will select the second option **Dynamically display images from a document library**, then all the images will be displayed from a particular SharePoint Document Library.

5. You can select your document library from the dropdown menu and display all the images in the image gallery web part. Moreover, you can check the **Include subfolders** option as shown below.

6. Moreover, the image gallery web part allows you to display a maximum of 255 images. Refer to the following figure for your guidance:

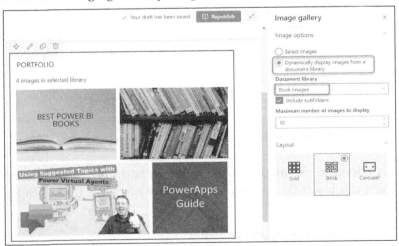

Figure 7.12: Various image options in Image gallery Web part

You can also change the image's caption, alternate text for those who cannot see the image, and title for each image.

Quick links web part in SharePoint Online

You can quickly add links to your page for easy access using the quick links web part. The link could lead to a document, images, videos, etc. Follow the given steps:

1. To add the quick links web part, choose a section on the site page | Click on the + icon | Select **Quick links** under the **Text, media, and content** section as shown:

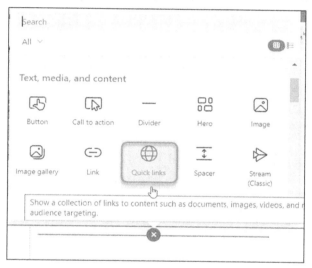

Figure 7.13: SharePoint Online Quick links Web part

2. You can add some links by using the **+ Add links** button in the quick links web part.

3. Also, you have a variety of layout choices for the links:

   a. **Compact**

   b. **Filmstrip**

   c. **Grid**

   d. **Button**

   e. **List**

   f. **Tiles**

4. Moreover, you can change the title text, icon appearance, button appearance, and alignment. Furthermore, audience targeting is possible.

5. You can modify the following for each unique link as shown in *Figure 7.14*:

a. Title

b. Thumbnail (can be auto selected, custom image, or icon)

c. Alternate text field for thumbnail image

d. Description

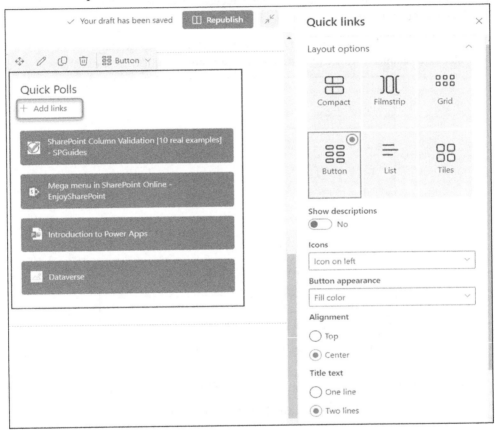

Figure 7.14: Add links in SharePoint Quick links Web part

News web part in SharePoint Online

Since it is a convenient way to post notices, status updates, and people news, the news web part is frequently utilized in communication sites.

1. To add the news web part, choose a section on the site page | Click on the + icon | Select **News** under the **News, people and events** category, as illustrated below:

Figure 7.15: *SharePoint Online News Web part*

2. You can configure this web part in many ways, including:

    a. News source (the same site or from other sites in your tenant)

    b. Layout (including title, commands, number of posts to show, number of views, etc.)

    c. Filter

    d. Audience targeting

    e. Order of the news posts

3. Also, the title of news from official or authoritative websites has a distinctive color block to indicate its distinction and significance.

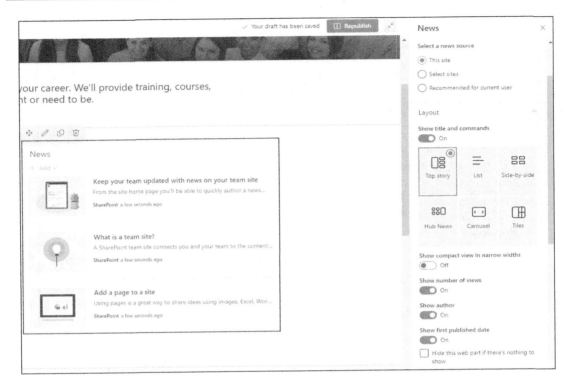

Figure 7.16: News Web part Layouts in SharePoint Online

- Selecting a news source:

  The page's library receives new posts that have been published. You can select the source from which the news will be sourced while working on a news web part. Follow the instructions listed below to do so:

1. On the edit mode, choose the edit icon of the news web part (if you are in published mode).

2. Under the Select a news source (from the right-side pane), Choose **This site** or **Select sites**.

3. When you choose **Select sites**, then all the SharePoint sites will appear below it. You can select one or more sites by searching for it. Refer to the figure below:

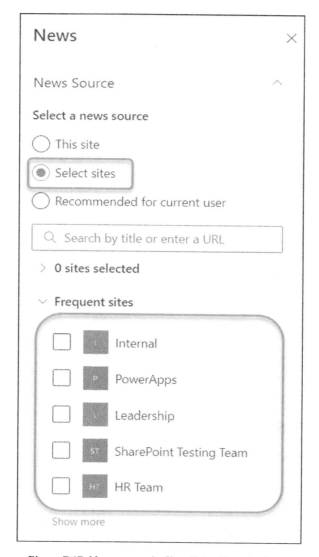

Figure 7.17: News source in SharePoint News Web part

4. The posts that you want to display in your news web part can also be filtered by title, recently added or altered, generated by or modified by, and page properties.

5. Furthermore, you can enable audience targeting and sort and organize the news order in the news web part.

The following figure explains the **Filter** window:

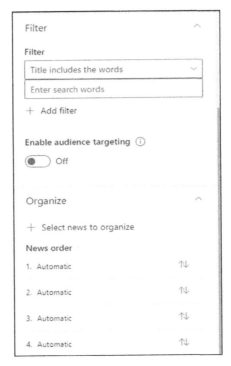

Figure 7.18: SharePoint Online News Web part Filter

Add a news post by link

You can only add a news post into the news web part in the publishing mode. You cannot add a news post in edit mode.

Follow the instructions below to display a post using a link from your site or another site:

1. From the News web part, expand **+ Add** button | Click on the **News link** option as shown below:

Figure 7.19: Add a news link to SharePoint News Web part

2. Next, the **News link** window will appear on the right side of the web part where you can view all the below fields:

    a. **Link**: Provide the news post link that you want to display on the site page.

    b. **Preview image**: Here, the preview image will appear by default. If you want to change it, then click on **Change** and upload a new image.

    c. **Title**: Provide a title for the news post.

    d. **Description**: Provide the news post description.

3. Once everything is done, click on the **Post** button as shown:

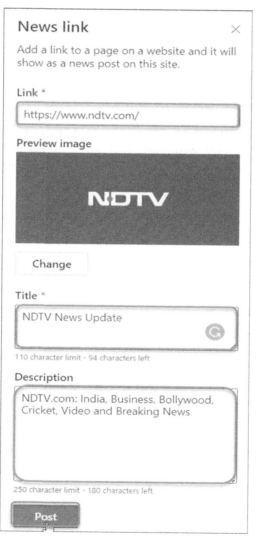

Figure 7.20: Provide News link details to SharePoint News Web part

Once we post the news, then the news web part will be displayed like the image below:

Figure 7.21: View SharePoint Online News Web part

Removing the news web part

Every time we add news to the news web part, a page for that news is automatically created in site pages with the page title. The site pages are listed under site content. The steps listed below can be used to delete the news item:

1. Go to the **Settings** icon (On the top right corner of SharePoint site) | Click on **Site contents** | Select **Site Pages**. The following figure illustrates this step:

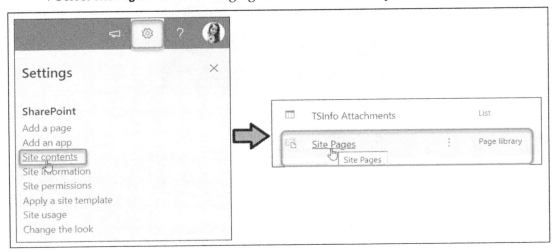

Figure 7.22: Remove News Webpart from SharePoint Online

2. Under the **Site Pages**, select the news post | Click on ellipses **(...)** | Select **Delete** as shown below:

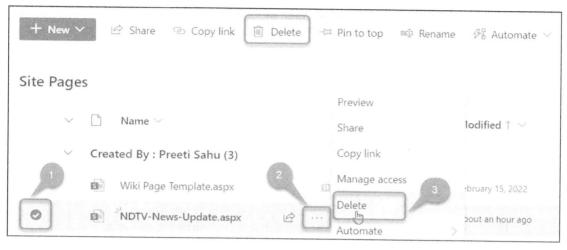

Figure 7.23: Delete SharePoint Online News Web part

3. Once you click on the **Delete** option, a confirm pop-up window will appear. If you are sure to delete that news post, then click on the **Delete** button. The pop-up window will look something like the following figure:

Figure 7.24: Delete News Web part in SharePoint

4. If you want to delete the news web part itself, go into editing mode, hover over the news web part, and select delete from the left-hand menu.

People web part in SharePoint Online

The people web part is helpful in case you want to display users on your page. It displays the person's profile link and contact details.

Considering this, it would be a good idea to have the admin's profile visible on the page in case someone needs to get in touch with them right away.

1. To add the people web part, choose a section on the site page | Click on the + icon | Select **People** under the **News, people and events** category, as shown:

Figure 7.25: SharePoint Online People Web part

2. There are total of three layouts in the people web part. They are:

   a. **Small**

   b. **Medium**

   c. **Large**

3. Additionally, you can provide a title to the people web part (like **INSTRUCTORS**). Refer to the following figure:

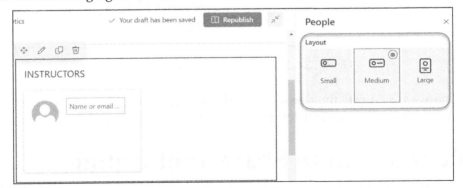

Figure 7.26: SharePoint People Web part Layouts

4. Enter a user's email address inside the people web part, and the specific user will automatically populate below. When you choose a certain user, their profile image will also appear in the people web part as shown:

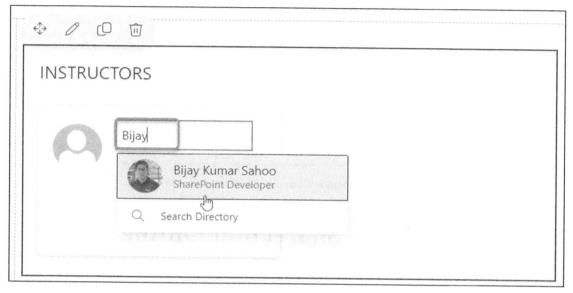

Figure 7.27: Add people in SharePoint People Web part

5. Once you have added the user, you can see a **+ Add a profile link** option under the user. To add any profile link like Linked in, Twitter, etc., click on the link and put the profile URL under the Address field.

6. Also, you can add a text to display the user profile and then **Save** it, as shown in the following figure:

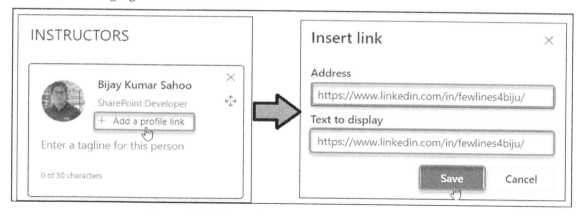

Figure 7.28: Add a profile link to SharePoint People Web part

7. Similarly, we can add multiple users in the SharePoint people web part and that will look like the screenshot below:

Figure 7.29: Display Multiple users in SharePoint People Web part

Button web part in SharePoint Online

A button with your own label and URL can be added to your page using this web part. The alignment of the buttons on the page can also be changed.

1. To add the button web part, choose a section on the site page | Click on the + icon | Select **Button** under the **Text, media, and content** category, as shown below:

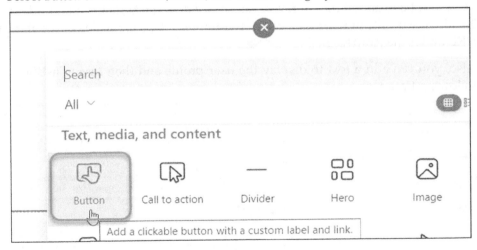

Figure 7.30: SharePoint Online Button Web part

2. Then, the button web part will be added into the site page. These are the properties below that we need to fill:

   a. **Label**: Provide a label or text that will display on the button.

   b. **Link**: Provide a site link that will open when the user taps on the button.

   c. **Button alignment**: You can align the button as left, center, or right as per your need.

3. As the button color is already a part of the accent color for the site theme, you are unable to change it in edit mode.

4. Once everything is done, just publish the SharePoint site page.

The following figure shows the button properties:

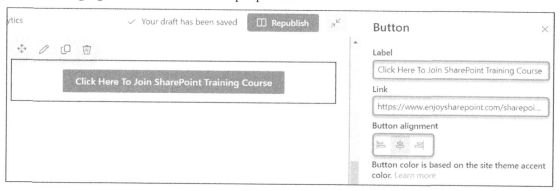

Figure 7.31: Button web part properties in SharePoint Online

5. Click on the **Click Here To Join SharePoint Training Course** button and then the specific URL will launch in a new tab as shown below:

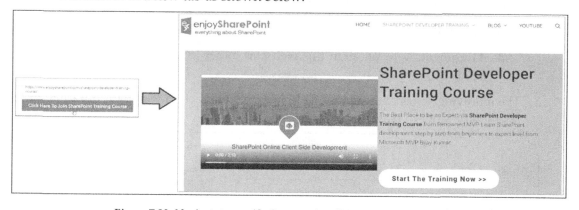

Figure 7.32: Navigate to specific Screen using SharePoint Button Web part

Call to action web part in SharePoint Online

If you need an upgraded button web part, then this web part is what you need. With this one, you may give users a Call to action button.

By using this Call to action web part, we can directly click on the button and then go to the specific website or page that what exactly we need. Follow the given steps:

1. To add the Call to action web part, choose a section on the site page | Click on the + icon | Select **Call to action** under the **Text, media, and content** section, as shown:

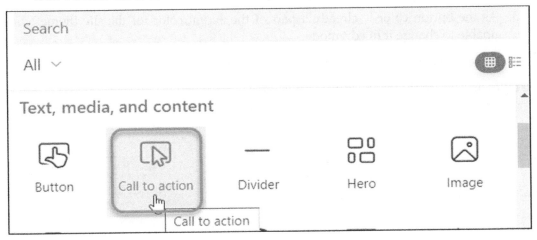

Figure 7.33: SharePoint Online Call to action Web part

2. Below are the **Call to action** web part properties:

    a. **Background image:** You can change the background image of the Call to action web part.

    b. **Button label:** Provide the button label or text that will display on the button.

    c. **Button link:** Provide the link that will launch when the user taps on the button.

    d. **Alignment:** You can align this web part either left, center, or right as per your need.

3. The following screenshot represents how the Call to action web part looks like in the SharePoint Modern page:

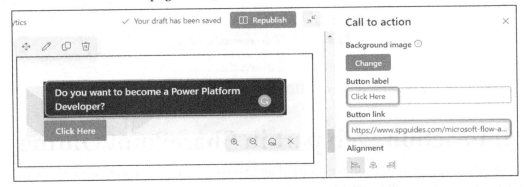

Figure 7.34: Call to action properties in SharePoint Online

Hero web part in SharePoint Online

The hero web part is found on communication sites by default, although you can still add it to any modern site page.

The goal of this web part, as implied by its name, is to attract readers' attention and interest in order to force them to pay attention to the contents on this page.

Layout options are only available for an appropriate window size and screen resolution. If you are using this web part in a 1/3 or 1/2 column section, move the web part to a 2/3 or full-width column.

Although a video can be added to this web part, the viewer must click through it to access the video player or link source in order to watch it. Follow the given steps:

1. To add the Hero web part, choose a section on the site page | Click on the + icon | Select **Hero** under the **Text, media, and content** section. The following figure shows this step:

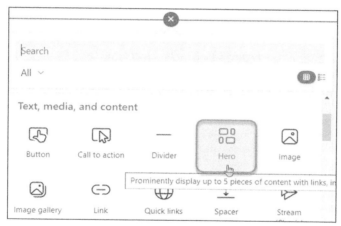

Figure 7.35: SharePoint Online Hero Web part

2. A maximum of five items may be displayed here, including:

    a. Images

    b. Insert Links (to a file, library, or even site)

    c. New upload

3. Also, there are two types of layouts in the hero web part. They are:

    a. **Tiles**

    b. **Layers**

These options are shown in the following figure:

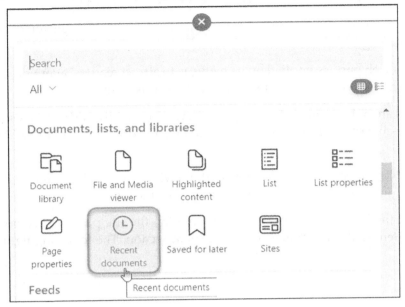

Figure 7.36: Hero Web part Layouts

4. To insert a link in the hero web part, click on the **Select link** button in any of the hero content, as shown:

Figure 7.37: Select link in Hero Web part

5. Once you click on the button, the window shown in *figure 1.38* will appear where you need to choose any image or files from Web search, OneDrive, Site, etc.

6. Select any image or file and then tap on the **Insert** button below:

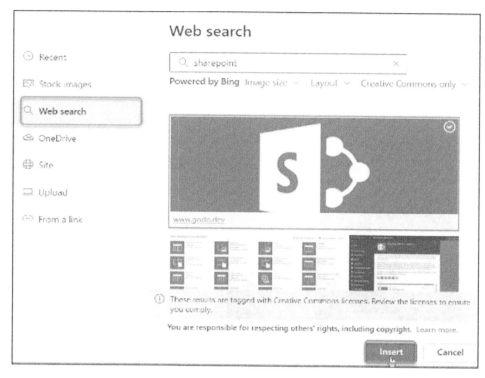

Figure 7.38: Add links to SharePoint Hero Web part

7. Once you add all the images, then the hero web part will look like the screenshot below:

Figure 7.39: Hero Web part in SharePoint Online

8. Additionally, you can provide the hero web part title and change the link as per your need.

9. You can view three types of background images as shown in *figure 1.40*:

    a. Auto-selected image

    b. Custom image

    c. Color block

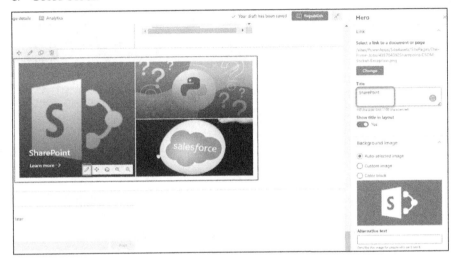

Figure 7.40: Provide Title to SharePoint Online Hero Web part

10. There are several customization possibilities as well, including the ability to change an image's focal point, rearrange the tiles or layers, or even include a call to action button.

11. You can provide any web site link or any URL in the Call to action link option, as shown:

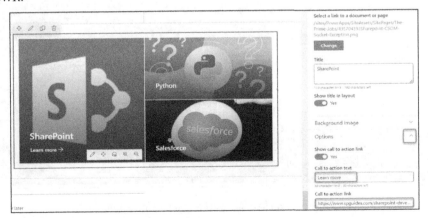

Figure 7.41: SharePoint Online Hero Web part Properties

12. When a user will tap on the link, then the specific given site will launch in a new tab as shown below:

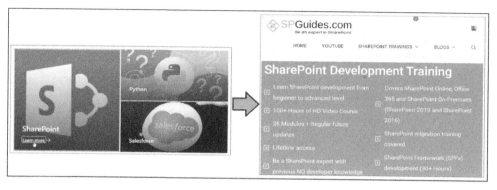

Figure 7.42: *Use SharePoint Online Hero Web part*

Document library web part in SharePoint Online

You can display a browsable document library using the document library web part (in a specific view or to a specific folder).

This web part nevertheless respects the permission level that you have established for your users. The files on the online section can only be added to, edited, or viewed by those with the proper permissions. Follow the given steps to add this web part:

1. To add the Document library web part, choose a section on the site page | Click on the + icon | Select **Document library** under the **Documents, lists, and libraries** section. Refer to the following figure:

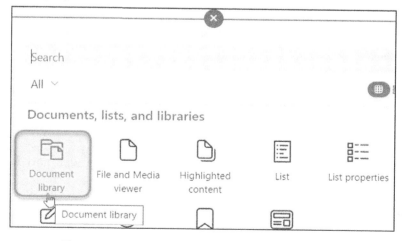

Figure 7.43: *SharePoint Online Document library Web part*

2. Select a SharePoint Document Library (like **Book Images**) to add to the page:

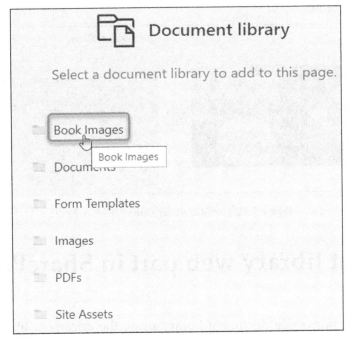

Figure 7.44: Add SharePoint Online Document Library

3. When a user with the necessary access chooses a file, that user has the option to download, rename, delete, or even pin the chosen file to the library's top.

4. Also, you can configure a dynamic list filtering on the web part to base the files displayed on a choice made from another list or library.

5. You can see below the properties available in the document library web part:

   a. Folder

   b. Size

   c. Show command bar

   d. Show **See all** button

   e. Dynamic filtering

Here in the below image, you can see how a Document library web part looks like on the

SharePoint modern page:

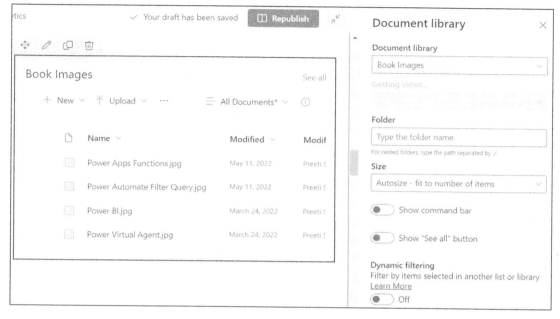

Figure 7.45: Document library Properties in SharePoint Online

File and Media viewer web part in SharePoint Online

With the File viewer web part, you can display or insert a file directory directly onto the page.

Since it was first released, the files that this web part supports have advanced significantly. It supports several preferred file types, including:

- Excel
- Word
- PowerPoint
- Visio
- PDF
- 3D models
- Videos

Image files are not supported by the file viewer web part. If you want to add a picture to the page, the image web part element can be used. To add the File and Media viewer web part, follow these steps:

1. Choose a section on the site page | Click on the + icon | Select **File and Media viewer** under the **Documents, lists, and libraries** section, as shown:

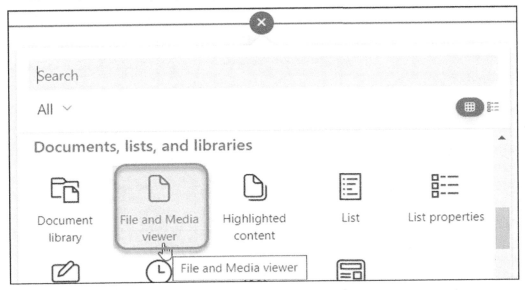

Figure 7.46: SharePoint Online File and Media viewer Web part

2. Once we click on the File and Media viewer web part, the window below will appear where we need to upload the files either from OneDrive, Site, From a link, etc.

3. Select any of the options and upload the file from your system or OneDrive as shown in the following figure:

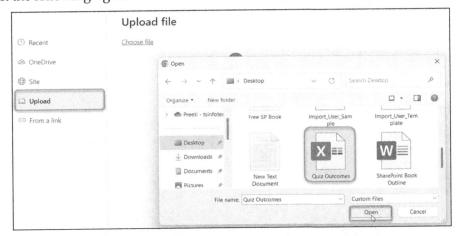

Figure 7.47: Upload file in File and Media viewer web part

4. Finally, tap on the **Add file** button to upload the file into the **File and Media viewer** web part as shown:

Figure 7.48: *Add file in SharePoint Online File viewer web part*

5. Now the uploaded file will be displayed as shown below. The file you added has a significant impact on the options you can specify in the edit mode. Moreover, you can upload files to the web part:

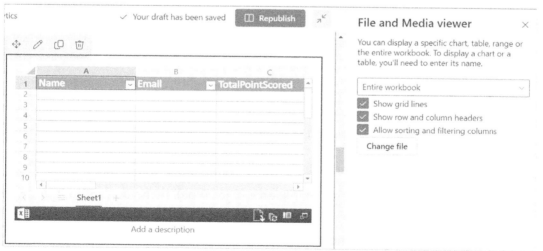

Figure 7.49: *Display uploaded file in SharePoint File viewer Web part*

6. In accordance with the user's selections in the document library web part, you can also utilize dynamic filtering and display files in a dynamic manner.

Modern SharePoint highlighted content web part

One of the web parts that advanced users frequently use is the **Highlighted Content Web Part**, also known as **HCWP**.

You can dynamically show content from a document library (typically), sites, a site collection, or even from all sites using this web part. Follow the given steps:

1. To add the highlighted content web part, choose a section on the site page | Click on the + icon | Select **Highlighted content** under the **Documents, lists, and libraries** section. The following figure explains this step:

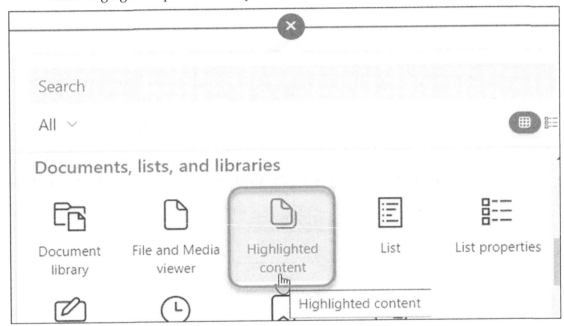

Figure 7.50: SharePoint Online Highlighted content Web part

2. To limit search results for the web part, you can use a filter or a custom query.

3. Also, if you want to add any other source (Site, Type), then you can do it under the Content category.

4. Options for custom query include:

   a. Source

   b. Query text (KQL)

   c. Sort by

    d. Enable audience targeting

    e. Group-level caching

    f. Layout

    g. Show title and commands

    h. Show up to this many items at a time

The basic filter options are shown below:

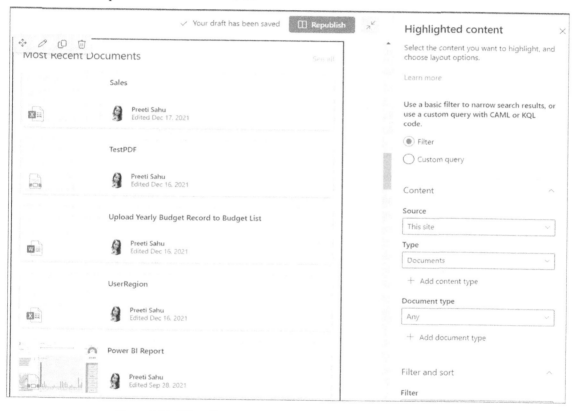

Figure 7.51: Filter SharePoint Online Highlighted content web part

5. Options for filtering include:

    a. Content source, type, and document type

    b. Sort by

    c. Enable audience targeting

    d. Group-level caching

    e. Layout

f. Show title and commands

g. Show up to this many items at a time

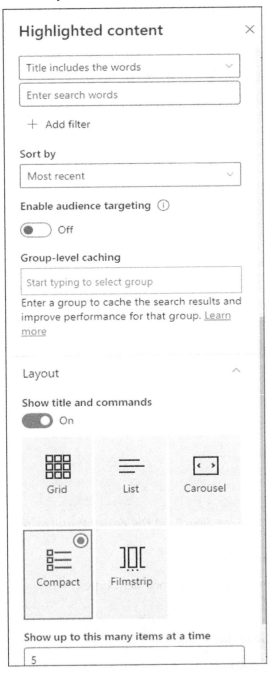

Figure 7.52: Highlighted content Web part Layouts

6. The layout, title and commands, how many items are shown at once, and hiding the web part if there is nothing to show, are all customizable.

List web part in Modern SharePoint Online

Using the list web part, you may embed or display a list directly on the page and give it a specific title, view, and size. To add the list web part:

1. Choose a section on the site page | Click on the + icon | Select **List** under the **Documents, lists, and libraries** section as shown:

Figure 7.53: SharePoint Online List Web part

2. Here, various list kinds can be seen, including:

   a. Custom lists

   b. Announcement lists

   c. Issue tracking lists

   d. Contact lists

3. Select a SharePoint list to add to the page. Once you select any list, then you can select the list View and Folder.

4. When the SharePoint list is displayed, the user can use most of its features and even add a new item to the list. The features are shown in the following figure:

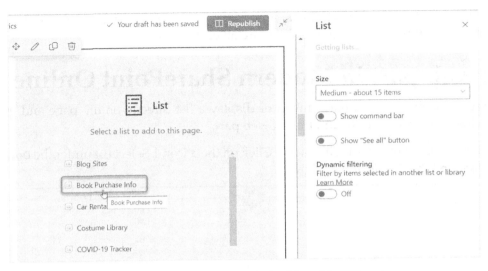

Figure 7.54: Add a SharePoint Online List to List Web part

5. You can use dynamic filtering, show or hide the command bar, and click **See all** just like with the document library web part. The screenshot below represents how the SharePoint list looks like in the SharePoint Modern Page:

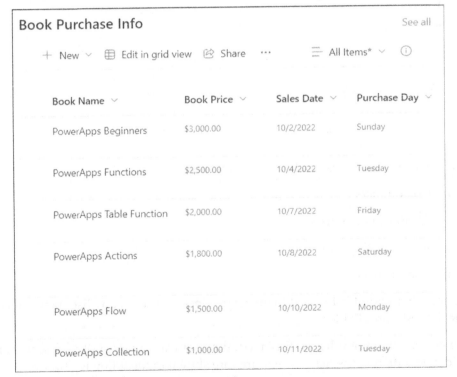

Figure 7.55: Display SharePoint List in List Web part

Recent documents web part in SharePoint Online page

By using the recent documents web part, the most recent documents that a user has accessed on the site may be shown. It is similar to a history section, but with only the recent documents displayed. Follow these given steps for the recent documents web part:

1. To add the recent documents web part, choose a section on the site page | Click on the + icon | Select **Recent documents** under the **Documents, lists, and libraries** section. The following figure illustrates this step:

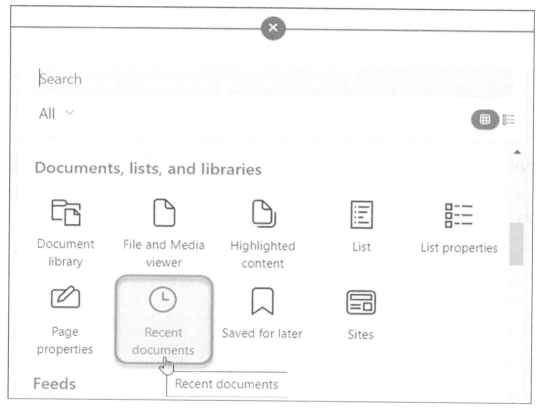

Figure 7.56: *SharePoint Online Recent documents Web part*

2. You can choose how many documents the user will see at once, as you can see in the image below. Also, as the user accesses other documents, this web part will continue to update:

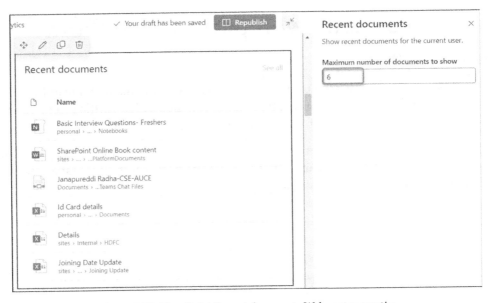

Figure 7.57: SharePoint Recent documents Web part properties

Events web part in Modern SharePoint Online

With the help of the events web part, you can display future events on your page in an attractive manner. The steps for the same are given below:

1. To add the Events web part, choose a section on the site page | Click on the + icon | Select **Events** under the **News, people and events** section as displayed:

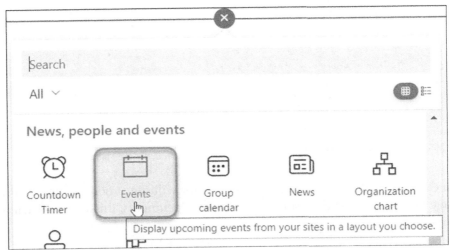

Figure 7.58: Events Web part in SharePoint Online

2. There are many ways to customize this web part:

   a. Source (where to get the events from)

   b. Category

   c. Date range

   d. Layout

   e. Show up to this many items at a time (How many items are shown at once)

   f. Enable audience targeting

   g. Group-level caching

   h. Show event images

The following figure shows the events window:

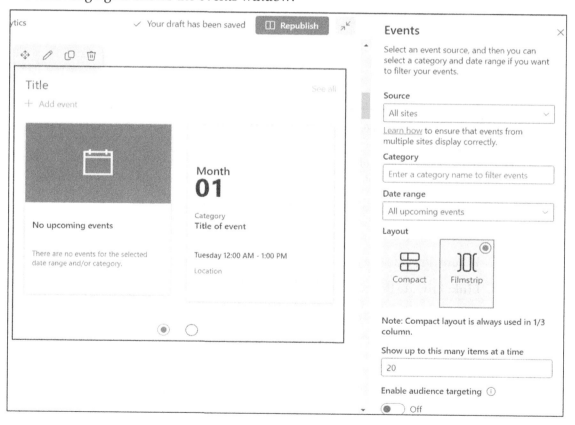

Figure 7.59: SharePoint Events Web part Layouts

Adding events in events web part

Follow the given steps to add events:

1. We can add an event inside the event web part once after publishing the SharePoint Modern Page. In the edit mode, we cannot add a single event inside the event web part.

2. Click on the + **Add event** option on the event web part:

Figure 7.60: Add an event to SharePoint Events Web part

3. When we click on the **+ Add event** option, then a new page will appear where we need to create a new event. Below represents all the information that we need to fill on it:

   a. **Title:** Provide a title for the event.

   b. **When:** Select the start date and end date including timing.

   c. **Where:** Provide the address where you want to perform the event.

   d. **Link:** Provide the event address or link. Also, enter the display name as well.

   e. **Category:** Enter a category for the event.

   f. **About this event:** Give a description of the event.

   g. **Event participants:** If you want to add some participants to attend the event, then provide their names over here.

4. Once everything is filled up, then click on the **Save** button as shown:

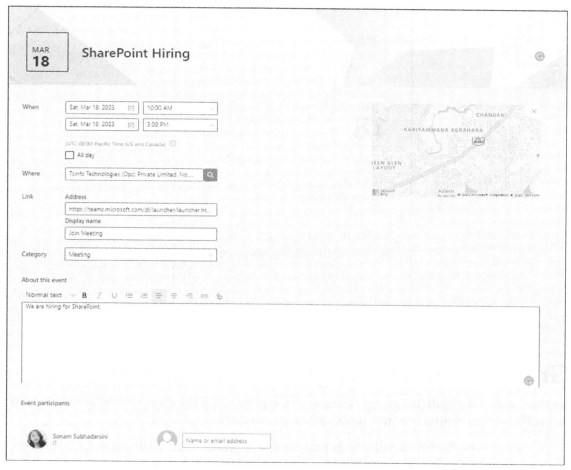

5. Finally, go to the SharePoint modern page and refresh it. You can see the Event web part has added with the upcoming events as shown below:

Figure 7.62: Display SharePoint Events Web part

Group calendar web part in SharePoint Online

You can add a Microsoft 365 group calendar to the page using the group calendar web part so that colleagues can quickly notice future activities. To do this:

1. To add the Group calendar web part, choose a section on the site page | Click on the + icon | Select **Group calendar** under the **News, people and events** section as shown in the following figure:

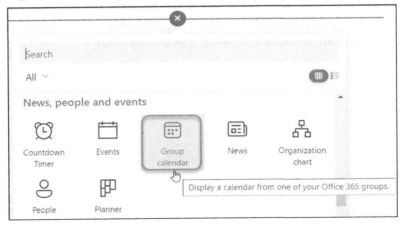

Figure 7.63: SharePoint Online Group calendar Web part

2. You can select any group name under the Group calendar web part property and as well as the number of events per page as shown:

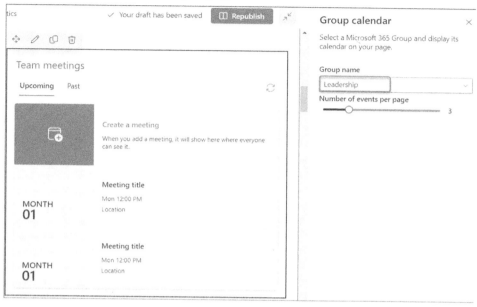

Figure 7.64: SharePoint Group calendar Web part

3. To create a new meeting, click on **Create a meeting** link. Then, Office 365 Outlook will appear where you need to create a new event.

4. Go to the **Home** tab | Click on **New event** option as shown below.

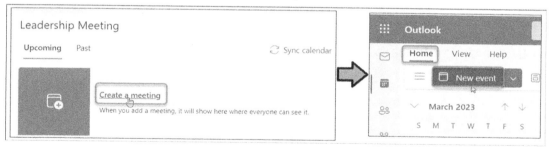

Figure 7.65: Create a meeting in SharePoint Group calendar Web part

5. Next, provide all the necessary fields to create a new event like:

   a. Add a title

   b. Invite required attendees

   c. Suggested times

6. Once the above things are done, click on **Send**. Then the new events will be created in Office 365 Outlook as shown in the following figure:

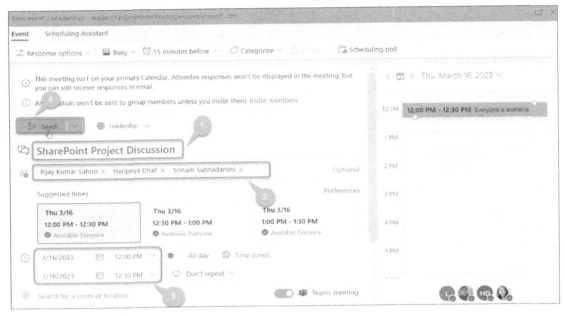

Figure 7.66: View new event in Office 365 Outlook

7. Finally, come to the SharePoint Modern page where you have added the Group calendar web part. Click on the **Sync calendar** option as in the image below:

Figure 7.67: Sync calendar in Group calendar Web part

8. Now we can see all the upcoming events appearing in the group calendar web part and we can join the meeting on the page itself.

9. Additionally, you can also view all the past events by clicking on the **Past** tab in the Group calendar web part. The following figure shows the tabs:

Figure 7.68: Display SharePoint Group calendar Web part

10. Only team sites can use the group calendar because this web part necessitates the existence of a group. Outlook allows for the addition of events.

Organization chart web part in SharePoint Online

You can use the organization chart web part to add a chart showing the visual hierarchy of the business or organization to the page.

To put it simply, this web part is used to show an organization chart with structure and connections for a selected person. To add the organization chart web part:

1. Choose a section on the site page | Click on the + icon | Select **Organization chart** under the **News, people and events** category as shown:

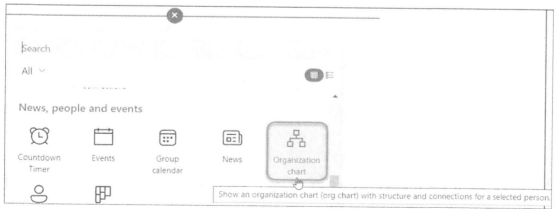

Figure 7.69: SharePoint Online Organization chart Web part

2. In the organization web part, enter the username to whom people are reporting as shown below:

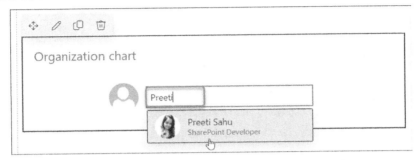

Figure 7.70: Add user to SharePoint Organization chart Web part

3. Furthermore, you can provide the title to this chart web part. Also, there is one more option called **Number of reporting levels up**. It will show the level up reporter in this web part.

4. For example, as mentioned, the number of reporting levels up is **1**, so the below three people (Haripriya, Roselin, and Sonam) are reporting to Preeti and Preeti is reporting to Bijay. This is the hierarchical structure of the organization, displayed through the organization chart:

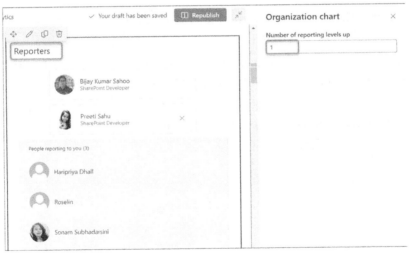

Figure 7.71: Specify the number of reporting levels in Organization chart Web part

Microsoft forms web part in SharePoint Online

A fantastic, simple-to-use tool for creating surveys and polls is Microsoft Forms. You may incorporate the form into your page using this web part by following these steps:

1. To add the Microsoft forms web part, choose a section on the site page | Click on the + icon | Select **Microsoft Forms** under the **Data analysis** category as shown in the following figure:

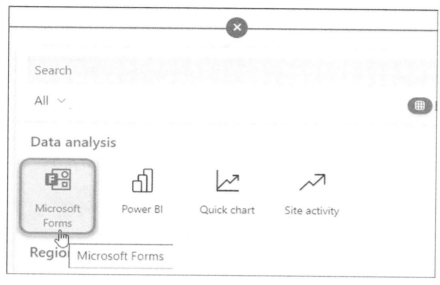

Figure 7.72: Microsoft Forms Web part in SharePoint Online

2. With this Microsoft forms web part, we can use an existing form or create a new one.

3. Now, when you edit this Microsoft forms web part, you can choose to collect responses (from the site users) or show form results as shown:

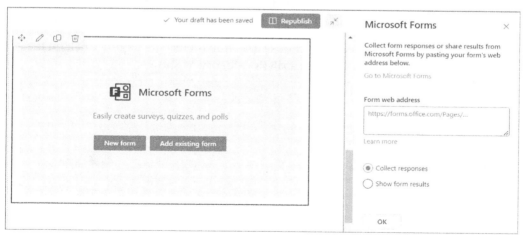

Figure 7.73: Edit SharePoint Online Microsoft Forms Web part

4. Provide the Form web address and then click on **OK**.

5. Once you publish the modern page, you can view the Microsoft form similar to the image below:

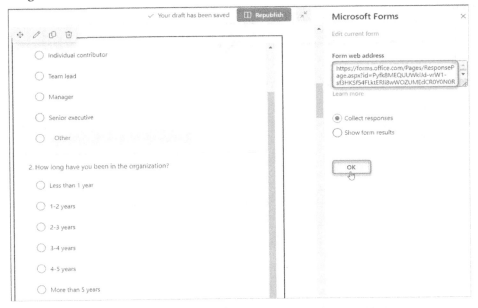

Figure 7.74: SharePoint Online Microsoft Forms Web part properties

Quick chart web part in SharePoint Online

The quick chart can be used if you need to display a basic column or pie chart on the page (instead of creating one on Power BI or on Excel).

1. To add the quick chart web part, choose a section on the site page | Click on the + icon | Select **Quick chart** under the **Data analysis** category as shown:

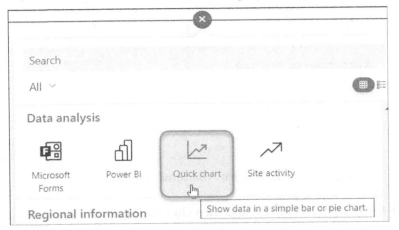

Figure 7.75: SharePoint Online Quick chart Web part

2. The web part will look like this once you have added it to the page: Here, you may give the chart a name in the **Name your chart** option.

3. Once the properties panel has opened, click on the Edit icon of the chart web part to start configuring it in SharePoint Online.

4. The SharePoint quick chart web part lets us display two different sorts of charts. They are:

    a. **Column chart**: The column chart can be used to compare data changes to other elements. The categories are shown here on the horizontal axis, while the values are shown on the vertical axis.

    b. **Pie chart**: The percentage of a whole will be shown on the pie chart. The pie chart can be used if you have fewer items (less than the recommended seven).

5. There are two data types available for the SharePoint Online Quick chart web part:

    a. Enter data (manually)

    b. Get data from a SharePoint list or library on this site

Figure 7.76: Provide Data to SharePoint Quick chart Web part

6. You can enter your own data for the data or get data from the site's existing list or library.

7. On the chart, you can also specify the following elements:

   a. List or library with a number column

   b. Column that has the data to display

   c. Horizontal (category) axis label (for column chart only)

8. Finally, when you add the data into the quick chart, then the web part will be displayed as below:

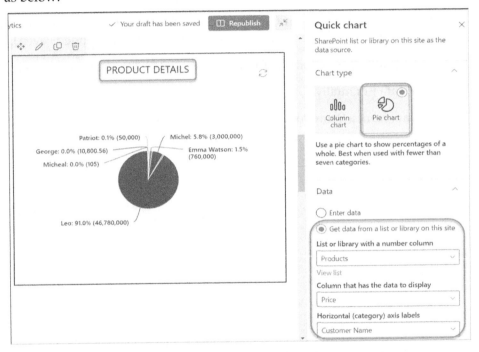

Figure 7.77: SharePoint Online Quick chart Web part properties

Site activity web part in SharePoint Online

The site activity web part can be useful if you want a function that makes it possible to quickly see site updates. To add this web part:

1. To add the site activity web part, choose a section on the site page | Click on the + icon | Select **Site activity** under the **Data analysis** category. Refer to the following figure:

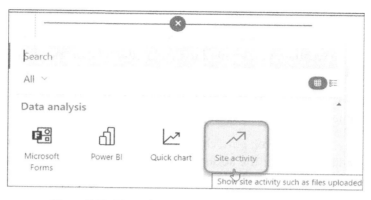

Figure 7.78: Site activity Web part in SharePoint Online

2. Fundamentally, this web part will automatically show the user any recent site action that has occurred (like new uploads, edits, lists, etc.)

3. The maximum number of items to show at once is the only configuration you have here. The things described above are not under your control either. The configuration would look like the following figure:

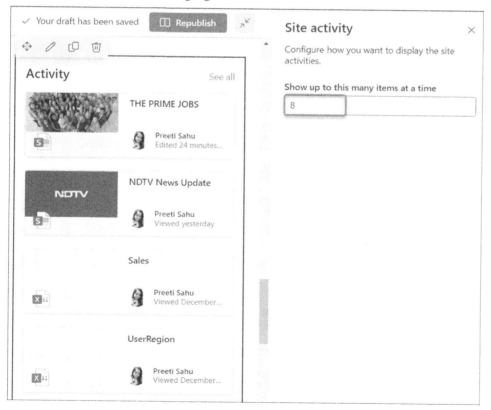

Figure 7.79: Specify the item number in SharePoint Online Site activity Web part

World clock web part in SharePoint Online

What if, instead of the weather, you wanted to display the time of specific locations along with how many hours ahead or behind they are with respect to the initial location?

Now, we have a World clock web part in SharePoint Modern Page that helps to display the current date and time from various locations.

1. To add the world clock web part, choose a section on the site page | Click on the + icon | Select **World clock** under the **Regional information** section. Refer to the following figure for your help:

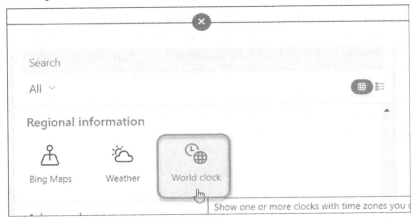

Figure 7.80: World clock Web part in SharePoint Online

2. Once the world clock web part has been added to the site page, then you need to enter or add the location to display the current time and date, as shown:

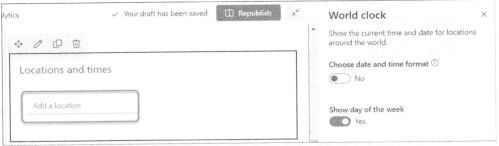

Figure 7.81: Add a Location in SharePoint Online World clock Web part

3. You can set up the following with the world clock web part:

   a. Date format (can also be set to default)

   b. Time format (can also be set to default)

   c. Show day of the week

4. When we add the location into the web part, then the current time and date (including day) is displayed as shown in the image below:

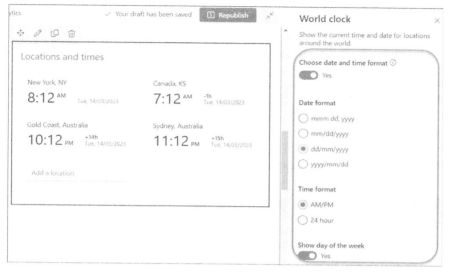

Figure 7.82: SharePoint Online World clock Web part properties

Code snippet web part in SharePoint Online page

By using this SharePoint Code snippet web part, we can display the code on the site page itself. Follow these given steps:

1. To add the code snippet web part, choose a section on the site page | Click on the + icon | Select **Code Snippet** under the **Advanced** section, as shown:

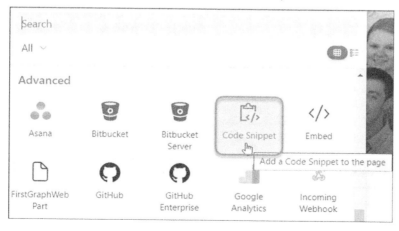

Figure 7.83: Code snippet Web part in SharePoint Online

2. You can customize the following options while using the code snippet web part:

   a. The programming language (the web part will then detect the syntax)

   b. Show numbered lines or not

   c. Configure the color theme (dark or light theme)

   d. Line wrap

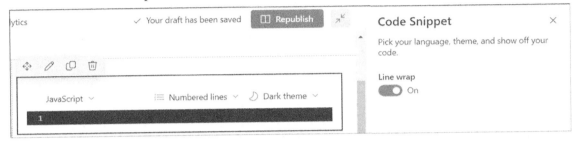

Figure 7.84: SharePoint Online Code Snippet Web part properties

3. You can expand the language and select any language like **C**, **C++**, **C#**, **CSS**, **Python**, etc. The code snippet will open based upon the selected language. Refer to the following figure:

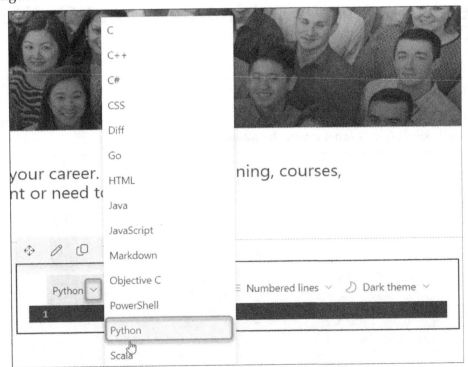

Figure 7.85: Select the Code Language in Code Snippet Web part

4. Inside the code snippet web part, you can write your code or syntax. The syntax is also auto corrected by the web part. The screenshot below represents how the code snippet looks like in the SharePoint Modern Page:

Python ⌄   ≣ Numbered lines ⌄   ☽ Dark theme ⌄

```
1 number= input('Enter a Binary number:')
2 dec_number= int(number, 2)
3 print('The decimal conversion is:', dec_number)
4 print(type(dec_number))
```

Figure 7.86: Output of SharePoint Online Code Snippet Web part

Embed web part in SharePoint Online Page

You can display content from other websites that allow embedding by using the embed web part. Links from well-known websites like Sway, YouTube, Vimeo, etc. is sufficient for the same.

Always try to paste the embedded code from the site instead. Embed code must be iframe-based. Script tags are not supported in the embed web part. To add the embed web part:

1. Choose a section on the site page | Click on the + icon | Select **Embed** under the **Advanced** section, as shown:

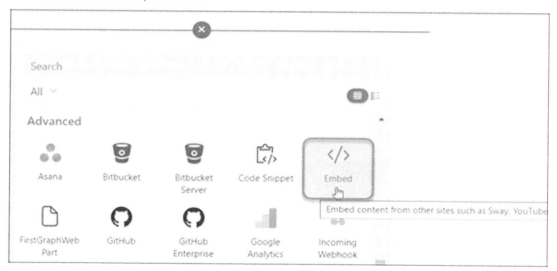

Figure 7.87: Embed Web part in SharePoint Online

2. You can also connect to a list or library to dynamically change your embed code by selecting the ellipses (...) and connect to source as shown below:

Figure 7.88: Connect to source in SharePoint Embed Web part

3. When you apply the website address or any embed code inside the code box, then you can see that specific website or video in the embed web part, as shown:

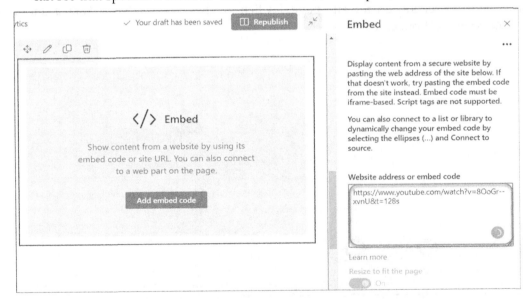

Figure 7.89: Provide Website address in SharePoint Embed Web part

4. As we have put the YouTube video URL inside the embed web part, that is why we can view and play the video on the site page itself. The following figure illustrates this step:

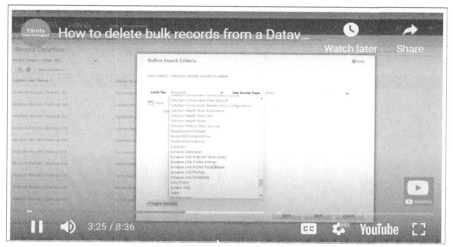

Figure 7.90: Display Output of SharePoint Embed Web part

The embed web part also offers more advanced capability that allows you to use another web part to display dynamic content.

Conclusion

In this chapter, we discussed what SharePoint Online web part is, how to add, remove, and duplicate a web part in SharePoint Online Modern Page. Also, we learned how to customize the various SharePoint web parts like Text, Image, gallery, Quick links, News, and so on.

In the next chapter we will see what Power Apps is, how to connect and integrate Power Apps with SharePoint Online, and much more.

Join our book's Discord space

Join the book's Discord Workspace for Latest updates, Offers, Tech happenings around the world, New Release and Sessions with the Authors:

https://discord.bpbonline.com

## CHAPTER 8

Power Apps

Introduction

In this chapter, we will explore Power Apps in depth. We will cover what Power Apps is, its benefits and drawbacks, permissions, connectors, integrating with SharePoint, working with controls, saving, publishing, and sharing apps. By the end of the chapter, you will have a solid understanding of Power Apps and how to utilize its features effectively.

Structure

This chapter includes an overview of Power Apps as well as examples of how they can be quickly built by a user. We will cover the following topics in the chapter:

- Introduction to Power Apps
- Different Components in Power Apps
- Working with Power Apps connectors
- How to integrate SharePoint with Power Apps?
- SharePoint lists customization with Power Apps
- How to work with Power Apps Form using SharePoint Data?

- Working with Power Apps gallery control

- How to filter SharePoint data in Power Apps?

- Working with Power Apps Button

- Save, Preview, and Publish Power Apps

- Share Power Apps with SharePoint Group

- What is SharePoint Power Apps Delegation?

Objectives

This chapter is a comprehensive guide for beginners or those new to Power Apps. By the end of the chapter, readers will have a solid foundation in understanding and using Power Apps. Topics covered include creating, saving, previewing, and publishing apps, sharing them with others, working with SharePoint lists, customizing them with Power Apps, and more. Whether it is building simple or advanced applications, this chapter provides the necessary knowledge and skills to get started with Power Apps.

What is Power Apps?

A Microsoft-based solution called Power Apps assists in creating personalized apps using the company's data. With the help of different data connectors, including Microsoft Dataverse, online data sources, and on-premises data sources such as SharePoint, OneDrive, Excel Spreadsheet, SQL Server, JIRA, Microsoft 365, and Dynamic 365, we can easily create custom apps.

The advantage of using Power Apps is that we can design our own bespoke business application without any programming or development experience. A bespoke app can be simply created by anyone utilizing our own data sources.

Microsoft IE11, Google Chrome, and Microsoft Edge, as well as any mobile devices (Android, Windows, iOS, etc.), tablets, etc., all provide direct access to our application.

A user can easily connect to any external data source in Power Apps as well. Our customized app can be saved, published, and shared with the team members of the organization.

Different Components in Power Apps

There are mainly four types of components in Power Apps as follows:

- **Canvas apps:** Power Apps Canvas app is an interface where a user may select how they want to create an app. Simply imagine it as an empty container, and we will design it by adding various controls or elements.

Like this, the blank canvas app has a large number of controls, images, forms, and so on, that we can easily drag and drop to customize it according to our business requirements.

There is no restriction on the type of data source in the Power Apps Canvas app. More than 200 data source connections, including those for Microsoft 365, Dynamic 365, SharePoint, SQL Server, and so on, can be used to retrieve data in Power Apps.

- **Model-driven apps:** In the model-driven app, a user can build a unique app by combining different elements including dashboards, forms, views, and charts. By employing minimum to no code, we can create basic and even complicated applications.

  You can immediately select the Model-driven app whenever we are creating an app to manage a complex process like Employee Onboarding, Product Sales, Leave Approval, and so on.

  The most significant fact about this app is that a user cannot construct a model-driven program without using Microsoft Dataverse. So, to use it, Dataverse is required.

  Configuring Power Apps' forms, processes, and some business rules require Microsoft Dataverse. The Model-driven app can be made by anyone using the Power Apps site.

- **Cards (preview):** Cards (preview) are mini applications that don't require any coding knowledge or IT skills and may be utilized in a variety of applications.

  Through Power Platform connectors, you can quickly build and develop cards that can surface business data, or you may utilize your own business logic for further customization.

- **Microsoft Dataverse:** The data platform included with Power Apps, called Dataverse, enables you to model and store business data. It serves as the foundation for the development of Dynamics 365 apps, including those for sales, customer service, field service, marketing, and project service automation. Your data is already present in Dataverse if you are a Dynamics 365 customer.

  You can use Dataverse to safely store and manage data in a collection of pre-built and custom tables, and you may add columns as you need them.

NOTE:

Previously, there were three different categories of Power Apps. But it's been updated now. Before, there was a Portal or Website app in addition to the Canvas and Model-driven apps. However, Power Pages are increasingly being used as a reference.

What is Power Pages?

Microsoft Power Pages is a low-code, secure, enterprise-grade SaaS platform for building, hosting, and managing contemporary external-facing company websites.

Power Pages gives you the ability to quickly build, configure, and publish websites that function across web browsers and devices whether you are a low-code creator or a professional developer.

Working with Power Apps connectors

Another significant component of Power Apps is data. We cannot create any bespoke Power Apps application without data and data sources. Data sources and connectors are important to build the application.

In essence, the data is stored on a data source (such as SharePoint, Dataverse, Excel, OneDrive, and so on.) and connected to the app through a connector. Moreover, we can link the app to the On-premises data source.

Certain Power Applications connectors are in high demand. Office 365 Users, Dataverse, SharePoint, Azure AD, SQL Server, Office 365 Outlook, and so on.

To create a new connection in Power Apps, go to **Apps** | Click on **Connections** as illustrated in the following figure:

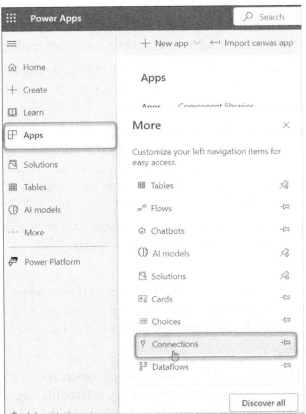

Figure 8.1: Power Apps Connectors

You can view many connections like **Azure, Bing Maps, Dataverse, SharePoint, MSN Weather,** and so on, as shown in the following figure:

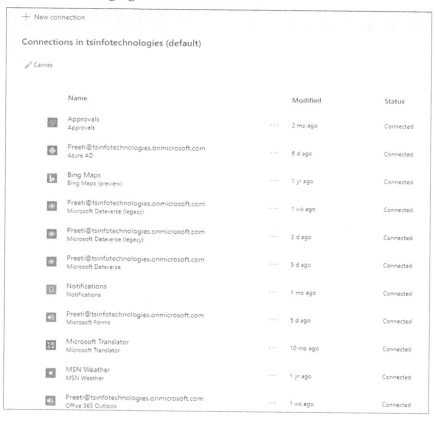

*Figure 8.2: **Various** Connectors in Power Apps*

How to connect Power Apps with various connectors

We can connect Power Apps to several well-known Data connectors. The following sections lists a few of them.

Excel

One of the data sources in Power Apps is Excel. Data can be stored in an Excel spreadsheet, and the app can be linked to this excel data source.

Go to the **Data** tab (from the left menu) and click **+ Add data** to link the Excel data source. In the search box or by expanding the Connectors section, choose **Excel** or **Import from Excel** as seen in the figure:

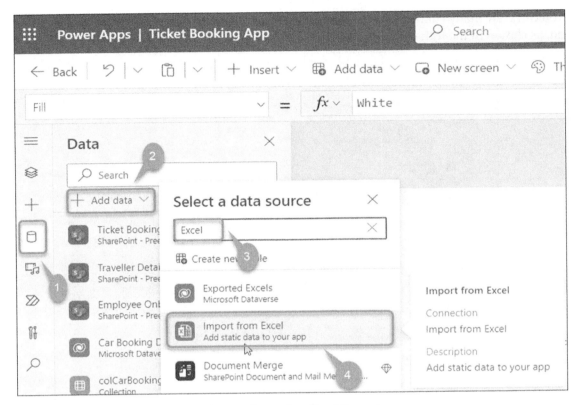

Figure 8.3: Power Apps Excel Connector

SharePoint

Power Apps frequently use the connector for SharePoint Data source. Company's data is stored in a list or document library on SharePoint, and it is linked to the app using a connector called SharePoint.

Go to the **Data** tab (from the left menu) | Click on **+ Add data** | Search **SharePoint** in the search box to link the **SharePoint** data source.

Afterwards, we can use a new or pre-existing SharePoint connection to connect to it. Then, to link our SharePoint site to the app, we can select a list and our SharePoint site as shown in the following figure:

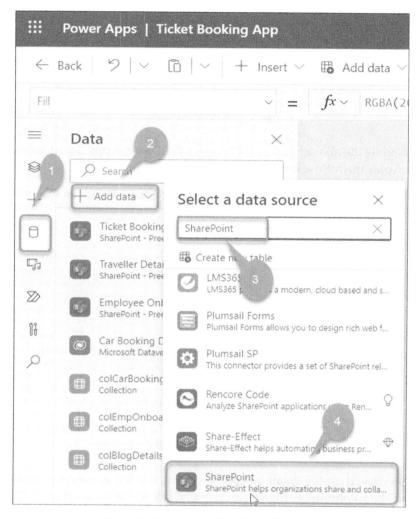

Figure 8.4: *Power Apps SharePoint Connector*

How to integrate SharePoint with Power Apps

In the next step we will create an app from the SharePoint list. That means how we can integrate the SharePoint list with Power Apps. Refer to the instructions below to achieve it:

We have a SharePoint list named **Blog post Scheduler** having different types of columns such as: **Blog Title** (Default one), **Blog Status** (Choice column), **Blog type** (Choice column), **Draft Date and Publish Date** (Date and time column), as displayed in the following figure:

Figure 8.5: *SharePoint List*

Now, we will integrate the above SharePoint list with the Power Apps. To integrate a SharePoint list with Power Apps, the follow the given steps:

1. On the SharePoint list, click on **Integrate | Power Apps | Create an app**. As illustrated in the following figure:

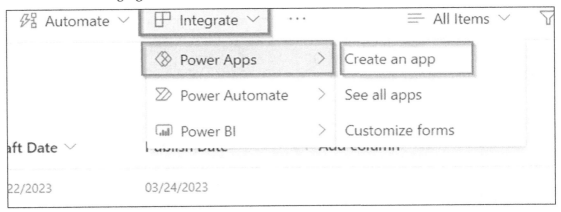

Figure 8.6: *Integrate SharePoint with Power Apps*

2. Once you clicked on the **Create an app,** it will ask to give a name to build a custom app based on SharePoint list using Power Apps. Click on **Create**, as shown in the following figure:

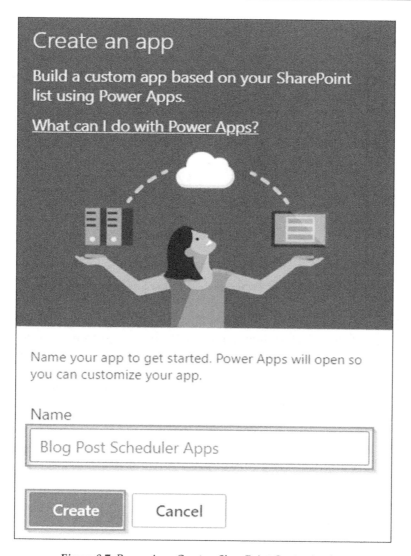

Figure 8.7: *Power Apps Create a SharePoint Customize App*

3. It will redirect to the Power Apps custom app that contains 3 different screens with various functionalities. The three screens are as follows:

   a. **Browse Screen**: This screen has a gallery that displays all the items that are retrieved from the SharePoint list. Along with this, the screen includes a **Search bar** to search the contents, a **Refresh icon** to refresh the data source, a **Sort-updown icon** to display the items by sorting them, an **Add icon** to add a new item to the list, and a **Navigation arrow** to navigate to another screen (that is Details screen), as illustrated in the following figure:

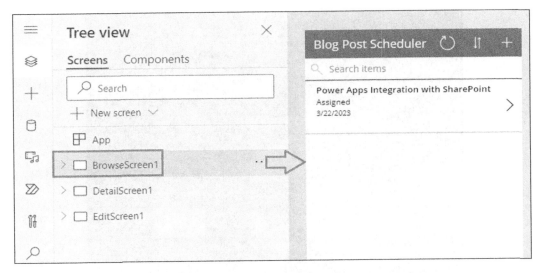

Figure 8.8: Power Apps Browse Screen

b. **Details Screen:** This screen has a Power Apps display form that will display the details of the selected item. Along with this, the screen has three more options such as **Navigation arrow** to navigate to the previous screen, a **Trash icon** to remove the details or item from the app as well as from the list, and an **Edit icon** to edit the details of the item by navigating to another screen (That is Edit screen), as shown in the following figure:

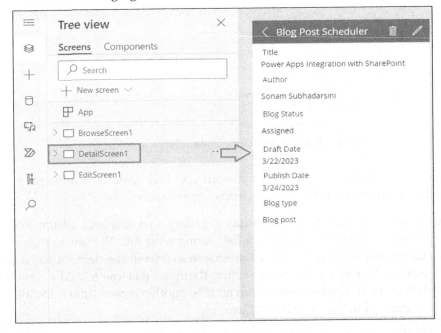

Figure 8.9: Power Apps Detail Screen

c. **Edit Screen**: This screen has a Power Apps edit form that allows you to edit a selected item. Along with it, the screen has two other icons such as tick and close icons.

4. When the user clicks on the **Tick** icon, the form will submit and save into the SharePoint list. Also, the submitted data will be represented in the **Browse screen** of the custom app.

5. Similarly, when the user clicks on the **Close** icon, the form will reset and back to the previous page, as displayed in the following figure:

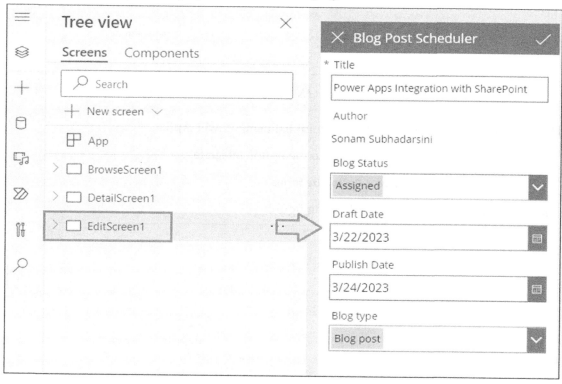

Figure 8.10: *Power Apps Edit Screen*

SharePoint lists customization with Power Apps

Customizing SharePoint lists with Power Apps is a great way to extend the functionality of a SharePoint site. Once the SharePoint list is customized (based on your requirement) with the Power Apps, it will appear as shown in the following figure:

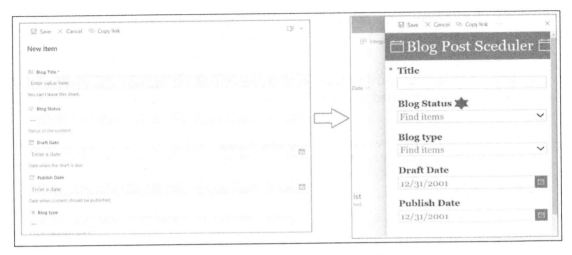

Figure 8.11: SharePoint List Customization with Power Apps

Here are the steps to customize a SharePoint list using Power Apps:

1. On the SharePoint list, navigate to the option **Integrate**.

2. Click on the **Power Apps | Customize forms**.

These steps are illustrated in the following figure:

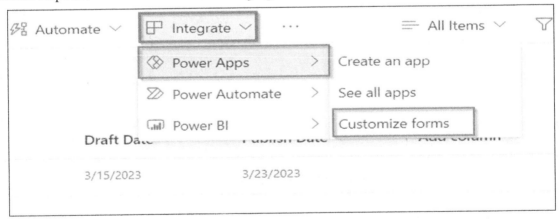

Figure 8.12: Power Apps Customization Form in SharePoint

It will redirect to the Power Apps, where we can build the SharePoint list customized form. Now you will find a simple app with one single screen called **Form screen.** Also, we will find an object named **SharePointIntegration** that defines the app we customize in the Power Apps, is a SharePoint customized list-based app as shown in the following figure:

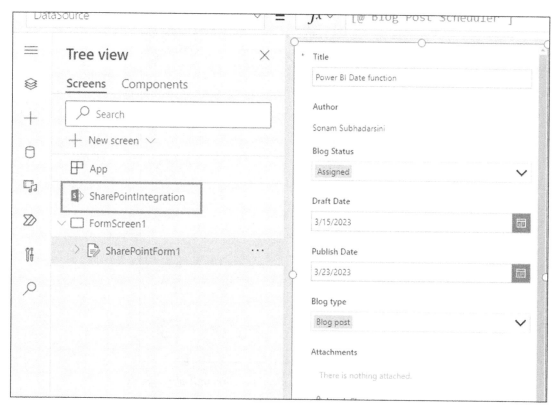

Figure 8.13: SharePoint integration form in Power Apps

Let us remove the unnecessary columns from the form, such as: **Author**, **Attachments**. Select **SharePointForm1** from the left navigation bar and click on **Edit fields** from the properties panel. There you can remove the columns from the form.

Customize the SharePoint list form in Power Apps

Let us customize the SharePoint list form in Power Apps using a **Text label control**, using the given steps:

1. Add a **Text label** control to the **FormScreen,** place the text label on top of the screen as header, and resize the **SharePointForm** to fit the screen resolution.

2. Format the **Text label** control by giving a background color, give a text for heading, font size, font style, and so on. Once the customization is done, the form will appear as the following figure:

Figure 8.14: Customize SharePoint List form in Power Apps

Power Apps Add icon to SharePoint list Customization form

It allows you to add an icon or logo as the form's heading that will be reflected on the SharePoint list as well. Let us add a **Calendar** icon on both sides of the header.

You can customize the color of the icon too.

The screen will appear as follows:

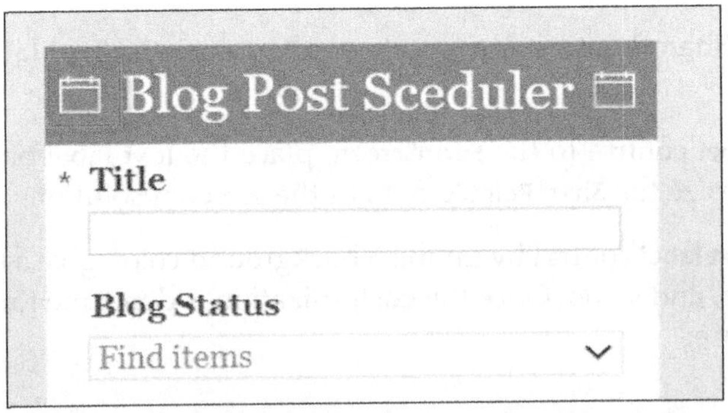

Figure 8.15: Add icon to SharePoint list customization form

Customize the SharePoint list form in Power Apps using conditional formatting

You can put conditions to the SharePoint list form. Suppose let us add a shape that will change the colors based on the **Blog Status**. That means when the user selects the blog status as planned, then the color of the shape will change according to conditions. Similarly, if the user selects any options from the **Blog Status,** the color will be changed accordingly.

To customize the form based on the conditions, add a shape (For example: **Star**) to the form screen and place it beside the **Blog Status.**

Select the **Star shape** and insert the expression below on the Shape's **Fill** property, take a look at the following steps:

```
Fill = Switch(DataCardValue3.Selected.Value,"Planned",Color.DarkBlue, "Assigned",
Color.LightBlue,  "Ready  to  publish",  Color.DarkSeaGreen,"Published",Color.
IndianRed,Color.DarkGreen)
```

Where the **DataCardValue3** defines the name of the **Blog Status's Combo box Control**. As shown in the following figure:

Figure 8.16: Power Apps Customize SharePoint List Form using Conditional Formatting

Publish the custom list form in SharePoint via Power Apps

Once the custom form is ready, it needs to be published on SharePoint. As a result, the customization will apply to the SharePoint list. To publish the custom list form into SharePoint, follow the given steps:

1. On the Power Apps studio, click on the **Save icon** to save the app.

2. Next, click on the **Publish** icon. It will ask for confirmation **Publish to SharePoint.** Select that button to publish the list form inside SharePoint. Refer to the following figure:

Figure 8.17: Publish to SharePoint

How the customization form looks in SharePoint List

Now open your SharePoint list and click on **+ New** to add an item. You can see the customization is applied to the SharePoint list via Power Apps, as shown in the following figure:

Figure 8.18: Display PowerApps Customization Form in SharePoint List

How to work with Power Apps form using SharePoint Data

In this section, we will discuss how to work with Power Apps Form using SharePoint List Data.

In Power Apps, there are two types of forms as given:

- **Edit form:** This Power Apps Edit form control allows you to make changes to one or more fields in a single record (or create a new record with default values) and save the updated information back to the original data source.

- **Display form:** This Power Apps Display form control helps to show the details of a record.

Now, we will view a scenario that shows how to work with Power Apps Form using SharePoint List Data.

Scenario:

There is a SharePoint list called **Hotel Guest Registration** having various columns (with various data types) like **First Name, Last Name, Street Address, City, Email,** and so on as illustrated in the following figure:

Figure 8.19: Create SharePoint List

1. Open Power Apps **(https://powerapps.microsoft.com/en-us/)** And create a blank canvas app.

2. Connect the SharePoint DataSource connector and choose the specific SharePoint list (Hotel Guest Registration) to the app.

3. Create four new screens and rename them as follows:

    - **Welcome Screen**

    - **Main Screen**

    - **Success Screen**

    - **Details Screen**

The following figure illustrates the same:

Figure 8.20: Create Power Apps Screens

Now we will explore all four Power Apps screens one by one.

Welcome Screen

Figure 8.19 represents the first screen, called the Welcome Screen. Here, you can see the following controls are available on this screen:

- **Welcome To the Mark Hotel**: This is a Text Label control that helps to display the Hotel name.

- **Guest Details**: This is a button input control. When a user clicks this button, it will navigate to the Details screen (where all the guest information will appear).

- **+ New Guest:** This is a button input control. When a user clicks this button, it will navigate to the Main Screen (where a user can register or book the room).

- The following code snippet represents the code that is used for **+ New Guest** button (**OnSelect** property):

```
OnSelect = Navigate('Main Screen')
```

- **Main Screen:** This is the second screen in Power Apps where a user can enter the record using the Power Apps Edit form. Refer to the following figure to know more details about this screen:

Figure 8.21: *Power Apps Welcome screen*

Main Screen

Case 1(What happens when we click on the **+ New Guest** button):

- Suppose a user clicked on the **+ New Guest** button (from the Welcome screen). The user will be redirected to the second screen named **Main Screen**.

- This screen has a Power Apps Edit form where a user can enter details like **First Name, Last Name, Street Address**, and so on.

- Finally, when the user taps on the **Submit** button, all the user entries will be stored in the specific SharePoint list (Hotel Guest Registration).

The following Power Apps controls are available on the second screen:

- **Guest Registration Form:** This is a Label control that helps to display the form name.

- **Refresh:** This is a Power Apps Refresh icon that helps to reset the edit form when user taps on it.

  First Name, Last Name, Street Address, and so on: These are the SharePoint columns retrieved from the specified SharePoint list. According to your SharePoint Column data types, the fields will display with the specific Power Apps input control. For example, as the Check-in Date is a Date time column in SharePoint list, that is why this field is displaying with a Date picker control by default in the Power Apps Edit form.

- **Submit:** This is a button control that helps to submit the user entry in the SharePoint list.

The following figure displays the various controls available:

Guest Registration Form

First Name	Last Name
Marie	Gold

Street Address	City
123 5C	America

Email	Contact
Gold@gmail.com	3267284637

Check-in Date	Check-out Date
3/22/2023	3/23/2023

Room Type	Free Shuttle Service
Double	Off

Submit

Figure 8.22: Power Apps Main Screen

The Power Apps formulas that we have used on the **Main Screen** are as follows:

Refresh

Select the Refresh icon and apply the code below on its **OnSelect** property as:

```
OnSelect = ResetForm(Form1);
```

Where,

ResetForm: The **ResetForm** function restores a form's contents to their original state, prior to any changes made by the user.

Form1: Power Apps Edit form name.

As illustrated in the following figure:

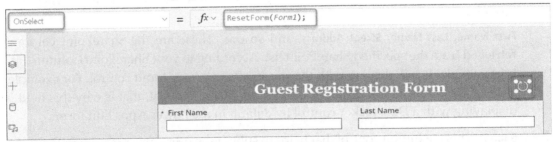

Figure 8.23: Refresh Power Apps Form

Submit

Select the Submit button and apply the code below on its **OnSelect** property as:

OnSelect = SubmitForm(Form1);

where,

SubmitForm: Any changes made to a Form control can be saved to the data source by using the **SubmitForm** function in the **OnSelect** property of a Button control.

Form1: Power Apps Edit form name.

As shown in the following figure:

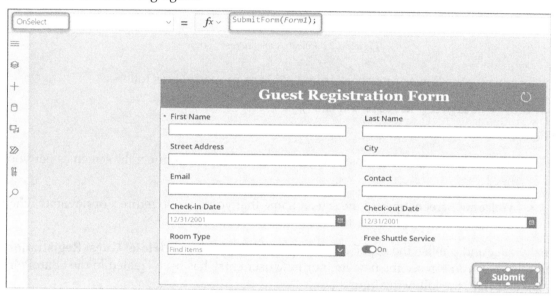

Figure 8.24: *Submit Power Apps Form*

Success Screen

Once the user taps on the Submit button (from the Main Screen), the user is redirected to the next screen that is **Success Screen**. This screen displays the successful message to user as **Your Form has been Submitted Successfully**.

The Power Apps input controls that are available on the success screen are given here:

Check icon: This is a Power Apps icon that helps to display a check mark on the screen.

Your Form has been Submitted Successfully: This is a Label control that displays the successful message.

Back icon: This is a Power Apps back icon that helps to redirect to the specific screen.

The following figure illustrates the same:

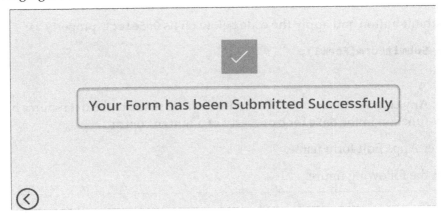

Figure 8.25: Power Apps Success Screen

The formula for the Power Apps back icon (**OnSelect** property) is as follows:

OnSelect = Navigate('Welcome Screen')

Where,

- **Navigate**: This Power Apps Navigate function helps to redirect the screen as per your need.

- **Welcome Screen:** Specify the screen name that you want to redirect or navigate when user taps on it. In our case, this is the first screen.

Finally, save and publish the app. Go to the specific SharePoint list (**Hotel Guest Registration**) and refresh it. You can see the new item or new user entry has been created in the SharePoint list, as shown in the following figure:

Hotel Guest Registration ☆ ⊙

First Name	Last Name	Street Address	City	Email	Contact	Room Number	Check-in Date	Check-out Date
Peter	Crush	15 Rue de Verdun	France	Peter@gmail.com	4864783371	M-101	03/15/2023	03/16/2023
Jaffery	Archery	3559 avenue Royale	Canada	Jaffery@hotmail.com	4956739287	M-102	03/16/2023	03/18/2023
Smith	RD	67 Marloo Street	Australia	RD@gmail.com	3576338364	M-103	03/19/2023	03/20/2023
Zakir	Patel	Apt 3B	America	ZPatel@hotmail.com	4752847848	M-104	03/20/2023	03/21/2023
Stane	MC	123 Dreamland Street	Brazil	StaneM@gmail.com	1246377450	M-105	03/21/2023	03/23/2023
Marie	Gold	123 SC	America	Gold@gmail.com	3267284637	M-106	03/22/2023	03/23/2023

Figure 8.26: Refresh SharePoint List

By using the preceding process, we can create a new item in SharePoint list by using a Power Apps Edit form and a Button control.

Case 2:

In this case, we will check how to work with a Power Apps Display form.

From the first screen (**Welcome Screen**), click on the **Guest Details** button. When we click on this button, it redirects to the last screen, that is **Details Screen**.

The following code is used for **Guest Details** button (**OnSelect** property):

```
OnSelect = Navigate('Details Screen')
```

Where,

Details Screen: This is the third screen in Power Apps, as illustrated in the following figure:

Figure 8.27: Click Guest Details from Welcome Screen

Details Screen

Figure 8.26 represents the **Details Screen,** where you can see all the guest details or information using a Power Apps Display form.

Here, *Figure 8.26* represents a Power Apps Vertical Gallery, and *Figure 8.27* represents a Power Apps Display form.

For example, let us suppose a user wants to view the information of **Room Number: M-104**, then he/she will click on the navigation icon. Once the user clicks on the icon, the specific guest information will display in the display form as shown in the following figure:

MARK GUEST DETAILS

Room Number: M-101	>	First Name	Last Name
Room Number: M-102	>	Zakir	Patel
Room Number: M-103	>	Street Address	City
Room Number: M-104	>	Apt 3B	America
Room Number: M-105	>	Email	Contact
Room Number: M-106	>	ZPatel@hotmail.com	4752847848

Check-in Date 3/20/2023   Check-out Date 3/21/2023

Figure 8.28: Click Navigate button to view the item details

The following codes are applied on the navigation screen:

Next Navigation icon: When a user clicks on the next icon of a specific record (from the gallery), the guest details will appear in the display form. For this, select the next navigation icon and apply the code on its **OnSelect** property as given:

```
OnSelect = Navigate(

   'Details Screen',

  ScreenTransition.Fade,

  {selectedId: Gallery1.Selected.ID}

)
```

Where,

- **Details Screen:** Current screen name

- **selectedId:** Here, we have created a context variable. So, provide a content variable name.

- **Gallery1:** Specify the Gallery control name

- **ID:** SharePoint list ID column

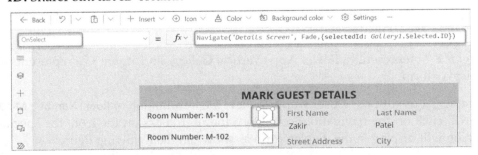

Figure 8.29: Power Apps Next Navigation Icon

- **Next Navigation icon color change**: Whenever a user taps on the next navigation icon, it changes color to Blue. For this, select the next navigation icon and apply the code below on its **Color** property as:

```
Color = If(
    ThisItem.IsSelected,
    Color.Blue,
    Color.Coral
)
```

where,

Blue, Coral: This is the color you need to provide based on your condition. As displayed in the following figure:

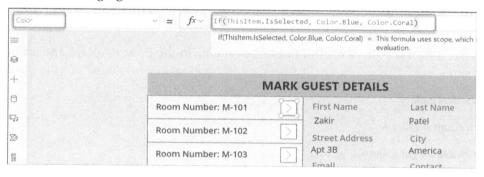

Figure 8.30: Provide color to navigation button

Moreover, if you want to add more SharePoint list fields inside the Power Apps Display form, select the Power Apps Display form | Click **Edit fields** from the **Properties** pane | Tap on **+ Add field** and insert the SharePoint fields as per your need, as shown in the following figure:

Figure 8.31: Add Fields to Power Apps Display Form

In this approach, we can use Power Apps Forms using SharePoint Online list.

Working with Power Apps Gallery Control

A control called Power Apps Gallery can hold numerous entries from a database, each containing different types of data.

A gallery control can display collections of data and handle multiple Power Apps input controls.

Consider the scenario where we want to use a gallery control to show some **Gadget Details**. After that, we may display all the relevant information, such as the Gadget Name, Gadget Id, Gadget Color, Quantity, Gadget Sales Date, Total Sales, and so on.

If we alter the template in any way, the entire gallery control will be affected.

Items, Selected, Default, AllItems, DelayItemLoading, Fill, LoadingSpinner, NavigationStep, Selectable, ShowScrollbar, ShowNavigation, TemplateSize, Transition, WrapCount, Visible, and so on, are some of the major gallery control properties.

There are six different gallery control options available in the Power Apps Canvas app. They as follows:

- **Vertical gallery**
- **Horizontal gallery**
- **Flexible height gallery**
- **Blank vertical gallery**
- **Blank horizontal gallery**
- **Blank flexible height gallery**

This is illustrated in the following figure:

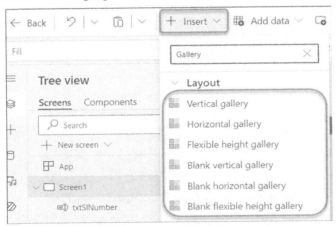

Figure 8.32: Various Power Apps Gallery Controls

To insert any gallery control in the app, expand the **+ Insert** tab | Search **Gallery** in the search box | Expand **Layout** | Select the gallery as per your requirement, as illustrated in the following figure:

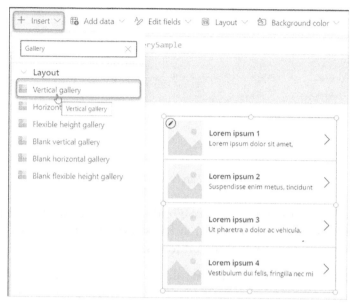

Figure 8.33: Insert Power Apps Vertical gallery control

Connect and use SharePoint with Power Apps Gallery Control

Here, we will look at how to connect and use a Power Apps Gallery control with a SharePoint list.

For example:

Figure 8.32 represents a SharePoint list named **TSInfo Attachments**. This list has various columns with different data types, such as:

- **ID:** Number

- **Title:** Single line of text

- **Attachment Types:** Choice

- **Attachment Costs:** Currency

- **Attachment Created Date:** Date and time

- **Book Author:** Person/Group

- **IsReceived:** Yes/No

Also, you can see that the SharePoint list has some attachment records like **PowerApps Beginners**, **Power BI Reports**, and so on, as shown in the following figure:

TSInfo Attachments							
ID	Title	Attachment Types	Attachment Costs	Attachment Created Date	Book Author	IsReceived	
1	PowerApps Beginners	Microsoft Document	$2,000.00	04/13/2022	Preeti Sahu	✓
2	Power BI Reports	PPT	$1,500.00	04/25/2022	Preeti Sahu	
3	Power BI Beginners	PDF	$3,500.00	05/22/2022	Sonam Subhadarsini	✓
4	PowerApps Sales Sheet	Excel	$1,000.00	05/02/2022	Haripriya Dhali	
5	SharePoint Beginner	PDF	$3,500.00	05/15/2022	Bijay Kumar Sahoo	✓
6	PowerApps Sample PDF	Excel	$4,000.00	05/08/2022	Sonam Subhadarsini	✓
7	Sample PDF	PDF	$2,000.00	05/10/2022	Bijay Kumar Sahoo	

Figure 8.34: SharePoint Online List

We utilize the SharePoint list mentioned above to display every attachment in a Power Apps Gallery control. Additionally, users can search for a certain document and display it in the gallery control if they want to view that file or document.

Using the above SharePoint list, we display all the attachments in a Power Apps Gallery control. Also, if a user wants to view a particular file or document, they can search the specific document and display it in the gallery control.

For example, in the first image given below, it shows all the attachments that are available in the SharePoint list. When we searched documents related to PowerApps (in the second image), it showed us all the attachments that are related to PowerApps only as shown in the following figure:

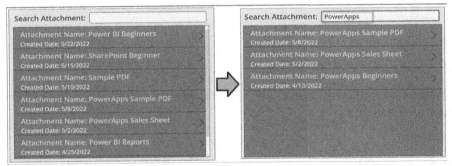

Figure 8.35: Search Document and Filter Power Apps Gallery

We can view the attachments in Power Apps gallery control following the given steps:

Step 1:

First, we need to connect the SharePoint connector and SharePoint list to Power Apps. To connect the SharePoint with Power Apps gallery, go to **Data** tab (from the left navigation) |

Click on **+ Add data** | Search **SharePoint** in the search box | Click on **SharePoint.** This is shown in the following figure:

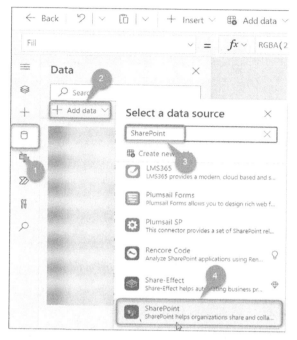

Figure 8.36: Add SharePoint Connector to Power Apps

Step 2:

Add a new SharePoint connection (if it is a first-time user) using valid Microsoft 365 credentials. Otherwise, click and connect on the existing SharePoint connection, as illustrated in the following figure:

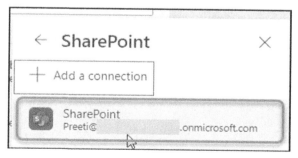

Figure 8.37: Add a new or existing SharePoint Connection

Step 3:

Once the SharePoint connection is done, you need to connect to your SharePoint site. Provide the **SharePoint URL** for the location of your list and connect it. Further, you can get your specific

SharePoint site (here, **PowerApps**) under the section of the **Recent site**. Select it, as illustrated in the following figure:

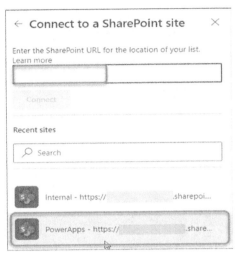

Figure 8.38: Connect SharePoint Site

Step 4:

Then you will be redirected to the list pane where you need to choose your SharePoint list. Select **TSInfo Attachments** and then click on **Connect,** as shown in the following figure:

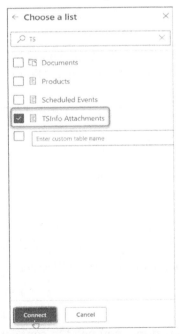

Figure 8.39: Choose SharePoint List and Connect

Finally, the SharePoint list (**TSInfo Attachments**) has been connected to Power Apps app as shown in the following figure:

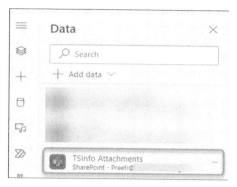

Figure 8.40: SharePoint List Added in Power Apps

Step 5:

Insert a **Text label** control where the user can search any files or documents. Expand **+ Insert** | Select **Text input** under the **Popular** section.

Once it is added to the screen, you can rename it to **txtSearchAttach**. Additionally, you can provide the background color to the text input. This step is illustrated in the following figure:

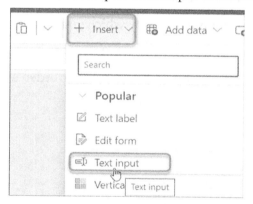

Figure 8.41: Insert Power Apps Text input Control

Step 6:

Next, add a vertical gallery control and select the gallery **layout** to **Title and subtitle.** Also, you can design your gallery control by using various properties like Color, Background color, Font, Font size, and so on.

Then, select the gallery and apply the code below on its **Items** property as given in the following code:

```
Items = SortByColumns(

    Filter(

        'TSInfo Attachments',

        txtSearchAttach.Text in Title

    ),

    "AttachmentCreatedDate",
    SortOrder.Descending

)
```

where,

SortByColumns: The table can also be sorted using the **SortByColumns** function based on one or more columns.

Filter: The filter function locates table records that matches with the formula. You can identify a set of records using Filter and eliminate that do not meet one or more criteria.

TSInfo Attachments: SharePoint list name

TxtSearchAttach: Text input control name

Title: Specify the SharePoint column name by which you want to search

AttachmentCreatedDate: SharePoint list Date column name

SortOrder.Descending: A table is sorted in descending order using the Sort function. As illustrated in the following figure:

Figure 8.42: Filter Power Apps Gallery Control

Step 7:

Select the **Title** from the gallery control, and apply the following code on its **Text** property as:

Text = "Attachment Name: " & ThisItem.Title

where,

"Attachment Name: ": This text will be displayed in the title box in gallery control.

Title: As we want to display the list title value in this title box, that is why we put **ThisItem. Title**, illustrated in the following figure:

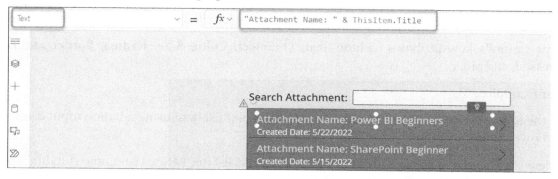

Figure 8.43: Add SharePoint Title value to Text input control

Step 8:

Similarly, in the subtitle box, we want to view the attachment created date. Select the **Subtitle** in the gallery control and apply the formula below on its **Text** property as:

Text = "Created Date: " & ThisItem.'Attachment Created Date'

where,

"Created Date: ": This text will be display in the subtitle box in the gallery control.

'Attachment Created Date': As we want to display the list created date value in this subtitle box, that is why we put **ThisItem.'Attachment Created Date'.** And shown in the following figure:

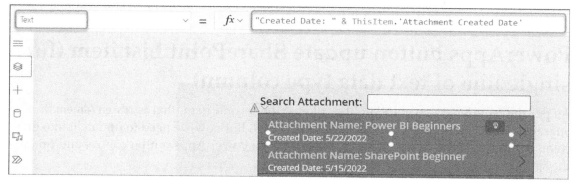

Figure 8.44: Add SharePoint Date Value to Text input control

Working with Power Apps button

Power Apps Button control is a type of input control that helps to perform an action when a user clicks or taps on it.

A user can tap on the PowerApps Button control to interact with the app. It is a form of input control. This implies that when a user clicks the button, something will happen within the app.

This control's key attributes include **Text, OnSelect, Color, Size, Radius, Border radius, Pressed,** and others.

For Example:

In the following scenario, we will update the SharePoint list item using a button input control in PowerApps.

There is a SharePoint list named **Car Rental Services**. This list has various columns with different Data types like **Car Name, Car Type, Daily Price, Rent Date,** and so on. Refer to the *Figure 8.43*.

Among all these columns, we have two more columns named **Location (Choice)** and **Car Color (Single line of text).** And we update these two column values using Power Apps Button control. So, let us see how we can achieve this as shown in the following figure:

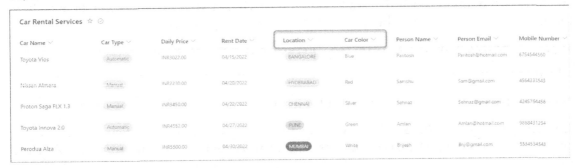

Figure 8.45: Create Different Columns in SharePoint Online List

PowerApps button update SharePoint List item (for single line of text data type column)

As per the requirement, we update the color of the second item, that is **Nissan Almera**. In the SharePoint list, you can see the color of that car is Red. But now we need to update it into grey color. For this purpose, in Power Apps, we can take a Power Apps button control and update the specific value by clicking on it.

To work with this in Power Apps, we insert a Gallery control and a Button. Change the button Text property to **Grey**.

Refer to the following figure that shows how the app looks like in Power Apps:

Figure 8.46: *Power Apps Button Update SharePoint List Item*

Ensure that you place the button control within the initial section of the gallery. Once you have added the button to the gallery, it will be displayed for each item within the gallery. As shown in the following figure:

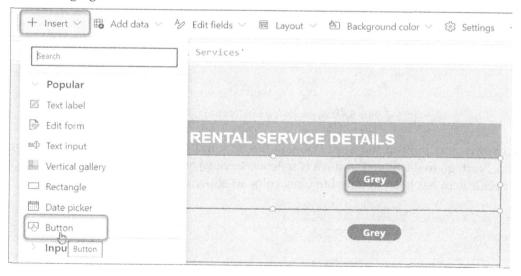

Figure 8.47: *Insert Power Apps Button Control*

Select the **Button control (Grey)** and set its **OnSelect** property to the code below:

```
OnSelect = Patch(
    <Car Rental Services>,
    ThisItem,
    {<Car Color>: "Grey"}
)
```

where,

- **Patch:** Power Apps Patch function helps to modify or create one or more records in a data source, or merges records outside of a data source.

- **'Car Rental Services':** Provide the SharePoint List name.

- **'Car Color':** Single line of text column from SharePoint list.

- **"Grey":** Specify the value that you want to update in the SharePoint list. The following figure shows displayed screen:

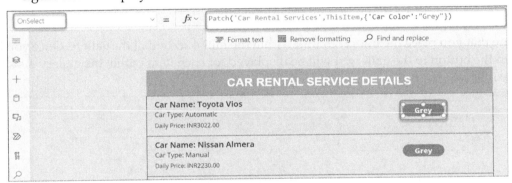

Figure 8.48: Apply Code on Button's OnSelect Property

Finally, save and publish the app. Preview the app and then click on the second item **Grey** button. Next, go to the SharePoint list (**Car Rental Services)** and refresh the list once. You can see the specific item has been updated to Grey color, as shown in the following figure:

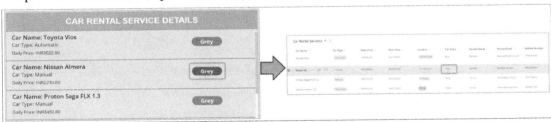

Figure 8.49: Click button and update the value in SharePoint List

Power Apps button update SharePoint List item (for choice data type column)

Next, we will learn how to update a SharePoint list choice column using Power Apps Button Control.

In the SharePoint list, you can observe that there is a **Choice** column called **Location.** If we need to update a specific location of a particular item, we can use the Power Apps Button control and make it possible.

In the same process, we add another button inside the gallery control and change its **Text** property to **BANGALORE**.

Select the button control (**BANGALORE**) and use the code below on its **OnSelect** property as:

```
OnSelect = Patch(

    ‹Car Rental Services›,

    ThisItem,

    {

        Location: {

            Value: "BANGALORE",

                        ‹@odata.type': "#Microsoft.Azure.Connectors.SharePoint.
SPListExpandedReference"

        }

    }

)
```

where,

- **Location**: SharePoint list Choice column name.

- **"BANGALORE"**: Specify the choice value that you want to update in the SharePoint list. As illustrated in the following figure:

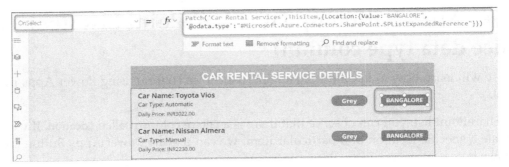

Figure 8.50: *Click Power Apps Button and Update SharePoint Choice Column*

Finally, save and publish the app. Preview the app and then click on the fourth item **BANGALORE** button. Next, go to the SharePoint list (**Car Rental Services**) and refresh the list once. You can see the specific item has been updated to **BANGALORE** location as illustrated in the following figure:

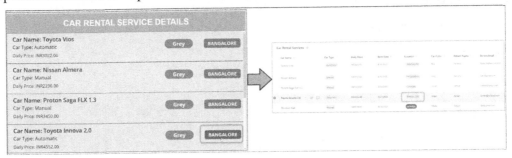

Figure 8.51: *Update SharePoint Choice Value on Power Apps Button Click*

Save, Publish, and Preview Power Apps

Once our app is completed, it is essential to save and publish it. Failure to do so will result in an app that lacks any of the components or functionalities you have built. Let us take a look at how to save the app.

Save Power Apps

In Power Apps, to save an app, we can directly tap on the **Save** icon button (from the top right corner). If we have previously saved our app, then we can only use the **Save** option. The app will prompt us to add a Version note or comment when we save it.

When we expand the **Save** button, three types of save options are available as follows:

- **Save with version notes:** About the updates you have made, save and add notes.

- **Save as:** Create a copy of the app by saving it under a different name.

- **Download a copy:** We can download a local copy of the app.

This is illustrated in the following figure:

Figure 8.52: Save Power Apps App

Power Apps also provides an automatic saving feature, which saves the app every two minutes. This means that once the application has been initially saved, Power Apps will continue to periodically save new versions without the user having to push or tap the **Save** button.

By navigating to **Setting | General**, authors can enable or disable the **Auto save** feature. As displayed in the following figure:

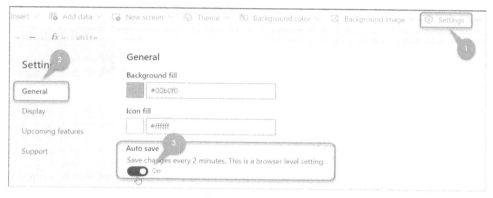

Figure 8.53: Enable Auto save feature in Power Apps

NOTE: Every time you publish a canvas app, it will be updated to run on the most recent version of Power Apps, giving it access to all the newest features and performance improvements we have implemented since you last published. If you haven't published an update in a while, you will probably notice an improvement in performance right away by doing so right away.

Some information will be locally kept on users' devices in the browser cache to enable users to obtain app details more quickly when the app opens. Details about the app, environment, and connection will all be stored. Depending on the storage limitations of each browser, this data will continue to be stored there. According to each browser's instructions, users can clear saved data.

Publish Power Apps

Once you have saved the Power Apps, you need to publish it. The environment will publish the version of your application.

To publish the Power Apps:

1. Click on the **Publish** button (Right side of the **Save** button). Also, you can use *Ctrl + Shift + P* button to publish an app.

2. In the Publish window, click on the **Publish this version** button as shown in the following figure:

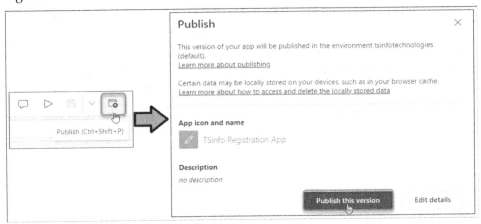

Figure 8.54: Publish Power Apps App

Preview Power Apps

The user can view and use the app while it is in preview mode before publishing. The **Preview** button allows us to test out things swiftly. This mode enables the user to check whether the application is functioning properly or not.

Also, we can test the app directly on the canvas by double-clicking to write in controls and holding down the **Alt** key to activate buttons and other controls as illustrated in the following figure:

Figure 8.55: Preview Power Apps App

Share Power Apps with other members

Next, we will see how to share Power Apps app with other users or members:

- When the customized Canvas app is complete, we may distribute it to other teams inside our company. For that, we must grant users the ability to change, run, and re-share the application.

- One of the most crucial things we should be aware of is the necessity of saving the app in the cloud (not locally) and publishing it before sharing it with others.

- Office 365 Groups include the SharePoint Group. Now, PowerApps only allows us to share an app with specific users or security groups in Azure Active Directory.

- There is presently no solution in PowerApps to meet your demands if you wish to share an app with an SP Group (Office 365 Group).

- As a substitute, you may think about creating a Security Group in your Azure Active Directory, adding your end users to it, and then sharing your canvas app with this Security Group. You can refer to this link for more details: **https://learn.microsoft.com/en-us/power-apps/maker/canvas-apps/share-app**

If you are inside the current Power Apps Canvas app, then you can directly click on the **Share icon** from the top right of the page to share the app with others or members as shown in the following figure:

Figure 8.56: Share Power Apps App with other users

The other method, open the Power Apps | Select **Apps** (from the left navigation) |Select the app to share and click on **More commands** options (...) | Click on **Share**. Also, we can directly share the app from the top Command bar as shown in the following figure:

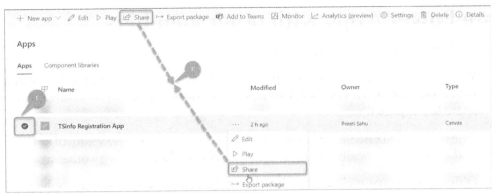

Figure 8.57: Different ways to Share Power Apps

On the Sharing screen, enter any username, email address, or Everyone to share the app with.

Enter any username or email address, or Everyone to share the app with on the Sharing screen. Also, provide an Email message and upload an image to showcase what your app looks like (if necessary).

If you want to send an email invitation to the new users while sharing, then check on the **Send an email invitation to new users**, so that the specific user(s) will get a sharing notification.

We can select the **Co-owner** option to grant the ability to use, change, and re-share the app to a specified person. Finally, press the **Share** button, the screen displays as shown in the following figure:

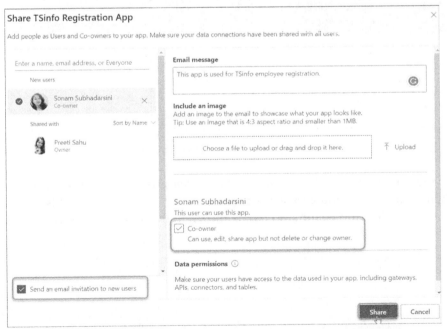

Figure 8.58: Enable Co-owner and Send email invitation in Sharing method

Finally, you will get a success sharing notification on the top of the page like **All permission changes were saved successfully**, as illustrated in the following figure:

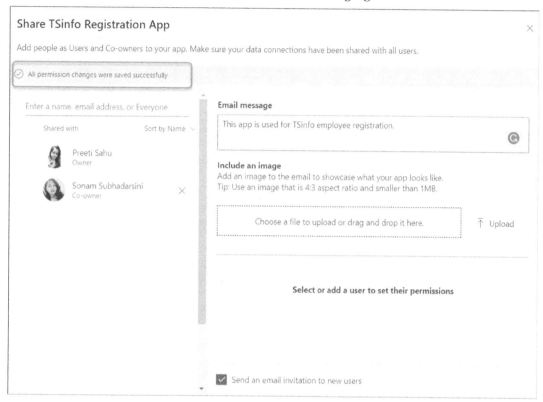

Figure 8.59: Get Successful Permission Notification

Two users cannot edit the app simultaneously. The other user can only run the app while the editor is working on it, they are unable to make changes.

What is SharePoint Power Apps Delegation

We must understand the significance of *Delegate* before working with the Power Apps Delegation. Delegate is the act of assigning someone a specific assignment to complete.

In fact, PowerApps Delegation includes assigning the data processing to specific data sources, such as SharePoint, Excel, SQ Server, Dataverse, and so on, after the data has been obtained from those sources.

When there are numerous data sets accessible in the data sources, but they cannot load simultaneously, Power Apps Delegations occur. Power Apps can retrieve a set amount of data, which speeds up the program.

The Power Apps Delegation limit is set to 500 by default. This means it can only retrieve 500 items at a time from any of the data sources. The user will receive a warning message called a Delegation warning if the item limit exceeds 500.

You will get a message like: **Delegation warning. The highlighted part of this formula might not work correctly with column "Title" on large data sets.** This is illustrated in the following figure:

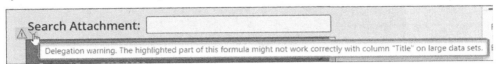

Figure 8.60: SharePoint Power Apps Delegation

We can also increase the delegation limit from 500 to 2000. As a result, it may now take up to 2000 items from the data source, rather than just 500.

Go to **Settings** | Click on **General** | Set 2000 under **Data row limit** section as shown in the following figure:

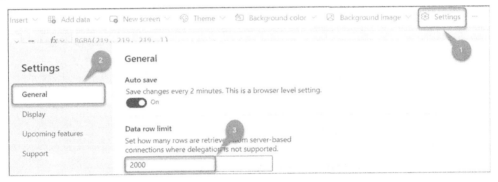

Figure 8.61: Set Data row limit in Power Apps Settings

Many data sources are provided for use in Power Apps. A few of them can be delegated. These data sources include Dynamic 365, SharePoint, SQL Server, and Dataverse.

The following Power Apps features can also be delegated: Search, Sort, Sum, Max, Filter, LookUp, and so on.

Visit this page to learn more about Power Apps Delegation, including how to avoid it and possible solutions: **https://docs.microsoft.com/en-us/powerapps/maker/canvas-apps/delegation-overview**

Conclusion

Power Apps is a tool for building any business application that is subscription-based. With the help of the Power Apps Studio tool, anyone can create any kind of app. Also, we may use any browser, desktop, or mobile device to execute the software.

This chapter covers every aspect of power apps, including their types and their advantages. Also, we will learn some tips on how to design, save, publish, preview, and share a canvas app in Power Apps quickly and efficiently.

We have also learned how to use Power Apps to integrate SharePoint, how to interact with PowerApps forms using SharePoint, how to use a Power Apps gallery control and button, and much more.

In the next chapter, we will understand all about Power Automate or Microsoft Flow.

Points to remember

- You can rapidly read and comprehend some of the chapter's most crucial learning points like:

  o Power Apps, a Microsoft product, helps develop customized apps using the organization's data. We can quickly build unique apps with the help of many data connectors, such as Microsoft Dataverse, online data sources, and on-premises data sources, including SharePoint, OneDrive, Excel Spreadsheet, SQL Server, JIRA, Microsoft 365, and Dynamic 365.

- There are four various components in Power Apps. Such as:

  o Canvas app

  o Model-driven app

  o Cards (preview)

  o Dataverse

- Connectors and data sources are essential for building the application. Essentially, the information is kept on a data source (such as SharePoint, Dataverse, Excel, OneDrive, and so forth) and linked to the app through a connector. Additionally, we can connect the app to the on-premises data source. There are different types of connectors that we can connect with Power Apps like:

  o Excel

  o SharePoint

  o Dataverse

  o Azure

  o Bing Maps etc.

- Also, we can integrate SharePoint with Power Apps from the SharePoint List itself.

- An excellent method to increase the functionality of a SharePoint site is by customizing SharePoint lists using Power Apps. We can save our time by integrating SharePoint list and build the app directly in Power Apps.

- Also, we can apply various conditions and publish the SharePoint list form using Power Apps.

- **Power Apps form using SharePoint Data**: Add and set up a Display form control in a canvas app to display all fields in a record. A record can be added, an edit form control can be added and configured, and you can modify any field in a record while adding a record and saving your changes back to a data source.

- Power Apps Gallery can store several database entries, each containing a different kind of data. Multiple Power Apps input controls can be managed by a gallery control, which can also display collections of data.

- We can connect and use SharePoint List with Power Apps Gallery Control.

- Power Apps Button Control is a type of input control that allows user to perform an action by clicking on it. By using this Button control, we can update the SharePoint List item (Using Various Columns like Single line of text, Choice type).

- **Save, Publish, and Preview Power Apps**: Once Power Apps app is ready, we need to save and publish the app. Otherwise, the changes will miss or not reflect to other users. Also, we can preview the app to test it.

- **Share Power Apps with Other Users**: One of the most important things we should be aware of is the requirement to publish the app first before sharing it with others and to save it in the cloud (not locally). Presently, PowerApps only enables us to share an app with Azure Active Directory security groups or individuals. To distribute the app with other members, we need to share the Power Apps.

- **SharePoint Power Apps Delegation**: Power Apps Delegations happen when multiple data sets are available in the data sources, but they cannot load at once. Power Apps can speed up the program by retrieving a predetermined amount of data.

  The default setting for the Power Apps Delegation limit is 500. As a result, it is limited to retrieving 500 items at a time from any data source. If the item limit goes over 500, the user will see a warning message called a delegation warning.

## CHAPTER 9

Power Automate

Introduction

This chapter will discuss Power Automate, the advantages of Power Automate, various types of connectors, triggers, and actions available on Power Automate, what is flow, and different types of automated flows.

Along with that, users will get to know how to create different types of flows based on SharePoint, how to share this flow with their respective colleague or team member, how to do export and import operations with a flow, turn on and off a flow, delete a flow, and so on.

Structure

This chapter contains general information about Power Automate as well as scenarios that demonstrate how it can be easily created by a user. The table of contents below is an outline of the chapter:

- Introduction to Power Automate
- Advantages of Power Automate
- Power Automate Licensing and Pricing
- What is flow?

- Different types of flows available in Power Automate

- Various connectors in Power Automate

- What are triggers and various types of actions available in Power Automate?

- Different types of flows available in Power Automate

- Create a Power Automate flow using SharePoint

- Create a manual trigger flow within Power Automate

- Create a scheduled flow in Power Automate

- Sharing a flow to another user

- Export and import Power Automate flow

- Turn On/ Turn Off a Power Automate flow

- Delete a flow in Power Automate

- SharePoint with Power Automate flow [With 10 Examples]

Objectives

This chapter will help the reader if they are new to Power Automate or have no idea what it is or how to use it.

The user will have a basic understanding of Power Automate's usage and functionality, as well as how to create a simple flow in Power Automate, after reading this entire chapter.

Users can get an idea about building conditional flows, recurring flows, sharing a flow with another, deleting a flow, and many more. Along with this, users will get ideas about creating flow with Microsoft Teams, SharePoint list, working with approval flow, and so on.

Introduction to Power Automate

Microsoft Flow, a cloud-based software application, was released in April 2016. In October 2019, Microsoft renamed the Microsoft Flow to Power Automate for branding purposes, and it is now used by over 350,000 organizations.

It is a component of the Microsoft Power Platform that enables users to automate repetitive business processes using built-in connectors such as SharePoint, Excel, Microsoft Team, Outlook, OneDrive, Google Drive, Dynamic 365, or by directly using API.

As it is a low-code or no-code environment, it enables the end user to build their flow and automate their workflow without any developer knowledge. When the automated flow is created, it will be triggered whenever a task occurs in the assigned platform, such as SharePoint, Excel, Outlook, etc.

The following figure is an example of a Power Automate cloud flow that will send an email to the specified user(s) and then update the item in the SharePoint list when an item is created or modified:

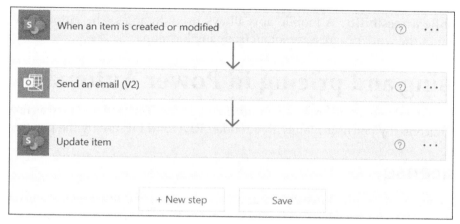

Figure 9.1: Example of an automated cloud flow

Further than basic workflow, it allows you to send a reminder or notification about a previous task, move data from system to cloud, or exchange data between systems on a schedule using triggers and actions. Once the flow is created, we can access Power Automate from the mobile app.

Advantages of Power Automate

Using automation in your business improves the efficiency of your business processes. It can also boost productivity, communication, and collaboration. Here are some of the most important advantages of using Power Automate:

- **User friendly:** This platform is a low-code or no-code-based platform that allows end users to easily set up and use the Power Automate by utilizing pre-built connectors and templates.

- **Eliminates workload**: Because the primary benefit of Power Automate is to automate repetitive tasks, it diminishes work pressure, human errors, and saves time.

- **Update daily tasks:** Using Power Automate, users can assign a priority to a business meeting or events, so that they receive an alert when a high-priority email arrives. They will never miss an email as a result of this.

- **Prebuilt templates:** With over 100 pre-built templates available in the Power Automate Platform, these can be set up without putting effort in your daily business.

- **Associate with AI and Virtual Agent:** For robotic process automation, Power Automate recently integrated with Artificial Intelligence and Power Virtual Agent.

- **Seamlessly share and transfer data:** There are over 275 connectors available in Power Automate that allow users to access data easily. They can also transfer files and folders from one location to another using connectors.

- **Mobile accessibility:** A mobile app allows users to access the automated flow and monitor the work progress remotely from any location.

Licensing and pricing in Power Automate

Each service in the Power Platform has a unique license based on its plans, such as Free, License by per user, License by per-user plan with attended RPA, and License by the per-flow plan.

Free License

This free license works with Office 365 and allows for up to 250 flows per month. However, there is a limit of 30 days of using the free trial version. RPA and AI services are not available.

License by per user (with unattended RPA)

The following list represents all the Power Automate licenses per user basis (with unattended RPA). If any user wants to buy this plan, then he/she can get all the below benefits:

- This license allows the user to create an unlimited number of cloud flows based on their needs. Users can also review their flow, but RPA and AI services are not included in this license. You can use them if you purchase them separately.

- This license costs $15 per user per month.

- It consists of prebuilt connectors, on-premises connectors, and custom connectors.

- It allows for a database capacity of 50MB and a file size of 200MB.

License by per user (with attended RPA)

The following list represents all the Power Automate licenses per user basis (with attended RPA). If any user wants to buy this plan, then he/she can get all the below benefits:

- It enables each user to create an unlimited number of cloud flows and analyze their process.

- Users can also automate legacy applications using Robotic Process Automation and Artificial Intelligence. This license costs $40 per user per month.

- This license includes 5,000 monthly service credits for AI builders, and it allows for a database capacity of 50MB and a file size of 200MB.

License by the per-flow plan

The following list represents all the Power Automate licenses per flow basis. If any user wants to buy this plan, then he/she can get all the below benefits:

- It enables the implementation of cloud flows with limited capacity for an infinite number of users in your community.

- It requires the permission of a global or billing administrator in the Microsoft 365 admin center.

- The total cost for this license begins at $500.

Click on the following link to get more ideas about Power Automate licensing and pricing (**https://powerautomate.microsoft.com/en-us/pricing/**) Provided by Microsoft.

Getting started with Power Automate

We can get Power Automate from the **https://www.office.com/** app list with our respective Microsoft credential and get the Power Automate app from the App launcher.

The following figure is what you will see once you login with Office365. You can get the Power Automate app from the App launcher:

Figure 9.2: Getting started with Power Automate

You can also browse Power Automate (**https://powerautomate.microsoft.com/en-us/**) directly by using your personal Microsoft ID and Microsoft credentials. In the following sections, we will learn how to create various types of flows in Power Automat by utilizing various connectors, triggers, actions, and templates.

What is flow?

Microsoft Flow is a cloud-based software that enables users to build and automate workflows and tasks all over various applications and services without requiring the additional support of developers. These automated workflows are known as cloud flow.

Different types of flows available in Power Automate

Microsoft Power Automate offers four types of flows: automated cloud flow, instant cloud flow, scheduled cloud flow and desktop flow. To see the different types of flow available, go to **https://flow.microsoft.com** and select **Create**, as shown:

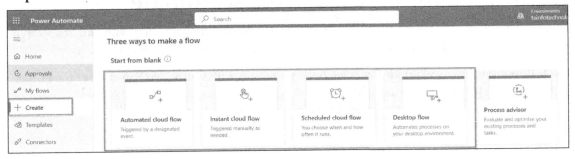

Figure 9.3: Types of flows available in Power Automate

- **Automated cloud flow**: With the automatic cloud flow, we can build automation that is triggered by a specific event, such as receiving an email notification from a specific person, creating a file in a document library, someone mentioning your company's name or a specific term in social media, and so on.

- **Instant cloud flow:** As the name indicates, it will generate an immediate flow that automates the procedure with a button tap and manually starts the flow as needed. It enables the user to operate the flow from the mobile app or the desktop. For example, we can generate a reminder for the team or a group with a push-button from the mobile app.

- **Scheduled cloud flow**: This flow is triggered by a specific date and time, allowing you to choose when and how frequently it runs, such as daily data updates to SharePoint, an excel sheet, or any database.

- **Desktop flow:** As the names suggest, we may automate repetitive processes on the web or the desktop. It enables us to begin creating desktop flows based on **Robotic Process Automation (RPA)**.

Templates available in Power Automate

In Power Automate, Microsoft provides numerous prebuilt cloud-based templates that allow us to automate our process in under a minute by adding intelligence.

Once you signed in the Power Automate, navigate to **Template.** You can find all the templates provided by Microsoft here:

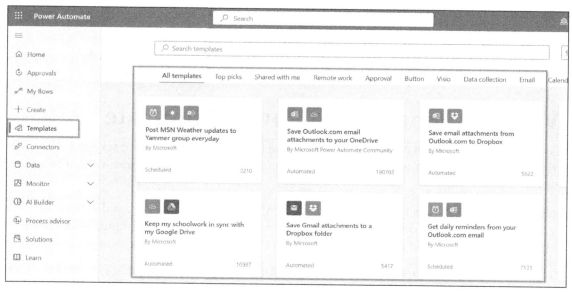

Figure 9.4: Displaying the prebuilt templates available in Power Automate

To use the prebuilt templates in your business, follow these steps:

1. Select any prebuilt template from the templates section. (Ex: Send an email to responder when response submitted in Microsoft Forms)

2. It will check for the connector's connection.

3. Click on **Continue** as shown:

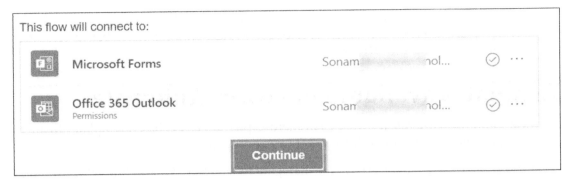

Figure 9.5: Creating flow using Power Automate prebuilt templates

4. Configure the flow as per the requirements.

5. Click on **Save and Test**. Now, the flow will automatically be triggered when a response is submitted in Microsoft Form, notifying the responder via an email.

Various connectors in Power Automate

Connectors allow you to communicate from one server to another. It is packaged with some triggers and actions in Power Automate. We can use them to create a workflow that meets our needs.

It enables users to connect their accounts and configure prebuilt triggers and actions to create workflows and apps. Connectors are divided into two categories: standard and premium, which are not included in the free licensing plan.

You can find the list of connectors in the Power Automate platform provided by Microsoft. On the Power Automate, navigate to **Connectors** as illustrated in the following figure:

Figure 9.6: Displaying connectors in Power Automate

Triggers available in Power Automate

Microsoft Power Automate provides the connectors, and the connectors (not all of them) provide the pre-defined triggers used to build a cloud flow.

A trigger is an event that starts a flow. For example, selecting a connector SharePoint will redirect you to the page where you can find all the triggers that come under that connector such as, when a file is created, when an item is deleted, when an item or a file is modified, etc.

Go to **Connectors** | **SharePoint** | **Select**.

Refer to the following figure for a better understanding:

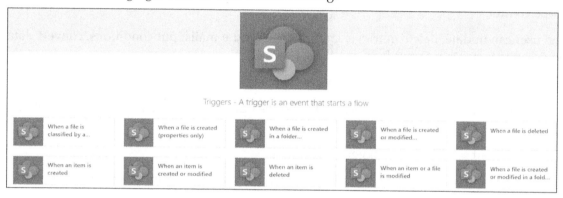

Figure 9.7: Displaying triggers available under a connector

Types of Power Automate triggers

Triggers are classified into several types based on flow types and connectors, because they serve as a starting point in the creation of a flow. Triggers come in three varieties:

- **Event trigger or automated trigger**: One of the best features of Power Automate is automated workflow. To create an automated workflow, we must use an automated trigger that will automatically start the flow when an event takes place. Some examples of the automated triggers are: When an item is created in the SharePoint list, When a new task is created in the Microsoft planner, When an HTTP request is received, When a new e-mail arrives in outlook's inbox and so on.

- **Scheduled trigger:** These triggers are used to implement a scheduled-based workflow in which the flow will automatically get triggered on a regular basis. For example, you need to send your report to the team lead on a weekly basis, you need to pay bills of your EMI on the monthly basis etc. In such cases, we can use scheduled trigger to notify the user on a specific time period.

- **Instant trigger:** The button flow or instant flow trigger contains a push button that, when pressed, triggers the flow. The flow implementation is not based on an automated process. However, the flow will run when we manually enable it. This trigger has an amazing feature that can be accessed remotely from any location.

Actions available in Power Automate

A Power Automate flow starts with a trigger and finishes with an action. A flow can include one or more actions to complete it as needed. The action will initiate once the flow has been triggered. Microsoft Power Automate includes a variety of actions. Several different actions are available for each connector.

Even Microsoft allows the user to group actions that fall under the condition action by using scope control.

The user can update, delete, retrieve, create items, send e-mails, put conditions, convert data types, and many other things by using these actions.

To find the actions under a specific connector, the following steps are:

1. On the Power Automate, click on the **Create** | Select any cloud flow (i.e., Instant cloud flow).

2. Without selecting any trigger, click on **Skip.**

3. Search for a connector name on the Search bar (Ex: SharePoint) | **Actions,** as shown in the following figure:

Figure 9.8: Displaying actions available under a connector

Users can retrieve additional information about the action, such as, how to use it, what purpose it will serve, what properties it will require, and so on, by selecting the appropriate information icon, as shown:

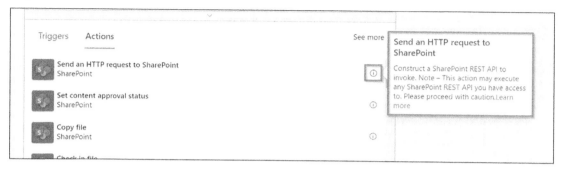

Figure 9.9: Displaying information of a selected action

Creating a Power Automate flow using SharePoint

As Power Automate was designed to automate workflows by utilizing various types of cloud flows, this article will demonstrate how to create a Power Automate flow using SharePoint.

Consider an automated flow that will be triggered when a new item is created in a specific SharePoint list and will send a notification to the specified user via Microsoft Teams.

There is a SharePoint list named **Interviews** having different types of columns such as, single line of text column, choice column, date columns, and people column. As per the automated flow, each time a new item is added to the SharePoint list, the mentioned user will be notified via Teams. Refer to the following figure as an example:

Figure 9.10: Example of a SharePoint list to build an automated flow

To create this Power Automate flow, follow these steps:

1. On the Power Automate, navigate to **Create**.

2. Selected **Automated Cloud Flow**.

3. Provide a name to the cloud flow and select the trigger to start the flow, that is, When an item is created.

4. Click on **Create** as shown:

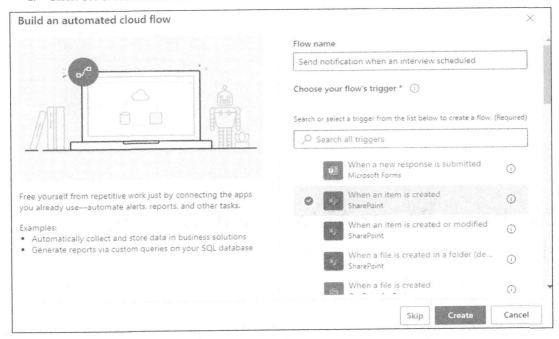

Figure 9.11: Select trigger to build an automated flow

5. It will redirect to the page, where the trigger is added to the flow. Configure the trigger by providing the **Site Address** and the **List Name.**

6. Next, add an action to the flow. Click on **New step** | Search action **Post message in a chat or channel** | **Select.**

7. Configure the action's properties such as:

   a. **Post as:** Flow bot

   b. **Post in:** Chat with Flow bot

   c. **Recipient:** Assign any specific person's name

   d. **Message:** Provide message using dynamic contents that will display on the specified user's teams.

The following figure shows the mentioned properties:

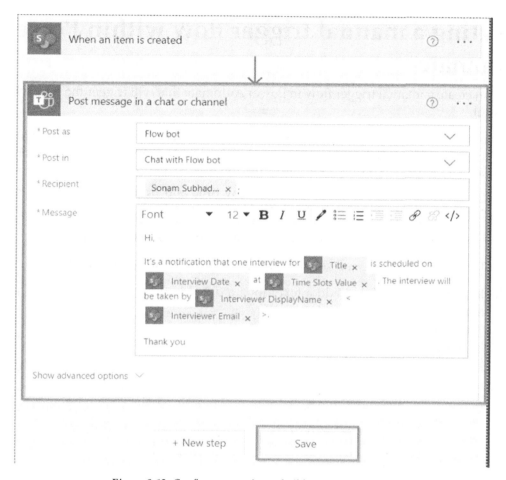

Figure 9.12: Configure an action to build an automated flow

8. Click on **Save** | **Test**.

9. For testing purposes, insert a new item into the above specified SharePoint list, which is, **Interviews**. Once a new item is created in the list, the flow will automatically send a notification to the user via Microsoft Teams as shown below:

Figure 9.13: Power Automate flow with SharePoint list and Microsoft Teams

Creating a manual trigger flow within Power Automate

Users can create a manual trigger flow in Power Automate that will trigger the flow whenever they want.

For example, the HR may want to connect with an employee via Outlook email or Microsoft Teams to inform them about the monthly session. In this case, HR can use the instant cloud flow to send a notification to a specific user with the click of a button.

You can control this flow from your phone at any time and from any location. To build an instant cloud flow, the following steps are:

1. On the Power Automate, click on the **Create** I **Instant cloud flow** I select.

2. Provide a flow name and select the trigger as **Manually trigger a flow** I Create.

3. Expand the trigger and add a text input, a date input to insert the monthly session's name and date, as shown:

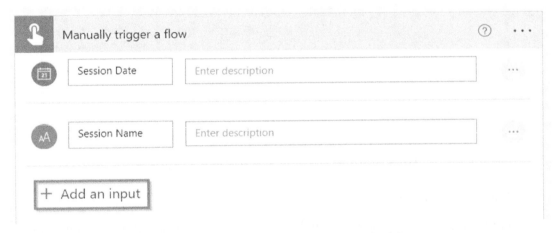

Figure 9.14: Build a Power Automate Instant cloud flow

4. Click on **New step** I Search and select the action **Send an email (V2)** under Outlook connector. Provide the components such as to whom you want to send this message, **Subject**, and **Body** of the email using the dynamic contents from the trigger. Refer to the following figure as an example:

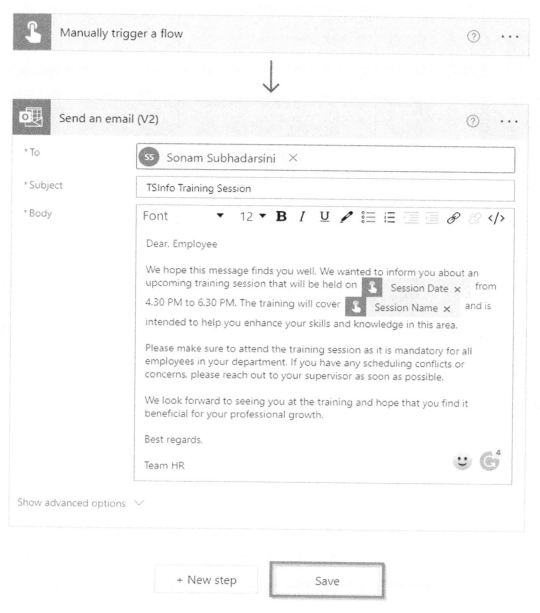

Figure 9.15: Building an Instant cloud flow to send notification

5. To test the flow, click on **Save** | **Test** | select **Manually** | **Test flow** | Specify the session name and date | **Run flow,** as shown:

Figure 9.16: Testing an Instant cloud flow to send notification

6. Immediately, it will send a notification to the user via email as shown in the following figure:

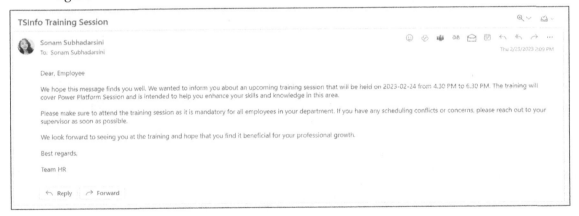

Figure 9.17: Getting notification on Outlook via instant cloud flow

Creating a scheduled flow within Power Automate

Similarly, Power Automate enables the user to create a scheduled cloud flow, which will automatically trigger the flow based on the time period specified. Let us create a Power Automate scheduled cloud flow that will send a mobile notification every 1 minute or an email notification to the user's specified email address at a periodic interval. Follow the given steps:

1. On the Power Automate, Navigate to **Create** | **Scheduled cloud flow.**

2. Provide a name to the Scheduled cloud flow, specify the flow **Starting date and time.**

3. Set the recurring time by editing the **Repeat every** | **Create.** The window will look something like this:

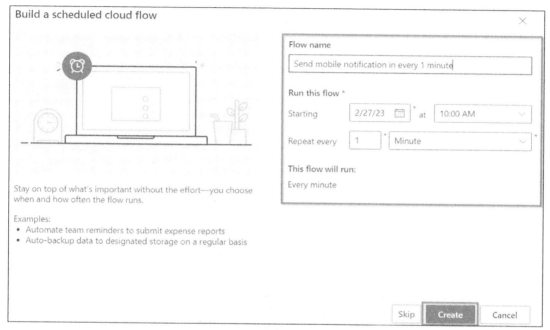

Figure 9.18: Building a Power Automate Scheduled Cloud Flow

4. To add more trigger configurations, select the trigger and expand the **Show advanced options.** We can choose the time zone and set the start time in YYYY-MM-DDTHH:MM:SSZ format. The **Recurrence** dialog box looks like this:

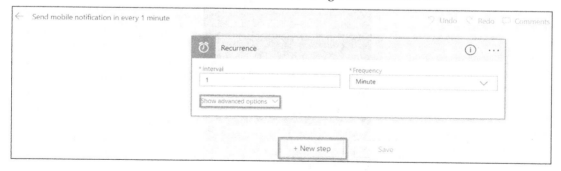

Figure 9.19: Configuring Scheduled Cloud Flow trigger

5. To add an action, click on the **New step** | Search the action **Send me a mobile notification.** Give text or message in the **Text** property of the action as shown below in *Figure 9.20:*

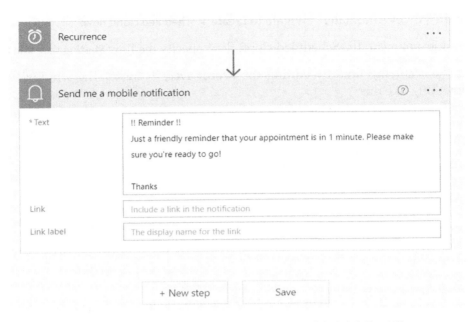

Figure 9.20: Configuring action for Power Automate Scheduled Cloud Flow

6. To test the flow, click on the **Save | Test**. You can see it will send a notification to the user's phone every 1 minute:

Figure 9.21: Configuring action for Power Automate Scheduled Cloud Flow

Sharing a flow with another user

On Power Automate, there is an option to share a flow with another user. We can share a flow with a colleague who shares the same tenant address, or we can add another owner who can edit, update, and delete the flow. All owners can also view the run history and add or remove other owners. When an owner is removed from the flow, he/she is no longer able to access the flow.

When a flow is shared with another user, it sends an email with a link to the owner. Follow these given steps:

1. On the Power Automate, go to **My Flows** and hover over the flow that you want to share.

2. Click on the **Share** icon.

3. It will redirect to the page, where you can add user or a group as an owner of the flow.

4. It also allows the user to remove the user from the list of flow-owners by clicking on the **Delete** icon.

5. Along with these steps, it also requires access to all connectors when sharing a flow with another, as shown:

Figure 9.22: Sharing a Power Automate flow to another user

Export and import Power Automate flow

In Power Automate, we can perform export and import a flow, which means we can export a flow as a zip file in Power Automate and then import that file into another environment.

Exporting a Power Automate flow

The following steps are to export a flow in Power Automate:

1. Go to **My flows** | **Select a flow** that you want to export.

2. Click on the **ellipses (More commands)** | **Export** | **Package(.zip)** as shown:

Figure 9.23: Exporting a Power Automate flow

3. It will redirect to a page where you need to give the package details and click on **Export**.

4. It will be converted into a zip file and downloaded to your system which can be shared with an external user.

Importing a Power Automate flow

Similarly, to import a Power Automate flow, the following steps are:

1. On Power Automate, go to **My flows** | **Import.**

2. If you want to import a flow from a zip file, select **Import Package,** as shown:

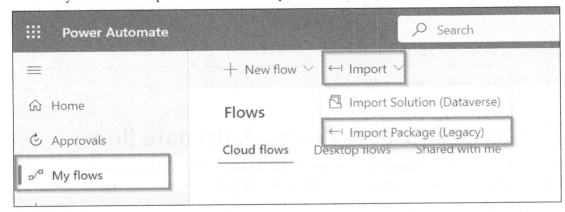

Figure 9.24: Import a Power Automate flow

3. Choose a .zip package file to upload and click on the **Update** (on the **Review Package Content**) as shown:

Figure 9.25: Import a flow to Power Automate

4. Choose Setup as **Create as new** and provide a name to the Resource name. Click on **Save**.

5. Similarly, configure the Related resources and click on **Save**.

6. Click on the **Import** button as shown:

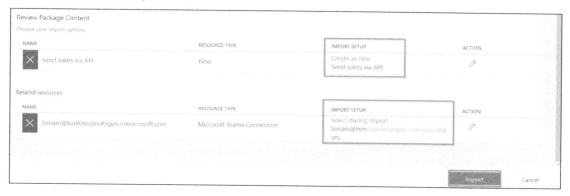

Figure 9.26: Importing a flow to Power Automate

7. It will redirect to another page where you can find a link to **Open flow:**

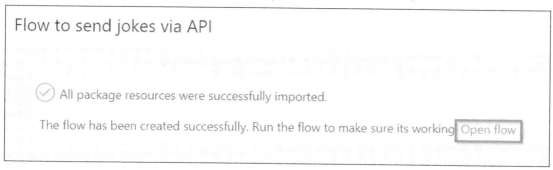

Figure 9.27: Open an imported flow in Power Automate

Turn On/ Turn Off a flow

We may want to stop the flow at times to prevent it from continuing. We must turn off the flow during this time. To turn off the flow, follow the steps outlined below:

1. On the Power Automate, navigate to **My flows** | **Select a flow** that you want to stop.

2. Click on the **More commands** | press **Turn off** as shown:

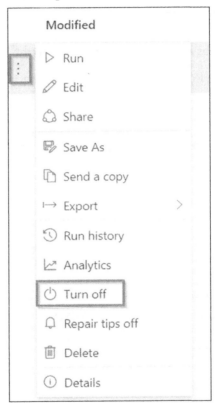

Figure 9.28: Turning off a flow in Power Automate

Alternatively, you can restart the flow by turning it on. It will continue to run if we turn off the flow while it is running. If we delete the flow while it is still running, the current run will be cancelled.

Deleting a flow

To delete an existing Power Automate flow, follow these given steps:

1. Select the flow from the list of **My flows** section that you want to delete.

2. Click on the **Vertical ellipses** | click on **Delete**, as shown in the following figure:

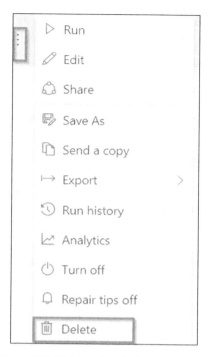

Figure 9.29: *Delete a flow in Power Automate*

Select **Delete** to confirm that you want to delete the flow. This action deletes the flow for all users and cannot be reversed. After deleting the flow, your **My flows** page loads, displaying a list of all your flows.

Power Automate with SharePoint (Examples)

Let us create some different types of Power Automate cloud flows based on various scenarios, such as flow triggers based on conditions, a SharePoint list is automatically updated once the Microsoft form is submitted, getting a specific item from the SharePoint list, posting a message when an item is created in the list, copying a document from one location to another via flow, building a SharePoint list using API via flow, and many more.

Save attachment into SharePoint library based on condition via Power Automate

In many organizations, email is a primary means of communication and collaboration. Often, email messages contain important documents such as Excel files, which are shared among team members for analysis and decision-making.

However, managing email attachments can be time-consuming and error-prone, particularly when dealing with large volumes of data. To avoid that, let us create an automated flow that will run when an email arrives and will check to see if it contains an excel file. If there are any excel files, then the flow will save those excel files to the specific SharePoint document library.

To create the automated flow, the following steps are:

1. On Power Automate, build an automated cloud flow.

2. Select the trigger **When a new email arrives (V3)** | **Create**.

3. On the trigger, select the **Folder** as **Inbox** and expand the **Advanced options.** Set **Yes** for the **Include Attachments.**

4. Next add a condition action to check whether the attachment is an excel file or not. Click on the **New step** | **Condition.** Set the Condition values as below:

5. Attachments Name contains .xlsx or **.xls**

Note: Attachments Name is the dynamic contents that taken from the trigger's output.

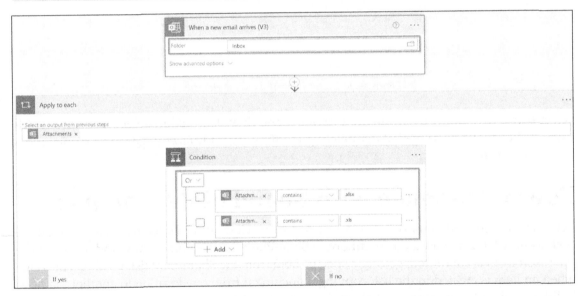

Figure 9.30: Apply condition to check whether the file is excel or not

6. If the attached file is in Excel format, then the flow will proceed forward to save it in a specific SharePoint document library folder. For that, add a **Create file** action inside the **If yes** section.

7. On the If yes section, click on **Add an action** | **Create file.** Configure the action with the SharePoint site address, Folder path to store the excel, take **File name and File content** from the dynamic contents as shown:

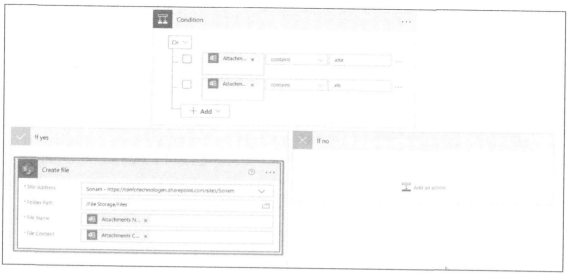

Figure 9.31: *Using action to store excel file inside the SharePoint folder*

Let us save the flow, and for testing purposes, send an email to yourself with the attachment of Excel file(s). We can see that once the email arrives, the flow will automatically save the Excel attachment to the SharePoint library folder, as shown:

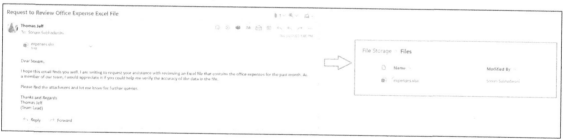

Figure 9.32: *Stores excel file from email to SharePoint using Power Automate condition*

Working with Microsoft forms using Power Automate

In this flow example, we will look at using Power Automate to work with Microsoft forms. When working with the Microsoft form, we may need to save the details from the form to our database.

In this case, we can use an automated flow that will be triggered when a Microsoft form or a new response is submitted, then retrieve all the information from the Form and save the details in the SharePoint list.

The following steps are:

1. We build a Microsoft form based on **Event Preference Survey** on **Forms** (**https://forms. office.com/**) that contains some general information such as responder name, organization, email address, and whether the user joined the event virtually or in person. Refer to the following figure:

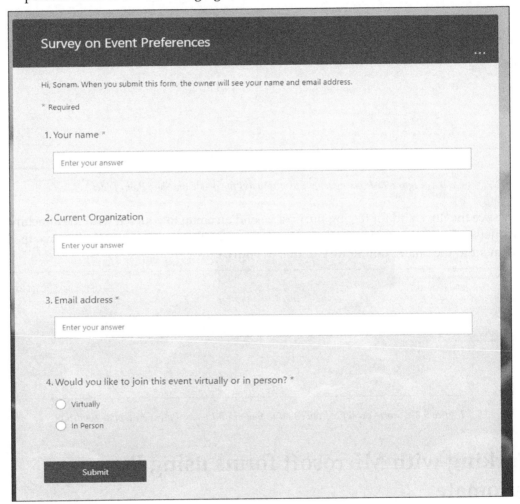

Figure 9.33: Displaying a Microsoft Form

2. Similarly, we have built a SharePoint list having 3 single lines of text columns and 1 choice column to store the information from Microsoft Forms. It will look like the following figure:

Figure 9.34: Displaying a SharePoint list based on Microsoft Form

To create the flow, the following steps are:

1. On the Power Automate, navigate to **Create | Automated cloud flow.**

2. Provide a name to the flow and select the trigger **When a new response is submitted** under Microsoft Forms connector | **Create.**

3. Configure the trigger by giving the **Form Id**, that is, **Survey on Event Preferences.**

4. Next, add an action to retrieve the responses from the submitted form. Click on the **New step | Search** and select the action **Get response details.** Set the **Form Id** and **Response Id** (select it from the dynamic content) within the action, as shown:

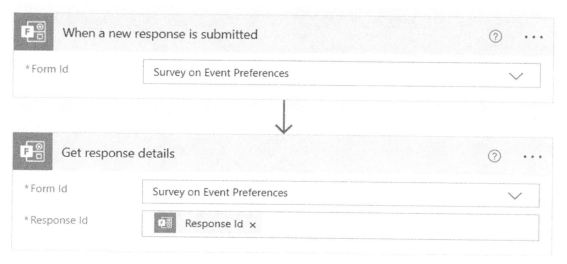

Figure 9.35: Configuring trigger and action on the Power Automate flow

5. Next, add another action to create a new item inside the specific SharePoint list. Click on **New step | Create item** (Under SharePoint connector). Configure the SharePoint site address, list name.

6. Also, set the Responder Name, Organization, Email address, etc. from the dynamic content, as displayed in the following figure:

Figure 9.36: Flow to create item in SharePoint list from the Microsoft Form

To run the flow, click on the **Save | Test | Manually | Test.** Let us submit a new response via Microsoft Forms. Once the forms submitted, the responses will be saved in the SharePoint list as shown below:

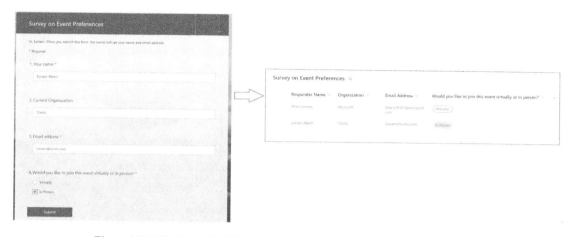

Figure 9.37: Working with Microsoft Forms in SharePoint list via automated flow

Getting SharePoint list items using Power Automate

By using Power Automate flow, we can get SharePoint list items based on specific conditions or filter queries.

There is a SharePoint list named Products list having different types of columns along with a choice column, which is **Company**, as shown in the following figure:

Title ∨	Order Date ∨	Company ∨	Price ∨
MacBook Pro with M2 chip	01/19/2023	Apple	$1,225.88
Apple Airpods Gen 2	01/26/2023	Apple	$229.32
Therabody Wave Roller	01/16/2023	Other	$126.23
Meta Quest Pro	01/21/2023	Meta	$1,499.73

Figure 9.38: An example of SharePoint list

Let us create a flow that will retrieve only those data whose **Company is equal to Apple.**

1. On the Power Automate, navigate to **Create | Instant cloud flow.**

2. Provide a flow name and choose the trigger to start the flow, which is, **Manually trigger a flow.** Click on **Create**.

3. Next, add an action to get the items from the SharePoint list. Click on **New step | Get items.** Configure the **Site Address and List name.**

4. On that action, expand the **Advanced options.** Insert the below expression to **Filter Query** to filter the SharePoint data.

```
Company eq 'Apple'
```

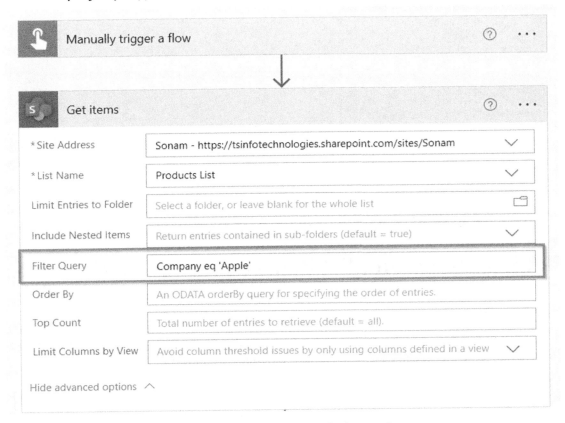

Figure 9.39: Using filter query in Get items action

5. To display the retrieved data, add a **Compose** action and configure it with the Product's Title, Company, order date, and price, as shown:

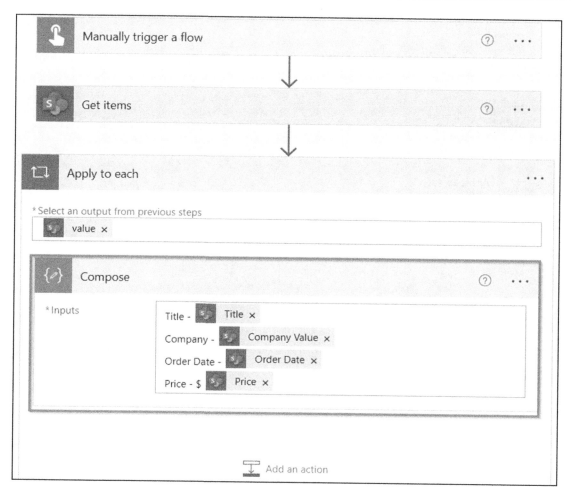

Figure 9.40: Get items from the SharePoint list using Power Automate

6. While testing the flow, the result will appear in the compose action as shown below:

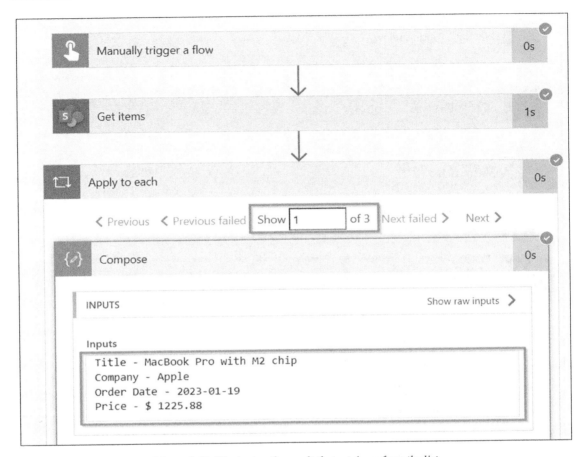

Figure 9.41: Displaying the result that retrieves from the list

When you click on **Next,** it will display the rest two items from the SharePoint list that satisfy the filter query.

Post message when a SharePoint item is created via Power Automate

Power Automate allows you to post messages in the Microsoft Teams channel or chat to the respective mentioned person when an item is created in the SharePoint list.

Suppose you have a SharePoint task list having different types of columns such as Task's Title, description, start date, and status. Along with these, there is another person column labelled **Assigned To,** as shown:

Title ⌄		Description ⌄	Assigned To ⌄	Start Date ⌄	Status ⌄
Build a flow using API		Build a Power Automate flow using API that will create a SharePoint list	User1	03/01/2023	Not Started

Figure 9.42: Example of a SharePoint task list

Let us build an automated flow, when a new task is created in the above SharePoint list, it will notify the respective assigned user about the task via Microsoft Teams. To build the flow, take a look at the following steps:

1. On the Power Automate, navigate to **Create | Automated cloud flow.**

2. Give a name to the flow and select the trigger as **When an item is created** under SharePoint connector and press **Create.**

3. Configure the trigger by giving the SharePoint site address and list name.

4. Next, click on the **New step |** search and select the action **Post message in a chat or channel** under Microsoft Teams connector. Set the action properties as below, also shown in *Figure 9.43*:

    a. **Post as:** Flow bot

    b. **Post in:** Chat with Flow bot

    c. **Recipient:** Assigned to Email (Select this value from the dynamic contents)

    d. **Message:** Specify the message using the dynamic contents that will display in the user's Teams

Figure 9.43: Post a message in Microsoft Teams via Power Automate

To test the flow, click save and test. Run it manually. To see the result, create a new item within the SharePoint list and assign the task to a user. We can see, immediately it will notify that assigned user via Microsoft Teams chat as shown below:

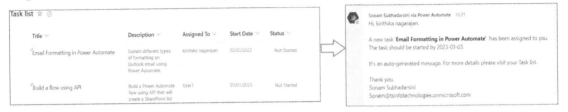

Figure 9.44: Flow to post message to the Teams when a task is assigned

Copy folder using Power Automate

By using Power Automate, we can copy the folder including files and documents from one location to another SharePoint document library.

Assume you have a folder in a specific SharePoint document library, and you want to copy all the files along with that folder to another location on a recurring basis, say once per day.

In this case, we can create an automated scheduled cloud flow and copy the folder from the source to the destination. The following steps are required to create the cloud flow:

1. On the Power Automate, go to **Create** | **Scheduled Cloud Flow**.

2. Give a name to the cloud flow.

3. Configure the Starting date and time, recurring time | Create.

4. Once the trigger is configured, add an action to copy folder from source location to destination. Click on **New step** | **Copy Folder** (Under SharePoint connector)

5. Provide all the details of mandatory fields inside the action such as Current Site Address, Folder to Copy, Destination Site Address, Destination Folder, and set a value from the dropdown list (that is, Copy with a new name) for the **If another folder is already there** option, as shown:

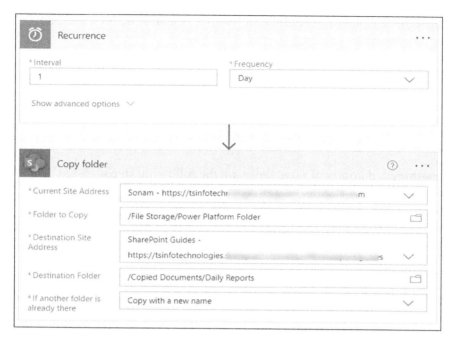

Figure 9.45: Copy folder from one SharePoint site address to another

Now run the flow to see if it copies the folder from the source SharePoint document library to the destination SharePoint document library.

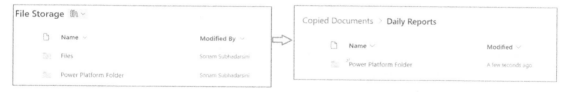

Figure 9.46: Copying folder from one SharePoint library to another

This flow will run automatically on a scheduled basis, that is, once a day.

Working with approvals using Power Automate

Power Automate can be used to create approvals and receive responses from the specified users, such as leave approvals, invoice approvals, approvals for vacation requests, approvals for documents that require sign-off, financial document approvals, and so on.

There is a SharePoint list where the user will enter the data for applying for leaves. Once the data is entered, it will automatically generate an approval request and send it to the specified approvers (Team lead and Manager) to be approved at the same time. When they approve the request, it will notify the user who requested it, and the approval status, along with their comments, will be updated in the SharePoint list.

The following figure displays the SharePoint list to let the user insert their data:

Figure 9.47: Displaying a SharePoint list for applying leave

To create the automated approval flow, these are the following steps:

1. On the Power Automate, go to **Create** | **Automated cloud flow**.

2. Give a name to the flow and select a trigger **When an item is created** under the **SharePoint connector** | **Create**.

3. Specify the SharePoint site address and list name.

4. To create an approval request, add an action under the trigger, that is, Start and wait for an approval. Configure the action's properties as below:

    a. **Approval type:** Approve/Reject - Everyone must approve.

    b. **Title:** Specify the approval title using the dynamic contents.

    c. **Assigned to:** Assign the HR's user ID.

    d. **Details:** Provide some details for the approval request.

5. To send the approval request to both the team lead and manager, we need to add a parallel branch. For this, in between the trigger and the approval action, click on the + icon. Select **Add a Parallel branch.**

6. Again, add another **Start and wait for an approval** on the other side of the parallel branch and configure the action accordingly, as shown in the following figure:

Figure 9.48: Create an approval request when an item is created in SharePoint list

7. Next, add a **Condition** action to check whether both the requests are approved or not. If both are approved. Click on **New step | Condition.** Set the conditions as below:

    a. Outcome is equal to Approve [Start and wait for an approval – Team Lead]

    b. Outcome is equal to Approve [Start and wait for an approval – Manager]

Note: Take both Outcome(s) from the above approval actions respectively.

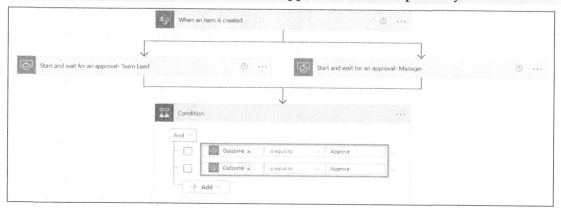

Figure 9.49: Use condition to check the approval's outcomes

8. Then the flow will send email notifications to the user who created the item to notify them whether the approval is approved or rejected.

9. Add **Send an email** action in both the **If yes** and **If no** section. Click on **Add an action | Send an email.**

10. Configure the properties such as:

    a. **To:** Created by email (select it from the trigger's dynamic content)

    b. **Subject:** Specify the email's subject

    c. **Body:** Specify the body using the action's dynamic contents.

Note: While using the dynamic contents from the above action it will create an 'Apply to each' loop.

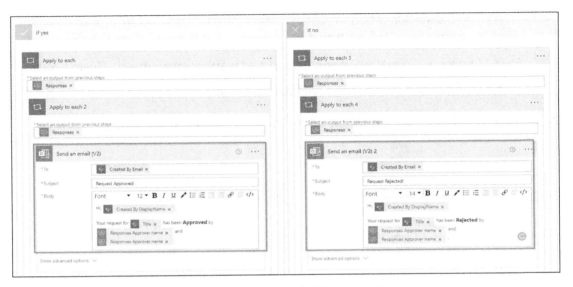

Figure 9.50: Sending an email with approvers' names

11. To update the approver's comments along with the approval status within the SharePoint list, add an action outside of the **Send an email** action. Make sure to add this action inside the **If yes** section.

12. Click on the **Add an action** (inside the **If yes** section) | **Update item** (Under SharePoint connector). Configure the properties as below:

    a. **Site Address:** Provide the SharePoint site address.

    b. **List Name:** Specify the list where the item will update.

    c. **ID:** Select ID from the trigger's dynamic content.

    d. **Title:** Select title from the trigger's dynamic content.

    e. **Status Value:** Choose **Approved** from the dropdown menu.

    f. **TeamLead Comment:** Choose **Approver comment** from the approval action's dynamic content.

    g. **Manager Comment:** Choose **Approver comment** from the approval action's dynamic content.

13. Do repeat the same process in the **If no** section too. Set the **Status Value** as **Rejected.** Refer to the following figure:

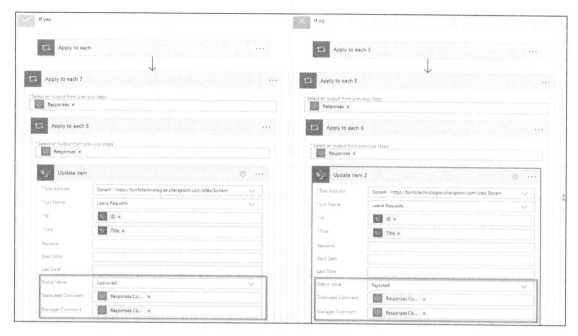

Figure 9.51: Update SharePoint items based on the Approval responses using Flow

Now, save the flow, and for testing, create an item in the SharePoint list. Once the item is created in the SharePoint list, it will create approval requests and send it to both the approvers parallelly. If both the approvers approved the request, it will send an email to the user who created that request, as shown:

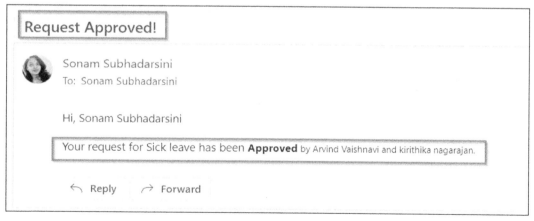

Figure 9.52: Notify the user once the approval is approved

14. As you can see, it will update the SharePoint list with the status and comments from the approvers:

Figure 9.53: Update SharePoint item based on approval using Automated flow

Use API to create SharePoint list via Power Automate

API stands for **Application Programming Interface**. We can use Power Automate with REST API to manage the cloud flow and the SharePoint list, such as creating a list to update items, delete files, retrieve items, and so on.

Let us build an instant cloud flow using REST API that will create a list within the SharePoint site. For this, the following steps are:

1. On the Power Automate, build an Instant cloud flow.

2. Select the trigger **Manually trigger a flow**.

3. To create a list within SharePoint, we need to call the HTTP request. Click on **New step | Send an HTTP request to SharePoint**. Configure the action properties as below:

    a. **Site Address:** Specify the SharePoint site address where the list will be created.

    b. **Method:** Post

    c. **Url:** _api/web/Lists/

    d. **Headers:** Here, you need to provide the Key and Value.

Enter key	Enter value
Accept	application/json;odata=verbose
content-type	application/json;odata=verbose

Table 9.1: Power Automate HTTP request

Body:

```
{ '__metadata': {'type': 'SP.List' ,
'AllowContentTypes': true,
'BaseTemplate': 100,
```

```
'ContentTypesEnabled': true,
'Description': 'My list description',
'Title': 'Budget Management'}
```

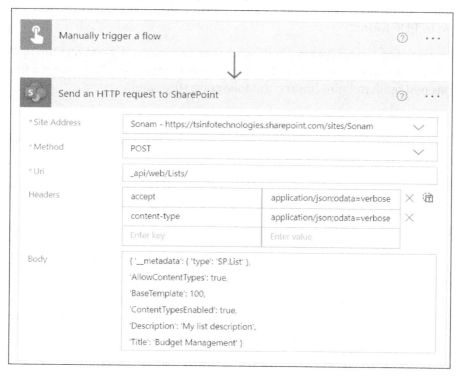

Figure 9.54: Build a SharePoint list using Power Automate flow

4. Once you run the flow, a SharePoint list named **Budget Management** will be created in the specified SharePoint site, as shown below in *Figure 9.55*:

Figure 9.55: Build a list in the SharePoint site via Power Automate flow

Converting file to PDF format and storing in Power Automate

Converting a text file to a PDF format and storing it in SharePoint via Power Automate is a process that can be automated using different tools and platforms. Power Automate is one of these platforms that can simplify the conversion and storage process by providing an intuitive and easy-to-use interface.

Assume you have a folder in your SharePoint document library that allows users to upload documents such as text or Excel, which is easily modifiable by others. It may take longer if we convert them to PDF format.

However, by using the Power Automate flow, we can automatically convert the uploaded file to PDF format and securely store it in a SharePoint document library. To convert a file into PDF format and store it in SharePoint library, the following steps are:

1. On the Power Automate, build an Automate cloud flow.

2. Give a name to the flow. Select the trigger **When a file is created (properties only)** under SharePoint connector | Create.

3. Configure the trigger by provide the SharePoint site address, Library name, and folder (give the folder path where users can upload the files).

4. Click on the **New step** | add action **Get file content** under SharePoint connector.

5. Provide the SharePoint site address and select the **File Identifier** from the trigger's output.

6. Next, add another action under the **Get file content** to create the file in secondary storage (that is, OneDrive). Click on **New step** | **Create file** (under OneDrive connector). Configure the action's properties such as:

    a. **Folder Path**: Where you want to create the file in OneDrive, or you can give '/' as the root folder.

    b. **File Name**: Select **File name with extension** from the trigger's dynamic contents.

    c. **File Content**: File content from the action's dynamic content.

The following figure shows these configurations:

Figure 9.56: Add actions to convert a file into PDF format in Power Automate

7. Once the file is created under secondary storage, it will convert that file to PDF format via Power Automate. Click on **New step | Convert file** (under OneDrive connector). Configure the action with the below properties:

   a. **File**: Id (From the Create File's dynamic contents)

   b. **Target type:** PDF.

8. Once it is converted into PDF, add another action to create this PDF file inside the SharePoint folder. Click on **New step | Create file** (Under SharePoint

connector). Provide the values to properties as below, and as shown in *Figure 9.57*:

a. **Site Address:** Specify the SharePoint site address

b. **Folder Path:** Give the folder path where the PDF will create

c. **File Name:** File Name.pdf (Select File Name from the trigger's dynamic content)

d. **File Content:** File content (select File content from the dynamic content of the Convert file)

Figure 9.57: Add actions to convert file to PDF and create in SharePoint folder

9. Once the PDF file is created, the flow will delete the earlier file from the SharePoint folder as well as the secondary storage. Click on **New step** | **Delete file** (under OneDrive). Select the File as Id from (OneDrive - Create file dynamic contents).

10. Similarly, add another action to delete file from the SharePoint list. Click on **New step** | **Delete File** (under SharePoint connector). Configure the action with the SharePoint site address and **File identifier** as **Identifier** (select this from the trigger's dynamic content), as shown in the following figure:

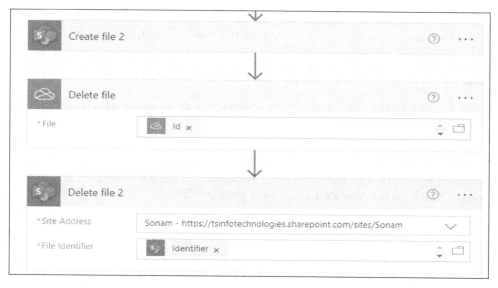

Figure 9.58: Add actions to delete files from the SharePoint and OneDrive

Now, save and test the flow. To see the result, upload a text file and Excel file into the specified SharePoint library folder. You can see, it will convert those files into PDF files and delete those uploaded files from the document library:

Figure 9.59: Convert files to PDF format via Power Automate

Create task in Planner from SharePoint list using Power Automate

Creating tasks in Planner from a SharePoint list can be a time-consuming process when done manually. Fortunately, Power Automate can automate this process, making it faster and easier to manage tasks across both platforms.

The process typically involves configuring Power Automate to read the contents of a SharePoint list and create corresponding tasks in Planner. The platform can then be set up to automatically assign the tasks to designated team members, set due dates, and even send email notifications when tasks are assigned or updated.

There is a SharePoint list called **Task List** that has a default column (Title), a person column (Assigned To), a start date and an end date (Date and Time). When the team leader adds an item to the SharePoint list, it creates a task in the user's planner. This whole process will go through based on the Power Automate. To create the flow, the following steps are:

1. On the Power Automate, build an automated flow. Click on **Create** | **Automated cloud flow.**

2. Give a name to the flow and choose the trigger as **When an item is created** under the SharePoint connector. Click **Create**.

3. Specify the SharePoint Site address and the list name.

4. To get the user profile from the list's Assigned To column, add an action under the trigger. Click on the **New step** | Get user profile (V2).

5. Set the **User (UPN)** as **Assigned to Email from the dynamic contents of the trigger**, as shown below:

Figure 9.60: Get user profile from the SharePoint list via Power Automate

6. To create a task within the user's Planner, add another action under the Get user profile. Click on **New step** | **Create a task** (Under the Microsoft planner connector). Set the properties as below:

   a. **Group ID:** Select your group id from the dropdown.

   b. **Plan ID:** Choose the plan ID.

   c. **Title:** Choose **Title** from the dynamic content

   d. **Bucket ID:** To-do

   e. **Start Date Time:** Choose it from the trigger's dynamic content.

    f. **Due Date Time:** Choose it from the trigger's dynamic content.

    g. **Assigned User Ids:** Select Id from the **Get user profile's** dynamic content.

You can also refer to the following figure:

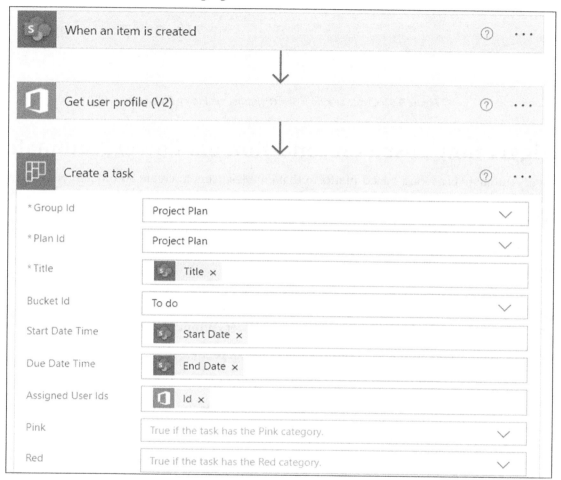

Figure 9.61: Adding action to create a task from the SharePoint list via flow

For testing purposes, add an item in the specified SharePoint list, it will create a task in the user's planner as shown below:

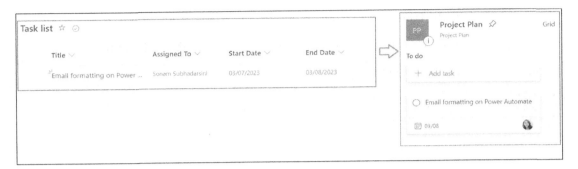

Figure 9.62: Create task from SharePoint list via Power Automate

Trigger flow based on condition via Power Automate

Power Automate is a cloud-based platform that enables users to create automated workflows that can streamline their day-to-day tasks. One of the key features of Power Automate is the ability to trigger workflows based on specific conditions. This means that workflows can be customized to run only when certain conditions are met, such as a specific data point being entered, a file being uploaded to a specific folder, an item being modified in the SharePoint list, etc.

Assume there is a SharePoint list named Task list containing a choice column Task Status. Let us build a flow, when the user completes the task and changes the task status to Completed, the flow will retrieve and display those values on Power Automate via a Compose action.

To create a flow based on this scenario, the following steps are:

1. On Power Automate, create an automated cloud flow and provide a name to the flow.

2. Select the trigger as **When an item is created or modified** under the SharePoint connector.

3. Specify the SharePoint site address and list name.

4. Click on the Horizontal ellipses of the trigger and go to **Settings**.

5. Insert the expression below on the Trigger Conditions. As a result, the flow will trigger based on the condition:

   ```
   @equals(triggerBody()?['TaskStatus']?['Value'], 'Completed')
   ```

Where the Task Status is the internal name of the SharePoint choice column and Completed is the name of the choice column value:

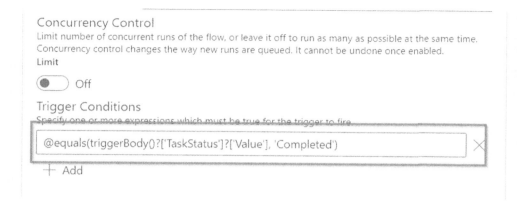

Figure 9.63: *Applying condition on Power Automate trigger*

6. Add a Compose action under the trigger to retrieve the task details.

7. Click on **New step** | **Compose**.

8. Add details from the trigger's dynamic contents. Refer to the following figure for a better understanding:

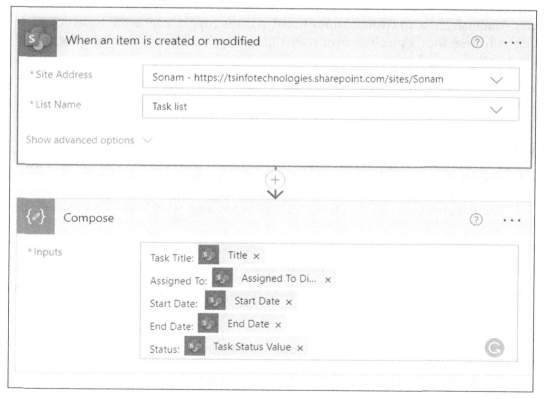

Figure 9.64: *Using Compose action to get the details from the list via Power Automate*

Let us save the flow and to test it, edit a task status to Completed on the SharePoint list. You can see the details will be retrieved and displayed in the Power Automate compose action as shown below:

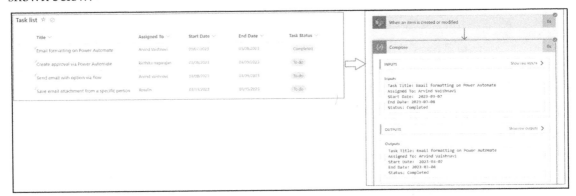

Figure 9.65: Flow runs based on Power Automate trigger condition

Conclusion

In this chapter, we discussed what Power Automate is, different types of flows available in Power Automate, how to create various flows, what is trigger, connector, actions, and so on. Along with these, the chapter has covered ten different types of flow examples using SharePoint list and libraries based on use cases.

In the next chapter, we will see what Power BI is, how to connect and integrate Power BI with SharePoint Online to create different visuals, reports, dashboards, and many more.

Points to remember

- Microsoft Flow is cloud-based software that enables users to build and automate workflows and tasks all over various applications and services without requiring the additional support of developers. These automated workflows are known as cloud flow.

- Using automation in your business improves the efficiency of your business processes. It can also boost productivity, communication, and collaboration.

- In Power Automate, each service has a unique license based on its plans, such as Free, License by per user, License by per-user plan with attended RPA, and License by the per-flow plan.

- Microsoft Power Automate offers four types of flows:

  o **Automated cloud flow**: The flow will run automatically when an event occurs.

  o **Instant cloud flow**: Users can create a manual trigger flow in Power Automate that will trigger the flow whenever they want.

o **Scheduled cloud flow**: It enables the user to create a scheduled cloud flow, which will automatically trigger the flow based on the time period specified.

o **Desktop flow**: Everyone who does simple or sophisticated rule-based operations on their workstations is essentially addressed by desktop flows. Users can use the automation features of Power Automate to design processes, interact with common tools like email and Excel, or work with both modern and legacy applications, whether they are at home, in small businesses, corporations, or larger companies.

• Microsoft Power Automate provides numerous prebuilt cloud-based templates that allow us to automate our process in under a minute by adding intelligence.

• The main components of the Power Automate are:

o **Connector**: Connectors allow you to communicate from one server to another. It is packaged with some triggers and actions in Power Automate. We can use them to create a workflow that meets our needs.

o **Trigger**: A trigger is an event that starts a flow. Triggers come in three varieties: Event trigger or automated trigger, Scheduled trigger, Instant trigger.

o **Action**: The action will initiate once the flow has been triggered. Microsoft Power Automate includes a variety of actions. Several different actions are available for each connector.

• We can share a flow with a colleague who shares the same tenant address, or we can add another owner who can edit, update, and delete the flow.

• Power Automate allows to export and import a flow that means we can export a flow as a zip file in Power Automate and then import that file into another environment.

• It allows to prevent the flow from continuing by turn off it.

Join our book's Discord space

Join the book's Discord Workspace for Latest updates, Offers, Tech happenings around the world, New Release and Sessions with the Authors:

https://discord.bpbonline.com

CHAPTER 10
Power BI

Introduction

In the previous chapter, we learned about Power Automate, the advantages of Power Automate, licensing and pricing in Power Automate, and how we can create different types of flow with SharePoint that is, scheduled flow and manually triggered flow. Also, we saw how we can share, export/ Import, and delete the flow.

In this chapter, we will see what Power BI is, the different components of Power BI, and how we can connect SharePoint data sources. Also, we will see how we can transform and clean data in Power Query; then, we will see how we can create a report and dashboard.

Lastly, we will see how to publish and share reports in the Power BI service. Further we will explore how we can embed the report in SharePoint Online page.

Structure

This chapter overviews Power BI and how users can easily create a report and dashboard. The following topics will be discussed in the chapter:

- What is Power BI
- Introduction to Power BI Desktop
- Key features of Power BI

- Various data sources in Power BI

- Connecting to SharePoint data sources

- Introduction to Power BI report

- What is Power Query

- Transforming the data using Power Query

- Overview of visualization in Power BI

- Creating Power BI reports using SharePoint Online data source

- What is Power BI Service

- What is a workspace in Power BI

- Publishing and sharing report in Power BI

- Embedding Power BI report with SharePoint Online

- Creating Power BI Dashboard

- How to automatically refresh SharePoint data in Power BI

Objectives

If the reader is new to Power BI or has no idea what it is or how to use it with SharePoint data source, this chapter will be very helpful. After reading this chapter, the reader will have a fundamental understanding of Power BI usage and features, as well as building interactive reports and a dashboard.

The content covers the creation, publication, and sharing of reports within Power BI, among other essential aspects. Furthermore, readers will delve into working with SharePoint list data and discover how to effectively visualize and analyse information stored in SharePoint lists through Power BI reports.

What is Power BI

Power BI from Microsoft is a data analytics service that allows users to visualize and analyze data with greater speed, reliability, and insight. BI offers a variety of data analysis tools, including data transformation, data modeling, different types of visualization, and publishing reports.

Users can connect to a large variety of data sources using Power BI, including Excel, SharePoint Online list, Cloud-based and on-premises databases, and third-party applications.

Further, the users can also use Power Query to transform and clean the data, which provides a simple easy, intuitive user interface to clean and transform data with less effort.

Once the data is prepared, reporters can use Power BI's drag-and-drop interface to create interactive reports that include a variety of charts, graphs, and other data visualizations. They can also create reports and dashboards that can be shared inside and outside the organization, and they can also be embedded in other applications.

Also, Power BI offers different collaboration functionalities, like real-time collaboration and the ability to make comments, as well as governance functionality for enterprise-level deployments and advanced security.

Power BI is further subdivided into three elements:

- **Power BI desktop:** This is the authoring tool where you can connect to data, transform, and model the data, and create visualizations, reports, and dashboards. We need to install this tool on our desktops to access it.

- **Power BI service:** This is a Cloud-based platform where you can publish and share the reports and dashboards created in Power BI Desktop. It provides additional features like collaboration, sharing, and administration.

- **Power BI mobile:** This is the mobile app that allows you to access your Power BI content from your mobile devices, including smartphones and tablets. It allows you to view and interact with your reports and dashboards on the go and stay up to date with your data.

Introduction to Power BI Desktop

Power BI Desktop is a powerful data visualization and business intelligence tool developed by Microsoft. It allows users to connect to and analyse data from a wide range of sources, including Excel spreadsheets, databases, and Cloud-based services.

Power BI Desktop offers a variety of tools for creating interactive reports, dashboards, and visualizations, including charts, graphs, maps, and tables. These visualizations can be customized and arranged on a canvas to create a compelling narrative that helps users better understand their data.

The tool also includes advanced features such as data modeling and transformation, allowing users to shape and manipulate their data to fit their specific needs. Additionally, Power BI Desktop integrates with Microsoft's other business intelligence tools, such as Power BI Service and Excel, allowing users to seamlessly move their data between these platforms.

Overall, Power BI Desktop is a powerful and flexible tool that allows users to gain valuable insights from their data and communicate those insights effectively to others in their organization.

How to install Power BI Desktop

To download and install in Power BI Desktop on our local computer, follow the given steps:

1. Open the browser on your computer, and navigate to this link:

2. **https://www.microsoft.com/en-us/download/details.aspx?id=58494.**

3. Then click on the **Download** button based on your system requirements and your language.

4. Once it is installed on your local desktop, you can open and access the Power BI Desktop. Refer to the following figure for a better understanding:

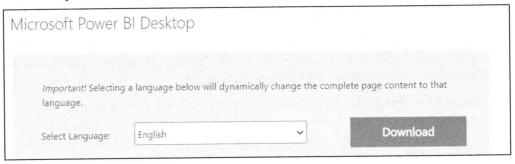

Figure 10.1: Download Power BI Desktop

UI of Power BI Desktop

Microsoft Power BI Desktop is a business analytics tool that allows you to visualize and analyze data from a variety of sources. Its user interface is designed to be intuitive and user-friendly, with the following main components:

1. **Ribbon:** The ribbon is located at the top of the Power BI Desktop window and contains all the main commands and tools for designing and managing your reports and visualizations.

2. **View tab:** It is divided into three parts. These are report view, data view and model view.

3. **Filter pane:** The filter pane is located on the right side of the window and before the filter pane. You can filter the visualization from the filter pane to get the required information.

4. **Visualizations pane:** The visualizations pane is located on the right side of the window and contains all the available visualizations that you can add to your report.

5. **Fields pane:** The fields pane is located on the right side of the window and displays all the available data fields that you can use in your visualizations.

6. **Report canvas:** The report canvas is the main working area of Power BI Desktop and is located in the center of the window. This is where you can design and customize your visualizations and create your reports.

7. **Page view:** Power BI Desktop allows you to switch between two pages and we can add new pages to our report.

The following figure illustrates the UI of Power BI Desktop:

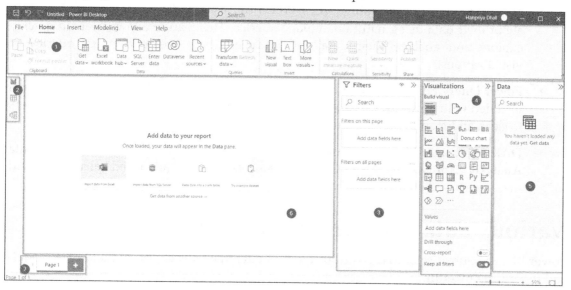

***Figure 10.2:** UI of Power BI Desktop*

Key features of Power BI

Microsoft Power BI Desktop is a powerful data analytics and visualization tool that enables users to connect to and transform data from various sources, create interactive visualizations and reports, and share insights with others. Some of the key features of Power BI Desktop are:

- **Data connection and transformation:** Power BI Desktop allows users to connect to various data sources, including Excel spreadsheets, databases, cloud-based services, and web-based sources. Users can also transform and clean the data using various tools and functions.

- **Data modeling:** Power BI Desktop provides advanced data modeling capabilities, including the ability to create relationships between tables, create calculated columns and measures, and define hierarchies and KPIs.

- **Interactive visualizations:** Power BI Desktop enables users to create interactive and compelling visualizations, such as matrix, charts, graphs, maps, and tables. Users can also add custom visuals from a wide range of third-party providers.

- **Dashboard:** Power BI Desktop enables users to build interactive dashboards that provide key metrics and insights in real time. The dashboard's layout and design can also be altered by users to suit their needs.

- **Collaboration and sharing:** Users of Power BI Desktop can collaborate with one another by exchanging reports and dashboards. They can also manage the access to the reports and dashboards and work in real-time collaboration.

- **Natural Language Processing (NLP):** Power BI Desktop allows users to ask questions about their data using natural language queries. This feature allows users to quickly explore and analyze their data without needing to create complex queries or visualizations.

- **Power Query Editor:** The Power Query Editor is a powerful data transformation tool included with Power BI Desktop. With an easy-to-use interface, this tool enables users to clean and manipulate data from many sources.

- **DAX Language:** Power BI Desktop uses a powerful formula language called **Data Analysis Expressions (DAX)** that enables users to create advanced calculations and measures based on their data.

Various data sources in Power BI

Power BI data sources refer to the various types of data that can be used to build data models and reports in Power BI.

Power BI supports a wide range of data sources that can be used to extract, transform, and load data into the Power BI environment for analysis and reporting. To access this wide range of data sources in Power BI, there is option that is, **Get data**.

Here is the list of data sources in Power BI is categorized into:

- **All data sources:** It contains all data connection types.

- **File-based data sources:** These data sources include files like Excel spreadsheets, CSV files, and text files. Power BI can connect to these files directly or through a local or Cloud-based file-sharing service such as OneDrive or SharePoint.

- **Database data sources:** These data sources include structured databases such as SQL Server, Oracle, MySQL, and PostgreSQL. Power BI can connect to these databases directly or through an on-premises data gateway or a cloud-based gateway.

- **Power platform data sources:** These data sources contain Power BI datasets, DataMart's, Dataverse, etc.

- **Azure data sources:** These data sources contain Azure SQL database, Azure Blob storage, Azure Databricks, Azure Table Storage, and many more.

- **Online Service data sources:** These data sources contain SharePoint Online list, Microsoft Exchange Online, Adobe Analytics, QuickBooks Online, Quick base, and many more.

- **Other data sources:** These contains data sources like Web, SharePoint list, OData Feed, R script and many more.

The following figure lists these data sources:

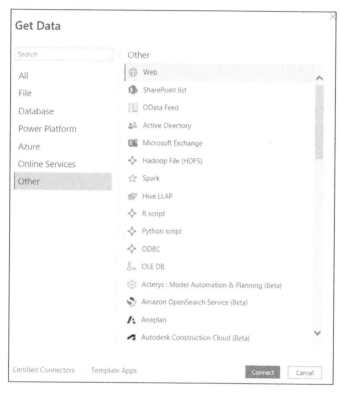

Figure 10.3: Different data sources in Power BI

Connecting to SharePoint data sources

SharePoint is a popular document management, collaboration, and data storage platform. Many industries use SharePoint to manage critical business data such as customer information, sales information, and project information.

You can easily connect to SharePoint data sources and create rich, interactive reports that provide valuable insights into their data using Power BI.

You can use the SharePoint Online List or SharePoint Folder connectors to connect Power BI to SharePoint data sources. These connectors enable you to easily access SharePoint lists and folders, as well as document libraries, and import data for analysis into Power BI.

After importing the data into Power BI, you can create powerful reports and dashboards that provide a comprehensive view of their data. You can use a variety of visualizations, such as charts, tables, and maps, to analyze and present your data in a way that makes sense to your audience. You can drill down into the data and gain deeper insights into their business operations by using Power BI's advanced filtering and slicing capabilities.

To connect Power BI Desktop with SharePoint list, we need to follow the below steps:

1. Login to Power BI Desktop, with your Microsoft 365 credential.

2. Then click on **Get data** from the ribbon in the **Home** tab | click on **More options**.

3. Now the Get data window will open | Search for SharePoint Online List | Click on **SharePoint Online list** connector.

4. Then click on **Connect** as shown:

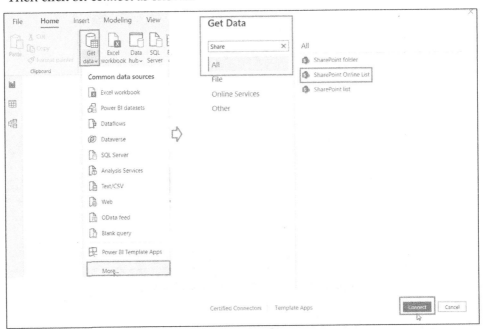

Figure 10.4: SharePoint Online list Connector

5. Now SharePoint Online list window will open | Provide the URL of the site.

6. Then select **2.0**(Beta), under implementation.

7. Expand the **Advanced** options, select the **View mode** as **Default**.

8. Then click on **OK**.

9. Next, select the Microsoft account and click **Sign In** | Select the SharePoint site from the list under **Select which level to apply these settings to**.

10. Click on **Connect** as shown below:

Figure 10.5: Connect SharePoint Online List to Microsoft Power BI

11. Then the **Navigator** window will open, and select the SharePoint Online list, in this case, it is the **Financial Sample** list. Also, this is where you can see the preview list.

12. If you do not want to customize the data, then directly click on **Load**, else you can click on **Transform data**; it will redirect the data to the Power Query editor, where you can transform and shape your data. Refer to the following figure to get a better understanding of these steps:

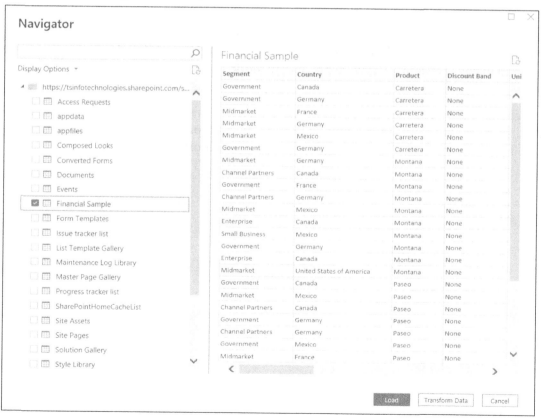

Figure 10.6: SharePoint Online list connect to Power BI

To summarize, connecting Power BI to SharePoint data sources allows users to analyze and visualize their data in new ways, providing valuable insights that can inform decision-making and drive business success. The integration of these two powerful platforms makes it easier for organizations to leverage their SharePoint data and gain a competitive advantage.

Introduction to Power BI report

A report in Power BI is a collection of visualizations and insights created from one or more data sources. The report gives users an interactive and meaningful view of their data, allowing them to explore and analyze it to gain insights and make informed business decisions.

Power BI reports can be created with Power BI Desktop, a Windows-based application that provides a powerful set of tools for creating and editing reports. Reports can also be created using the Power BI web service, which allows users to create reports directly in their web browser.

Power BI reports can include various visualizations such as charts, tables, matrices, gauges, and maps. Users can also add text boxes, images, and other types of content to their reports to provide context and additional information.

Power BI reports are extremely interactive, allowing users to interact with their data in real time. Users can filter, drill down, and drill through data to gain a better understanding of their data and uncover insights that were previously hidden.

After creating a report, it can be published to the Power BI service, which is a Cloud-based service that allows users to access their reports from any location and on any device. Reports can also be shared with others, allowing users to collaborate and share insights into their data. The following figure is an example of a Power BI report:

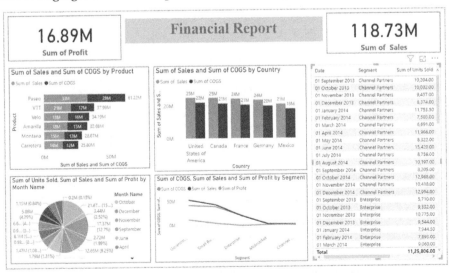

Figure 10.7: Power BI Report

Overall, Power BI reports give users a powerful set of tools for creating, sharing, and analyzing data, allowing them to gain deeper insights and make more informed business decisions.

What is Power Query

The data preparation and transformation tool included in Microsoft Power BI and Excel is called Power Query. It enables users to connect different data sources, then transform and shape the data and load it into the Power BI.

Users can quickly combine and shape data from many sources using Power Query, remove unnecessary columns or rows, replace missing values, split or merge columns, pivot and unpivot data, apply calculations and aggregations, and much more.

With the use of Power Query's graphical user interface, users may create data transformations by following a step-by-step procedure. Each transformation step can be seen and edited by users, and Power Query generates the matching M language code automatically in the background.

Power Query can access data from a variety of sources, including files, databases, web-based data sources, and other types of data stores. It also includes a variety of connectors that enable users to connect to almost any data source they can think of.

After transforming data with Power Query, it can be loaded into Power BI for analysis and reporting using Power BI's powerful visualization and analytics tools.

Overall, Power Query is a powerful data preparation tool that enables users to transform data quickly and easily into an analysis and reporting-ready format.

Accessing Power Query Editor in Power BI

To access Power Query Editor in Power BI, follow the below steps:

1. In Power BI Desktop, click on the **Transform data** from the ribbon; it will open the Power Query editor.

2. If you have the data in Power BI, then it will reflect on Power Query, else you can upload data directly to Power Query, using **Get data** option. Refer to the following figure:

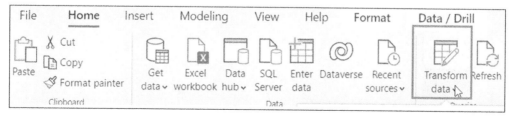

Figure 10.8: Transform data icon in Power BI Desktop

UI of Power Query Editor

The Power Query Editor in Power BI is a powerful tool for data transformation and cleaning. The Power Query Editor's user interface is intended to provide an intuitive and simple interface for users to manipulate data using various transformations.

The Power Query Editor contains the following key UI elements:

1. **The navigation pane:** It appears on the left side of the screen and displays a list of the queries available in the workbook.

2. **Query editor:** This is where you will do most of your data transformations. It has several tabs, such as Home, Transform, Add Column, View, and Options.

3. **The formula bar:** It is located at the top of the editor, displays the formula for the currently selected step.

4. **Current view:** Here you can see the data based on the queries selected.

5. **Query parameters:** This appears in the right-hand pane and displays information about the selected query, such as its name, source, and steps used.

6. **Applied steps:** This is located in the right-hand pane and displays a list of steps that have been applied to the data thus far. You can edit or remove a step by clicking on it.

7. **Preview pane:** It is located at the bottom of the editor and displays a preview of the data after the applied steps have been completed.

8. **Status bar:** Here you can see the relevant information about the query like total columns and rows, execution time, and processing status.

The UI of Power Query Editor looks something like this:

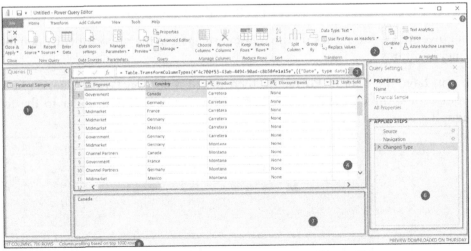

Figure 10.9: UI of Power Query Editor

Transforming the data using Power Query

Power Query Editor is a powerful data transformation and manipulation tool within Power BI that allows you to clean, reshape, and transform your data into a more suitable format for analysis. You can use Power Query Editor to perform data transformations such as filtering, sorting, aggregating, joining, and pivoting, to name a few.

These transformations can be performed without the need for complex coding or manual data manipulation, making it easier and faster to transform and analyze your data. In this tutorial, we will look at how to use Power Query Editor to transform data in Power BI, allowing you to make the most of your data and improve your data analysis process.

In the next sections, we will perform a transformation on financial sample data that we have uploaded from SharePoint, that is, SharePoint List. These transformations are:

- Renaming the column name
- Changing the data type
- Replacing values
- Merging column
- Splitting column

Renaming the column name

Rename refers to changing the name of a column or table in a query in Power Query Editor. Renaming is a common data preparation operation because it allows you to give more descriptive and meaningful names to columns and tables created by data transformation.

Follow the below steps to rename the column name:

- In Power Query Editor | Go to the **Transform** tab | Select the column name.
- Then click on **Rename**, and write the name based on the requirement, as shown below:

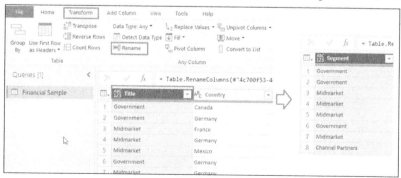

Figure 10.10: Rename the column in Power Query Editor

Changing the data type

A data type is a classification of data in Power Query Editor that specifies the type of values that can be stored in a specific column of a table. A data type determines the type of data that can be stored in each column in a table, such as text, numbers, dates, or logical values.

Data types are significant because they govern how data is stored and processed, as well as how data is displayed and used in Power BI reports. For example, if a column is defined as a text data type, it can only store text values, whereas a numeric data type can only store numerical values.

Power Query Editor supports a wide range of data types, including:

- Text
- Decimal number
- Currency
- Percentage
- Date/time
- Logical (Boolean)
- True/false
- Duration
- Binary

When you import data into Power Query Editor, it automatically assigns data types based on the format of the data. However, you can change the data type of a column to suit better your needs, such as changing a text column to a numeric column or a date column to a text column.

Let us see how we can change the data type in Power Query Editor:

1. In Power Query Editor | Go to the home tab.

2. Select the column | Click on **Data type** (here you can see the data type of the column) | Select the required data type, as shown in the following figure:

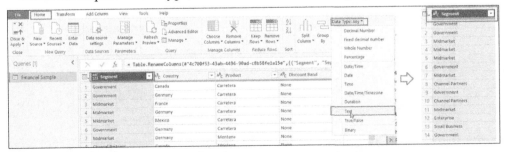

Figure 10.11: Change the data type in Power Query Editor

Replacing Values

The Replace Values feature in Power Query Editor allows you to replace specific values in a column with new values. This is useful when cleaning up or transforming data that contains errors or inconsistencies.

Follow the below steps to replace values in a particular column:

1. Select the value in a column, and then in the Home tab | click on **Replace Value**.

2. Now the Replace value window will open. You can provide the replaced value, so it will reflect in the whole column where the value is used which one you want to replace. It will look like the following figure:

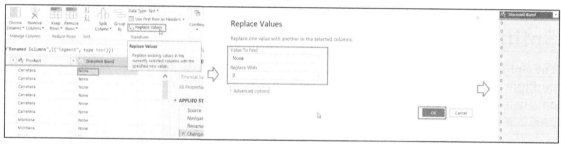

Figure 10.12: Replace value in Power query editor

Merging Columns

The Merge Columns operation in the Power Query editor allows you to combine the contents of two or more columns into a single column. When you have data that is split across multiple columns and need to consolidate it for further analysis or reporting, this operation can be useful.

Follow the below steps to Merge column in Power Query editor:

- In Power query editor, select the columns you want to merge by pressing the *Ctrl+* select Column.

- Then the **Merge Columns** window will open, select the **Separator**, and provide the column name.

- Click on **OK**, as shown:

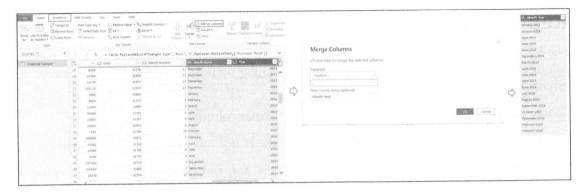

Figure 10.13: Merge column in Power Query editor

Splitting Column

The Split Column feature in Power Query Editor allows you to split a single column into multiple columns based on a specified delimiter or number of characters. When you have data in a single column that needs to be separated into multiple columns for easier analysis or presentation, this is useful.

Follow the below steps to split the column in Power Query Editor:

1. Select the column you want to split.

2. Then go to home tab | Click on **Split Column** | Select **By Delimiter**

3. In **Split Column By Delimiter** window, select or enter the delimiter | Select Split at **Each occurrence of the delimiter**.

4. Click on **OK**.

5. Then rename the column based on the split data, as shown:

Figure 10.14: Split column in Power Query editor

Overview of visualization in Power BI

Visualization in Power BI refers to the process of creating graphical representations of data in the form of charts, graphs, tables, and other visual elements. These visualizations enable users to easily understand and analyze complex data sets, as well as gain insights into business performance.

Power BI includes a wide variety of visualization types, such as bar charts, line charts, pie charts, tables, matrices, maps, gauges, and many more. Users can select the appropriate visualization type based on the data they want to present and the insights they want to gain.

Power BI visualizations are highly interactive, with users able to drill down into data, apply filters, and highlight specific data points. Slicers can be used to filter data across multiple visualizations.

Power BI visualizations are dynamically linked to the underlying data, so any changes to the data will be reflected in the visualizations. This allows users to keep their reports and dashboards up to date with the most recent data.

Custom visuals, which are third-party visualizations created by the community, are also supported by Power BI. These graphics can be downloaded and imported into Power BI reports creating one-of-a-kind and engaging visualization. The visualizations will look something like this:

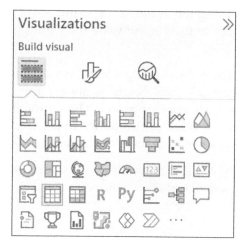

Figure 10.15: Power BI Visualization

Let us discuss some of the visualizations below, which you can access from the visualization pane in Power BI. To create the below visuals, we are going to use financial sample data:

- Bar chart
- Area chart
- Pie chart
- Card
- Table

Bar chart

A bar chart in Power BI is a type of visualization that uses rectangular bars that are proportional in length to the values they represent to display data. The bars can be displayed horizontally, and each bar's length represents a numerical value.

Bar charts are frequently used to compare the values of various data categories or groups. A bar chart, for example, can be used to compare sales figures for various products, regions, or time periods.

The bar chart is further divided into:

- **Stacked bar chart:** A stacked bar chart is a type of chart that shows multiple series of data stacked on top of each other, with each segment representing a specific series' contribution to the total value of each category or group. Stacked bar charts can be used to show the overall size of various categories or groups, as well as the relative contributions of each series to the total.

- **Clustered bar chart:** A clustered bar chart shows multiple series of data side by side, with each bar representing the value of a specific series for each category or group. Clustered bar charts can be used to compare the values of various series within each category or group.

- **100% Stacked bar chart:** A 100% stacked bar chart is similar to a regular stacked bar chart, except that each bar's total height is always the same, representing 100% of the total value for each category or group. The segments within each bar continue to represent each series' relative contributions to the total, but the chart is useful for comparing the proportions of each series within each category or group.

Below in *Figure 10.16* you can see the above three bar charts available in Power BI which represent the **Sum of sales** and **Sum of Profit** by Country:

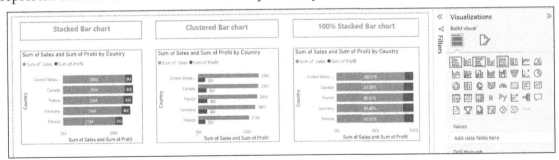

Figure 10.16: Bar chart in Power BI

Similarly in Power BI, we can create a Column chart, which is further divided into Stacked column chart, Clustered column chart, 100% Stacked column chart. And the appearance of Column chart is vertical bars.

Area chart

An area chart in Power BI is a type of visualization that shows quantitative data as a series of points connected by a line, with the area below the line colored. Area charts are useful for displaying how values change over time or across categories, as well as comparing the relative sizes of different series.

As in Power BI contains two Area charts that is, Area chart and Stacked area chart, you can see in the following image:

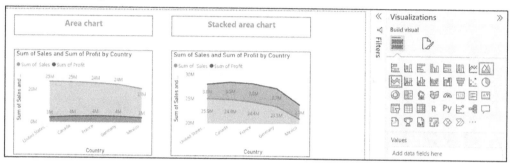

Figure 10.17: Area chart in Power BI

Pie chart

In Power BI, a pie chart is a type of visualization that shows data as a circle divided into slices, with each slice representing a portion of the total value. Pie charts are useful for displaying the relative sizes of various categories or groups, as well as the proportions of each.

Below you can see the Pie chart representing sum of sales, sum of profit by country in Power BI Desktop:

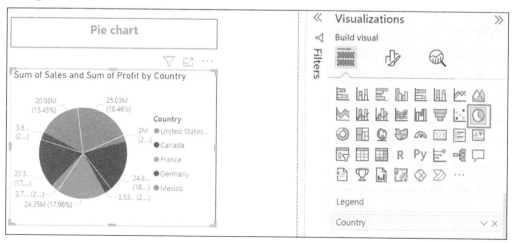

Figure 10.18: Pie chart in Power BI

Card

The Power BI card visual is a simple yet effective visualization that displays a single value or metric in a clear and concise manner. It is frequently used to emphasize a **key performance indicator (KPI)** or a summary statistic, such as sales revenue, profit margin, or customer satisfaction score.

Below you can see the card visual, which show the **Sum of Sales**:

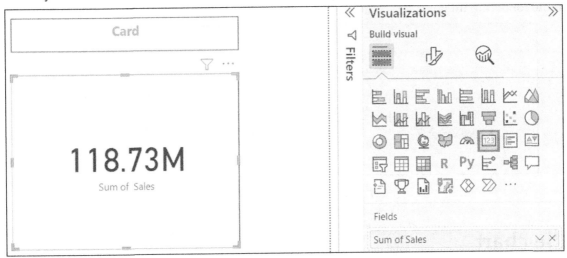

Figure 10.19: Card visual in Power BI

Table

The Power BI table visual is a type of visualization that displays data in a tabular format, much like a spreadsheet or database table. It is frequently used to display detailed data and to enable filtering and sorting.

Below you can see a table visual, having detailed data on financial report in Power BI Desktop:

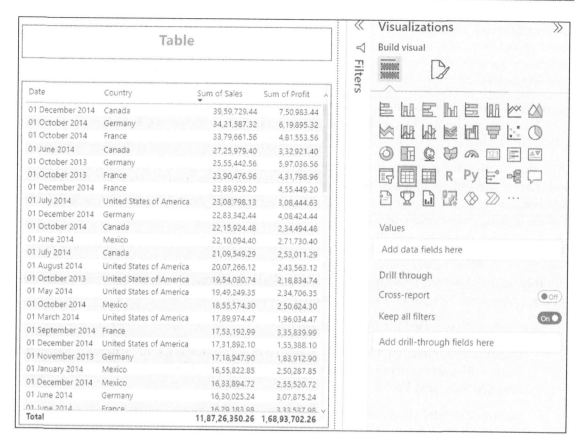

Figure 10.20: Table visual in Power BI

Creating Power BI reports using SharePoint Online data source

Power BI is an advanced data visualization tool that enables you to analyze and visualize data in meaningful ways. SharePoint Online is a Cloud-based collaboration platform for storing, organizing, and sharing information with others. Power BI makes it simple to connect to SharePoint Online data sources and create visually stunning reports to aid in data-driven decision-making.

You must first connect to the data source before you can create a Power BI report with SharePoint Online data. This is done by selecting **SharePoint Online List** from the list of available data sources after clicking the Get Data button in the Power BI Desktop Home tab. The URL and credentials for your SharePoint Online site will then be requested.

Once connected, you can import the data you want to analyze into Microsoft Power BI by selecting the list or library that contains it. You can then begin creating your report by dragging and dropping visualizations from the visualization pane such as bar charts, tables, and maps, onto the canvas.

Power BI also includes customization options to help you in customizing the report based on your business needs. You can add filters, perform custom calculations, and style your visuals to fit your branding.

Once done with your report creation on Power BI Desktop, publish it to the Power BI service and share it with others in the organization or outside the organization. This enables real-time collaboration with colleagues, stakeholders, and customers, as well as providing a powerful tool for making data-driven decisions.

As we have already connected the Financial SharePoint list to the Power BI in the above topic *Connect to SharePoint Data source*. So here we will see how we can create a report that is, a monthly financial report. This report typically includes information such as revenue, expenses, profits, losses, cash flow, and other key financial metrics.

In this report, we have used the following visuals:

- **Clustered bar chart:** In this, we have used Sales, Profit and Country fields, to represent Sum of sales and sum of profit based on Country. Also, it helps you to compare the data between Sales and Profit

- **Waterfall chart:** In this we have used profit, gross sales and segment fields, to represent sum of profit, the sum of gross sales based on segment.

- **Table visual:** In this we have used date, segment, country, sales, gross sales, and profit columns. Here you can see the detailed view of the data.

- **Slicer:** In this we have added Month (Date field). We will use the monthly slicer to slice all the visual, to get the Monthly financial report.

- **Card:** In this report, we have used three card visual, which represents Sum of sales, Sum of profit, and Sum of gross sales

- **Pie chart:** In this visual, have used sales, profit, gross sales, unit sold, and product field. This represents Sum of Profit, Sum of sales, sum of gross sales, sum of unit sold based on the product field.

The financial report will look something like the following figure:

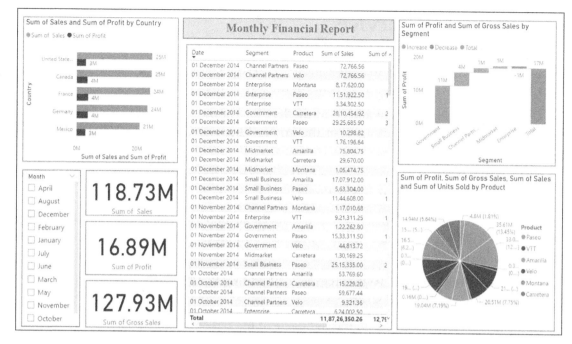

Figure 10.21: *Monthly Financial Report in Power BI*

What is Power BI Service

Microsoft's Power BI Service provides a Cloud-based business intelligence platform where users can create, publish, and share interactive reports, and dashboards. Power BI Service is one of the tools in the Power BI, which also includes Power BI Desktop, Power BI Mobile, and Power BI Embedded.

In Power BI Service, we can connect to a different data source, such as Excel, databases, or SharePoint data sources. After connecting the data source, users can use Power Query available in Power BI Desktop to clean, transform, and arrange the data for analysis.

Then, using a drag-and-drop interface or by writing custom DAX queries, users can create interactive reports. Report visualization can be combined to create dashboards in Power BI service, which offer a high-level view of key metrics and KPIs.

In Power BI service, users can collaborate and share reports and dashboards with others, either internally within their organization or externally with clients and partners, using Power BI Service. Reports and dashboards can be published to the Power BI Service and shared by linking to them or embedding them in other applications or websites.

To help users manage and monitor their reports and dashboards, Microsoft Power BI Service includes capabilities like data refresh schedules, and usage metrics alerts. Power BI Service integrates with other Microsoft products such as Dynamics 365, Teams, and SharePoint.

UI of Power BI service

The Microsoft Power BI Service **User Interface (UI)** is designed to provide a user-friendly and interactive experience for users to access and helps to interact with their data. Here are some of the most important features and elements of the Power BI Service UI:

1. **Navigation pane:** It is available in the left side of the screen and provides easy and quick access to different areas of the Power BI Service, including Datahub, Browse, Workspaces, and Apps.

2. **Top menu:** It is available at the top of the screen and provides you with access to extra features like search, help and settings.

3. **Report canvas:** This is place where we can create and view their reports. Also, we can display their data by adding charts, tables, and other visualizations to the canvas to create report in the Power BI service.

4. **Icon buttons with labels:** for sharing, embedding the Power BI report, exporting the report, bookmarks, and so on.

5. **Visualizations pane:** It is on the right side of the screen; gives you access to a different visualization that you can use in your report.

6. **Filters pane:** This is on the right side of the screen and allows you to apply filters to the data in the dashboard or report.

7. **Data pane:** This is on the right side of the screen, and allows you to access the data sources and fields used in the dashboard or report.

The UI of Power BI Service looks something like this:

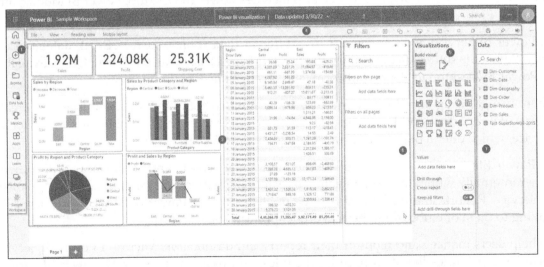

Figure 10.22: UI of Power BI Service

What is workspace in Power BI

In Microsoft Power BI, a workspace is a collaborative environment where we can publish the report, and multiple users can work together to create and share reports, dashboards, and datasets. Workspaces in Power BI Service enable individuals to share data and insights with others in their organization, thus making it simpler to collaborate on business intelligence projects.

In a Power BI service, users can create and manage content such as reports, dashboards, and datasets within a workspace. They can also collaborate with other workspace users by sharing content, providing feedback, and changing shared assets. Workspaces can be configured to give users varying levels of access, with some users having read-only access and others having editing permissions.

Workspaces in Power BI Service can be created for specific projects, departments, or teams, and they can be managed by workspace admins who have access to permissions and settings. Organizations can improve collaboration and streamline data analysis workflows by using workspaces in Microsoft Power BI.

Publishing and sharing report in Power BI

Microsoft Power BI is a robust data visualization and reporting tool that allows users to create interactive and dynamic Power BI reports from different data sources. We can publish a report created in Power BI Desktop to the cloud-based Power BI service and share it with others in your organization or beyond. Also, collaborate with other users and make data-driven decisions based on shared insights by publishing and sharing Microsoft Power BI Report.

Publishing and sharing a report in Power BI involve two main steps:

Publishing the report

Firstly, we will publish the report from the Power BI Desktop to the Power BI service. From the Power BI service, everyone can access and collaborate in one place. Log in to your Power BI account and select the workspace where you want the report to be published. Also, we can change the name, description, and permissions of the report.

So here we will Publish financial reports, which have a report page and Monthly Financial report page from Power BI Desktop to Power BI service. For this follow the steps below.

1. First, save the report on your local desktop.

2. Then click on the **Publish** icon available on the home page, which is displayed in the following figure:

Figure 10.23: Publish the report in Power BI

1. Then select the default workspace which is **My workspace** else, you can create your own workspace. So, here we are selecting my own workspace: **Sample Workspace** from **Publish to Power BI** window.

2. Click on **Select** as shown:

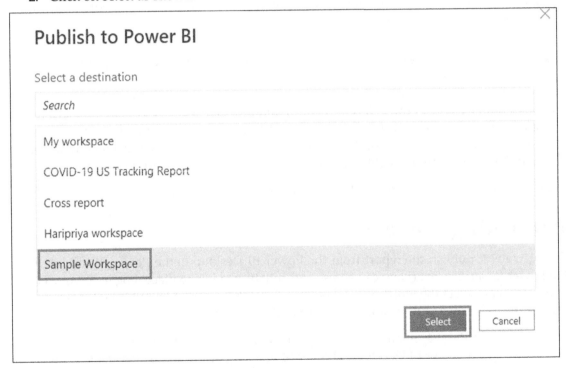

Figure 10.24: Publish the report in Power BI Workspace

Once it is published you can see the success message below and by clicking on the link you can redirect to the published report in Power BI Service. Then click on **Got it** as displayed below:

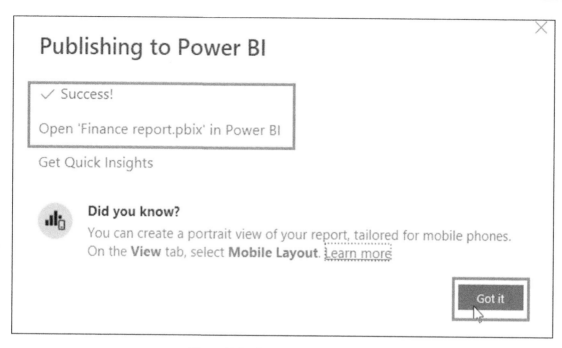

Figure 10.25: *Power BI report published*

Sharing the report

You can share the Power BI report with others after it has been published by granting them access to the report. This includes giving each user-specific permissions, such as view-only or edit access, and sending them a link to the report. The report can also be embedded in other applications or websites, such as SharePoint or Teams.

If your report is opened, you can click on the Share icon | Provide the name you want to share report in your organization | Click on **Send** as illustrated:

Figure 10.26: Share the report in Power BI service

Once you send the link, you can see the below successful message pop on the screen:

Figure 10.27: Successfully shared the report

Embedding Power BI report with SharePoint Online

Power BI is a powerful data analytics and business intelligence platform that allows users to design interactive reports and dashboards. The capacity to embed reports and dashboards in other applications or websites, such as SharePoint Online, is an important feature of Microsoft Power BI.

Users can view and interact with a Power BI report embedded in SharePoint Online without having to switch between applications or open multiple windows. Users' productivity and workflows can be improved because they can access the information, they need in one place.

Embedding a Power BI report in SharePoint Online is a simple procedure that involves generating an embedded code from Power BI and pasting it into the SharePoint Online page where the Power BI report is to be embedded. You can personalize the appearance and functionality of the embedded report to your specific requirements by selecting the size of the report to embed.

To embed the report in SharePoint using embedded code, the **Publish to web** feature must be enabled. If it is not enabled, ask your Power BI administrator to enable it, and if you are the Administrator, follow the steps below to enable:

1. Click on the **Settings** | **Admin Portal** in Power BI Service.

2. Then Admin Portal window will open | Click on **Tenant Settings**.

3. Toggle on the **Enable** button.

4. Under Choose how embedded code works, select Allow existing and new codes.

5. Under **Apply to**, select the **The entire organization** option. Click on **Apply** as shown:

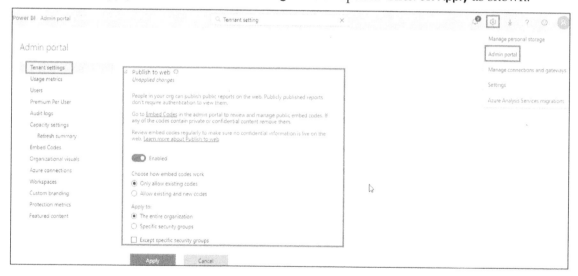

Figure 10.28: Power BI Admin Portal

Embedding Power BI report to SharePoint Online

To embed Power BI report to SharePoint Online using embed link, follow the below steps and refer to the following figure for reference:

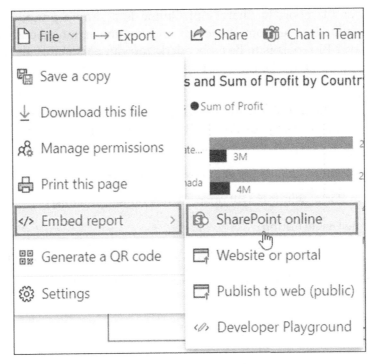

Figure 10.29: Power BI embed report

1. The embed link for SharePoint window will open, from there copy the link. It will look something like this:

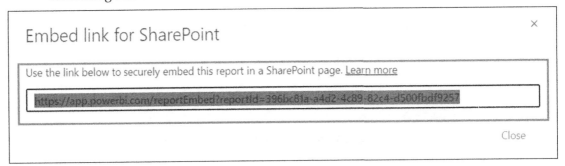

Figure 10.30: Embed link in SharePoint

2. Then edit the SharePoint Page where you want to embed the report.

3. Then click on **+** icon after each part | Search for **Power BI**.

4. Then click on **Power BI** as shown in the following figure:

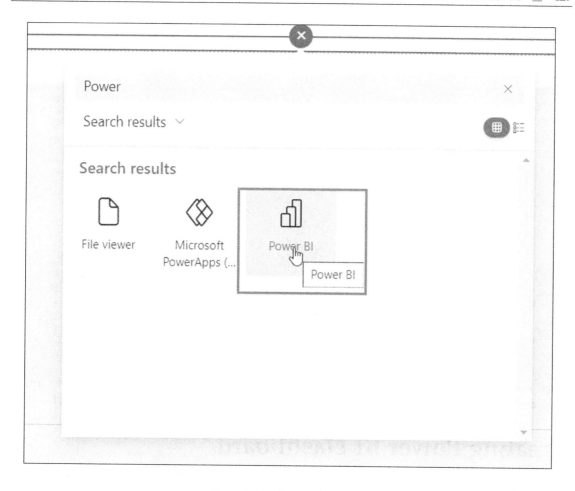

Figure 10.31: *Power BI web part*

5. Then click on **Add a report option** | Provide the report link in the **Power BI Report Link.**

6. Provide Page name and change the display.

7. Enable or disable the navigation, filter, and action pane based on your requirement.

8. You can preview the report on the left side of the window. Then click on **Republish**, as shown below:

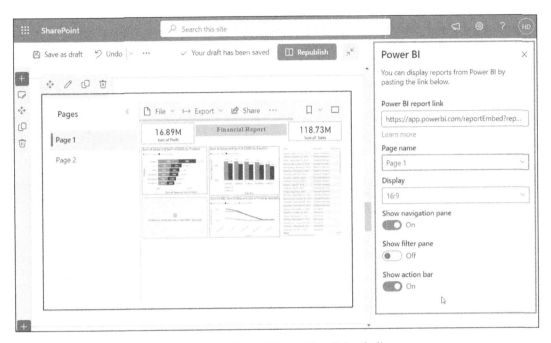

Figure 10.32: Embed Report link in SharePoint Online page

Once you click on **Republish**, the Power BI report is embedded into the SharePoint Online Page and anyone in the organization have access to the report can analyze the report.

Creating Power BI Dashboard

A Power BI dashboard is a collection of visualizations and reports that provides a high-level view of **Key Performance Indicators (KPIs)** and important business metrics in Power BI. Dashboards in Power BI enable users to monitor the health and performance of their business quickly and easily by visually appealing and interactively presenting relevant data.

Power BI dashboards can be built by combining multiple visualizations from one or more reports, and they can include charts, tables, maps, gauges, and other visual elements. Users can customize the layout and appearance of their dashboards, as well as drill down into the data and gain deeper insights using interactive features such as filters and slicers.

Dashboards in Power BI are highly interactive, allowing users to view underlying data or navigate to other related reports and dashboards by clicking on a visual element. Dashboards can also be shared internally and externally by publishing them to the Power BI Service or embedding them in other applications or websites.

Power BI dashboards can be used for a variety of business purposes, such as tracking marketing campaigns, analyzing customer behavior, and managing supply chain operations. Power BI dashboards assist organizations in making data-driven decisions and driving business growth by providing a clear and concise view of critical business metrics.

Steps for creating a Power BI Dashboard

To create Power BI Dashboard from the report, follow the below steps:

1. In Power BI Service, go to the Workspace and open the report.

2. Then select the visualization, you want to pin on the dashboard | Click on the pin icon on the top of the selected visual.

3. Now **Pin to dashboard** option | Select **Existing dashboard** and **New dashboard**. Here we have selected **New dashboard**, so I will provide the Dashboard name as **Finance Analysis Dashboard** | Click on **Pin**, as shown:

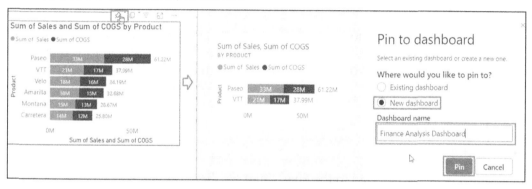

Figure 10.33: *Pin visuals to Dashboards in Power BI service*

Then open the dashboard from the Workspace, you can see above visual is reflected on Dashboard in Power BI service. Like that you can add other visuals also from the same report as well as from different report. The following figure shows the Power BI dashboard:

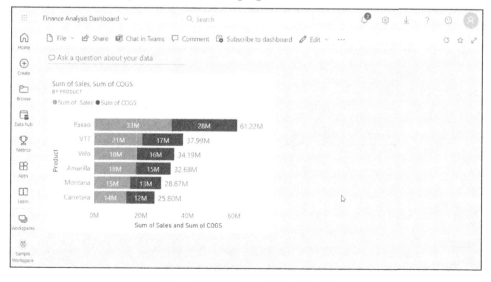

Figure 10.34: *Power BI Dashboard*

How to automatically refresh SharePoint data in Power BI

The data refresh in Power BI is the way of updating the data in the Power BI report and dashboard based on the latest change from the underlying data sources. This is important to make sure that the insights and visualizations in the report reflect the most recent data available.

Our Power BI report is connected to different data sources like Excel, SharePoint Online list, and many more. Then the data is imported to the data model once it is cleaned and transformed to support reporting and analysis.

Data refresh can be scheduled to happen automatically at regular intervals or done manually as needed. Power BI queries the underlying data sources, retrieves the most recent data, and updates the data model and visualizations accordingly during data refresh.

As data refresh is divided into two types:

- Manually refresh data
- Schedule refresh data

As our Report data is connected to the SharePoint list, here we will see how we can schedule the data refresh. For this follow the below steps:

1. In Power BI Service, open the workspace (Sample workspace) | Go to **Datasets + dataflows**.

2. Hover over the report; you can see the two options: **Refresh now** and **Schedule refresh**. Here, select schedule refresh as illustrated below:

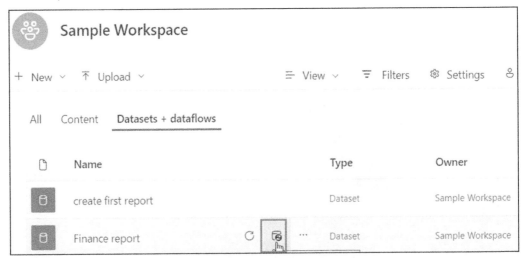

Figure 10.35: Power BI Schedule refresh

3. Next under **Datasets** | Expand the **Data source credentials** | Click on **Edit credentials**.

4. In Configure Financial report, **SharePointSiteURL**, by default detected, | Under Authentication method, check the **OAuth2**.

5. Under the Privacy level setting for this data source, select **Organizational**. Click on **Sign in**.

6. Then provide credentials and password for Microsoft account. Refer to the following figure:

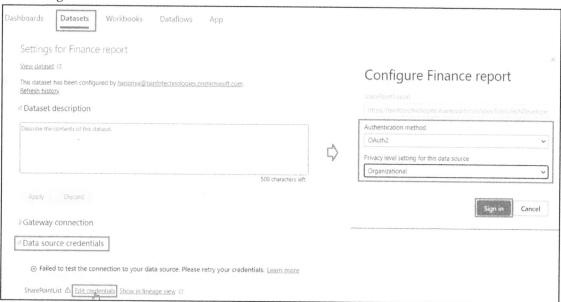

Figure 10.36: Sign in with your credentials

7. Now expand the schedule refresh section | Under **Keep your data up to date**.

8. Then toggle on to configure the data refresh. Next select the **Refresh frequency** | as weekly or daily. If you select weekly, select the days you want to schedule refresh.

9. Then select the time zone.

10. By clicking **Add another time**, you can provide another time to schedule.

11. Under **Send refresh failure notification to**, mention data owner and these contacts.

12. Click on **Apply** as shown:

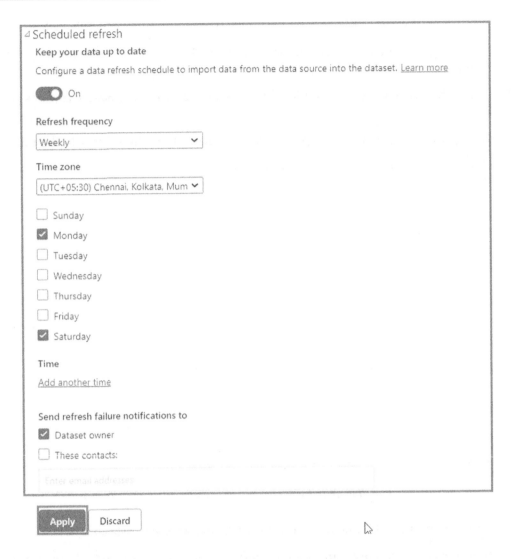

Figure 10.37: Schedule refresh for SharePoint Online data resources

Once you click on **Apply**, you can successfully schedule the refresh for Power BI Desktop, as shown:

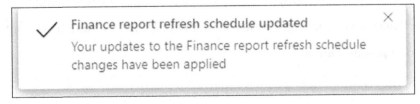

Figure 10.38: Successfully schedule the refresh

Conclusion

To summarise, Power BI is a robust business intelligence application that enables users to see and analyse data in an interactive and intuitive manner. It includes a number of critical features and functionalities, such as data transformation with Power Query, data visualisation, and the ability to connect to a variety of data sources, including SharePoint.

Users can utilise Power BI Desktop to build informative reports and dashboards, which can then be published and shared via the Power BI Service. Furthermore, Power BI integrates seamlessly with SharePoint Online, allowing users to embed reports and automatically refresh data from SharePoint sources.

Overall, Power BI enables businesses to make more informed decisions and obtain important insights from their data.

In the next chapter, we dive into the world of **SharePoint Framework** (**SPFx**). We will start by discussing the SPFx and its importance in designing SharePoint solutions. We will then walk you through setting up the SPFx environment, making sure you have all of the required tools and setups in place.

Next, we will walk you through the process of building your first client-side web part, which will allow you to add dynamic and interactive components to your SharePoint pages. We will also look at web component properties and the property pane, which allow you to customize and configure your web parts. Furthermore, we will go through SharePoint Framework Extensions, such as application customizers, field customizers, command sets, and form customizers, which extend SharePoint's capabilities and enable you to increase its usefulness in a variety of ways.

Points to remember

- Power BI is a complete data analytics service that provides a variety of tools for data visualization and analysis.

- Users using Power BI can connect to a variety of data sources, such as databases, Excel, and SharePoint Online.

- Processes for cleaning and transforming data are made easier by Power Query.

- A drag-and-drop interface is provided by Power BI Desktop for building interactive reports and visualizations.

- Reports and dashboards can be shared both inside and outside of the company, and they can be integrated with other applications.

- Three components that makeup Power BI are Power BI Desktop, Power BI Service (a platform for publishing and sharing data in the cloud), and Power BI Mobile (a mobile app for accessing data from Power BI on smartphones and tablets).

- Powerful reports and dashboards can be created using visualizations like charts, tables, and maps.

- Advanced filtering and slicing capabilities provide deeper insights into business operations.

- The ability to embed reports in other applications or websites, such as SharePoint Online, is a fundamental feature of Power BI.

- Enabling the **Publish to web** function and following the appropriate procedures in Power BI and SharePoint allows Power BI reports to be seamlessly included in SharePoint Online.

- Users of Power BI can publish reports built with Power BI Desktop to the Power BI Service Workspace.

- Power BI Service workspaces are collaborative environments in which numerous users may develop, share, and manage reports, dashboards, and datasets. They enhance collaboration and provide varying levels of access and rights to users.

Join our book's Discord space

Join the book's Discord Workspace for Latest updates, Offers, Tech happenings around the world, New Release and Sessions with the Authors:

https://discord.bpbonline.com

CHAPTER 11
SharePoint Framework

Introduction

In the previous chapter, we learned what Power BI is and how it works with SharePoint data source. Also, we saw how we can transform and clean data from SharePoint list using power Query. We also discussed what is visualization and discussed some of the default visualization available in Power BI. Thereafter, we created a report and dashboard, and then we saw how to publish, share, and schedule refresh the report in Power BI.

In this chapter, we will discuss the only development environment of the modern SharePoint site, **SharePoint Framework (SPFx)**. First, we will see, step by step, how to set up a development environment for SPFx development. Then, once you set up the development environment, we will create a client side webpart, and discuss web part properties and property pane. Moving forward in this chapter, we will learn how we can create extensions in SharePoint Framework.

After that, we will see some examples of Application, Field, and Form customizer using SharePoint Framework.

Structure

This chapter will provide an overview of SharePoint Framework, and how we can use SPFx to customize SharePoint Online. We will discuss the following topics:

- Introducing SharePoint framework
- Setting up SPFx environment
- Creating your first client side webpart
- Web part properties and property pane
- Introduction to SharePoint Framework Extensions
- Application customizers
- Field customizers
- Command sets
- Form customizer

Objectives

The goal of this chapter is to provide a detailed overview to readers about SharePoint framework and its features. After reading this chapter, the readers will understand stepwise how to set up development environments and create client side webparts with SharePoint framework. The readers will also learn about working on Web part properties and property pane. Further, this chapter will introduce extension and customization for applications, fields, and forms.

By the end of this chapter, readers should have a strong grasp on SharePoint Framework and its various components, as well as the skills and knowledge required to create custom SharePoint solutions using SharePoint Framework.

Introducing SharePoint framework

A development model for customizing and adding SharePoint Online and SharePoint on-premises is called **SharePoint Framework (SPFx)**. SPFx is a set of technologies for building web parts and extensions for Microsoft Teams and SharePoint. It is a modern web development platform for building SharePoint personalization like web parts, extensions, and SharePoint add-ins with open-source tools and client-side development technologies such as HTML, CSS, and JavaScript.

We can use modern web technologies and tools in the desired development environment to build productive experiences and applications that are mobile ready and responsive with the SharePoint Framework.

In 2016, Microsoft introduced SPFx based on the most recent web development technologies and trends. Developers can use it to create responsive, scalable, and easily maintainable customizations.

Key features of SharePoint Framework

The following are some of the SharePoint Framework's important features:

- It operates in the browser's current user and connection context. No iFrames are used for the modification (JavaScript is embedded directly to the page).

- In the typical page DOM, the controls are rendered.

- The controls are responsive and easy to use.

- It gives the developer access to the lifecycle as well as render, load, serialize and deserialize, configuration changes, and other features.

- It is framework independent. You are free to implement any JavaScript framework you want, which is not restricted to Knockout, React, Angular, and Vue.js.

- NPM, TypeScript, Yeoman, Webpack, and Gulp are among the popular open-source client development tools used by the developer toolchain in SPFx.

- SPFx provides consistent performance.

- The tenant administrator approved the client-side solution in SPFx, which can be used in end user, available for all sites, including groups, personal sites, or self-service teams.

- To extend Microsoft Teams, we can use SPFx solutions.

Setting up SPFx development environment

SPFx offers tools and a contemporary client-side development approach to developers so they may create responsive, mobile-ready SharePoint experiences. Both SharePoint Online and SharePoint Server 2016/2019 and later versions, like the SharePoint subscription edition, are supported by SPFx.

We highly recommend checking **https://learn.microsoft.com/en-us/sharepoint/dev/spfx/set-up-your-development-environment**, the official Microsoft article to know what the recent versions are supported.

To work with SPFx, you must first create a development environment. We need the following prerequisites for that:

- Code Editor (such as Visual Studio code, Atom etc.)

- Install Node.js (**Long term support (LTS)** version – 18.15.0 LTS)

- Install SPFx development toolchain like:

  o Install Gulp

  o Install Yeoman

  o Install yeoman SharePoint generator

- Modern Web browsers (Install any browser like Google Chrome, Firefox, and Microsoft Edge)
- Configure Self signed developer certificate

Now, let us see one by one how we can install all the above prerequisites to set up SharePoint Framework development environment.

Installing Code Editor

As per the Microsoft guidelines, we can install any code editor or IDE which supports client-side development like building webpart.

Here, we are going to use Visual Studio code editor. To install it click on this https://code.visualstudio.com/. Then, click on **Download** for Windows (based on the OS):

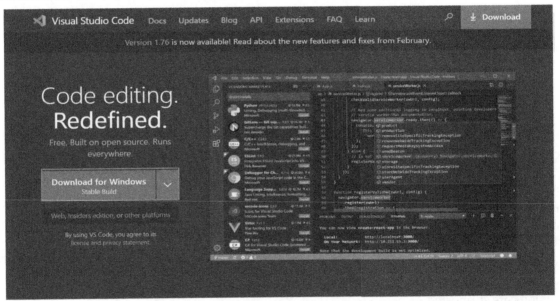

Figure 11.1: Install visual studio code

Installing Node.js

To install node.js on your local desktop based on your OS, click on: **https://nodejs.org/en**. Make sure whenever you install node.js, you always install the **long-term support (LTS)** current version as shown in the following screenshot:

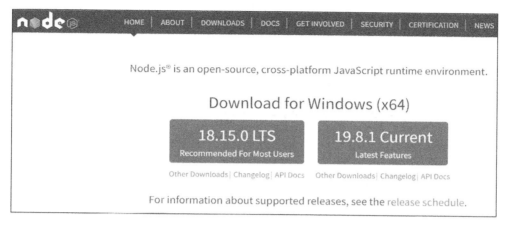

Figure 11.2 : Install node js

To check the node.js installed or note, also check the version of the node.js by following these steps:

1. Open the **Node.js command prompt** as Administrator.

2. Write the command to check the version of node.js: **node -version** as shown in the following figure:

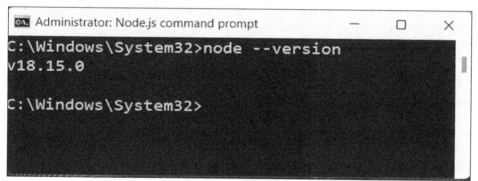

Figure 11.3: *Check node.js version on command prompt*

Installing SPFx development toolchain

Several popular open-source tools are used in SharePoint Framework development and build toolchain. While most dependencies come with each project, a few must be installed globally on your workstation.

Here, we are going to install three tools. You can install these tools globally with a single command: **npm install gulp-cli yo @microsoft/generator-sharepoint -global**.

Else, you can install it separately too.

Installing Gulp

Gulp is a task runner that uses JavaScript to automate repetitive operations. Gulp tasks are used by the SharePoint Framework to build projects, create JavaScript packages, and the resulting bundles are used to deploy solutions.

To install gulp globally, write the following command in the Command prompt:

```
npm install gulp-cli -global
```

Installing Yeoman

Yeoman assists you in launching new projects and suggests best practices and tools to keep you productive. For developing new web parts, SharePoint client-side development tools includes a Yeoman generator. The generator includes common build tools, boilerplate code, and a playground website for testing web parts.

To install Yeoman globally, write the below command in the command prompt:

```
npm install yo --global
```

Installing yeoman SharePoint generator

The Yeoman SharePoint web part generator aids in the rapid creation of a SharePoint client-side solution project with the appropriate toolchain and project system.

To install yeoman SharePoint generator, write the below command in the command prompt:

```
npm install @microsoft/generator-sharepoint -global
```

Configure Self signed developer certificate

When testing the custom SPFx solutions from your development environment, the SharePoint Framework's local webserver uses HTTPS by default. This is accomplished by using a development self-signed SSL certificate. Your developer environment does not trust self-signed SSL certificates. To proceed, set up your SharePoint Framework development environment to trust the certificate.

Once you create your first project, make sure you will run the below command only once in your local web server.

```
gulp trust-dev-cert
```

Now, to check whether the package is installed globally or not in your local environment. Write the below command in the command prompt: `npm list --global --depth=0` as shown in the following figure:

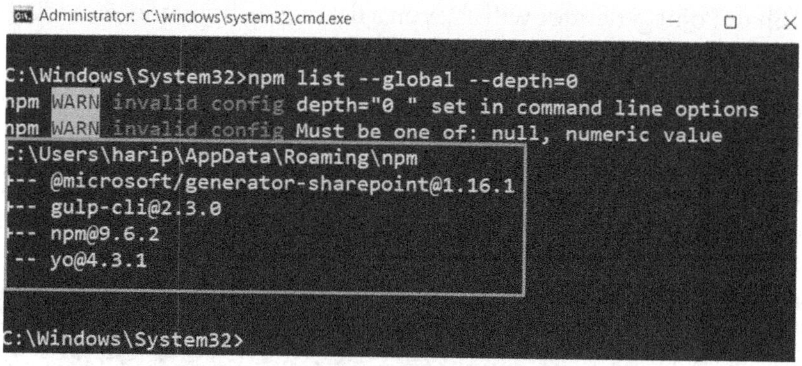

Figure 11.4: *Check the version of all installed package*

Once you install all the prerequisites, set up the develop environment for SharePoint Framework and move forward to create the first client side webpart.

Creating your first client side SPFx webpart

A form of web component known as a client-side web part can be added to SharePoint sites and is rendered on the client side, which means the user's browser executes the code. Writing TypeScript code for a client-side web part in SPFx entails having it compiled into JavaScript and packaged as a SharePoint solution.

In the previous section, we have already set up a development environment. Now let us see the step-by-step procedure to create and deploy the first client-side web part for SharePoint online using SPFx.

To follow the steps, create a SharePoint site where you want to add the client side webpart, and open the node.js command prompt:

1. In the command prompt, go to the drive on your local desktop, where you want to create the project folder. To change the drive, run the below command, if you are in the drive, then move to the next step:

   ```
   cd /d H:\
   ```

2. When we are in the required drive, we will create a project folder and navigate to it by using the following command:

   ```
   mdir "spfx projects"

   cd  "spfx projects"
   ```

3. Once you have created the folder, run the following command to create a new project. By running the Yeoman SharePoint generator in the new directory, you can create the new project:

   ```
   yo @microsoft/sharepoint
   ```

Then, Yeoman SharePoint generator will ask you a list of questions and provide the information based on your requirement:

- **? What is your solution name? client-webparts** (here you can provide you solution name if you do not want the recommended one)

- **? Which type of client-side component to create? WebPart** (here, you will get four options: Webpart, Extension, Library, and Adaptive Card Extension; you can choose from them), as shown in the following figure:

```
See https://aka.ms/spfx-yeoman-info for more information on how to use this generator.
Let's create a new SharePoint solution.
? What is your solution name? client-webpart
? Which type of client-side component to create? (Use arrow keys)
> WebPart
  Extension
  Library
  Adaptive Card Extension
```

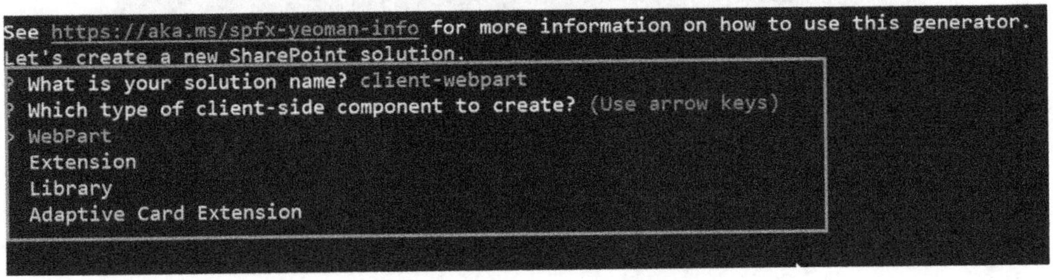

Figure 11.5: Provide solution name and type of client-side component

- **? What is your Web part name? Event Webpart** (here you can provide your web part name or else choose the generated name for web part)

- **? Which template would you like to use? No framework** (there will be three options, Minimal, No framework, and React, choose one based on your requirements) as shown in the following figure:

```
See https://aka.ms/spfx-yeoman-info for more information on how to use this generator.
Let's create a new SharePoint solution.
? What is your solution name? client-webpart
? Which type of client-side component to create? WebPart
Add new Web part to solution client-webpart.
? What is your Web part name? Event Webpart
? Which template would you like to use?
  Minimal
> No framework
  React
```

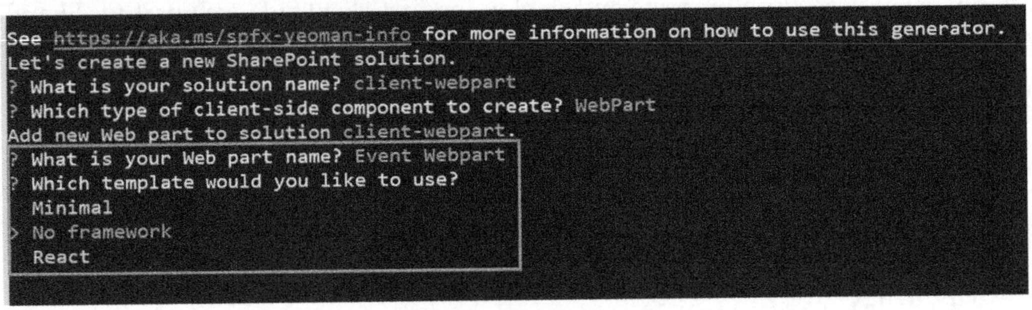

Figure 11.6: Provide webpart name and choose the template

After that, it will take some time to install all the dependencies for the project. Then, it will show you the following success message:

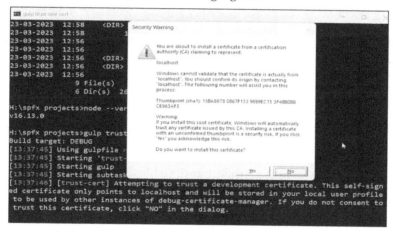

Figure 11.7: Successfully created client-side web part solution

- Since this is the first time, we are creating the first client-side web part solution, we need to certify our local web server. For this, run the following command:

```
gulp trust-dev-cert
```

Then, the security warning window will pop up, click on **Yes** to certify the local web server by installing the certificate as shown in the following figure:

Figure 11.8: Certify local web server

Now our client-side web part is created successfully. Also, we certify the local web server, open the code editor (Visual studio code) by using the command below or open it manually and then add the project folder:

```
code . (code space dot)
```

On the left-hand side of the visual studio code, you can see the client-side web part project structure in the visual studio code as shown in the following figure:

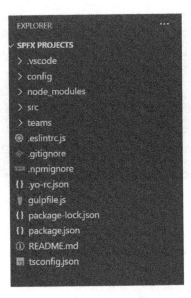

Figure 11.9: *Client-side web part project structure*

Let us understand the above folder structure of client-side web part in SharePoint Framework:

- **src**: This is the main folder, where we will use files most of the time to add functionality to the web parts.

- **config**: This folder includes all the configuration files; we will also change some of the files in this folder.

- **dist**: This folder includes the distributable files, as well as the typescript files that are compiled into JavaScript files.

- **lib**: This directory contains compilation-time files.

- **node_modules**: This directory contains all the dependency's files. For the SPFx development environment to function, these are necessary.

- **temp**: The SPFx development environment uses this folder to store temporary files.

- **.gitignore**: This file tells Git which files to ignore.

- **.npmignore**: This file tells npm which files to ignore.

- **gulpfile.js**: This is a configuration file for Gulp. It runs the Gulp command in this directory.

- **package.json**: The npm uses this file to define dependencies and their versions.

- **README.md**: This is the documentation file for the web part.

- **tsconcfig.json**: TypeScript compilation options are contained in this file.

Test Client-side web part in SPFx local web server

Before you run the project, we need to update the workbench URL, to test our project easily.

A workbench is a place where we can test the solutions before we deploy them. There are two types of workbenches available:

- **Local workbench**: Gulp serve opens the solution in your local Workbench. As a result, you will be able to add and test the components in the local workbench before making your solution available to your tenant.

- **SharePoint workbench**: This is used to test solutions in SharePoint before they are deployed to the SharePoint App catalog. To access SharePoint Workbench, add/layouts/15/workbench.aspx to any of your SharePoint sites.

For testing, when we run the project in the local web server by using the gulp serve, by default it will open a browser with a specified hosted workbench URL. So, in a new project, the default URL for the hosted workbench points to an invalid URL.

To solve this problem, in visual studio we will add SharePoint site to the workbench. For this, follow these steps:

1. In visual studio code, folder structure, expand the config folder and open the **server. json** file.

2. Then in the 'initial page' properties provide the site URL in 'enter-your-SharePoint site' (**https://enter-your-SharePoint-site/_layouts/workbench.aspx**), so when we run the gulp serve, it will run the solution in Site workbench.

Here is the code for reference:

```
{

"$schema":"https://developer.microsoft.com/json-schemas/spfx-build/spfx-serve.
schema.json",

"port": 4321,

"https": true,

"initialPage":"https://tsinfotechnologies.sharepoint.com/sites/
TsInfoTechDeveloper/_layouts/workbench.aspx"

}
```

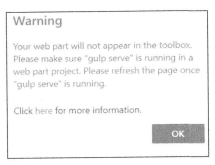

Figure 11.10 : Setup workbench for testing

3. Now, write the below command in the command prompt to run the project and you can test the solution hosted in the local workbench:

```
gulp serve
```

4. Once your project starts running, you will get the **Warning** window, click on **OK**, as shown:

> ## Warning
>
> Your web part will not appear in the toolbox. Please make sure "gulp serve" is running in a web part project. Please refresh the page once "gulp serve" is running.
>
> Click here for more information.
>
> **OK**

Figure 11.11: Warning window while running SPFx client web part solution

5. Now click on the Plus **+** icon and search the web part or Under the Local section, you can see your web part as shown in the following screenshot:

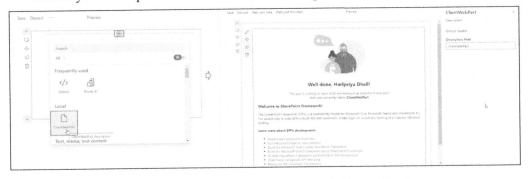

Figure 11.12: Add your custom web part to the site workbench

To stop running the solution in Workbench, write the Ctrl+ C command, and then type Y and press enter.

Deploy SharePoint Framework client web part to SharePoint Online App catalog

To use client-side web parts on modern SharePoint server-side pages, the web part must be deployed and registered with SharePoint. First, we should package the web part. Then, we will deploy the package in the SharePoint App catalog.

In Visual studio code, under **config** folder, open the **package-solution. Json** file, you can see the code having package metadata as shown in the following screenshot:

Here is the code for reference:

```
{
"$schema":"https://developer.microsoft.com/json-schemas/spfx-build/package-solution.schema.json",
"solution": {
"name": "web-part-client-side-solution",
"id": "143604d4-662e-467a-9c4c-37e5830d9675",
"version": "1.0.0.0",
"includeClientSideAssets": true,
"skipFeatureDeployment": true,
"isDomainIsolated": false,
"developer": {
"name":"",
"websiteUrl":"",
"privacyUrl":"",
"termsOfUseUrl":
"mpnId": "Undefined-1.16.1"
},
"metadata": {
"shortDescription": {
"default": "WebPart description"
},
"longDescription": {
```

```
"default": "WebPart description"

},

"screenshotPaths": [],

"videoUrl":"",

"categories": []

},

"features":[

{

"title": "web-part Feature",

"description": "The feature that activates elements of the web-part solution.",

"id": "eafe6b11-2d6e-4cce-a5f7-e07e35c666dc",

"version": "1.0.0.0"

}

]

},

"paths": {

"zippedPackage": "solution/web-part.sppkg"

}

}
```

To bundle the solution, write the command below in the command prompt.

`gulp bundle`

To package the solution, write the command below in the command prompt.

`gulp package-solution`

Once you run the command, it will create a package: **\sharepoint\solution\web-part.sppkg**.

To **deploy** the solution in the SharePoint App catalog follow these steps:

1. Open the SharePoint Admin center (https://<tenant name>-admin.sharepoint.com/) | Click on **More features** | under **Apps**, click on **Open**. Then, the **Manage apps** window will open, click on the **Upload** icon and upload the solution, that is, the web-part.sppkg file:

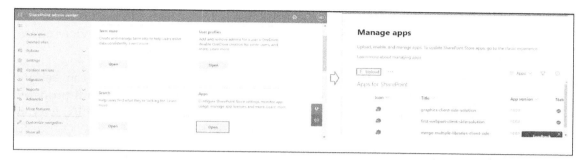

Figure 11.13: Manage Apps in SharePoint Admin center

2. Next in the **Enable App** window, under **App availability**, there will be two options:

   a. **Enable this app**: It will only enable this app. Also, you will install the solution from my app page and then you can use it.

   b. **Enable this app and it to all sites**: It will enable this app and automatically add the solution to the SharePoint site.

   c. So, select **Enable this app and it to all sites**. Click on **Enable App**. You can see the solution is now available in SharePoint App catalog, as shown in the following figure:

Figure 11.14: Deploy the solution in App catalog

Once you deploy the web part in SharePoint App catalog, you can install the webpart in your SharePoint site from **My apps**. It will also be available in the Site contents based on the option you choose while enabling the app. Then, you can use it in your SharePoint page.

Web part properties and property pane

A web part property is a customizable setting in SharePoint Framework that controls the actions or appearance of a SharePoint web part. The web part's title, description, the number of items to show, and the background color are some examples of web part properties.

The property pane is a user interface element that allows users to view and modify web part properties. It appears when a user selects a web part on a SharePoint page and provides a way to customize the web part's behavior without requiring any code changes.

In the SharePoint Framework solution, by using the property pane object, we can declare the web part properties and their respective controls, which gives a list of prebuilt property controls like dropdowns, checkboxes, text fields, and custom controls. Also, in SPFx, we can create custom controls with React, and use them in the Property pane of web parts

To use the Property Pane in an SPFx web part, we can declare the web part's properties and associated controls in a property pane object setup. The web part Property Pane components in SPFx receives this object and displays the property pane UI with the predefined controls.

Configure your SharePoint client-side web part with property pane and properties

In SPFx, end users are allowed by property pane to configure the properties in particular web parts. In SPFx webpart solutions, properties of property pane are declared in the propertyPaneSettings section in the webpart code.

A property pane contains three important metadata: a page, an optional header, and at least one group as explained below:

- Page: It allows you to separate complex interactions and place them on one or more pages. Pages include a header and groups.

- An optional header: You can specify the title of the property pane using headers.

- Groups: It enables you to choose which sections or fields in the property pane should be used to categorize your field sets.

The property pane supports the list of fields:

- Multi-line Text box

- Text box

- Toggle

- Slider

- Link

- Dropdown

- Horizontal rule

- Choice group

- Button

- Checkbox
- Custom

Field types can be found as modules in **@microsoft/sp-property-pane**. Before you can use the objects in your web parts, you must first import them into a module:

```
import {

PropertyPaneTextField,

PropertyPaneDropdown

PropertyPaneCheckbox,

PropertyPaneSlider

PropertyPaneLabel,

PropertyPaneLink,

PropertyPaneToggle

} from '@microsoft/sp-property-pane';
```

Handling field changes in SPFx

To handle field changes in SPFx, we need to handle the property pane. There are two ways for this:

- **Reactive:** The change event is triggered in reactive mode whenever a field control in the property pane is changed. The reactive behavior updates the web part's properties with the new values automatically. The reactive mode is the web part's default mode.
- **Non-Reactive:** While the reactive mode is sufficient for many scenarios, there are times when non-reactive behavior is required. Non-reactive does not automatically update the web part unless the user confirms the changes.

If you want to enable the non-reactive mode, you need the below code for the spfx solution:

```
protected get disableReactivePropertyChanges(): boolean {

  return true;

}
```

Creating Property pane in SPFx

First, we need to create a new folder for your project using the following command:

```
mkdir "client-webpart"
```

Now, navigate to the directory and write the following command:

`cd "client-webpart"`

Run the SharePoint Yeoman generator to create a new project in the project file:

`yo @microsoft/sharepoint`

Then the Yeoman SharePoint generator will ask you a list of questions related to the solution, as show in *Figure 11.15*:

- `? What is your solution name? event-list` (here you can provide you solution name if you do not want the recommended one)

- `? Which type of client-side component to create?` Webpart (here, there will be four options that you can choose from:

  o `Webpart,`

  o `Extension,`

  o `Library,`

  o `Adaptive Card Extension,`

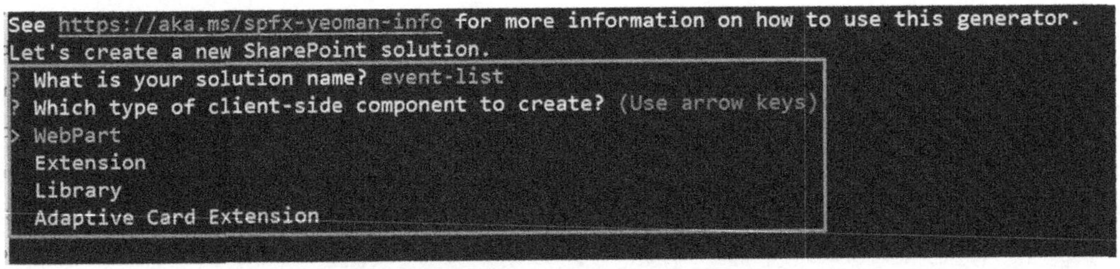

Figure 11.15: Provide solution name and client side component

- `? What is your Web part name? Event Webpart` (here you can provide your web part name or else choose the generated name for web part)

- `? Which template would you like to use? No framework` (there will be three options that you can choose from based on your requirements, as shown in *Figure 11.16*:

  o `Minimal,`

  o `No framework,` and

  o `React,`

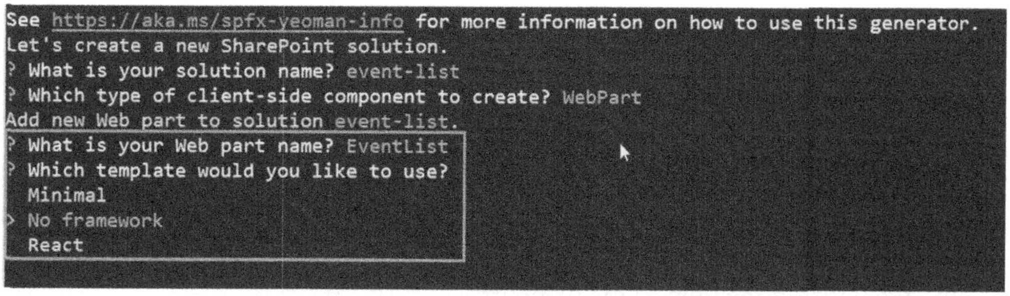

Figure 11.16: *Provide web part name, and template*

It will take some time to install all dependencies required to create solutions. After that you can see the success message for event list solutions:

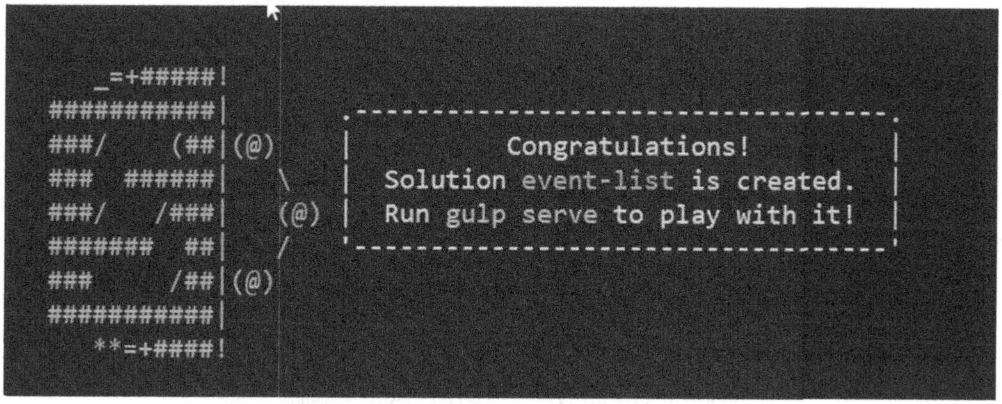

Figure 11.17: *Solution event list successfully created*

Once we successfully create the project, then write the below code to open visual studio code:

`Code . (code space dot)`

Then run the project with the below command and make sure you have provided the site URL to the workbench:

gulp serve

Now you can see your project is running in the local server. If you click on the edit icon on the top left corner of web part, you can see the property pane. In this property pane you can see the default field, that is, the Description field.

Now, let us see how we can add a field to our Event list web part. For this, follow the steps below:

1. In the visual studio code navigate to the **EventListWebpart.ts**, located in "\event list webpart\src\webparts\eventList\EventListWebPart.ts." Here, first add the field to the interface like below:

```
export interface IEventListWebPartProps {
  eventName: string;
  eventDate:string;
  description: string;
}
```

2. Then, in the same file add the below code to **getPropertyPaneConfiguration()**. By this, we will add the field to the webpart:

```
protected getPropertyPaneConfiguration(): IPropertyPaneConfiguration {
  return {
    pages: [
      {
        header: {
          description: strings.PropertyPaneDescription
        },
        groups: [
          {
            groupName: strings.BasicGroupName,
            groupFields: [
              PropertyPaneTextField('eventName', {
                label: strings.EventNameFieldLabel
              }),
              PropertyPaneTextField('eventDate', {
                label: strings.EventDateFieldLabel
              }),

              PropertyPaneTextField('description', {
                label: strings.DescriptionFieldLabel
              })
            ]
          }
        ]
      }
```

```
        ]
    };
}
```

3. In the same file change the **render()** code, with below code:

```
public render(): void {
    this.domElement.innerHTML = `
            <section   class="${styles.eventList}   ${!!this.context.sdks.
microsoftTeams ? styles.teams : ''}">
        <div class="${styles.welcome}">
          <img alt="" src="${this._isDarkTheme ? require('./assets/welcome-
dark.png') : require('./assets/welcome-light.png')}" class="${styles.
welcomeImage}" />
      <h2>Well done, ${escape(this.context.pageContext.user.displayName)}!</
h2>
          <div>${this._environmentMessage}</div>
          <div>Event Name: <strong>${escape(this.properties.eventName)}</
strong></div>
          <div>Event Date: <strong>${escape(this.properties.eventDate)}</
strong></div>
              <div>Event Description: <strong>${escape(this.properties.
description)}</strong></div>
        </div>
    </section>`;
}
```

4. Now, navigate to the manifest.json file, which is located in H:\event list webpart\src\ webparts\eventList\EventListWebPart.manifest.json. In the **preconfiguredEntries part**, write the below code:

```
"preconfiguredEntries": [{
    "groupId": "5c03119e-3074-46fd-976b-c60198311f70",
    "group": { "default": "Advanced" },
    "title": { "default": "EventList" },
    "description": { "default": "EventList description" },
    "officeFabricIconFontName": "Page",
    "properties": {
```

```
    "eventName": "",
    "eventDate":"",
    "description": ""
  }
}]
```

5. Then navigate to the en-un.js file, which is located in the **\event list webpart\src\ webparts\eventList\loc\en-us.js**, then write the below code:

```
define([], function() {
  return {
    "PropertyPaneDescription": "Description",
    "PropertyPaneEventName":"Event Name",
    "PropertyPaneEventDate":"Event Date",
    "BasicGroupName": "Group Name",
    "EventNameFieldLabel":"Event Name",
    "EventDateFieldLabel": "Event Date",
    "DescriptionFieldLabel": "Description",
    "AppLocalEnvironmentSharePoint": "The app is running on your local
environment as SharePoint web part",
    "AppLocalEnvironmentTeams": "The app is running on your local environment
as Microsoft Teams app",
    "AppLocalEnvironmentOffice": "The app is running on your local environment
in office.com",
      "AppLocalEnvironmentOutlook": "The app is running on your local
environment in Outlook",
    "AppSharePointEnvironment": "The app is running on SharePoint page",
    "AppTeamsTabEnvironment": "The app is running in Microsoft Teams",
    "AppOfficeEnvironment": "The app is running in office.com",
    "AppOutlookEnvironment": "The app is running in Outlook"
  }
});
```

6. Lastly, navigate to **myStrings.d.ts** file, which is located in **\event list webpart\ src\webparts\eventList\loc\mystrings.d.ts** write the below code:

```
declare interface IEventListWebPartStrings {
  PropertyPaneDescription: string;
```

```
    BasicGroupName: string;

    DescriptionFieldLabel: string;

    EventNameFieldLabel:string;

    EventDateFieldLabel:string;

    AppLocalEnvironmentSharePoint: string;

    AppLocalEnvironmentTeams: string;

    AppLocalEnvironmentOffice: string;

    AppLocalEnvironmentOutlook: string;

    AppSharePointEnvironment: string;

    AppTeamsTabEnvironment: string;

    AppOfficeEnvironment: string;

    AppOutlookEnvironment: string;

}
declare module 'EventListWebPartStrings' {

    const strings: IEventListWebPartStrings;

    export = strings;

}
```

Now, if your solution is running in the local server, you can refresh the page, and edit the webpart. You can also see that the field is added to the property pane, and provide the value, like shown in *Figure 11.18*. If your solution is not running, then write **gulp serve** in the command prompt:

Figure 11.18: Add properties to the property pane using spfx

Introduction to SharePoint Framework Extensions

The SharePoint Framework Extensions are one of the primary elements of the SharePoint Framework. It enables users to expand the functionality of SharePoint and alter the look and feel of SharePoint Modern sites like toolbar, area including notifications, forms, and list data views.

It provides a powerful way to extend and customize the SharePoint user experience using modern web technologies and frameworks. These modern web technologies include React, Angular, and TypeScript.

Extensions in SPFx are client-side components that enable users to build customizations. Also, it allows the use of the familiar SPFx tools and libraries to add new functionality or modify existing features of SharePoint sites.

There are mainly four types of extensions in SharePoint Framework:

- **Application Customizers:** This category of extensions in SPFx allows us to add unique CSS and JavaScript to a SharePoint page and change how it looks or behaves. We can also use these extensions to integrate external services and add unique branding elements.

- **Field Customizers:** This category of extensions mainly focuses to customize the look and behavior of fields that we use in a SharePoint library or list. For instance, we can use it to display a progress bar for a task list or to display an icon next to a document that indicates its status.

- **Command Sets:** This extension allows us to alter the functionality of existing buttons or add new menu items to the command bar. These extensions are useful tools for adding custom functionality to a SharePoint site.

- **Form Customizers:** With the help of these extensions, you may alter the look and behavior of the forms that are used to add, update, and view the contents of a SharePoint list or library. Form Customizers can be used to develop custom forms using cutting-edge web technologies like React or Angular, as well as to change the behavior of SharePoint forms by default.

Application customizers

The application customizer is a client-side extension in a SharePoint Framework which enables users to customize the look and feel of modern pages in SharePoint Online and gives additional features to the user interface of SharePoint.

This customizer is a JavaScript based extension that runs on the client side and is applied on the SharePoint modern page header. This means that the customization made using application customizer are only applied to the current page and do not affect other pages of the SharePoint site.

By using application customizer, we can add our own HTML, CSS and JavaScript code to the page header to create customized UI components such as custom branding, navigation menu, and notification. The application customizer also provides the feature to interact with SharePoint API, and Office 365 services to retrieve and display or perform other custom operations.

The advantage of using application customizer is for us to build customizations without changing the underlying code base of SharePoint. This means that application customizations are portable across different environments, and updates to SharePoint will not break the customizations

Now, let us see how we can create an application customizer extension in SPFx to customize SharePoint look and feel.

Creating Application customizer extensions in SPFx

Let us start by creating the project folder by following these steps:

1. Open node.js command prompt and then write the below command to create project folder:

```
mkdir AppCustomizer
```

2. Navigate to directory using the below command:

```
cd AppCustomizer
```

3. Then, to create the project, run the below command in the folder, so that the Yeoman SharePoint generator will create the project with the required dependencies:

```
yo @microsoft/sharepoint
```

4. Then, Yeoman will prompt the list of questions related to your solution, as shown in *Figure 11.19*:

   a. **What is your solution name? app-customizer** (here you can provide the name of the customizer and also you can select the name suggested by the yeoman)

   b. **? Which type of client-side component to create? Extension** (here you can see four choices, that is, Webpart, Extension, Library, Adaptive Card Extension, and select Extension)

   c. **? Which type of client-side extension to create?** Application Customizer (here it provides five options: **Application Customizer**, **Field Customizer**, **ListView Command Set**, **Form Customizer**, **Search Query Modifier**, from this choose **Application customizer**)

```
See https://aka.ms/spfx-yeoman-info for more information on how to use this generator.
Let's create a new SharePoint solution.
? What is your solution name? app-customizer
? Which type of client-side component to create? Extension
? Which type of client-side extension to create? (Use arrow keys)
> Application Customizer
  Field Customizer
  ListView Command Set
  Form Customizer
  Search Query Modifier
```

Figure 11.19: Yeoman generated questions

d. **? What is your Application Customizer name? AppCustomizer** description (here provide the application customizer name, or select the generated name), as shown:

```
See https://aka.ms/spfx-yeoman-info for more information on how to use this generator
Let's create a new SharePoint solution.
? What is your solution name? app-customizer
? Which type of client-side component to create? Extension
? Which type of client-side extension to create? Application Customizer
Add new Application Customizer to solution app-customizer.
? What is your Application Customizer name? AppCustomizer description
```

Figure 11.20: Application customizer name

Now it will take some time to install all dependencies and create our project. Once it is created, you can see the following success message:

```
   _=+#####!
##########|
###/    (##|(@)    .------------------------------------.
### ######|  \     |         Congratulations!           |
###/  /###|  (@)   | Solution app-customizer is created. |
###### ##|  /      | Run gulp serve to play with it!    |
###    /##|(@)     '------------------------------------'
##########|
   **=+####!
```

Figure 11.21: Successfully created App customizer extensions

The Folder structure of app customizer extension look like the following figure:

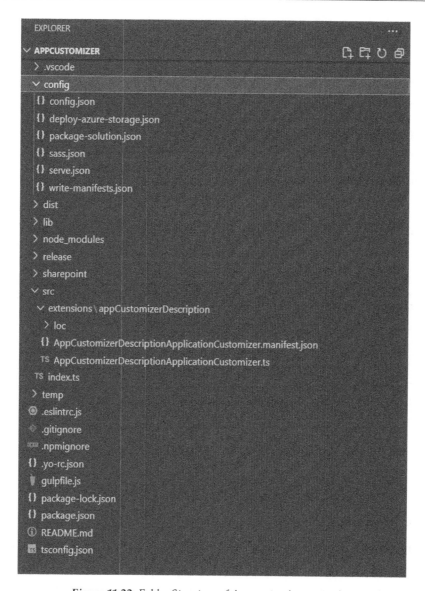

Figure 11.22: Folder Structure of App customizer extension

As we cannot run the application customizer in the local workbench, we need to provide the page URL of a particular site where you want to apply the customization.

For this, expand the config folder in the project structure | open **serve.json** file | then, give the URL of the page.

Here is the code for reference:

```
{
"$schema": "https://developer.microsoft.com/json-schemas/spfx-build/spfx-
serve.schema.json",

"port": 4321,

"https": true,

"serveConfigurations": {

"default": {

"pageurl": "https://tsinfotechnologies.sharepoint.com/sites/
TsInfoTechDeveloper/SitePages/ProjectHome.aspx",

customActions": {

"d9a50d0d-56d4-4506-95ab-9fdd7ef17544": {

"location": "ClientSideExtension.ApplicationCustomizer",

"properties":{

"testMessage": "Test message"

}

}

}

},

"appCustomizerDescription":

"pageUrl": "https://tsinfotechnologies.sharepoint.com/sites/
TsInfoTechDeveloper/SitePages/ProjectHome.aspx" ,

customactions : {

"d9a50d0d-56d4-4506-95ab-9fdd7ef17544": {

"location": "ClientSideExtension.ApplicationCustomizer",

"properties": {

"testMessage": "Test message"

}

}
```

```
        }

    }

  }

}
```

Now, open the **manifest.json** file of your project which is in "**appCustomizer****src****extensions**\\ **appCustomizerDescription****AppCustomizerDescriptionApplicationCustomizer.manifest. json**". This file specifies your extension's type as well as a unique identifier. This ID will be required later when you debug and deploy your extension to SharePoint.

Here is the code for reference:

```
{

    "$schema":  "https://developer.microsoft.com/json-schemas/spfx/client-side-
extension-manifest.schema.json",

  "id": "d9a50d0d-56d4-4506-95ab-9fdd7ef17544",

  "alias": "AppCustomizerDescriptionApplicationCusto",

  "componentType": "Extension",

  "extensionType": "ApplicationCustomizer",

  // The "*" signifies that the version should be taken from the package.json
  "version": "*",

  "manifestVersion": 2,

  // If true, the component can only be installed on sites where Custom Script
is allowed.

  // Components that allow authors to embed arbitrary script code should set
this to true.

  // https://support.office.com/en-us/article/Turn-scripting-capabilities-on-or-
off-1f2c515f-5d7e-448a-9fd7-835da935584f

  "requiresCustomScript": false
}
```

When the client-side extension is first initiated on the SharePoint page, the **onInit()** method is called, which also contains the logic for your Application Customizer. This happens after **this.context** and **this.properties** have been assigned. **OnInit()**, like web parts, returns a promise that can be used to perform asynchronous operations.

The **onInt()** is located in the **AppCustomizerDescriptionApplicationCustomizer.ts** file **'\appCustomizer\src\extensions\appCustomizerDescription\AppCustomizer DescriptionApplicationCustomizer.ts'**. You can see the below code by default that displays the alert message by default.

Here is the code for reference:

```
public onInit(): Promise<void> {

 Log.info(LOG_SOURCE, `Initialized ${strings.Title}`);

 let message: string = this.properties.testMessage;

 if (!message) {

   message = '(No properties were provided.)';

 }

 Dialog.alert(`Hello from ${strings.Title}:\n\n${message}`).catch(() => {

   /* handle error */

 });

 return Promise.resolve();

}
```

Run the following command to compile your code and host the compiled files from your local computer:

gulp serve

To continue loading scripts from your local host, navigate to your browser and select **Load debug scripts** as shown in the following figure:

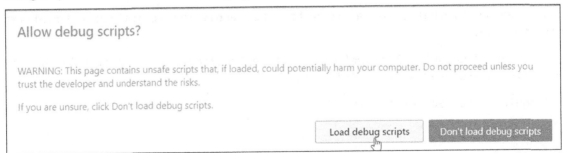

Figure 11.23: Load debug scripts

Now, you can see the dialog message window.

Your SharePoint Framework Extension has thrown this dialogue. The **testMessage** property is included in the alert message because you provided it as a part of the debug query parameters. You can set up your extension instances using the client component properties passed to the instance during runtime as shown in the following screenshot:

Figure 11.24: Alert pop up box

Deploy Application customizer extension to SharePoint Online

To deploy the Application customizer extension to SharePoint Online follow the below steps:

1. First terminate the solution from running with the below command:

   Ctrl+C

2. To get the basic structure ready for packaging, run the following command on your client-side solution that includes the extension:

   gulp bundle

3. Then, write the below command to create the solution package:

   gulp package-solution

4. Now, the solution is created in this location of folder structure, "/**appCustomizer\ sharepoint\solution\app-customizer.sppkg**" as shown in the following figure:

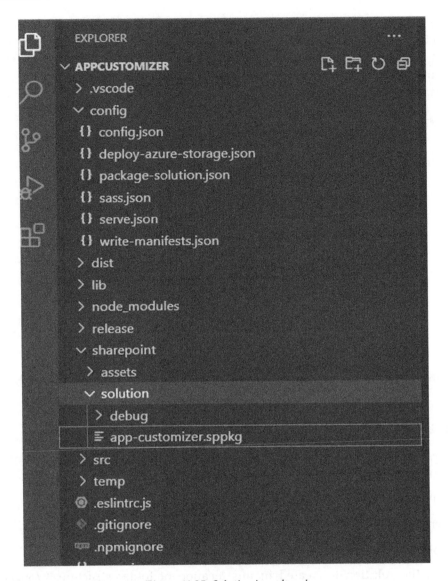

Figure 11.25: Solution is packaged

5. Then, navigate to SharePoint App catalog and upload the solution file.

6. Next, the Enable app window will open. From here, select the **Only enable app** option as shown in the following figure: After that you can see the app has been enabled.

Figure 11.26: Enable the App

Then you can see that the app is added to the App catalog, now it is available in My app page in SharePoint Online site:

Figure 11.27: Upload the solution for SharePoint catalog

7. Navigate to the SharePoint site and click on **+New** icon on the Home page | select the app. It will redirect the My app page of SharePoint site.

8. Then, click on **Add** button as shown in the following screenshot:

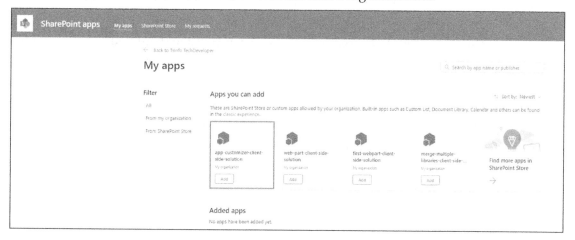

Figure 11.28: Add apps to your site from My apps

Now you can use the app or application customizer solution in your SharePoint site page based on your requirements.

Field customizer

The Field customizer in SPFx is a feature that allows users to change the design of fields in a SharePoint library or list to customize the look and feel of the library or list.

We can use this customizer to change how data is displayed and responded to in SharePoint columns by adding custom User Interface components such as menus, dialogues, and buttons.

This is also used to show extra information that is not available in the primary list item or document, as well as to implement custom business logic according to the field's value.

Creating Field customizer in SPFx

Let us start by creating the project folder by following these steps:

1. Open node.js command prompt and then write the below command to create project folder:

   `mkdir FieldCustomizer`

2. Navigate to directory using the below command:

   `cd FieldCustomizer`

3. Then, to create the project, run the below command in the folder, so Yeoman SharePoint generator will create the project with required dependencies:

   `yo @microsoft/sharepoint`

4. Then Yeoman will prompt the list of questions related to your solution, as shown in *Figure 11.29*:

   a. `What is your solution name?` `field-customizer` (here you can provide the name of the customizer and select the name suggested by the Yeoman)

   b. `? Which type of client-side component to create?` `Extension` (here you can see four choices, that is, `Webpart`, `Extension`, `Library`, `Adaptive Card Extension`; Select `Extension)` as shown in the following figure:

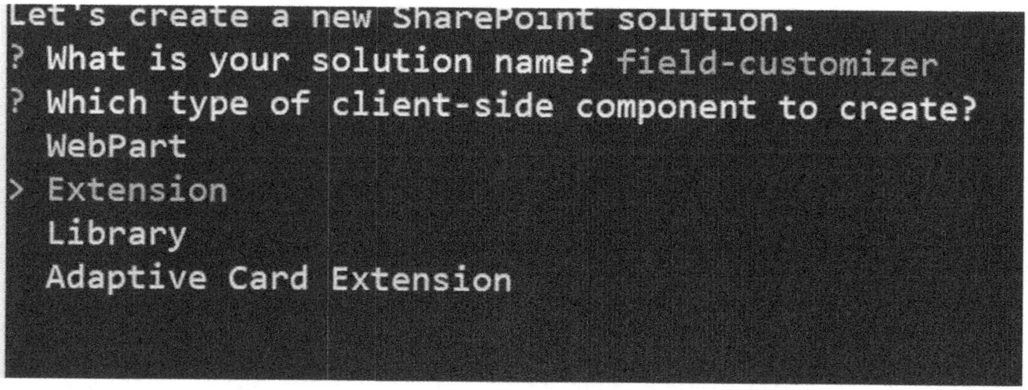

```
Let's create a new SharePoint solution.
? What is your solution name? field-customizer
? Which type of client-side component to create?
  WebPart
> Extension
  Library
  Adaptive Card Extension
```

Figure 11.29: Choose extension as client-side component to create

c. **Which type of client-side extension to create? Field Customizer** (here it provides five options: **Application Customizer**, **Field Customizer**, **ListView Command Set**, **Form Customizer**, **Search Query Modifier**; from this choose **Application Customizer**) This can be seen in the following figure:

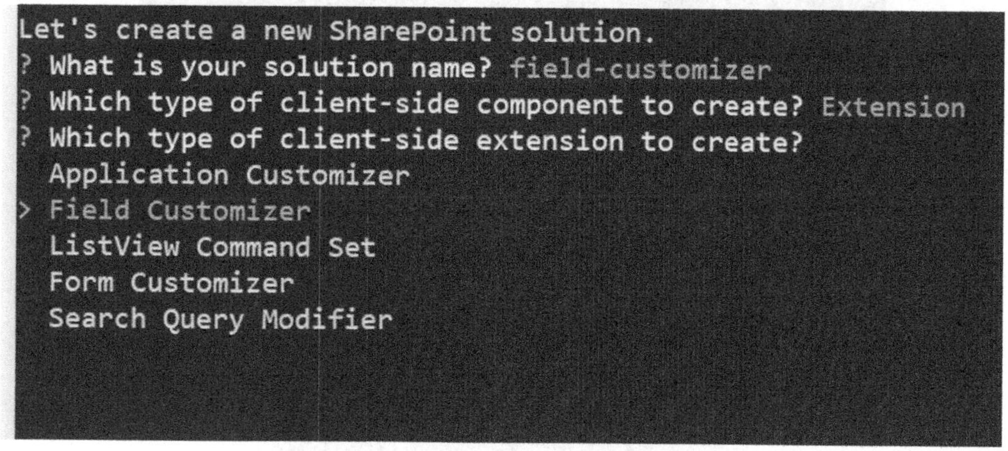

```
Let's create a new SharePoint solution.
? What is your solution name? field-customizer
? Which type of client-side component to create? Extension
? Which type of client-side extension to create?
  Application Customizer
> Field Customizer
  ListView Command Set
  Form Customizer
  Search Query Modifier
```

Figure 11.30: Field customizer as client-side extension

d. **? What is your Field Customizer name? FieldCustom** (provide the name for Field customizer or choose the default name)

e. **? Which template would you like to use? No Framework** (You will be provided with three options: **Minimal**, **No framework**, and **React**; choose one based on your requirements) as shown in the following screenshot:

```
Let's create a new SharePoint solution.
? What is your solution name? field-customizer
? Which type of client-side component to create? Extension
? Which type of client-side extension to create? Field Customizer
Add new Field Customizer to solution field-customizer.
? What is your Field Customizer name? FieldCustom
? Which template would you like to use?
  Minimal
> No framework
  React
```

Figure 11.31: Choose no framework as template for solution

5. It will take some time to install all dependencies for our solution. Then you can see the success message like the following figure:

```
   _=+#####!
###########|
###/    (##|(@)         --------------------------------------
### ######|   \        |         Congratulations!            |
###/   /###|  (@)       |  Solution field-customizer is created. |
####### ##|   /        |    Run gulp serve to play with it!   |
###    /##|(@)         --------------------------------------
###########|
  **=+####!
```

Figure 11.32: Successfully created field customizer solution

6. Let us open the visual studio code with the command **Code. (Code space dot)**. Below is our project structure:

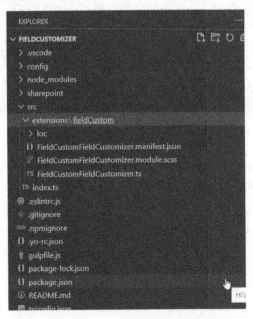

Figure 11.33: Folder structure of field customizer solution

7. Now, open the manifest.json file of your project which is in the "**FieldCustomizer\
src\extensions\fieldCustom\FieldCustomFieldCustomizer.manifest.json**". This file
specifies your extension's type as well as a unique identifier. This ID will be required
later when you debug and deploy your extension to SharePoint.

Here is the code for your reference:

```
{

    "$schema": "https://developer.microsoft.com/json-schemas/spfx/client-
side-extension-manifest.schema.json",

    "id": "b31d6f39-b010-425d-83bc-a6e48dc77aab",

    "alias": "FieldCustomFieldCustomizer",

    "componentType": "Extension",

    "extensionType": "FieldCustomizer",

    // The "*" signifies that the version should be taken from the package.
json

    "version": "*",

    "manifestVersion": 2,

    // If true, the component can only be installed on sites where Custom
Script is allowed.

    // Components that allow authors to embed arbitrary script code should
set this to true.

    // https://support.office.com/en-us/article/Turn-scripting-capabilities-
on-or-off-1f2c515f-5d7e-448a-9fd7-835da935584f

    "requiresCustomScript": false

}
```

8. The **sp-listview-extensibility** package which contains the SharePoint Framework
code needed by the Field Customizer is where the base class for the Field Customizer
is imported from, in the '**FieldCustomizer\src\extensions\fieldCustom\
FieldCustomFieldCustomizer.ts**'.

Here is the code for reference:

```
import { Log } from '@microsoft/sp-core-library';

import {

  BaseFieldCustomizer,
```

```
IFieldCustomizerCellEventParameters
} from '@microsoft/sp-listview-extensibility';
import * as strings from 'FieldCustomFieldCustomizerStrings';
import styles from './FieldCustomFieldCustomizer.module.scss';
```

9. The methods **onInit()**, **onRenderCell()**, and **onDisposeCell()** hold the logic for your Field Customizer:

   a. You will carry out the setup required for your extension in **onInit()**. This event happens after the assignment of **this.context** and **this.properties** before the page DOM is prepared. Like how web components work, **onInit()** returns a promise that may be used for asynchronous activities; **onRenderCell()** is not called until your promise has finished resolving. Just return **Promise.resolve()** if you do not require that.

   b. When a cell is rendered, the function **onRenderCell()** is called. It offers an event. Where the code can write its content is in the domElement HTML element.

   c. The function **onDisposeCell()** is called just before the event cellDiv has been removed. Any resources set aside for field rendering can be released using it. For instance, **onDisposeCell()** must be used to release a React element that was mounted by **onRenderCell()**; else, a resource leak would happen.

In the same **.ts** file you can see the methods **onInt()**, **onRenderCell()**, and **onDisposeCell()**.

Here is the code for your reference:

```
export default class FieldCustomFieldCustomizer
extends BaseFieldCustomizer<IFieldCustomFieldCustomizerProperties> {
public onInit(): Promise<void> {
}
// Add your custom initialization to this method. The framework will wait
// for the returned promise to resolve before firing any BaseFieldCustomizer
events.
Log.info(LOG_SOURCE,      'Activated     FieldCustomFieldCustomizer      with
properties:");
Log.info(LOG_SOURCE, JSON.stringify(this.properties, undefined, 2));
Log.info(LOG_SOURCE,      The     following     string     should     be     equal:
"FieldCustomFieldCustomizer" and "${strings.Title}**)
return Promise.resolve();
public onRenderCell(event: IFieldCustomizerCellEventParameters): void {
```

```
}
// Use this method to perform your custom cell rendering.
const text: string = "${this.properties.sampleText}: ${event.fieldValue}";
event.domElement.innerText = text;
event.domElement.classList.add(styles.fieldCustom);
public onDisposeCell(event: IFieldCustomizerCellEventParameters): void {
// This method should be used to free any resources that were allocated
during rendering.
// For example, if your onRenderCell() called ReactDOM.render(), then you
should
// call ReactDOM.unmountComponentAtNode() here.
super.onDisposeCell(event);
}
}
```

10. In *Figure 11.34*, you can see our SharePoint list, that is, task list which has a progress column (Number type):

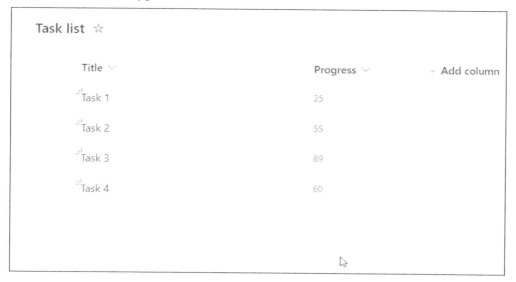

Figure 11.34: *SharePoint Online task list*

11. Let us see how we can enhance field customization rendering. For this locate to the **serve.json** file in the **'config\serve.json'**. Change the Page URL and internal name of column.

Here is the code for your reference:

```
{
    "$schema": "https://developer.microsoft.com/json-schemas/spfx-build/
spfx-serve.schema.json",
  "port": 4321,
  "https": true,
  "serveConfigurations": {
    "default": {
            "pageUrl": "https://tsinfotechnologies.sharepoint.com/sites/
TsInfoTechDeveloper/Lists/Task%20list/AllItems.aspx",
      "fieldCustomizers": {
        "Progress": {
          "id": "158d32590-eabc-4070-aa7b-8678f5d0ad40",
          "properties": {
            "sampleText": "Value"
          }
        }
      }
    },
    "fieldCustomizer": {
            "pageUrl": "https://tsinfotechnologies.sharepoint.com/sites/
TsInfoTechDeveloper/Lists/Task%20list/AllItems.aspx",
      "fieldCustomizers": {
        "Progress": {
          "id": "58d32590-eabc-4070-aa7b-8678f5d0ad40",
          "properties": {
            "sampleText": "Value"
          }
        }
      }
    }
  }
}
```

12. Now, navigate to the **.ts** file located in the **"\FieldCustomizer\src\extensions\ fieldCustom\FieldCustomFieldCustomizer.ts"**. In this file, change the **onRenderCell()**, with the following code:

```
public onRenderCell(event: IFieldCustomizerCellEventParameters): void {
    // Use this method to perform your custom cell rendering.
    if (this.context.field.internalName === 'Progress') {
        let value: number = parseInt(event.fieldValue);
        if(value<45)
        {
            event.domElement.innerHTML =`<div class='${styles.red}'>
            ${event.fieldValue}</div> `;
        }
        else if(value>45 && value<85)
        {
            event.domElement.innerHTML =`<div class='${styles.yellow}'>
            ${event.fieldValue}</div> `;
        }
        else
        {
            event.domElement.innerHTML =`<div class='${styles.green}'>
            ${event.fieldValue}</div> `;
        }
    }
}
```

13. Then navigate to **.scss** file and add the below CSS code for **.red**, **.yellow** and **.green** CSS class. This file is in:

"\FieldCustomizer\src\extensions\fieldCustom\FieldCustomFieldCustomizer. module.scss".

```
.green {
  background-color:green;
  width: 100px;
  height: 25px;
  color: white;
}
```

```
.red {
  background-color:red;
  width: 100px;
  height: 25px;
  color: white;
}
.yellow {
  background-color:yellow;
  width: 100px;
  height: 25px;
}
```

14. Now, run the below command to compile the code and you can see the solution will run in the local server:

    gulp serve

15. Choose the **Load debug scripts** when prompted to accept the loading of debug manifests as shown in the following figure:

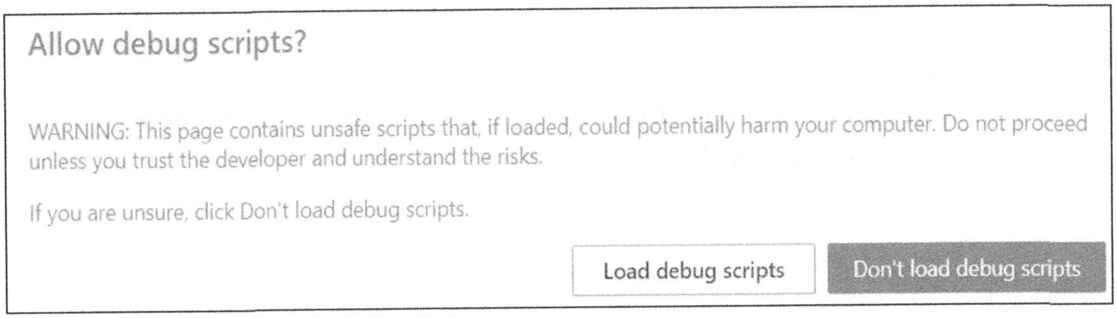

Figure 11.35: *Allow debug scripts window for field customization*

16. You can see the field customization in the SharePoint Online list view as shown in the following figure:

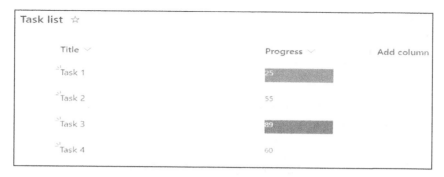

Figure 11.36: *Field customization applied to the SharePoint list view*

Deploying the Field customizer solution in SharePoint

Examine the XML in this file. The **ClientSideComponentId** property of your Field Customizer, which can be found in the file: **"sharepoint\assets\elements.xml"** has automatically been modified to reflect its unique ID. You must modify this file to reflect the type and specifics of your fields:

Here is the code for reference:

```
<?xml version="1.0" encoding="utf-8"?>

<Elements xmlns="http://schemas.microsoft.com/sharepoint/">

    <Field ID="{c1ac8f4a-83e1-4e1a-bb12-313e8d7d8e9d}"

            Name="SPFxPercentage"

            DisplayName="Percentage"

            Type="Number"

            Min="0"

            Required="FALSE"

            Group="SPFx Columns"

            ClientSideComponentId="58d32590-eabc-4070-aa7b-8678f5d0ad40">

    </Field>

</Elements>
```

1. Open the **package-solution.json** file at **./config**.

    The package metadata is defined in the **package-solution.json** file as seen in the following code. The default scaffolding of this file is altered to contain more information for a feature specification to guarantee that the elements.xml file is taken into consideration when the solution package is built. The elements.xml file is provisioned and executed using this feature definition.

Here is the code for your reference:

```
{
"$schema":"https://developer.microsoft.com/json-schemas/spfx-build/
package-solution.schema.json",
 "solution": {
"name": "field-customizer-client-side-solution",
"id": "44f73479-f2fd-4d3c-bd7d-25362d17913c",
"version": "1.0.0.0",
"includeClientSideAssets": true,
"skipFeatureDeployment": true,
"isDomainIsolated": false,
"developer": {
"name":"",
"websiteUrl":"" ,
"privacyUrl":"",
"termsOfUseUrl":"",
"mpnId": "Undefined-1.16.1"
},
"metadata":{
"shortDescription": {
"default": "field-customizer description"
},
"longDescription": {
"default": "field-customizer description"
},
"screenshotPaths": [],
"videoUrl": "",
"categories": []
},
"features":[
```

```
"title": "Application Extension - Deployment of custom action",

"description": "Deploys   a   custom   action   with   ClientSideComponentId
association",

"id": "5542bdd0-c58c-404f-a9cb-232c781086cf",

"version": "1.0.0.0",

"assets": {

"elementManifests": [

"elements.xml"

]

}

}

]

},

"paths": {

"zippedPackage": "solution/field-customizer.sppkg"

}

}
```

2. In the command prompt write the following command, to package the client solution, that contains command set extensions.

   gulp bundle -ship

3. To create the solution package solution, run the below command:

   gulp package-solution -ship

4. This will generate, **.spkg** solution file in **"sharepoint\solution\field-customizer. sppkg"**

5. Now, navigate to the manage app page of SharePoint, and upload the solution package for command set solutions. Once you upload the app, it will ask where the app will be available, like it will be available on the **My app** page, where you can install and use it, or it will automatically be installed and available on the SharePoint site.

6. From the Enable App window, click on the **Only enable this app** option. Then, select **Enable app** button. Then your app is enabled successfully, and you can see the message **This app is enabled** as shown in the following figure:

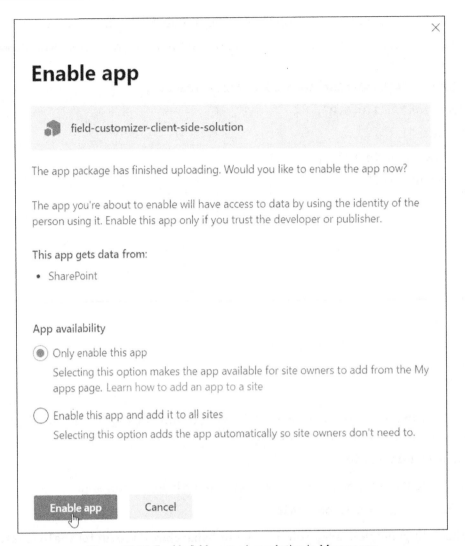

Figure 11.37: Enable field customizer solution in Manage app

7. Now you can see the solution for Field customizer extension is uploaded to the App catalogue of SharePoint, as shown in the following figure:

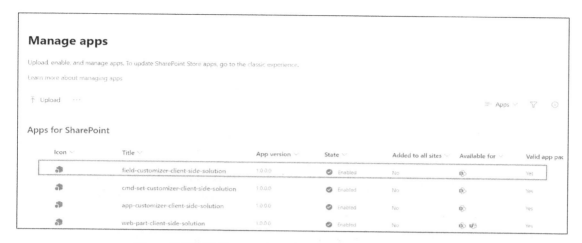

Now you can install the command set solution from **My apps** of SharePoint site, and then you can use it in the SharePoint list.

Command sets

A component of SPFx called Command sets enables programmers to add customized commands to the SharePoint modern **User Interface (UI)**. The Command Bar, List Views, and Document Libraries in SharePoint Online can all have buttons, menus, and other UI components added with the help of command sets.

Compared to the standard customization options offered by SharePoint, command sets enable developers to make more precise and targeted changes to the SharePoint Interface. Developers can implement custom business logic using command sets based on the context of the currently shown page or item, such as acting on chosen objects or visiting external pages.

Now let us see how we can create command set extensions using SharePoint Framework.

Creating Command sets extension

Let us start by creating the project folder by following these steps:

1. Open node.js command prompt and then write the below command to create project folder:

```
mkdir CmdSetCustomizer
```

2. Navigate to directory using the below command:

```
Cd CmdSetCustomizer
```

3. Then, to create the project run the below command in the folder, so the Yeoman SharePoint generator will create the project with required dependencies:

yo @microsoft/sharepoint

4. Then, Yeoman will prompt the list of questions related to your solution, as shown in *Figure 11.39*:

   a. **What is your solution name? cmd-set-customizer** (here you can provide the name of the customizer and you can select the name suggested by the yeoman)

   b. **? Which type of client-side component to create? Extension** (here you can see four choices, that is, **WebPart**, **Extension**, **Library**, **Adaptive Card Extension**, and **select Extension**)

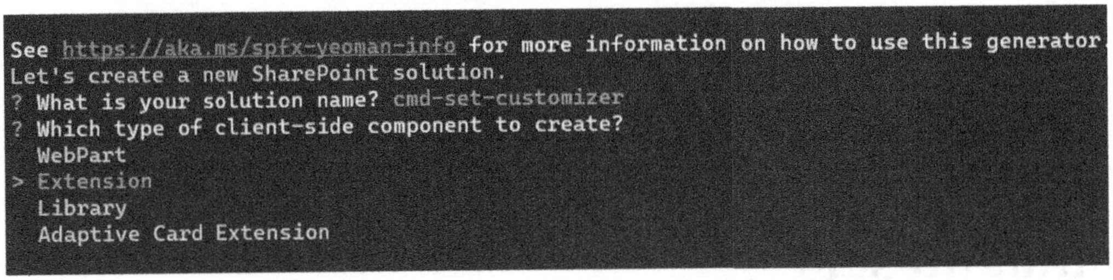

Figure 11.39: Choose client site component for command set customizer

   c. **Which type of client-side extension to create? List View Command Set** (here it provides five options: **Application Customizer**, **Field Customizer**, **ListView Command Set**, **Form Customizer**, **Search Query Modifier**, from this, choose **ListView Command Set**

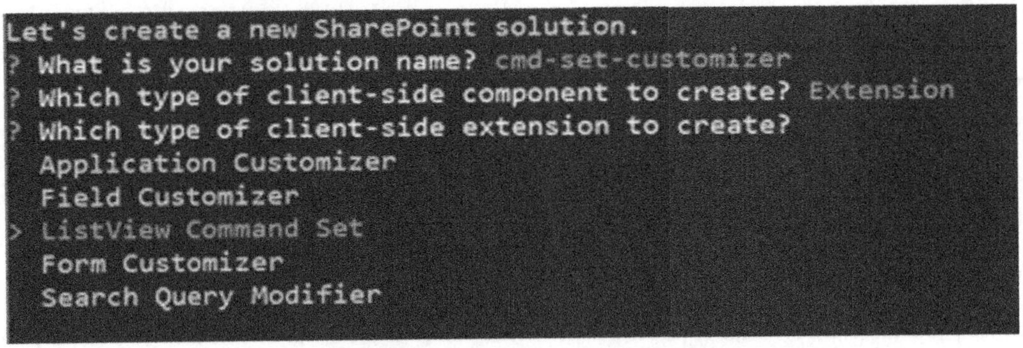

Figure 11.40: List view command set as client side extension

   d. **? What is your Command set name? CmdSet** (provide the name for Field customizer or choose the default name)

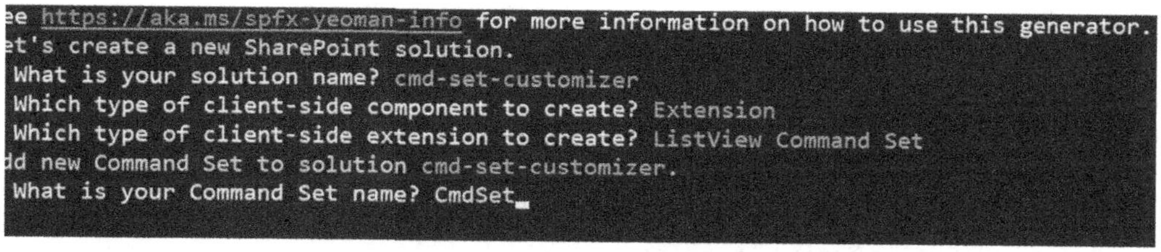

```
ee https://aka.ms/spfx-yeoman-info for more information on how to use this generator.
et's create a new SharePoint solution.
What is your solution name? cmd-set-customizer
Which type of client-side component to create? Extension
Which type of client-side extension to create? ListView Command Set
dd new Command Set to solution cmd-set-customizer.
What is your Command Set name? CmdSet
```

Figure 11.41: *what is your command set name*

5. Now, it will take some time to install the dependencies and create the project. Then, you can see the success message as shown in the following figure:

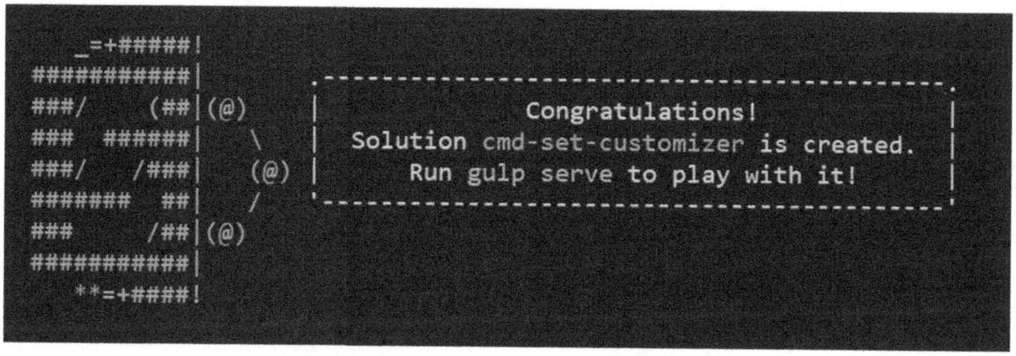

```
   _=+#####!
###########|
###/    (##|(@)    .--------------------------------------.
### ######| \     |            Congratulations!          |
###/   /###|  (@) |   Solution cmd-set-customizer is created. |
####### ##|  /    |      Run gulp serve to play with it!  |
###     /##|(@)    '--------------------------------------'
###########|
  **=+####!
```

Figure 11.42: *Successfully created Command set extension*

6. Let us open the visual studio code with the command **Code . (Code space dot)**.

7. Next, open the manifest.json file of your project which is in **"SP Solutions\ CmdSetCustomizer\src\extensions\cmdSet\CmdSetCommandSet.manifest.json"**. This file specifies your extension's type as well as a unique identifier. This ID will be required later when you debug and deploy your extension to SharePoint.

Here is the code for your reference:

```
{
"$schema":    "https://developer.microsoft.com/json-schemas/spfx/command-
set-extension-manifest.schema.json",

"id": "1aec144a-29db-41ef-9681-29172fde134f",

"alias": "CmdSetCommandSet",

"componentType": "Extension",

"extensionType": "ListViewCommandset",

// The "*" signifies that the version should be taken from the package.json
"version": "*",

"manifestversion": 2,
```

```
// If true, the component can only be installed on sites where Custom
Script is allowed. // Components that allow authors to embed arbitrary
script code should set this to true.
// https://support.office.com/en-us/article/Turn-scripting-capabilities-
on-or-off-1f2c515f-5d7e-448a-9fd7-835da935584f
"requiresCustomScript": false,
"items" : {
}
"COMMAND_1": {
},
"title": { "default": "Command One" },
"iconImageUrl": "icons/request.png", "type": "command"
"COMMAND_2": {
"title": { "default": "Command Two" },
"iconImageUrl": "icons/cancel.png",
"type": "command"
}
}
}
```

Please take note of the manifest file's actual command definitions. Based on the registration aim, these are the actual buttons that are displayed. Command One and Command Two are two distinct buttons that can be found in the basic template.

Understand the code of List View Command set extension

The sp-listview-extensibility package, which contains the SharePoint Framework code needed by the Field Customizer is where the base class for the List view command sets is imported. It is in the '**\CmdSetCustomizer\src\extensions\cmdSet\CmdSetCommandSet.ts**'.

Here is the code for your reference:

```
import { Log } from '@microsoft/sp-core-library';
import {
  BaseListViewCommandSet,
  Command,
```

```
        IListViewCommandSetExecuteEventParameters,

        ListViewStateChangedEventArgs

} from '@microsoft/sp-listview-extensibility';

import { Dialog } from '@microsoft/sp-dialog';
```

The **onExecute()** method defines the actions taken when a command is executed, such as selecting a menu item. The default implementation displays different messages based on the clicked button.

Here is the code for **onExecute()**:

```
public onExecute(event: IListViewCommandSetExecuteEventParameters): void {
    switch (event.itemId) {
      case 'COMMAND_1':
        Dialog.alert(`${this.properties.sampleTextOne}`).catch(() => {
          /* handle error */
        });
        break;
      case 'COMMAND_2':
        Dialog.alert(`${this.properties.sampleTextTwo}`).catch(() => {
          /* handle error */
        });
        break;
      default:
        throw new Error('Unknown command');
    }
  }
}
```

Access the SharePoint Online site, proceed to the list, or create a new one, and then copy the URL associated with the list.

This is necessary because our **ListView** command set is running and hosted from localhost, and we may use special debug query parameters to run the list view code.

Then, open the **serve.json** file in the config folder, provide the URL of the list page URL, where we can test the solution.

Here is the code for your reference:

```
{
    "$schema":    "https://developer.microsoft.com/json-schemas/spfx-build/spfx-
serve.schema.json",
  "port": 4321,
  "https": true,
  "serveConfigurations": {
    "default": {
                "pageUrl":    "https://tsinfotechnologies.sharepoint.com/sites/
TsInfoTechDeveloper/Lists/Task%20list/AllItems.aspx",
      "customActions": {
        "1aec144a-29db-41ef-9681-29172fde134f": {
          "location": "ClientSideExtension.ListViewCommandSet.CommandBar",
          "properties": {
            "sampleTextOne": "One item is selected in the list",
            "sampleTextTwo": "This command is always visible."
          }
        }
      }
    },
    "cmdSet": {
                "pageUrl":    "https://tsinfotechnologies.sharepoint.com/sites/
TsInfoTechDeveloper/Lists/Task%20list/AllItems.aspx",
      "customActions": {
        "1aec144a-29db-41ef-9681-29172fde134f": {
          "location": "ClientSideExtension.ListViewCommandSet.CommandBar",
          "properties": {
            "sampleTextOne": "One item is selected in the list",
            "sampleTextTwo": "This command is always visible."
```

```
                }
              }
            }
          }
        }
}
```

Compile the code and run the below command. You can see the solution will open in the local server:

```
gulp serve
```

Choose **Load debug scripts** when prompted to accept the loading of debug manifests as shown in the following screenshot:

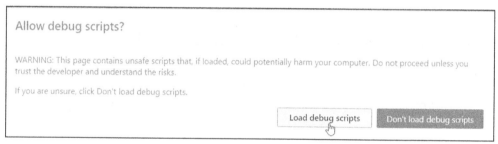

Figure 11.43: Load debug scripts for command set extension

Now, in the command bar you can see the **Command Two** button. By clicking on that, an alert box will pop up with a message, as shown in the following figure:

Figure 11.44: Alert box pops up by clicking on Command 2

Now, if you select any item from the list, and then click on more icon in the command bar, you can see **Command 1** and **Command 2** as shown in the following figure:

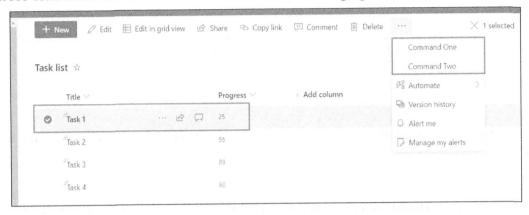

Figure 11.45: *Command 1 is also activated by selecting item in the list*

Deploying the solution in SharePoint

In elements.xml file, take note of the XML structure below. The **ClientSideComponentId** parameter has been changed to reflect the ListView Command Set's unique ID, which can be found in the **CmdSetCommandSet.manifest.json** file located in the. **/src/extensions/cmdSet** directory.

Here is the code for element.xml:

```
<?xml version="1.0" encoding="utf-8"?>

<Elements xmlns="http://schemas.microsoft.com/sharepoint/">

    <CustomAction

        Title="CmdSet"

        RegistrationId="100"

        RegistrationType="List"

        Location="ClientSideExtension.ListViewCommandSet.CommandBar"

        ClientSideComponentId="1aec144a-29db-41ef-9681-29172fde134f"

        ClientSideComponentProperties="{&quot;sampleTextOne&quot;:&quot;One item
is selected in the list.&quot;, &quot;sampleTextTwo&quot;:&quot;This command is
always visible.&quot;}">

    </CustomAction>

</Elements>
```

Follow these steps to deploy the solution in SharePoint:

1. Open the **package-solution.json** file at ./config.

2. The package metadata is defined in the **package-solution.json** file, as seen in the following code. The default scaffolding of this file is altered to contain more information for a feature specification in order to guarantee that the **elements.xml** file is taken into consideration when the solution package is built. The **elements.xml** file is provisioned and executed using this feature definition.

Here is the code for your reference:

```
{

  "$schema": "https://developer.microsoft.com/json-schemas/spfx-build/package-
solution.schema.json",

  "solution": {

    "name": "cmd-set-customizer-client-side-solution",

    "id": "c290edde-45a7-4946-90ce-d1a1623a389f",

    "version": "1.0.0.0",

    "includeClientSideAssets": true,

    "skipFeatureDeployment": true,

    "isDomainIsolated": false,

    "developer": {

      "name": "",

      "websiteUrl": "",

      "privacyUrl": "",

      "termsOfUseUrl": "",

      "mpnId": "Undefined-1.16.1"

    },

    "metadata": {

      "shortDescription": {

        "default": "cmd-set-customizer description"

      },

      "longDescription": {

        "default": "cmd-set-customizer description"

      },
```

```
    "screenshotPaths": [],
    "videoUrl": "",
    "categories": []
  },
  "features": [
    {
      "title": "Application Extension - Deployment of custom action",
      "description": "Deploys a custom action with ClientSideComponentId as-
sociation",
      "id": "68dae9f0-758d-484c-9b72-fc4184df725e",
      "version": "1.0.0.0",
      "assets": {
        "elementManifests": [
          "elements.xml",
          "ClientSideInstance.xml"
        ]
      }
    }
  ]
},
"paths": {
  "zippedPackage": "solution/cmd-set-customizer.sppkg"
}
}
```

3. In the command prompt write the below command, to package the client solution, that contains command set extensions:

    gulp bundle -ship

4. To create the solution package solution, run the below command:

    gulp package-solution -ship

    This will generate, .spkg solution file in **"\CmdSetCustomizer\sharepoint\solution\cmd-set-customizer.sppkg"**

5. Now, navigate to the manage app page, and upload the solution package for command set solutions. Once you upload the app, it will ask where the app will be available, for

example, it may be available in the My app page. Here you can install it and use, or it will automatically be installed and remain available on the SharePoint site.

6. Next, select **Only enable this app** option and then click on **Enable app** as shown in the following figure:

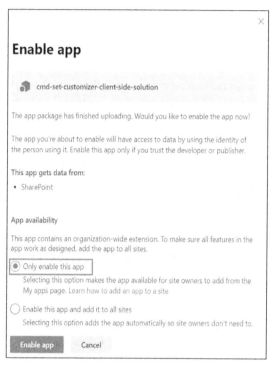

Figure 11.46: Enable app window, to manage apps in SharePoint site

7. Now, you can see that the solution for command set is uploaded to the App catalogue of SharePoint as shown in the following figure:

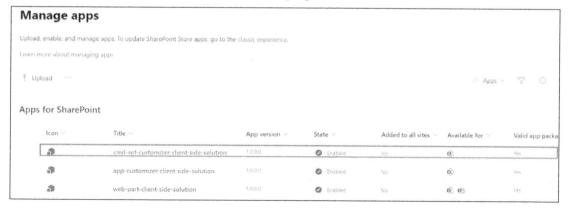

Figure 11.47: Command set customizer solution successfully uploaded to the App catalog

Now you can install the command set solution from My apps of SharePoint site and use it in the SharePoint list.

Form customizer

With the help of the Form Customizer feature in SPFx, developers can alter the appearance and functionality of SharePoint list and library forms. Developers can alter how SharePoint forms are displayed and how users interact with the data in the forms using Form Customizer.

In addition to modifying the structure, styles, and behavior of existing form elements, Form Customizer enables developers to add custom fields, sections, and groups to SharePoint forms. SharePoint forms can also have additional logic and validation rules added by the developers based on user input.

Form Customizer may be created by utilizing modern web technologies like TypeScript, React, and Office UI Fabric because it is built on top of the SharePoint Framework. With the help of this potent tool, users can build custom forms for SharePoint lists and libraries that satisfy their company requirements.

Creating Form Customizer extension using SharePoint Framework

To create form customizer extension using SharePoint Framework, follow these steps:

1. Let us start by creating the project folder, so open node.js command prompt and then write the below command to create project folder:

   `mkdir FormCustom`

2. Navigate to directory using the below command:

   `cd FormCustom`

3. Then to create the project, run the below command in the folder, so yeoman SharePoint generator will create the project with required dependencies.

   `yo @microsoft/sharepoint`

4. Then yeoman will prompt the list of questions related to your solution:

   a. **What is your solution name? form-custom** (here you can provide the name of the customizer and select the name suggested by the yeoman)

   b. **? Which type of client-side component to create? Extension** (here you can see four choices, that is, **Webpart**, **Extension**, **Library**, **Adaptive Card Extension**, and select **Extension**):

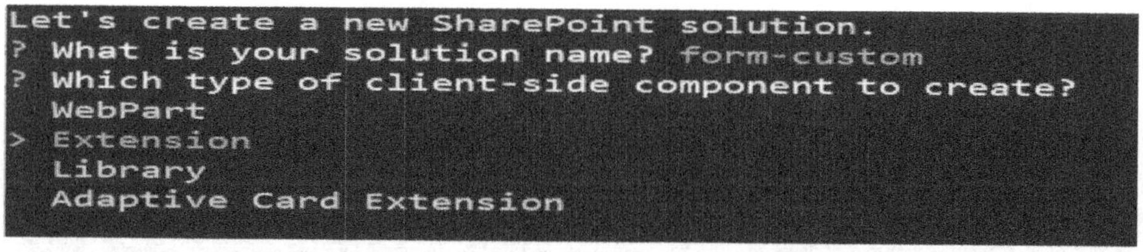

Figure 11.48: Solution name as form-custom and extension as client side component

c. **Which type of client-side extension to create? Form Customizer** (here it provides five options: Application Customizer, **Field Customizer**, **List View Command Set**, **Form Customizer**, **Search Query Modifier**, from this choose **Application customizer**):

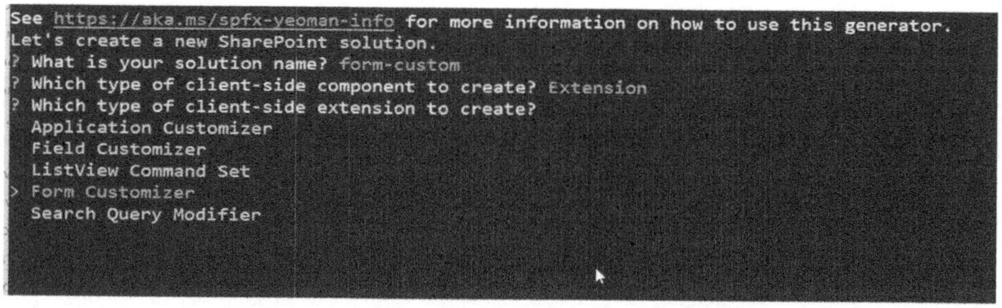

Figure 11.49: Form customizer as Client-side extension

d. **? What is your Form Customizer name? Form-custom** (provide the name for Field customizer or choose the default name):

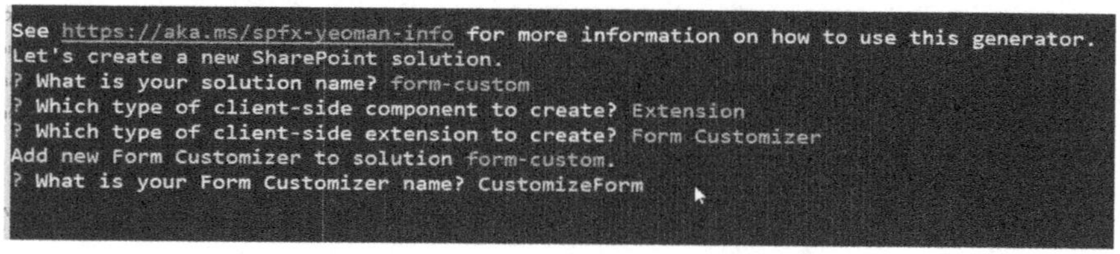

Figure 11.50: Select Form customizer name

e. **? Which template would you like to use? No Framework** (This provides you 2 options: **No framework**, React, choose based on your requirements):

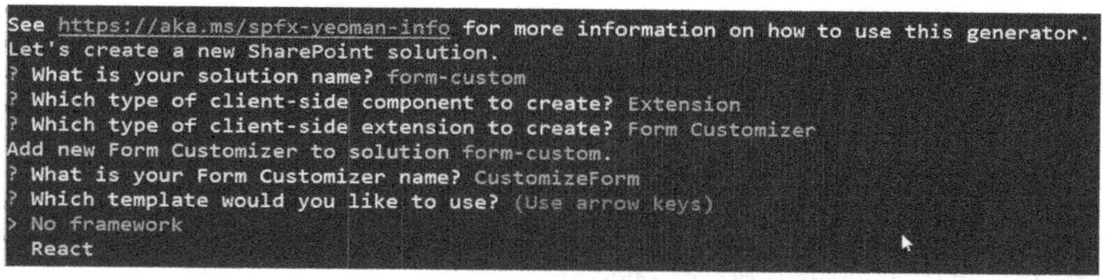

Figure 11.51: Select the Framework of the application

5. Now it will take some time to install the dependencies and create the project. Then you can see the success message as shown in the following figure:

Figure 11.52: Solution form-custom successfully created

6. Let us open the visual studio code with the command **Code** . (Code space dot).

7. Now open the **manifest.json** file of your project which is in **"src\extensions\ customizeForm\CustomizeFormFormCustomizer.manifest.json"**. This file specifies your extension's type as well as a unique identifier. This ID will be required when you debug and deploy your extension to SharePoint.

Here is the code for reference:

{

    "$schema": "https://developer.microsoft.com/json-schemas/spfx/client-side-extension-manifest.schema.json",

  "id": "848778db-7541-4942-a67e-d630e7b8e289",

  "alias": "CustomizeFormFormCustomizer",

  "componentType": "Extension",

  "extensionType": "FormCustomizer",

  // The "*" signifies that the version should be taken from the package.json

  "version": "*",

  "manifestVersion": 2,

  // If true, the component can only be installed on sites where Custom Script is allowed.

  // Components that allow authors to embed arbitrary script code should set this to true.

  // https://support.office.com/en-us/article/Turn-scripting-capabilities-on-or-off-1f2c515f-5d7e-448a-9fd7-835da935584f

```
  "requiresCustomScript": false

}
```

Understanding the code of Form Customizer extension

The sp-listview-extensibility package contains the SharePoint Framework code needed by the Form Customizer. It is where the base class for the **Formcustomizer** is imported from '**src\extensions\customizeForm\CustomizeFormFormCustomizer.ts**'.

Here is the code for reference:

```
import { Log } from '@microsoft/sp-core-library';

import {

  BaseFormCustomizer

} from '@microsoft/sp-listview-extensibility';
```

The **onInit()**, **render()**, and **onDispose()** methods each contain the logic for your Form Customizer.

- You will carry out the setup required for your extension in **onInit()**. This event happens following the assignment of **this.context** and **this.properties** before the page DOM is prepared. **Render()** is not called until your promise is resolved, just like with web components. But **onInit()** returns a promise that you may use to do asynchronous activities. Just return Promise if you do not require it, **resolve<void>();**.

- Here the promise mentioned in the sentence 'This event happens following the assignment of this.context and this.properties before the page DOM is prepared. Render() is not called until your promise is resolved, just like with web components.', signifies an asynchronous operation that needs to be completed before the Render() function is executed. The onInit() event, which takes place after the this.context and this.properties have been assigned, provides an opportunity to perform setup activities. It ensures that these setup actions are completed before any rendering occurs.

- When a component is rendered, **render()** is called. The event is provided, and the content of your code can be written in the **domElement** HTML element.

- Prior to the form host element being removed, **onDispose()** is called. All resources allotted for fo rm rendering can be released using it. For instance, if render() mounted a React element, it must be released using **onDispose()** to prevent a resource leak.

The default solution's **render()** and **onDispose()** contents are as follows:

```
public render(): void {
  // Use this method to perform your custom rendering.
  this.domElement.innerHTML = `<div class="${ styles.customizeForm }"></div>`;
}

public onDispose(): void {
  // This method should be used to free any resources that were allocated during rendering.
  super.onDispose();
}
```

Figure 11.53: Render method and onDispose method in .ts file of form customizer

Then we will create a blank list in SharePoint online. Here we have created a product list, as shown in the following figure:

Figure 11.54: Product list in SharePoint Online

1. Open the **./config/serve.json** file in Visual Studio Code.

In the preview steps, we built a URL for the list; update the page URL properties to reflect that URL and the root address will reflect the URL for list. Your **serve.json** file should now contain the following code:

Here is the code for reference:

```
{
    "$schema": "https://developer.microsoft.com/json-schemas/spfx-build/spfx-serve.schema.json",
  " port " : 4321,
  " https " : true,
```

```
" serveConfigurations " : {

  " default " : {

        " pageUrl " : " https ://tsinfotechnologies.sharepoint.com/sites/
TsInfoTechDeveloper/_layouts/15/SPListForm.aspx ",

     "formCustomizer": {

       "componentId": "848778db-7541-4942-a67e-d630e7b8e289",

       "PageType": 8,

       "RootFolder": "/sites/TsInfoTechDeveloper/Lists/Product%20list",

       "properties": {

         "sampleText": "Value"

       }

     }

  },

  "customizeForm_NewForm": {

        " pageUrl " : " https ://tsinfotechnologies.sharepoint.com/sites/
TsInfoTechDeveloper/_layouts/15/SPListForm.aspx ",

     "formCustomizer": {

       "componentId": "848778db-7541-4942-a67e-d630e7b8e289",

       "PageType": 8,

       "RootFolder": "/sites/TsInfoTechDeveloper/Lists/Product%20list",

       "properties": {

         "sampleText": "Value"

       }

     }

  },

  "customizeForm_EditForm": {

        " pageUrl " : " https ://tsinfotechnologies.sharepoint.com/sites/
TsInfoTechDeveloper/_layouts/15/SPListForm.aspx ",

     "formCustomizer": {
```

```
        "componentId": "848778db-7541-4942-a67e-d630e7b8e289",

        "PageType": 6,

        "RootFolder": "/sites/TsInfoTechDeveloper/Lists/Product%20list",

        "ID": 1,

        "properties": {

          "sampleText": "Value"

        }

      }

    },

    "customizeForm_ViewForm": {

        " pageUrl " : " https ://tsinfotechnologies.sharepoint.com/sites/
TsInfoTechDeveloper/_layouts/15/SPListForm.aspx ",

      "formCustomizer": {

        "componentId": "848778db-7541-4942-a67e-d630e7b8e289",

        "PageType": 4,

        "RootFolder": "/sites/TsInfoTechDeveloper/Lists/Product%20list",

        "ID": 1,

        "properties": {

          "sampleText": "Value"

        }

      }

    }

  }

}
```

Provide the page URL and root folder to each form in the serve.json file.

Adding editing capabilities to the form item

For the purposes of supporting and storing new items to the list, we will develop distinct rendering logic for the view, edit, and new forms. To add editing capabilities to the form items, follow these steps:

1. Add a new Title to the **ICustomizeFormFormCustomizerStrings** interface by opening the. '**src\extensions\customizeForm\loc\myStrings.d.ts**' file. The interface should look like this following your adjustments. Add title properties to interface of **mystring.d.ts**:

   Here is the code for reference:

```
declare interface ICustomizeFormFormCustomizerStrings {
    Save: string;
    Cancel: string;
    Close: string;
    Title: string;
}
declare module 'CustomizeFormFormCustomizerStrings' {
    const strings: ICustomizeFormFormCustomizerStrings;
    export = strings;
}
```

2. Add a new Title string to the **.src\extensions\customizeForm\loc\en-us.js** file. After your changes, the file's content should look like this:

   Here is the code for reference:

```
define([], function() {
    return {
        "Save": "Save",
        "Cancel": "Cancel",
        "Close": "Close",
        "Title": "Title"
    }
});
```

3. Open the **src\extensions\customizeForm\CustomizeFormFormCustomizer.module. scss** file and make the following changes to the styling definition. We are giving the component error style.

   Here is the code for reference:

```
.customizeForm {
    background-color: "[theme:white, default:#ffffff]";
    color: "[theme:themePrimary, default:#0078d4]";
```

```
      padding: 0.5rem;
    .error {
      color: red;
    }
  }
```

4. On the top of the **.ts** file, locate to **import styles** from **./CustomizeFormFormCustomizer.module.scss';** and then write the following code after that:

```
import { FormDisplayMode } from '@microsoft/sp-core-library'; import {
SPHttpClient, SPHttpClientResponse } from '@microsoft/sp-http';
```

5. As illustrated in this code sample, add the **private types_item** and **_etag** to the **CustomizeFormFormCustomizer** class. You will see that your code already contains the class definition:

```
export default class CustomizeFormFormCustomizer

   extends BaseFormCustomizer<ICustomizeFormFormCustomizerProperties> {

     // Added for the item to show in the form; use with edit and view form
private _item: {

Title?: string;

};

// Added for item's etag to ensure integrity of the update; used with edit
form

private _etag?: string;
```

6. As required, modify the **onInit()** method. This is used by this code. If more information is required, the selected list item is fetched after using **displayMode** to establish the rendering status:

```
public onInit(): Promise<void> {

  if (this.displayMode === FormDisplayMode.New) {

    // we›re creating a new item so nothing to load

    return Promise.resolve();

  }


  // load item to display on the form

  return this.context.spHttpClient

      .get(this.context.pageContext.web.absoluteUrl + `/_api/web/lists/
getbytitle('${this.context.list.title}')/items(${this.context.itemId})`,
```

```
        SPHttpClient.configurations.v1, {
            headers: {
              accept: <application/json;odata.metadata=none'
            }
        })
        .then(res => {
          if (res.ok) {
            // store etag in case we'll need to update the item
            this._etag = res.headers.get('ETag');
            return res.json();
          }
          else {
            return Promise.reject(res.statusText);
          }
        })
        .then(item => {
          this._item = item;
          return Promise.resolve();
        });
  }
```

7. Make the following changes to the **render** () method. Depending on the form's display mode, render the form either in display only or in edit mode. We currently use the same rendering for both the new and edited experiences, but, if necessary, you could easily create a dedicated option:

```
public render(): void {
  // render view form
  if (this.displayMode === FormDisplayMode.Display) {

    this.domElement.innerHTML =
                `<div class="${styles.error}">
                  <label for="title">${strings.Title}</label>
                  <br />
                    ${this._item?.Title}
```

```
                              <br />
                              <br />
                                <input type="button" id="cancel" value="${strings.
Close}" />
                          </div>`;


        document.getElementById('cancel').addEventListener('click', this._
onClose.bind(this));
    }
    // render new/edit form
    else {
      this.domElement.innerHTML =
                    `<div class="${styles.error}">
                      <label for="title">${strings.Title}</label><br />
                      <input type="text" id="title" value="${this._item?.Title
|| ''}"/>
                        <br />
                        <br />
                      <input type="button" id="save" value="${strings.Save}" />
                            <input type="button" id="cancel" value="${strings.
Cancel}" />
                        <br />
                        <br />
                        <div class="${styles.error}"></div>
                      </div>`;


        document.getElementById('save').addEventListener('click',  this._
onSave.bind(this));
        document.getElementById('cancel').addEventListener('click', this._
onClose.bind(this));
    }
}
```

8. The **CustomizeFormFormCustomizer** class's **_onSave** methods should be updated as follows:

```
private _onSave = async (): Promise<void> => {
    // disable all input elements while we're saving the item
            this.domElement.querySelectorAll('input').forEach(el    =>
el.setAttribute('disabled', 'disabled'));
    // reset previous error message if any
    this.domElement.querySelector(`.${styles.error}`).innerHTML = '';


    let request: Promise<SPHttpClientResponse>;
        const  title:  string  =  (document.getElementById('title')  as
HTMLInputElement).value;


    switch (this.displayMode) {
      case FormDisplayMode.New:
        request = this._createItem(title);
        break;
      case FormDisplayMode.Edit:
request = this._updateItem(title);
    }
    const res: SPHttpClientResponse = await request;
    if (res.ok) {
      // You MUST call this.formSaved() after you save the form.
      this.formSaved();
    }
    else {
      const error: { error: { message: string } } = await res.json();


        this.domElement.querySelector(`.${styles.error}`).innerHTML = `An
error has occurred while saving the item. Please try again. Error: ${error.
error.message}`;
                this.domElement.querySelectorAll('input').forEach(el    =>
el.removeAttribute('disabled'));
    }
  }
```

9. Next, we will add a new method to **CustomizeFormFormCustomizer** class, that is, **createItem()** as follows:

```
private createItem(title: string): Promise<SPHttpClientResponse> {
    return this.context.spHttpClient
        .post(this.context.pageContext.web.absoluteUrl + `/_api/web/
lists/getByTitle('${this.context.list.title}')/items`,        SPHttpClient.
configurations.v1, {
            headers: {
                <content-type': 'application/json;odata.metadata=none'
            },
            body: JSON.stringify({
                Title: title
            })
        });
```

10. Last method, we will add is **update()** in **CustomizeFormFormCustomizer** class. Provide the following code:

```
private updateItem(title: string): Promise<SPHttpClientResponse> {
    return this.context.spHttpClient
        .post(this.context.pageContext.web.absoluteUrl + `/_api/web/lists/
getByTitle('${this.context.list.title}')/items(${this.context.itemId})`,
SPHttpClient.configurations.v1, {
            headers: {
                <content-type': 'application/json;odata.metadata=none',
                <if-match': this._etag,
                <x-http-method>: <MERGE>
            },
            body: JSON.stringify({
                Title: title
            })
        });
}
```

11. Compile the code and run the below command, and you can see the solution will open in the local server:

gulp serve

12. Choose **Load debug scripts** when prompted to accept the loading of debug manifests as shown in the following figure:

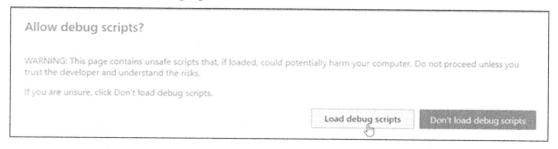

Figure 11.55 : Allow debug scripts window for field customization

Now you can see, the **Title** column is added in the form, in this form we can edit the text, as well as save the field that will be saved in the SharePoint list as shown in the following figure:

Figure 11.56: Added title field to the list form using Form customizer extension

Deploying the solution in SharePoint

To deploy the Form customizer extension to SharePoint Online follow these steps:

1. First terminate the solution from running with the below command:

   `Ctrl+C`

2. To get the basic structure ready for packaging, run the following command on your client-side solution that includes the extension:

   `gulp bundle`

3. Then write the below command to create the solution package:

   `gulp package-solution`

4. Now the solution is created in this location of folder structure: `sharepoint\solution\form-custom.sppkg`.

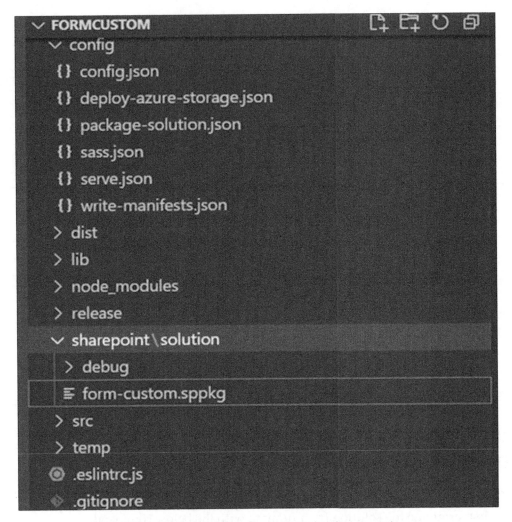

Figure 11.57: Form customizer solution bundle is created

5. Next, navigate to SharePoint App catalog page. Here, upload the solution package.

6. Once you upload the app, it will ask where the app will be available. It will be available on the My app page, where you can install it and use it, or it will automatically be installed and available on the SharePoint site. In this case, we have selected **Only enable this app**, that will make the app available for site owners to add from the **My apps** page as shown in the following screenshot:

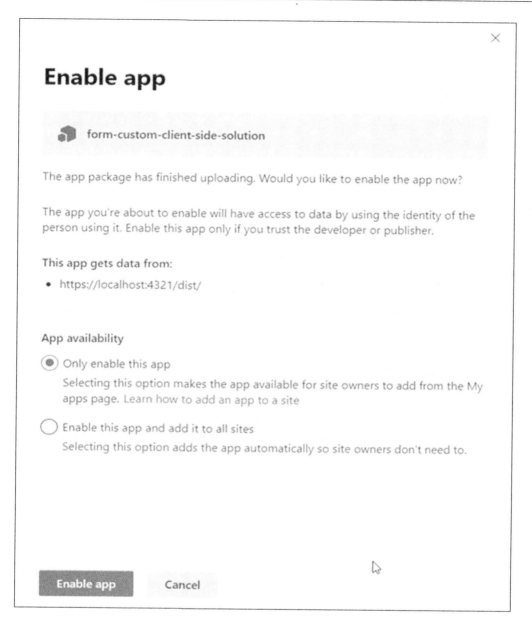

Figure 11.58: Deploy the form customizer extension in App catalog

7. Now you can see that the solution for Form customizer extension is uploaded to the App catalogue of SharePoint, as shown in the following screenshot:

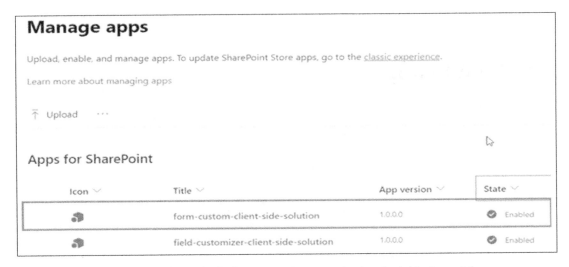

Figure 11.59: Solution for the form customizer extension is uploaded in App catalog

After this you can use the Form customizer that is uploaded successfully in the app catalog. You can now use it in your SharePoint list.

Conclusion

Finally, this chapter has gone through the fundamentals of **SharePoint Framework (SPFx)** and its role in customizing SharePoint Online. We discussed how to set up the SPFx environment and create a client-side web component.

Furthermore, we explored web part properties and the property pane, as well as the various types of SharePoint framework extensions, including application customizers, field customizers, command sets, and form customizers.

With this understanding, the readers should be able to properly customize SharePoint Online using SPFx.

Join our book's Discord space

Join the book's Discord Workspace for Latest updates, Offers, Tech happenings around the world, New Release and Sessions with the Authors:

https://discord.bpbonline.com

Index

Made in the USA
Middletown, DE
07 June 2025

76668962R00303